A literary history of the popular ballad

to MacEdward Leach (1896–1967)

A literary history of the popular ballad *by David C. Fowler*

Duke University Press   *Durham, N. C.*   1968

© 1968, Duke University Press
L.C.C. card number 68–19917
Printed in the United States of
America by Heritage Printers, Inc.

Preface

The idea for this history grew out of a curiosity about the connection between medieval romance and the popular ballad. The scope of my investigation turned out to be much larger than originally planned. In this study I present a chronology of ballad origin in development, and a description of the evolution of ballad style from the fifteenth through the eighteenth centuries in England and Scotland. I do not by any means discuss all of the ballads in the Child canon, but enough of the most important ones are included to avoid the charge of suppressing evidence in defense of a theory.

One important group of texts, however, is neglected in this study—namely the international ballads like "The Twa Sisters," "Lady Isabel and the Elf-Knight," and "Lord Randal," which begin to appear in Britain in the seventeenth century. For this reason I must acknowledge that my history is written from an insular point of view and needs to be placed in the larger context of the European ballad community. The importance of the international ballads in the development of English and Scottish balladry needs to be made manifest, and I hope that the present book will help make this next step possible. An excellent prospectus for future progress in that direction is contained in Holger Nygard's "Popular Ballad and Medieval Romance" in the festschrift for Wayland D. Hand, *Folklore International* (Hatboro, Pa., 1967), pp. 161–173.

Like so many other students in this field, I owe my scholarly interest in the ballad to MacEdward Leach, whose unforgettable class in the English and Scottish ballads I attended during the time I was an instructor in English at the University of Pennsylvania. His death on July 11, 1967 was a source of sorrow to his many friends and colleagues. This volume is dedicated to his memory. The debt which I owe to students in my own ballad class at the University of Washington is much greater than the occasional footnote references to their work would suggest. Indeed it is impossible to name here all of the people who, formally or informally, contributed in a major way to the substance of this book.

Above all I want to pay especial tribute to my family for making the whole effort possible, and even enjoyable. My mother, Mrs. Earle B. Fowler, and her sister, Miss Evabelle Covington, made a particular contribution (see chapter viii) by supplying a stanza of "Sir Hugh" recollected from their childhood days at Broadacre in Monroe, North Carolina. My two daughters, Sandra and Caroline, helped by singing (with a gay but untraditional modern beat) some of the ballads that find a place in this history. Finally, and perhaps crucially, my wife, Mary Gene Fowler, contributed immeasurably with her knowing but diplomatic criticism and her well-timed encouragement. I am glad for the opportunity to pay tribute to this talented, singing family and to thank them for their important part in the successful completion of my task.

I am grateful to Mrs. Arthur Bestor for compiling the index to this volume, and to the Agnes Anderson Fund of the University of Washington Graduate School for a subsidy covering costs connected with preparation of the index.

David C. Fowler

February, 1968

Contents

A literary history of the popular ballad

There's a classical definition of folk music that goes 'music made by an amateur,' but that no longer works because so many of us are professionals. We're like the minstrels of the Middle Ages. They were professional and so are we.

—*Pete Seeger*

1. The evolution of balladry*

The great collection of English and Scottish popular ballads made by Francis J. Child and published in 1898[1] includes 305 numbered ballads arranged according to a system which is difficult to describe. To some extent the list is chronological, so that we tend to think of a ballad with a low Child number as being old; yet among the first twenty ballads in his collection, numbers 3, 8, 15, 17, and 19 are not known in any form earlier than the nineteenth century. Within the general chronological pattern there are also groups formed according to subject or theme. Ballads 1–3 and 45–46, for example, contain riddles; numbers 4–44, 47–53, and 58–105 are ballads of romance and tragedy; the religious carols are 21–23, 54–56; and the Robin Hood ballads, in some ways the earliest group of all, are numbers 117–154. The position of a few ballads is no doubt accidental. Child tells us[2] that if he had discovered it sooner, "The Great Silkie" (113) would have been put following number 40; and some delay in the collection of materials probably accounts for the otherwise puzzling position of "King Edward the Fourth and a Tanner of Tamworth" (273).[3]

One effect of Child's arrangement has been to encourage the study of ballads without respect to time and place. Not only are they considered ageless, but their characteristics are statically conceived; a ballad either has certain stylistic features or it lacks them. As a result, the English and Scottish popular ballads have tended to be admired in isolation without ever being given an established position in the canon of English

* A slightly different form of this first chapter was read before the American Folklore Society meeting at Duke University on April 23, 1964, and was subsequently published under the title, "Toward a Literary History of the Popular Ballad," in the *New York Folklore Quarterly*, XXI (1965), 123–141.

1. Francis J. Child, *The English and Scottish Popular Ballads* (5 vols.; Boston and New York, 1882–1898; reprinted, New York, 1956); subsequently referred to as *ESPB*. In referring to the Child ballads I will customarily give the ballad number from this collection in parentheses following the title. Child also used a system of letters to designate particular versions of a ballad, and hence when-

ever necessary I will employ this system, as in the discussion below of the *Ever Green* version of "Johnie Armstrong" (169C). For a recent and illuminating discussion of the Child canon see Bertrand H. Bronson, *The Traditional Tunes of the Child Ballads* (Princeton, 1959–), I, xiii–xviii.

2. Child, *ESPB*, II, 494a*.

3. An alternative possibility (although it seems unlikely to me) is that Child was undecided about the admissibility of 273 and hence withheld his decision until the preparation of the fifth volume forced the issue. We know this to be true of 305 (see V, 190b†), where there are real grounds for hesitation.

3

literature. Although in some ways this may have been beneficial, since the genre extends over such a long period, it nevertheless has seriously hindered study of the literary development of the popular ballad.

In spite of the prevailing tendency to view the ballad in isolation from literary history, there have been several recent studies that represent new and important approaches. Hodgart's unpretentious but sensible book, *The Ballads* (1950), although to some extent bound by the traditional view, has two chapters that represent a significant advance over earlier studies.[4] These chapters are entitled simply "The Early History of the Ballads" and "The Later History of the Ballads." The scope of Hodgart's book was of course too limited for developing this approach beyond the merest sketch, but it was certainly a step in the right direction. Nygard's study of "Lady Isabel and the Elf-Knight" (4), published in 1958, contains an excellent critique of the Finnish method of ballad study and sets the pattern for future analysis of the international ballads.[5] D. K. Wilgus (1959) not only reviewed twentieth-century folksong scholarship but argued effectively for study of the ballad in a larger folksong context.[6] The most recent major book is Albert B. Friedman's *The Ballad Revival* (1961), which does for earlier balladry what Wilgus had done for that of the present century, and also contributes significantly to our understanding of the precise nature of the appreciation of ballads expressed by Joseph Addison and other neoclassicists of the eighteenth century.[7] Finally it is significant, I think, that the recent ballad anthologies of MacEdward Leach and Friedman show signs of a new freedom from the arrangement of texts which has in the past been dictated so completely by the organization of Francis J. Child's collection.[8]

The approach which I have adopted for the present study is fundamentally a chronological one. I believe, with Hodgart, that there is an early history and a later history of the ballads, and that it is only through

4. M. J. C. Hodgart, *The Ballads* (London, 1950).

5. Holger Olof Nygard, *The Ballad of Heer Halewijn, Its Forms and Variations in Western Europe: A Study of the History and Nature of a Ballad Tradition* (Helsinki [Folklore Fellows Communications No. 169] and Knoxville, Tenn., 1958).

6. D. K. Wilgus, *Anglo-American Folksong Scholarship Since 1898* (New Brunswick, N. J., 1959).

7. Albert B. Friedman, *The Ballad Revival: Studies in the Influence of Popular on Sophisticated Poetry* (Chicago, 1961).

8. MacEdward Leach, *The Ballad Book* (New York, 1955); Albert B. Friedman, *The Viking Book of Folk Ballads of the English-Speaking World* (New York, 1956; reprinted, 1963). Leach keeps the Child order, inserting American versions to compare with traditional English and Scottish texts, and then adds a section called "American Ballads by Origin or Adoption." Friedman organizes by types, the most suggestive and useful groups being the "Pastourelles" and the "Criminals' Goodnights." Hence Leach's anthology is best suited to the classroom, and Friedman's to the general reader.

4

a rigorously chronological analysis, with careful identification of the sources of every ballad, that we can come to recognize a most important and impressive historical phenomenon: the evolution of ballad style.

The lack of any extensive study of the evolution of ballad style cannot be blamed entirely on the tyranny of Child's edition. To a considerable extent this deficiency is attributable, I think, to an excessive current regard for the supposed autonomy of oral tradition.[9] It is very commonly assumed that the preservation of any ballad text is purely accidental, and that the date of the manuscript or printed collection in which it appears can be safely ignored, unless perhaps the date is so early that it can be used to impress the reader with the antiquity of the ballad in question. Although I do not want to be rigid about it, my aim is to adopt precisely the opposite attitude. I therefore assume that a given ballad took the particular shape it has about the time it was written down, unless there is specific evidence to the contrary. It is only in this way, I believe, that a literary history of the popular ballad can be written. The main task of such a history is of course the detailed analysis of particular ballads. But to provide a context for textual analysis, a preliminary sketch of the literary development of balladry is needed.

The ballad is a special narrative form within the larger context of folksong, of which it has become a part. It is important to remember, however, that there was a time in the past when the folksong tradition was flourishing and ballads were nonexistent. There is evidence of a strong tradition of folksong in England and in Europe generally from the twelfth century, when the vernacular literatures, especially French, began to flourish. In England, carols and religious lyrics appear in the thirteenth century, and increasingly in the fourteenth and fifteenth centuries.[10]

In assessing the nature of this early English folksong tradition, we must be careful to avoid two prevalent and false dichotomies. The first

9. Even Hodgart, who has come the nearest to freeing himself from current preconceptions, occasionally falls victim. See *The Ballads*, p. 104, where he says that the "rather lame ending" of the Motherwell version of "Edward" (13A) "has been transformed into" the dramatic conclusion ("The curse of hell frae me sall ye beir") of the *Reliques* version (13B). Of course Child invites this kind of interpretation by putting the versions in that order, but the fact is that the *Reliques* version appeared in 1765, while Motherwell's text can be no earlier than 1825. Furthermore, the "traditional" versions of Edward do not have this surprise ending; Motherwell's is almost certainly derived from the *Reliques* version. But see Archer Taylor, *"Edward" and "Sven I Rosengård"* (Chicago, 1931), pp. 3, 23, and refs.

10. See Richard L. Greene, *The Early English Carols* (Oxford, 1935), introduction; Friedman, *The Ballad Revival*, p. 3 and refs.

of these is the supposition that the "art" versus "folk" dichotomy we speak of today is applicable to the medieval scene. I do not think it is applicable at all. The early English carols and lyrics contain much of what we call "folklore" and various popular conceptions, but these were incorporated into artistic compositions of considerable skill and sophistication and did not exist in a stream of tradition apart from the dominant culture of the age. From this follows the second dichotomy we need to avoid, namely the notion of a separation between pagan and Christian or secular and religious songs. There were indeed love songs as well as carols, riddle songs as well as religious threnodies, but all of these floated in the same stream of tradition. In a strongly religious culture such as existed in the Middle Ages, it should not be surprising that such relics of folklore and myth as are to be found are preserved, as it were, by accident in songs of a markedly didactic and religious nature.[11]

In his quest for the beginnings of balladry in the later Middle Ages, Child hit upon certain early carols and songs which have been regarded as primitive examples of the ballad primarily because they contain a narrative element. The best-known example in the Child canon is "Judas" (23), found in a manuscript of the thirteenth century, but there are four or five others of this type, not including several more unknown to Child, of which the best example is undoubtedly the "Corpus Christi" carol.[12] There can be little doubt that carols of this kind were a prominent feature of the early folksong tradition. But they were not ballads. It is necessary to emphasize this because the influence of the Child canon is so strong that the mere fact of his including some of these religious songs in his edition makes us tend to think of them as ballads. Indeed I think it is fortunate that he included them, since, as we shall see, the carol was destined to play an important role in the development of the ballad; but

11. The earliest of Child's riddle texts, "Riddles Wisely Expounded" (1), is dated no later than 1445 (*ESPB*, V, 283 f.) and is entitled "Inter diabolus et virgo." In a contest of wit, a maid escapes the clutches of the devil.

12. Greene, *The Early English Carols*, pp. liv ff., xciv, xcvii f., 221 f., 411 f. I am trying to avoid Greene's folk-art dichotomy (see preceding discussion), but I must admit that the particular kind of carol I have in mind is better attested in oral tradition than it is in the manuscript sources used by Greene. It is for this reason that I use the "Corpus Christi" carol as my ex-

ample. There is a real crux here. Much as I admire Greene's introduction, I believe the entire direction of his argument is affected by an assumption that the stanza with internal refrain originates with the popular ballad and subsequently influences the traditional carol. Cf. Hodgart's brief but cogent discussion, *The Ballads*, pp. 80 ff. Erik Routley, *The English Carol* (London, 1958), has a valuable discussion of the "ballad carol" (pp. 43 ff.), but I think he too assumes the priority of a refrain ballad without really going into the problem.

6

the mere possession of a narrative element should not lead us to call a carol a ballad. To say this is not to reject the carol but rather to recognize its true nature and its position in the mainstream of folksong.

One of the most significant features of the early English folksong tradition was its stability. Oriented to the church calendar, its large body of religious songs were sung with a regularity and a propriety that no other group of songs could hope to match. There were carols for every major holy day throughout the year, and many narrative songs were based on the New Testament and even the Apocryphal Gospels as well. Nor must we make the mistake of picturing the populace as being reluctantly driven to this kind of activity by the indoctrination of a tyrannical clergy. If we may judge by the quality of the songs and lyrics of the thirteenth and fourteenth centuries, they were composed and sung with fervor, conviction, and delight. The carol in particular seems to have been sung as an accompaniment to various forms of dancing, a fact which has an important bearing on its development of internal and external refrains.[13] Love songs of course were also very popular and had their own kind of stability, but the artistic initiative remained with the predominantly religious folksong tradition.

There was nothing, however, in the folksong tradition which I have just described that in itself could have led to the development of the English and Scottish popular ballads. The tradition possessed a wealth of melodies and stanza forms ready for use and it had a few songs based on the Gospels, but something had to happen before a new type of narrative song could come into being. The event which sparked this development was the coming together of traditional song and medieval minstrelsy in the fifteenth and sixteenth centuries. During this period the popular ballad as we know it was born.

To understand the birth of the ballad we must first arrive at a definition of minstrelsy and then observe what was happening to this tradition in the fourteenth and fifteenth centuries just prior to the moment when it came into creative contact with folksong. By the middle of the thirteenth century in England the great French courtly romances of the twelfth century had joined with the native alliterative tradition to stimulate the composition of a group of English metrical narrative poems which retold to an eager new audience the earlier Germanic legends as well

13. See Greene, *The Early English   above.
Carols*, pp. xxix–lix. But see also n. 12,

as stories from the Charlemagne and Arthurian cycles and the Matter of Greece and Rome. Although these romances usually employed both meter and alliteration, meter was predominant, and a variety of stanza forms developed. Typical examples are *Sir Beues of Hamtoun, King Horn, Rauf Coilyear,* and *Sir Perceval of Galles.* Most of these were of course long poems, far too lengthy for recitation without pause. There were, however, briefer narratives, usually called Breton lays, that are perhaps for our present purpose best representative of English minstrelsy in the fourteenth century. In any case the achievement of English minstrelsy is fittingly represented by the contents of the Auchinleck manuscript, written probably before 1350.[14] Chaucer's "Knight's Tale" and *Troilus and Criseyde* were of course romances in the courtly tradition of Chrétien de Troyes; the nearest approach to the minstrel tradition in the *Canterbury Tales* is perhaps the "Franklin's Tale," modeled on the Breton lay. It is significant that in "The Tale of Sir Thopas" Chaucer parodies the metrical romance, for by this time, in the late fourteenth century, the art of the medieval minstrel was beginning to decline. An important reason for the decline of minstrelsy will be evident if we pause briefly to examine the social setting in which the art was practiced.

Although one tends to associate minstrels primarily with the king's court, which is indeed the way they are depicted in the early Tristan romances, nevertheless they flourished even more regularly in the halls of great lords of the realm. This was especially true in England in the later fourteenth century, when the court in London became an international cultural center demanding the sophistication of a Chaucer while perhaps deriding the provincial talents of the minstrel. Because of this cultural retreat of the minstrels from London, their fate became inevitably entwined with that of the great barons of the north and west, who were at that time engaged in a power struggle with the king.[15] The baronial opposition reached its zenith with the deposition of Richard II in 1399, but after this its decline was rapid, and the War of the Roses in the fifteenth century settled the question. London became supreme, and the great baronial centers were no longer able to sustain minstrelsy or other forms of culture on the grand scale. The departure of the minstrel from the baronial halls did not come suddenly, but when it did happen, in the fifteenth century, it provided the occasion for that fruitful con-

14. A. H. Billings, *A Guide to the Middle English Metrical Romances* (New York, 1901). For the Auchinlech MS, see *Englische Studien,* VII, 178–191.

15. For the significance of this struggle in relation to the alliterative revival, see J. R. Hulbert, "A Hypothesis Concerning the Alliterative Revival," *MP,* XXVIII (1931), 405–422.

8

junction of minstrelsy and folksong which I have already mentioned.

Many of the metrical romances that were composed in the fifteenth century reflect the altered circumstances of the minstrels who recited them. Conditions no longer permitted the leisurely reading or recitation of lengthy narratives, and hence a significant number of romances of this late period give the appearance of imperfectly remembered oral reconstructions of the minstrel's repertoire. To realize how far minstrelsy had declined, one need only compare that excellent fourteenth-century alliterative poem *Sir Gawain and the Green Knight* with the Gawain romances of the following century.[16] From this point of view, prospects for the future of minstrelsy were not encouraging. Removed from his accustomed setting and forced to rely reluctantly but increasingly on oral composition, the minstrel soon found that his narrative art was threatened with disintegration.

In the very midst of the decline just described, however, a basis for the regeneration of minstrelsy was being established. First of all, the pressures of oral composition naturally tended to shorten the average narrative to perhaps a thousand or fifteen hundred lines. Moreover, the various complex stanza forms and patterns of rhyme and meter drifted toward a normalized stanza of four lines alternating four and three stresses or simply four stresses throughout, with the second and fourth lines rhyming. This is of course the familiar quatrain destined to become the mainstay of balladry. Thus far, however, the stanza we are speaking of was still a unit of oral narrative; it was recited and not sung. It had undoubtedly developed rapidly in the fourteenth century, but in the next century it came to be regarded as a normal unit of the shorter metrical romances.

A final and most important development in the minstrel's art that came as a result of the influence of oral composition was the regeneration of a structural symmetry within the confines of the shortened narrative form. Plots tended to become regularized, and their symmetrical character was stressed by the studied repetition of motifs and descriptive detail. If a typical hero begins an adventure, for example, by putting on a coat of green and mounting his horse, we can be reasonably sure that at the end he will dismount and remove the coat of green in an exact mirror-image reversal of the initial stylized action. This device may have served initially as a memory aid, but it soon began to function with great effectiveness as a narrative technique and emerged finally as a positive

16. The group of Gawain poems is conveniently described in Billings, *A Guide* *to the Middle English Metrical Romances*, pp. 209–221.

artistic achievement in the new minstrelsy of the fifteenth and sixteenth centuries.

Although in a sense it is possible to explain the regeneration of minstrelsy as a response to the changing social and cultural conditions of fifteenth-century England, it seems highly unlikely that this rebirth would have occurred merely for the purpose of retelling romances of the older repertoire, nor would the themes built into these earlier romances have been of particular interest to the rapidly growing popular audience. The refurbishing and recasting of old stories did of course continue, but there can be little doubt that the vitality of the new form owes much to its association with the Matter of Sherwood Forest. "Rymes of Robyn Hood" were current, as we know, in the latter half of the fourteenth century, and in the space of less than a century these appeared to have expanded into a series of narratives resembling the earlier Arthurian cycle and echoing or parodying some of its characteristic motifs.[17] Especially significant is the fact that the earliest illustrations of that narrative symmetry which is characteristic of the new minstrelsy are to be found among the so-called Robin Hood ballads of Child's collection.[18] What needs to be stressed, however, is that these early texts, such as "A Gest of Robyn Hode" (117), "Robin Hood and the Monk" (119), and "Robin Hood and the Potter" (121), to mention only a few, were not ballads at all, which is to say that they were recited and not sung. They are, in fact, extant examples of those "Rymes of Robyn Hood" to which the allegorical figure of Sloth in *Piers the Plowman* was so hopelessly addicted.

In order to perceive clearly the way in which metrical narrative entered the mainstream of folksong it is important to be aware of a particular feature of the quatrain unit that is in one sense a structural weakness. I refer to the "filler," often the second or weak line in a four-line stanza, which because of its perfunctory or formulaic character gives the improvising minstrel a chance to plan his rhyme scheme and complete the stanza.[19] To illustrate this I will quote stanzas 81 and 82 of "Robin Hood and the Monk"(119):

17. W. W. Skeat (ed.), *Piers the Plowman*, B Text, V, 402 (2 vols.; Oxford, 1886), I, 166. The date usually given is 1377; a more likely date for the B Text, I think, is 1382. See David C. Fowler, *Piers the Plowman: Literary Relations of the A and B Texts* (Seattle, 1961), pp. 167–169. For an example of the Arthurian connection, see Child, *ESPB*, III, 51.

18. See "A Gest of Robyn Hode" (117). Here I will merely mention one example of the symmetry referred to. Compare stanzas 17–21 of the first fit with stanzas 208–213 of the fourth fit. The often repeated statement that the "Gest" is several ballads "stitched together" fails to recognize its carefully developed narrative structure.

19. This explanation of the "weak" line need not be limited in its application to pure oral composition, though it assumes an original oral situation.

Thus John gate Robyn Hod out of prison,
    Sertan withoutyn layn;
Whan his men saw hym hol and sounde,
    Ffor sothe they were full fayne.

They filled in wyne, and made hem glad,
    Vnder Þe levys smale,
And ȝete pastes of venyson,
    Þat gode was with ale.[20]

The "weak" line in the first of these two stanzas ("Sertan withoutyn layn") is typical. It does not advance the story, it adds nothing to the emotional impact, and in fact it says nothing except "I'll tell you no lie." Nevertheless, it is a very useful if uninspiring formula in the construction of stanzas and lends itself easily to such variations as "withoutyn lye," or "withoutyn doute," to fit the rhyme needed to complete the fourth line of the quatrain. The "weak" line of the second stanza quoted ("Vnder Þe levys smale") is more interesting and suggestive. It, too, is subject to variation, but formulas of this type, especially in the Robin Hood texts, are often richly suggestive of the Sherwood Forest setting, as in the line: "under the greenwood tree."

The point to remember here is that the "weak" line of the minstrel stanza, particularly the descriptive variety, bore a striking resemblance both in form and function to the internal refrain of the early English carol. When minstrelsy and folksong finally came together, it was this perhaps fortuitous resemblance that led to the creation of the first ballad. Whether we are fortunate enough to have in print in Child's collection this first of all ballads I hesitate to say.[21] But there can be little doubt that, as Child himself believed, the earliest of the popular ballads had a refrain. Only

20. Text is from Cambridge University Library MS Ff.5.48, fol. 128b (*ca.* 1450). Extracts from this MS are printed in Charles Henry Hartshorne, *Ancient Metrical Tales* (London, 1829), pp. 35–80, 151–208.

21. A definite possibility is "Robyn and Gandeleyn" (115), which Greene (*The Early English Carols*, p. lvi) calls a "rather puzzling piece." The refrain, "Robynn lyth in grene wode bowndyn," appears to be external, but whether it actually is such is not clear. Most of the other items in the MS are songs and carols of a conventional kind. Greene remarks (*ibid.*): "The scribe apparently recognized its unlikeness to its companion poems, for it is the only one in the entire manuscript written as prose and not marked off into stanzas." Of course this is true, but it is also true that the scribe evidently felt that it was for some reason appropriate to insert "Robyn and Gandeleyn" in this collection. The MS is Sloane 2593 in the British Museum, printed by Thomas Wright, *Songs and Carols* (London, 1856). For anyone interested in ballad origins, it is a fascinating MS to study. It contains what Greene calls "the ballad" of "St. Stephen and Herod" (22) and the riddle song related to the ballad "Captain Wedderburn's Courtship" (46) quoted by Child, *ESPB*, I, 415B.

one simple but miraculous step was needed to move from the "Corpus Christi" carol,

> He bare him up, he bare him down,
> *Lully, lulley, lully, lulley,*
> He bare him into an orchard brown,
> *The faucon hath born my make away.*

to the ballad of "The Cruel Mother" (20):

> She set her foot against a thorne,
> *Come bend and bear away the bows of yew,*
> And there she had two pretty babes born,
> *Gentle hearts, be to me true.*[22]

However, songs with internal refrain, like the "Corpus Christi" carol just quoted, obviously had a musical structure perfectly suited to the minstrel quatrain, and hence there exists also the possibility of the direct transfer of such a folk melody to the narrative stanzas of late medieval minstrelsy. It might even be argued that the interesting narrative symmetry of some of the rhymes of Robin Hood are attributable not to oral composition but to the shaping effect of a musical setting. This is indeed a possibility, but for the present I still think that most of the early Robin Hood pieces give no indication that they were ever sung.[23]

Whatever the truth about the Robin Hood texts, we know from a reference in *The Complaynt of Scotland* (1549) that "Chevy Chase" (162), for example, which is composed very much in the style of the new minstrelsy, was considered an old and popular song by the middle of the sixteenth century. There is also, of course, the well-known testimony of Sir Philip Sidney in the latter half of the century who remarked in his *Apology for Poetry*, speaking of "Chevy Chase:" "I never heard the old song of *Percy* and *Douglas* that I found not my heart mooved more than

22. See Edith C. Batho, "The Life of Christ in the Ballads," *E&S*, IX (1924), 70–97, esp. 93, where she prints the "Corpus Christi" carol as having an internal refrain. Greene rightly points out that the MS does not warrant this (*The Early English Carols*, p. 411), but I believe that in this case there is sufficient support in versions obtained from oral tradition to justify Miss Batho's interpretation. The stanza of "The Cruel Mother" is taken from the late seventeenth-century version printed by Child, *ESPB*, II, 500–

501. It should be obvious that I am using these two merely as examples of a carol and a ballad with internal refrain, and I am not implying a specific historical connection between them.

23. James A. H. Murray (ed.), *The Complaynt of Scotlande* (1549), (EETS, E.S. 17–18 [London, 1872]), lists a dance of "Robene hude," but "Robene hude and litil ihone" is found among the "tales" which are for the most part romances and definitely not "songs," which is a separate category.

with a trumpet; and yet it is sung but by some blinde Crowder, with no rougher voyce, than rude style."[24] Hence we must conclude, I think, that ballads of the type represented by "Chevy Chase" must have come into being by the end of the fifteenth century, presumably not long after the first refrain ballads had been composed.[25]

When we turn from inferences of this kind to see what can actually be found in the Child canon, however, the picture becomes complicated, partly because Child arranged the ballads in accordance with his theory that the earliest were those possessing refrains. Looking for the moment at the first twenty-eight Child ballads in the light of the preceding discussion, it is possible immediately to eliminate from consideration twenty of these twenty-eight on the grounds that they are either riddle songs, international ballads with completely different stanza structures, carols and other religious songs, or ballads recovered so recently as to make them of dubious value for the present purpose.[26] This leaves only eight items from this earliest group of refrain ballads. The first is "The Fair Flower of Northumberland" (9), published initially in Thomas Deloney's novel, *Jack of Newbury* (1597), where we are told it was sung by a group of maidens engaged in spinning and carding, "two of them singing the Ditty, and all the rest bearing the burden."

> It was a knight in Scotland borne,
> *Follow my love, leap over the strand,*
> Was taken prisoner and left forlorne,
> *Even by the good Earle of Northumberland.*
>
> · · · · · · · · · · · · ·
>
> And as in sorrow thus he lay
> *Follow my love, come over the strand,*
> The Earles sweet Daughter walkt that way,
> *And she the faire flower of Northumberland.*[27]

24. Quoted by Hodgart, *The Ballads*, p. 144.
25. The relevant ballads here, in addition to "Chevy Chase," are "The Battle of Otterburn" (161), "Sir Andrew Barton" (167), "Flodden Field" (168), and "Captain Car, or, Edom o Gordon" (178). I do not include "The King and the Barker" (273AppI), which is found, along with "Robin Hood and the Potter" (121), in Cambridge University Library MS Ee.iv.35.1 (*ca.* 1500).
26. These are three riddle ballads (Child 1, 2, 3), two international ballads (12, 13), three carols or religious songs (21, 22, 23), and twelve ballads of relatively recent date (4, 6, 7, 8, 15, 16, 17, 19, 24, 25, 27, 28). "Lady Isabel and the Elf-Knight" is of course an old ballad, but the relevant version here is Buchan's (4A), with couplet and refrain, published in 1828. This text is convincingly disposed of by Nygard, *The Ballad of Heer Halewijn*, pp. 311–316.
27. Francis O. Mann (ed.), *The Works of Thomas Deloney* (Oxford, 1912), pp. 33–36. I quote the first and third stanzas only.

This text is especially interesting, not only because it is the earliest known ballad with an internal refrain, but also because of the way in which the refrain is so directly involved in the story. The first of the two refrain lines does not change, but the second changes so radically and so often that the maidens who "bore the burden" must have had to be intimately acquainted with the ballad in order to participate in the singing.[28]

Four ballads with refrains appeared in the seventeenth century: "The Three Ravens" (26) was first published in Thomas Ravenscroft's *Melismata* (1611); "Sir Lionel" (18) is preserved in the Percy folio manuscript (*ca.* 1650), and the other two, "The Twa Sisters" (10) and "The Cruel Mother" (20), appear first in broadsides of the latter half of the seventeenth century.[29] "The Three Ravens" is actually a folksong, but Child rightly included it in the canon, for its stanza form, with threefold repetition of the first line and interlaced refrain, is to be found in a number of ballads and songs from the sixteenth century to the present day, including "Sir Lionel" and "The Twa Sisters."[30] This is certainly one of the most striking influences of folksong on the development of the ballad stanza. The remaining ballads in the early group are "Gil Brenton" (5), "The Cruel Brother" (11), and "Babylon" (14). All three have the normal internal refrain, and all first appear in the eighteenth century.

More could be said about the development of refrain ballads, but the point to be stressed here is that in spite of their importance in relation to ballad origins, they are a distinct minority group in the Child canon. This is in sharp contrast to the development of Danish ballads, for example, where both internal and external refrains are quite common,[31] and it is contrary to what might be expected in view of the observable tendency of ballads to drift toward a lyric abstraction of the "emotional core" of a narrative.[32] The fact is that the English and Scottish ballads, as

28. Stanzas 1 and 2 have "leap" over the strand, but thereafter it is "come."

29. Here I am concerned exclusively with the early refrain group in Child, 1–28. But it should be remembered that there is early evidence of a refrain tradition in the Robin Hood ballads. Leaving aside "Robyn and Gandeleyn" (115) as not strictly in the Robin Hood tradition, there is nevertheless the testimony of John Rastell's *The Interlude of the Four Elements* (*ca.* 1520). See edition of J. O. Halliwell ("Percy Society 22" [London, 1848]), pp. 50–51.

30. Child, 10, 18, 21, 26, 276; see B. H. Bronson, "The Interdependence of Bal-

lad Tunes and Texts," appearing originally in *California Folklore Quarterly* (now *Western Folklore*), III (1944), 185–207, reprinted in MacEdward Leach and Tristram P. Coffin (eds.), *The Critics and the Ballad* (Carbondale, Ill., 1961), pp. 77–102. For a valuable discussion of "The Three Ravens" stanza, see esp. pp. 83–88.

31. See Hodgart, *The Ballads*, pp. 80 ff.

32. For the "emotional core" concept, see Tristram P. Coffin, "Mary Hamilton and the Anglo-American Ballad as an Art Form," *JAF*, LXX (1957), 208–214; reprinted in Leach and Coffin, *The Critics and the Ballad*, pp. 245–256. I think

distinct from folksongs, maintained a strong narrative character until the beginning of the eighteenth century. The explanation for this, I believe, is to be found in what might be called the balance of power between the minstrel and folksong traditions which together determined the shape and development of the ballad form. Instead of subsiding into the musical patterns of folksong, the new minstrelsy of the Renaissance maintained the artistic initiative throughout the seventeenth century and for the most part forced the melodic tradition into a subservient role. That there were still men capable of composing symmetrical narratives in the traditional manner is evident not only in that remarkable ballad in the Percy folio manuscript, "Will Stewart and John" (107), but also in such eighteenth-century examples of baroque minstrelsy as "Dick o the Cow" (185) and "The Duke of Gordon's Daughter" (237).

Nevertheless, an important change did take place at the beginning of the eighteenth century, and I will therefore conclude the present sketch of the development of balladry by describing the nature of this change. Looking at the problem first from the purely social point of view, it could be said that a new development in the form of the popular ballad might be anticipated in view of the disintegration of the minstrel profession. Minstrels were sufficiently numerous in the sixteenth century to be satirized;[33] but in the seventeenth century they lost ground rapidly because of the centralization of culture in London and the gradual disappearance of the rural centers of social activity sponsored by the aristocracy. By the beginning of the eighteenth century the popular ballads were being sung by non-professional people in all ranks of society in both the urban and rural districts of England and Scotland. The minstrels had virtually disappeared, and such new ballads as were born in the post-minstrelsy age were for the most part composed by those talented individuals who sang them or by poets in touch with the ballad tradition.

The changes in social conditions affecting balladry coincided with a shift in the so-called balance of power mentioned above in connection with the relative strength of influence of minstrelsy and folksong. What happened around 1700 was that the traditional narrative emphasis of ballads gradually became subservient to the influence of melody, which

Coffin's thesis is applicable to ballads of the eighteenth century and following, but not earlier. See the discussion below of new developments in the eighteenth century and especially references to "Johnie Armstrong" (169C) and the development of a refrain. Later on there is a similar development in "The Lass of Roch Royal" (76H).

33. In F. J. Furnivall (ed.), *Robert Laneham's Letter* (London, 1907), pp. 36–43.

began to play a much more important part in determining ballad structure. Perhaps the best way to describe the general consequence of this new development is to say that there was at first a great intensification of narrative symmetry. This can be seen most readily, I believe, in a comparison of the *Wit Restord* version of "Johnie Armstrong" (169A), published in 1658, with the *Ever Green* version (169C), published in 1724 and obtained by Ramsay, significantly enough, from a member of the Armstrong family.[34] Aside from differences in the story itself, which is a separate problem, one notices immediately the insistent stanzaic parallelism. This occurs especially in the king's rejection of Johnie's offer, which in the seventeenth-century text occupies a single stanza, but in the Ramsay version is repeated no less than five times without verbal variation in response to an almost equally rigid series of offers by Johnie. It is interesting to note that Ramsay prints the first occurrence of the king's reply stanza in italics, and thereafter only part of the first line, italicized, followed by Etc., treating it as if it were a refrain.[35]

The consequences of this intensification of symmetry in the popular ballad at the beginning of the eighteenth century were very extensive and important, but space will permit mention here of only two. One of these is of course the rapid development of a treasury of commonplace stanzas, which it was felt increasingly appropriate to draw on in the creation and re-creation of ballads. This may have been due in part to a growing self-consciousness on the part of balladmakers in the eighteenth century. Realizing more and more the wealth of traditional song to which they were contributing, they perhaps composed with greater deference to and consciousness of a ballad style. Whatever the explanation, ballads of this period tend to have what I would call a mosaic quality. The unit of composition is no longer the line but the stanza. The stanzaic commonplaces are fitted together like pieces of colored glass to form the narrative design and achieve the desired effect. The beginning and the climax of this development can be seen in a comparison of "Johnie Armstrong" (169) and "Johnie Scot" (99).[36]

The second consequence of the intensification of narrative symmetry

34. Allan Ramsay, *The Ever Green: A Collection of Scots Poems Wrote by the Ingenious before 1600* (2 vols.; Glasgow, 1724; reprinted 1874), II, 190–196.

35. *Ibid.*, II, 192 f.

36. See James H. Jones, "Commonplace and Memorization in the Oral Tradition of the English and Scottish Popular Bal-lads," *JAF*, LXXIV (1961), 97–112. (Hereinafter referred to as "Commonplace and Memorization.") There is much truth in Friedman's critique immediately following (*JAF*, LXXIV, pp. 113–115), but I think there is more originality and value in Jones's approach than Friedman seems to allow.

was the sudden maturing of a device not unknown, but relatively rare, in earlier ballads: the device known as incremental repetition.[37] To some extent the rather sudden flowering of this feature might be explained generally as a result of the dominance of melody already mentioned. But it is also possible to see in this development a final contribution of the dying minstrelsy tradition. I have already described how the "weak" line of the minstrel quatrain, "for sothe I say to you," developed a descriptive line like "under the greenwood tree" which joined with folksong to create the earliest refrain ballads. But, of course, the refrain ballads are in the minority, and the older stanza form, complete with the "weak" line, continued to perpetuate itself. In the early eighteenth century, therefore, under these new conditions, the weak line became a source of stylistic strength as it yielded to melodic pressure and became an important link in the incremental repetition and the leaping and lingering technique so characteristic of the popular ballad as we know it today. One of the earliest typical but effective examples of the lingering technique can be seen in the *Tea-Table Miscellany* version of "The Gypsy Laddie" (200A), first published in 1740:

'Come to your bed,' says Johny Faa,
　'Oh come to your bed, my deary;
For I vow and I swear, by the hilt of my sword,
　That your lord shall nae mair come near ye.'

'I'll go to bed to my Johny Faa,
　I'll go to bed to my deary;
For I vow and I swear, by what past yestreen,
　That my lord shall nae mair come near me.

'I'll mak a hap to my Johny Faa,
　And I'll mak a hap to my deary;
And he's get a' the coat gaes round,
　And my lord shall nae mair come near me.'[38]

The eighteenth century is in one sense the golden age of balladry, and its achievement deserves more careful study than has thus far been devoted to it. But such a study must proceed chronologically; it must be duly aware of the major stylistic innovations of the period and not re-

37. See, for example, Child, 273App1, "The King and the Barker," stanzas 46–48, though I question whether this is a ballad; see n. 25, above. Many other examples could be cited if we include early carols and songs.

38. Allan Ramsay, *The Tea-Table Miscellany* (1740 ed.); I quote stanzas 5–7.

gard the ballad as having fixed, unchanging characteristics that do not evolve; and, above all, it must study stylistic features in the light of the sources of each version. The ballads collected by David Herd are one thing; those transcribed from the recitation of Mrs. Brown of Falkland are another. Ballads obtained through the good offices of David Dalrymple, Lord Hailes, are a third, quite different kind of thing.[39] We need no longer assume that ballads like these were being recovered by chance from an impervious oral tradition. The publication of these ballads in the late eighteenth and early nineteenth centuries was an event and not an accident. A recognition of this fact is an important prerequisite to stylistic analysis.

It is not my purpose to carry this sketch of the literary history of balladry beyond the end of the eighteenth century. One reason is that, just as is true of all historiography, it becomes increasingly difficult to see things in perspective the nearer one approaches the present age. Another is that a sudden distortion of the picture occurs in the early nineteenth century as a result of the tremendous increase in the number of ballad versions collected by eager antiquaries. Child's collection inevitably reflects this distortion; the majority of his versions were recovered in the nineteenth century. Although the ballad appears to have suffered a decline in the nineteenth century, to some extent it may be that I have merely failed to realize that the busy followers of Sir Walter Scott have thrust a magnifying glass before my eyes which distorts my view of the modern ballad tradition just as effectively as it did the fair skins of those English ladies mentioned by Lemuel Gulliver. A literary history of the ballad in modern times will of course need to adjust its view accordingly.

To summarize: the English and Scottish ballads originated in the fifteenth century when the metrical romance tradition of the later Middle Ages joined the mainstream of folksong to create a type of narrative song which we now call the ballad. When medieval minstrelsy passed through the folksong prism, it emerged in a colorful spectrum of stanza forms with refrain, reflecting the various structures then existing in folksong tradition; but the new minstrelsy, with its tendency to create strong symmetrical narratives, continued to dominate the musical setting which it had acquired, so that ballads having a refrain were in the minority. When the

39. See A. Watkin-Jones, "Bishop Percy and the Scottish Ballads," in *E&S*, XVIII (1933), 110–121; David Nichol Smith and Cleanth Brooks (eds.), *The Percy Letters*, esp. vol. IV, A. F. Falconer, (ed.), *The Correspondence of Thomas Percy and David Dalrymple, Lord Hailes* (Baton Rouge, 1954). (Hereinafter referred to as Falconer, *Percy-Hailes Correspondence*.)

tide turned at the end of the seventeenth century, the long-standing supremacy of minstrelsy ended, and the music of the ballad increasingly came to determine the course of its evolution. The resulting intensity of narrative symmetry, the growing reservoir of commonplaces, and the remarkable developments of style, especially the leaping and lingering technique, made the eighteenth century a major creative period in the history of balladry.

1. The evolution of balladry   19

2. The folksong tradition

If for the moment we pretend that the popular ballad never existed, there remains an important English and Scottish folksong tradition extending from the Middle Ages to the present day which is well worth studying for its own sake. I refer particularly to the secular and religious songs which as early as the thirteenth century began to appear in manuscript collections. Although the songs in this category are predominantly religious, they also contain a variety of other elements, including much popular lore and belief. Of the genres that might be included here the most important for our purposes are the riddle songs, the songs of romance and comedy, and the religious songs. A most interesting and significant early group of these is included in the Child canon. The riddle songs are "Riddles Wisely Expounded" (1), "The Elfin Knight" (2), "The Fause Knight upon the Road" (3), "King John and the Bishop" (45), and "Captain Wedderburn's Courtship" (46); the songs of romance and comedy are "The Three Ravens" (26), "Crow and Pie" (111), "The Baffled Knight" (112), "The Friar in the Well" (276), and perhaps "John Dory" (284); the religious songs are "The Maid and the Palmer" (21), "St. Stephen and Herod" (22), "Judas" (23), "The Cherry-Tree Carol" (54), "The Carnal and the Crane" (55), and "Dives and Lazarus" (56). In the latter category belong a number of other songs not included by Child in his collection, such as "The Bitter Withy," "The Holy Well," and the "Corpus Christi" carol.

There are several reasons for considering the early folksong tradition before giving detailed attention to the beginnings of balladry. For one thing, it is my contention that the songs listed above are on the fringes rather than at the center of Child's canon, and that they should therefore not be permitted to distort our vision or predetermine our expectations regarding ballad origins. Furthermore, the religious songs and carols are undoubtedly the earliest pieces to be dealt with in the present history, and it is therefore in accord with our chronological procedure to consider them first, in spite of the fact that particular songs in this group may not have been recovered before the nineteenth century. Above all it should be recognized that the religious songs and carols in particular were a powerful influence on balladry at certain stages of its development. To see this, we need to become familiar with the content and style of these songs before proceeding to a study of the ballads themselves. It is worth mentioning, finally, that whereas most ballads are born, flourish, and die within a relatively short period, there is evidence that, because of what might be called "stability of occasion," religious songs tend to live on for centuries in tradition.[1]

The riddle songs

Turning first to the riddle songs, we find that with the exception of "The Fause Knight upon the Road" (3), which first appeared in Mother-well's *Minstrelsy* (1827), all are found relatively early. "Riddles Wisely Expounded" (1) appears in a manuscript of 1445 or earlier; "The Elfin Knight" (2) exists in a broadside of about 1670; a version of "King John and the Bishop" (45) not known to Child has been found in a manuscript leaf of about 1550–1570; and although the narrative setting of "Captain Wedderburn's Courtship" (46) is first found in David Herd's manuscripts in the latter half of the eighteenth century, the riddle sequence on which it is partly based is contained in a manuscript of the first half of the fifteenth century.[2]

The deadly nature of the ancient riddling duel, re-created so effectively in Tolkien's description of the duel between Bilbo and Gollum,[3] is largely obscured in the riddle texts under consideration. Some of the tension of the contest lingers in the earliest version of "Riddles Wisely Expounded" (1), which in the manuscript is given the title "Inter diabolus et Virgo," for although the devil at first seems to be tempting the maid (sts. 2–4),

Thys spake Þe fend to Þe mayd:
'Beleve on me, mayd, to day.

1. A good illustration is provided by Richard L. Greene, "The Traditional Survival of Two Medieval Carols," *ELH*, VII (1940), 223–238. By applying the phrase "stability of occasion" to religious songs I mean to suggest merely that their position in relation to the Christian calendar of holy days has tended to strengthen these songs and preserve them from decay. There were of course frequent and appropriate social occasions for the singing of ballads, both during and after the age of minstrelsy, but the social conditions needed for ballad singing were less enduring than the occasions that call for the singing of religious songs. It is in this sense that the traditional carols surviving over such a long period of time owe their remarkable preservation to "stability of occasion."

2. The manuscript version of "Riddles Wisely Expounded" was not noticed by Child until late, and hence it appears under "Additions and Corrections," V, 283–284. For the version of "King John and the Bishop" not known to Child, see Roberta D. Cornelius, "A New Text of an Old Ballad," *PMLA*, XLVI (1931), 1025–1033.

3. J. R. R. Tolkien, *The Hobbit* (London, 1937), pp. 80–101.

'Mayd, mote y thi leman be,
Wyssedom y wolle teche the:

'All Þe wyssedom off the world,
Hyf Þou wolt be true and forward holde,'

nevertheless, after asking the riddles, he concludes threateningly (st. 12):

'But Þou now answery me,
Thu schalt for soÞe my leman be.'

In spite of the lateness of its recovery, a similar preservation of old features is evident in "The Fause Knight upon the Road" (3), which is a perilous contest of wits similar to the authentic and amusing shape-shifting duel described by T. H. White.[4] After the opening "polite" conversation, the exchanges are as quick as thought itself (sts. 6–9):

'I wiss ye were on yon Tree:'
'And a gude ladder under me.'

'And the ladder for to break:'
'And you for to fa down.'

'I wiss ye were in yon sie:'
'And a gude bottom under me.'

'And the bottom for to break:'
'And ye to be drowned.'

But the contest of wit in the riddle songs has been largely supplanted, of course, by the battle of the sexes. In the broadside version of "Riddles Wisely Expounded" (1A), the knight, having had his will of the girl, uses the riddles as a means of "trying her wit" before deciding whether to marry her! And in "Captain Wedderburn's Courtship" (46), the captain's plan for seduction is skilfully transformed by the girl's riddles into a marriage proposal. By the time we reach the song's last riddle, the "priest unborn" is standing outside the door, and indeed for poor Captain Wedderburn the handwriting is already on the wall next to which the ingenious girl has insisted she will not lie (46A18):

Little kent Grizey Sinclair, that morning when she raise,
'Twas to be the hindermost of a' her single days;
For now she's Captain Wetherburn's wife, a man she never saw,
And she man lye in his bed, but she'll not lye neist the wa.

4. T. H. White, *The Sword in the Stone* (New York, 1939), pp. 79–83.

The remarkable persistence of the riddle form is evident in a comparison of "Captain Wedderburn's Courtship" with its manuscript sources. Not only is the "cherry without a stone" sequence preserved with little change, but a few of the girl's six questions are in very close verbal agreement with "Riddles Wisely Expounded," where we find (1A15):

'Or what is greener than the grass,
Or what is worse then a woman was?'

To which the reply is (1A18):

'And poyson is greener than the grass,
And the Devil is worse than woman was.'

The reference to "a woman" here is of course to Eve, for the setting implied is that of the temptation as described in Genesis. But in David Herd's text of "Captain Wedderburn" the girl asks "What's war than a woman's wiss" (46A12), which in other versions appears as "women's wish" (B16) and even "woman's voice" (C8). Yet these variations in themselves are a remarkable testimony to the verbal stability of the riddles, which outlast the lovers who employ them.

Omnibus that it is, "Captain Wedderburn" also contains the motif of the wedding "tasks," which is however best illustrated in "The Elfin Knight" (2), where the knight and the girl set impossible tasks for each other. She must shape a sark to him without any cut or hem, etc., and he must harvest a crop for her under impossible conditions. The result is, in fact, a stalemate; he will keep his plaid and she her maidenhead. The structure of this particular text is very suggestive of the folktale, as we meet it, for example, in "Kulhwch and Olwen":

"Seest thou yonder vast hill?" "I see it." "I require that it be rooted up, and that the grubbings be burned for manure on the face of the land, and that it be ploughed and sown in one day, and in one day that the grain ripen. And of that wheat I intend to make food and liquor fit for the wedding of thee and my daughter. And all this I require done in one day."

"It will be easy for me to compass this, although thou mayest think that it will not be easy."

"Though this be easy for thee, there is yet that which will not be so. No husbandman can till or prepare this land, so wild it is, except Amaethon the son of Don, and he will not come with thee by his own free will, and thou wilt not be able to compel him."

2. The folksong tradition   23

"It will be easy for me to compass this, although thou mayest think that it will not be easy."[5]

Once the formula is established, as in "Kulhwch and Olwen," the teller of tales can spin out the story indefinitely, describing conditions of increasing complexity and difficulty.

The tasks in "The Elfin Knight," however, are relatively stable; the knight's instructions for making the sark change and expand very little. In the seventeenth- and eighteenth-century versions the girl is told merely how to sew the sark; but beginning with *Gammer Gurton's Garland* (1810), she is told to wash and dry it as follows (2G2–3):

'Can you wash it in yonder well,
Where never sprung water nor rain ever fell?

'Can you dry it on yonder thorn,
Which never bore blossom since Adam was born?'

Although washing the sark in a dry well can be regarded as reasonably difficult, drying it on the thorn seems unforgivably simple. And while the problem might be solved by recourse to Kinloch's 1826 version (2C9),

'And ye maun dry it on yon hawthorn,
Whare the sun neer shon sin man was born,'

I am doubtful of the authenticity of this homely allusion to difficult drying conditions. It seems rather like a rationalization of the Garland version. The development can best be explained, I think, as a phenomenon which we shall encounter frequently in our study of the ballads: it is an example of the influence of the religious carols. In this instance one recalls the concluding stanza of the Staffordshire version of "Corpus Christi" (1862):

At that bed's head there grows a thorn,
which was never so blossomed since Christ was born.

The sudden development of new refrains in the nineteenth century, especially the "Sing ivy, sing ivy" of the Halliwell nursery version (2K), can perhaps be regarded as confirmation of the carol influence on late versions of "The Elfin Knight."[6] In any case there can be little doubt of the

---

5. Lady Charlotte Guest (trans.), *The Mabinogion* (London, 1906), p. 113. For further information and modern translations, see Idris Ll. Foster, "Culhwch and Olwen and Rhonabwy's Dream," in R. S. Loomis (ed.), *Arthurian Literature in the Middle Ages* (Oxford, 1959), pp. 31–43.
6. See Bronson, *The Traditional Tunes of the Child Ballads*, I, 9 ff.

24

direction of influence, such as it may be, between the two songs. The allegorical thorn of the "Corpus Christi" carol is profoundly meaningful in its context, as we shall see; the thorn in late versions of "The Elfin Knight" is either introduced whimsically or by attraction of words from the carol tradition.

One problem about the riddle texts which has not yet been mentioned is the difficulty of being certain that the early manuscripts do indeed contain versions that were sung. Was "Inter diabolus et virgo" a song? It may never be possible to answer such a question with certainty, but perhaps it will be profitable to examine one further riddle text with this question in mind. Speaking of "King John and the Bishop" (45), Bronson remarks:

> The stuff of this ballad, as Child's introduction makes very clear, is out of the storehouse of tradition. On the other hand, Child's parallels—an impressive array—are almost wholly drawn from *tales* both popular and literary. The earlier we get in the English records, the less does the ballad resemble traditional verse.[7]

Let us therefore look briefly at the earlier versions of this ballad to see whether a structural comparison of them can shed any light on the problem.

The earliest known version of "King John and the Bishop" was discovered originally by Carleton Brown in an Oxford manuscript and subsequently printed by Roberta D. Cornelius in 1931.[8] The date of the leaf on which this text was copied is about 1550–1570, or nearly a hundred years earlier than Child's A text taken from the Percy folio manuscript. Neither of these versions has music, nor even a refrain that would indicate a singing tradition. Child's B text is a broadside of the late seventeenth century, with external refrain indicated at the end of the first stanza: "Derry down, down hey, derry down." From this point on, the musical tradition of "King John," though complex, is never in doubt. A particularly energetic New England tune for this ballad runs through my mind every time I see the words.[9]

The Oxford text of "King John," in addition to being the earliest, is also the fullest narrative. Moreover, this version, interestingly enough, has something of that symmetrical quality which I mentioned in the pre-

7. *Ibid.*, I, 354.
8. See n. 2, above. The text is on a leaf bound in the Corpus Christi College, Oxford MS.255.
9. See "Eight Traditional British-American Ballads" (Helen Hartness Flanders Collection, Middlebury College, Middlebury, Vt.), New England Folksong Series No. 1: "King John and the Bishop," sung by Elmer George.

2. The folksong tradition   25

ceding chapter as characteristic of minstrelsy narrative. King John, hearing how expensive and lordly is the life of the Bishop of Canterbury, sends for him with the idea of asking him three impossible questions and seizing his lands if he cannot answer. The following outline will indicate the narrative symmetry:

A. The Bishop came with one hundred men and knelt before the King.
   1. *King*: You are welcome.
   2. *Bishop*: I spend nothing but God's and my own.
   3. *King*: Answer my questions or lose your head.
      a. *first question*: What am I worth?
      b. *second question*: How soon may I go around the world?
      c. *third question*: What am I thinking?
INTERLUDE: The Bishop inquires at Oxford and Cambridge for the answers to these questions, but without success; he returns home despondent. A shepherd (his brother-in-law) persuades the Bishop to let him dress as the Bishop and go before the King to answer the questions.
B. The Shepherd came with one hundred men and knelt before the King.
   1. *King*: you have kept your day; now answer my questions.
   2. *Shepherd*: I spend nothing but God's and my own; what was your first question?
   3. *Exchange*:
      a. *first question*: what am I worth?
         answer: twenty-nine pence; one penny less than Jesus.
      b. *second question*: how soon may I go around the world?
         answer: follow the sun; it will take 24 hours.
      c. *third question*: what am I thinking?
         answer: you think I am the Bishop of Canterbury.
CONCLUSION: Bishop is pardoned and shepherd rewarded.

If we look at the Percy manuscript version with this structure in mind, we discover that while in certain respects the narrative has been compressed, in other ways the symmetrical parallelism has been increased. What I have called the "interlude" in the Oxford text has acquired two new stanzas (A16–17) that repeat the King's questions, and the implicit parallelism of the King's welcoming speech, first to the Bishop and then to the Shepherd-bishop, is made verbally explicit (A4, 21). On the other hand, the Bishop's defense of his spending (A5) and the King's threat to cut off his head (A6) are not repeated and hence these parallels are lost in the Percy folio version. The broadside version (45B) with refrain is about one-half the length of the Percy text and has lost all narrative parallels except the threefold repetition of the King's three questions. The result is a still higher proportion of stanzas repeated with slight variations. The "old abbot" (as he is now called in B) can inform the shepherd of what happened at court simply by paraphrasing and echoing the King's words (B10–12):

'Sad news, sad news I have thee to give,
For I have but three days space for to live;
If I do not answer him questions three,
My head will be taken from my body.

'When he is set so high on his steed,
With his crown of gold upon his head,
Amongst all his nobility, with joy and much mirth,
I must tell him to one penny what he is worth.

'And the next question I must not flout,
How long he shall be riding the world about;
And the third question I must not shrink,
But tell him truly what he does think.'

From what has been said thus far it might be concluded that the three early texts of "King John and the Bishop" illustrate a development from written to oral form analogous to that pointed out convincingly by Nygard with respect to "The Death of Queen Jane" (170).[10] Yet I think it is possible to regard the Oxford text of "King John" as something quite different from "The doleful death of Queen Jane" etc., which Nygard rightly calls a "wretched poem."

To a considerable extent, of course, the Oxford version is a sophisticated one. This is particularly evident in the introductory portion having no counterpart in either of the later versions considered. There is, for example, the unique passage naming King John's predecessor, Richard I, and his successor, Henry III (ll. 5–6), and the long passage describing

10. H. O. Nygard, "Ballads and the   Middle Ages," *TSL*, V (1960), 85–96.

the appearance of the King's messenger before the Bishop and the Bishop's reply (ll. 11–28). It is significant, I think, that although the Oxford text for the most part divides readily into four-line stanzas,[11] the passage just mentioned does not, as is illustrated in the following lines, quoted as Miss Cornelius gives them, following the manuscript, without modern punctuation or stanza divisions (ll. 11–24):

> when the purseuant came to canterburye
> he found the b. making full merye
> the purseuant sayd sire god you saue
> & to the byshipe a letter he gaue
> conteaninge this tenoure without leasing
> that he wos accuseid vnto the King
> the byshipe red therein awhille
> & unto himself sumthing he dyd smille
> & sayd I perceaue without leasing
> that I ame accused vnto the King
> for my housekepinge & for my good cheare
> but I trust his grace, will do me no deare
> for to his grace I wysh it wear knowne
> I spend nothing but godes & mine owne

Not only does this passage not divide readily into stanzas, it also seems strikingly different from the rest of the ballad in tone and perspective. The sudden insight or plan of action betokened by the Bishop's private smile is never made clear; and the lavish entertainment of the King's messenger, though it is an admirable touch, seems not in keeping with the rest of the story. Hence I conclude that this is an example of the transcriber's own creative contribution, stimulated perhaps by a momentary failure of memory. I doubt that it was ever sung.

Yet there is some evidence, I believe, that a sung version lies behind the Oxford text. As Miss Cornelius points out, the scribe more than once makes the kind of error that is clearly memorial and not visual.[12] Furthermore, although it is true that this text lacks the characteristic repetition of the King's questions in the "interlude," I cannot help feeling that these stanzas were present in our scribe's oral exemplar (if such a term is permissible), and that the following lines are an arbitrary abridgment of the repeated questions (ll. 85–88):

11. Other cases of imperfect stanzas may be attributed, as Miss Cornelius suggests, to a "slip of memory" ("A New Text of an Old Ballad," p. 1026).

12. *Ibid.*

What be tho questions the shepperd dyd saye
the byship shewed him without deleay
when he had shewd him the questions thre
the shepperd laughed ful hartelye.

I do not claim any great antiquity for "King John and the Bishop"; yet
I do believe that, like most of the pieces in the group we have just considered, it has been perpetuated in oral tradition for an unusually long
time, and in fact was being sung, perhaps "to its own tune," in the middle
of the sixteenth century.

Songs of romance and comedy

The songs to be considered here can be grouped under the heading
"romance and comedy" if we consider the term "romance" flexible enough,
for example, to apply to "The Three Ravens" (26). For the present purpose, however, it is particularly important to emphasize that, unlike the
earliest texts in the riddle group, we need have little hesitation in assuming that these romantic and comic pieces were sung from the very moment
of their creation. Three of them, indeed, first appear in the songbooks
of Thomas Ravenscroft: "The Baffled Knight" (112) and "John Dory"
(284) in his *Deuteromelia* (1609), and "The Three Ravens" (26) in his
Melismata (1611).[13] Two other pieces, "The Friar in the Well" (276)
and "The Knight and the Shepherd's Daughter" (110), are first found
in seventeenth-century broadsides, but the stanza form of "The Friar in
the Well," a delightful comic song, is like that of "The Three Ravens,"
and references, probably to "The Friar," are found as early as John
Skelton's "Colin Clout" (1522).[14] The final song in this group, "Crow
and Pie" (111), is the earliest, found in a manuscript of about 1500. The
text unfortunately lacks any indication of a tune.

Concerning "Crow and Pie" Child remarks (II, 478): "This is not a
purely popular ballad, but rather of that kind which, for convenience,
may be called the minstrel-ballad." Since in the present study I am
stressing the role of the minstrel in the creation of the popular ballad (as
was indicated in the preceding chapter), I prefer not to apply the term
"minstrel-ballad" to "Crow and Pie," even though I agree with what

13. These songbooks, the first two
originally published in 1609 and *Melismata* in 1611, have been reprinted by
the American Folklore Society as Vol.
XII of the Bibliographical and Special
Series: *Pammelia Deutromelia Melismata
by Thomas Ravenscroft* (Philadelphia,
1961). "John Dory" is *Deuteromelia* 1,
"The Baffled Knight" is *Deuteromelia* 22,
and "The Three Ravens" is *Melismata* 20.
14. See Child, *ESPB*, V, 100; Bronson,
"The Interdependence of Ballad Tunes
and Texts," pp. 85 ff.

seems to be the general intent of Child's remark. If this song was not always a typical minstrel's song, it is altogether likely that by this time (1500), if my theory is correct, it had certainly found its way into the increasingly diversified minstrel repertoire. As we shall see, it resembles to a considerable degree the light, secular love songs in the Sloane manuscript.[15]

In a sense "Crow and Pie" and its sequence, notably such pastourelles as "The Knight and the Shepherd's Daughter" (110) and "The Baffled Knight" (112), are sophisticated offshoots of the battle of the sexes found in the riddle songs. What had been a grim supernatural contest in "Riddles Wisely Expounded" (1A12),

'But Þou now answery me,
Thu schalt for soÞe my leman be,'

becomes a lighthearted seduction game in "Crow and Pie" (111, st. 5):

He toke then owt a good golde ryng,
    A purse of velweytt, that was soo fyne:
'Have ye thys, my dere swetyng,
    With that ye wylbe lemman myn.'

The girl's defenses, though finally ineffective, are replete with rationality and worldly considerations (st. 6):

'Be Cryst, I dare nott, for my dame;
    To dele with hym Þat I doo nott knowe;
For soo I myght dyspyse my name;
    Therfore the crow shall byte yow.'

But long before all the play is played, the girl's impish refrain line "Therfore the crow shall byte yow" has been supplanted by the boy's triumphant reply, "Therefore the pye hathe pecked yow." And just as the youngest daughter in "Riddles Wisely Expounded" is forced to ask (1A9),

'Now you have had your will,' quoth she,
'I pray, sir knight, will you marry me?'

so the girl in "Crow and Pie" inquires (111, st. 10):

'But sythe ye haue i-lyen me bye,
    Ye wyll wedde me now, as I trowe:'
'I wyll be adwysed, Gyll,' sayd he,
    'For now the pye hathe peckyd yow."

15. See subsequent discussion of British   Museum MS Sloane 2593 in this chapter.

30

But whereas the obliging northern knight of "Riddles Wisely Expounded" marries the young daughter, the gay young man of "Crow and Pie" abandons the girl to her fate. When she asks him (st. 13),

> 'Now sythe ye haue i-leyn me bye,
>   A lyttle thyng ye wyll tell;
> In case that I with chylde be,
>   What is your name? Wher doo ye dwell?'

his reply is a farewell (st. 14):

> 'At Yorke, at London, at Clerkenwell,
>   At Lycester, Cambryge, at myrye Brystowe;
> Some call me Rychard, Robart, Jacke, and Wyll;
>   For now the pye hathe peckyd yow.'

This same dialogue is echoed in the seventeenth-century broadside version of "The Knight and the Shepherd's Daughter" (110A5–6):

> 'Now you have had your wil, good sir,
>   And put my body thus to shame,
> Even as you are a courteous knight,
>   Tel me what is your name.'

> 'Some men do call me Jack, sweet heart,
>   And some do call me John,
> But when I come to the king's fair court,
>   They call me Sweet William.'

"The Knight and the Shepherd's Daughter" (110) and "The Baffled Knight" (112) are in a sense both elaborations of "Crow and Pie," the former providing a truce to the battle of the sexes through a denouement reminiscent of Chaucer's "Wife of Bath's Tale," and the latter allowing the complete triumph of the girl over her would-be seducer. In fact the crow continued to bite the baffled knight in a series of continuations that evidently became very popular in the late seventeenth or early eighteenth century. The same type of challenge and response can be seen operating on the literary level in "The Passionate Shepherd to His Love," ascribed to Christopher Marlowe, and "The Nymph's Reply to the Shepherd," sometimes ascribed to Sir Walter Raleigh.[16]

As we have seen, in addition to "The Baffled Knight," Ravenscroft

---

16. For the baffled knight continuations, see Child, *ESPB*, II, 491–493. To speak of "The Baffled Knight" as popular and the "Shepherd" poems as literary is perhaps to make an artificial distinction. See the remarks of Friedman, *The Ballad Revival*, pp. 52–53.

published two other songs that Child chose to include in his collection, "The Three Ravens" (26) and "John Dory" (284). The former is of course a beautiful work of art, justifiably famous for both its words and music, preserved in *Melismata*. "John Dory," on the other hand, though it enjoyed considerable popularity in the seventeenth century,[17] is not very well known but calls for some attention because it is the nearest thing to a popular ballad in the primary sense Child intended than any of the pieces we have considered in this group (284, st. 1):

> As it fell on a holy-day,
> > And vpon an holy-tide-a,
> Iohn Dory bought him an ambling nag,
> > To Paris for to ride-a.

There is a substantial narrative here. In Child's words:

> John Dory goes to Paris and offers King John, in return for a pardon asked for himself and his men, to bring the French king all the churls in England in bonds. Nicholl, a Cornish man, fits out a good bark, has an encounter with John Dory, and after a smart fight takes him prisoner. (*ESPB*, V, 131)

The text as Child prints it, however, fails to show very clearly the actual form of the song. Compare, for example, the above stanza quoted from Child with the same stanza as it appears in Ravenscroft's *Deuteromelia*, with all of the repetitions called for in the text:

> As it fell on a holy-day,
> As it fell on a holy-day,
> > holy-day,
>
> And vpon an holy-tide-a,
> And vpon an holy-tide-a,
> > tide-a,
>
> Iohn Dory bought him an ambling nag,
> Iohn Dory bought him an ambling nag,
> > ambling nag,
>
> To Paris for to ride-a,
> To Paris for to ride-a,
> > ride-a.

Perhaps it would be technically correct to call "John Dory" a ballad, but I think it would be misleading. Here we see a narrative completely at

17. See Child, *ESPB*, V, 131 f., and   Friedman, *The Ballad Revival*, p. 124.

the mercy of the tune. Such a composition belongs properly in the folk-song tradition, and as such may exert some influence in the history we are tracing; yet it can scarcely be regarded as of primary importance in the development of balladry. At the very time "John Dory" was flourishing, however, the old song of Percy and Douglas and other compositions of the new minstrelsy were converging to form the mainstream of the ballad tradition.

The Sloane manuscript

Before turning our attention to particular religious songs it will be desirable first to consider the context or manuscript setting in which they are found. Although the garlands, drolleries, and miscellanies in which some of the later Child ballads appear have been studied,[18] very little has been done by way of analysis of the manuscript collections in which Child found the earliest texts for his collection. There is no space in the present study for detailed examination of all the manuscript sources involved, but it will be well, I think, to consider one of these that is of particular interest: the British Museum manuscript Sloane 2593, dating from the first half of the fifteenth century.

Although various selections had been published earlier, the Sloane manuscript was first edited in its entirety by Thomas Wright for the Warton Club in 1856.[19] In the preface to this edition, Wright compares Sloane with a similar manuscript then in his possession and remarks that "they are both of them apparently the song-books of minstrels."[20] He does not expand upon this point, however, and I doubt that he really meant to imply anything more than that they were songbooks, which indeed they are.[21] The interesting thing about the Sloane manuscript for the present study is the fact that it contains two Child texts, "St. Stephen and Herod" (22) and "Robyn and Gandeleyn" (115), plus the riddle sequence of the cherry-without-a-stone, etc., which is utilized in "Captain Wedderburn's Courtship" (46). Hence it will be well to look at Sloane not only for its own sake as an important early folksong collection, but also for

18. See esp. Friedman, *The Ballad Revival*, chap. v, pp. 114–155.

19. *Songs and Carols from a Manuscript in the British Museum of the Fifteenth Century* (London, 1856). For date and convenient description of contents, see Greene, *The Early English Carols*, p. 330.

20. Wright, *Songs and Carols*, p. 3. The other MS referred to is now in the Bodleian Library, Oxford: MS English Poet.e.l. (Summary Catalogue No. 29734),

and was printed by Wright as Vol. XXIII of the Percy Society Series, *Songs and Carols, Now First Printed from a Manuscript of the Fifteenth Century* (London, 1847).

21. See Greene, *The Early English Carols*, speaking of Bodleian MS English Poet.e.l. (p. 338): "There is no external evidence that it was made 'presumably for the use of a professed minstrel' (Madan, *Summary Catalogue*)."

the opportunity it gives us to judge Child's criteria of selection of the two "ballads" he chose from this group. (There are seventy-four songs in the manuscript, and, to avoid confusion with the arabic numerals used in this study for Child ballad numbers, I will employ the roman numerals in Wright's edition to refer to these songs.)

Joseph Ritson was the first to draw on the Sloane manuscript, choosing only five of the seventy-four pieces for inclusion in his *Ancient Songs from the Time of King Henry the Third to the Revolution*, published in 1790. Significantly, two of these five were xxxv, "Robynn lyth in grene wode bowndyn" (=Child 115), and xLIV, "Seynt Stevene was a clerk" (=Child 22). The other three were a song on the martyrdom of St. Edmund (LI), a satirical piece on the power of the penny (LIII), and a Nativity carol (LXVIII). It seems evident from the nature of his collection that Ritson regarded all five of these as songs.[22]

In 1833 William Sandys, in *Christmas Carols, Ancient and Modern*, republished two of the songs chosen by Ritson, "Seynt Stevene" (xLIV) and the Nativity carol (LXVIII), plus two other carols, "Blyssid be that mayde Mary" (VI) and "Mary moder, meke and mylde" (XXIV). There can be little doubt that Sandys regarded all four of these, including the "Seynt Stevene" (=Child 22), as good examples of the ancient Christmas carol.

Although other selections from Sloane were published during the nineteenth century, they do not seem to have been based on formal considerations.[23] I do not wish to explore the complete history of publication of extracts from this collection; it will be illuminating, however, to pause long enough to see what use has been made of the Sloane songs in two major twentieth-century collections.

Richard L. Greene's *The Early English Carols* (Oxford, 1935) contains fifty-seven of the seventy-four pieces in the Sloane manuscript. In order to indicate the kinds of songs represented, I give below a list of those included by Greene, grouped in accordance with the system used in his collection. (The roman numerals are of course those found in Wright's edition of the songs; the arabic numerals following in parentheses represent Greene's numbered carols):[24]

Nativity: V (68), VI (24), IX (87), XXIII (86A), XXX (25), XLVII (27A), LVI (16), LVIII (28), LXVIII (7B), LXXII (8B).

22. Friedman remarks (*The Ballad Revival*, p. 238): "Ballad scholars universally commend Ritson for distinguishing between songs and ballads in his various collections."
23. See B. Fehr, "Die Lieder der Hs. Sloane 2593," *Archiv*, cix (1902), 33–70, esp. 40 f.
24. Where more than one MS version is known, Greene uses letters, upper and lower case, following the example of the Child collection.

St. Thomas: XLVI (114A).

Epiphany: XXXII (123B), XXXIV (124A), XXXIX (125A), LVII (122B).

Lullaby: XXXVII (148A), XXXVIII (145B), LXIX (143).

Passion: XLIII (168), XLV (157C), LIX (169).

Virgin: XIII (175C), XIX (188), XLVIII (180B), L (185A).

Five Joys: XXI (231).

Annunciation: XXIV (242), LX (236), LXIV (234C).

Saints: III (315), LI (312), LXXIII (316).

Eucharist: XXXIII (320), XLII (317).

Religious Counsel: VII (329).

Moral Counsel: II (336), XII (356A), XIV (339), XX (355A), LXIII (341).

Repentance: LII (357).

Doomsday: IV (365), XVII (363).

Mortality: XVI (368).

Satire: X (383), XI (390), XV (385), XVIII (381), LIII (392), LXII (384).

Women: VIII (395B), XXII (403).

Marriage: XLIX (405).

Picaresque: LIV (416), LXI (417).

Amorous: LXXIV (457).

Chanson d'aventure (fragment): I (Appendix V).

The three Latin songs in Sloane (XXXVI, LXV, and LXVI) do not of course appear in Greene. Hence this leaves fourteen English songs in the manuscript which Greene decided not to include. Of these, eleven can be classified without difficulty according to Greene's own system as follows:

Nativity: XL, XLIV (=Child 22), LXX.

Virgin: XXV, XXVIII.

Annunciation: LV.

Moral Counsel: XLI.

Satire: LXXI.

Amorous: XXVI, XXIX (cf. Child 46), XXXI.

The most obvious reason for Greene's exclusion of these Sloane pieces is that they are not in the dominant carol meter as he defines it (*aaab*).[25]

---

25. Greene's designation of XXXV and XLIV as "ballads" (see *The Early English Carols*, p. 330) seems to be based on the fact that Child included them. Anyone who re-enacts Child's decision and makes his own selection of "ballads" from the Sloane MS will find that criteria for distinguishing them are hard to come by, especially in the group of eleven listed above.

At the same time we must recognize that Greene *did* include at least five carols from our manuscript that also do not fit the customary metrical pattern.[26] This leaves three songs that do not fit Greene's thematic categories or his metrical scheme, and, perhaps significantly, all three are suggestive of minstrelsy: a drinking song (xxvii), a comic apology for a poor singing voice (lxvii), and "Robynn lyth in grene wode bowndyn" (xxxv), this last of course being Child's "Robyn and Gandeleyn" (115).

The other principal modern collection containing pieces from the Sloane manuscript is Carleton Brown's *Religious Lyrics of the Fifteenth Century* (Oxford, 1939). Greene's edition of the carols had already appeared, and therefore Brown admitted only a "representative selection" of these.[27] Of the twenty-eight lyrics common to Greene and Carleton Brown, twelve can be found in the Sloane manuscript. For convenience I retain the thematic categories used above, but this time the arabic numbers in parentheses are those assigned to texts in the Brown collection:

Nativity: xxiii (B. 79), xl (B. 78).
St. Thomas: xlvi (B. 123).
Epiphany: xxxii (B. 88), xxxiv (B. 87), lxx (B. 90).
Lullaby: xxxvii (B. 84).
Virgin: xxv (B. 81), xxviii (B. 83).
Annunciation: lv (B. 18), lxiv (B. 72).
Eucharist: xlii (B114).

Five of these twelve Sloane lyrics, however, were not in Greene: "I syng of a myden" (xxv), "Adam lay I-bowndyn" (xxviii), "As I went throw a gardyn grene" (xl), "Ave maris stella" (lv), and "Enmy Herowde, thou wokkyd kyng" (lxx). These five were perhaps regarded by Brown as falling more naturally in the "religious lyric" category.

From the history of classification of the Sloane manuscript songs it can perhaps be inferred that they constitute primarily a carol collection with the admixture of a few lyrics differing primarily in metrical form rather than in content. Furthermore, if we look for a principle of organization in the manuscript itself, a certain rough grouping appears. The most distinct unit by far is numbers xxv–xxxi, all in the quatrain or couplet form. As we have seen, these are generally excluded from Greene's canon, but he did include xxx (his no. 25), on which he has the following note:

The highly repetitive character of this carol, so like that of tra-

---

26. These are xxx (rhyming *abcb*), xxxvii (couplet), xxxix (bob and wheel), li (*abab*), and lxxiv (*abcb* or perhaps couplet).

27. P. xix.

ditional game-songs, indicates that its author was imitating closely the methods of folk-song. This is emphasized by the occurrence of the carol in the MS. among other pieces which are not carols, but which use the same device of repetition and are even more obviously affected by folk-song, e.g., 'I haue a yong suster,' which precedes the carol, and 'I haue an newe gardyn,' which follows it.[28]

The two adjoining pieces referred to by Greene are of course the riddle song (cf. Child 46) and an amorous song which seems to lie behind "The Twelve Days of Christmas."[29]

As was mentioned in the preceding chapter, however, I question whether it is possible to speak of folksong elements as a separate and recognizable feature distinct from other characteristics in the carol tradition. It is not possible to go into detail here, since this study is primarily to be concerned with the popular ballad, but I must at least consider briefly this one issue raised by Greene because it involves a stylistic trait (the "highly repetitive character" of the song) which is commonly associated with the ballad. The carol referred to in the above quotation is as follows:

REFRAIN: Al the meryere is that place
     The sunne of grace hym schynit in.

1 The sunne of grace hym schynit in
   In on day quan it was morwe,
 Quan our Lord God born was
   Withoute wem or sorwe.

2 The sunne of grace hym schynit in
   On a day quan it was prime,
 Quan our Lord God born was,
   So wel he knew his tyme.

3 The sunne of grace hym schynit in
   On a day quan it was non,
 Quan our Lord God born was
   And on the rode don.

4 The sunne of grace hym schynit in
   On a day quan it was vndyrn,

28. Greene, *The Early English Carols*, p. 357.
29. See Margaret Dean-Smith, *A Guide* to *English Folk Song Collections, 1822–1952* (Liverpool, 1954), p. 21.

Quan our Lord God born was
And to the herte stongen.[30]

This highly formalized stanza structure immediately reminds us of that incremental repetition so often cited as a prominent feature of ballad style:

10 She had not sailed a league, a league,
    A league but barely three,
    When dismal grew his countenance,
    And drumlie grew his ee.

11 They had not saild a league, a league,
    A league but barely three,
    Until she espied his cloven foot,
    And she wept right bitterlie.[31]

But it is not necessary to quote such a late ballad as "The Daemon Lover," and in Scott's version at that,[32] to illustrate this repetitive style. In the Sloane manuscript itself, "Robynn lyth in grene wode bowndyn" (=Child 115) has very nearly the same thing:

16 'Now xalt Þu neuer ȝelpe, Wrennok,
    At ale ne at wyn,
    Þat Þu hast slawe goode Robyn,
    And his knaue Gandeleyn

17 'Now xalt Þu neuer ȝelpe, Wrennok,
    At wyn ne at ale,
    Þat Þu hast slaw goode Robyn,
    And Gandeleyn his knaue.'

Although this lacks the progressive revelation by increments which is a common feature of the ballads (as in "The Daemon Lover"), there are numerous other songs in the Sloane manuscript which possess the incremental pattern. One example will have to suffice:

1 I syng of a myden
    Þat is makeles.

30. Sloane No. xxx, Greene No. 25.
31. "James Harris (The Daemon Lover)" (Child 243F), the version taken from Scott's *Minstrelsy* (5th ed., 1812), II, 427. One might as easily cite the formalized stanzas of "Queen Eleanor's Confession" (156), an earlier example of a similar but not identical development.

32. Incremental repetition is not so prominent in earlier versions of "The Daemon Lover." Compare 243B9–11.

Kyng of alle kynges
   To here sone che ches.

2 He cam also stylle
   Þer his moder was
As dew in aprille
   Þat fallyt on Þe gras.

3 He cam also stylle
   to his moderes bowr
As dew in aprille
   Þat fallyt on Þe flour.

4 He cam also stylle
   Þer his moder lay
As dew in aprille
   Þat fallyt on Þe spray.

5 Moder & mayden
   was neuer non but che—
Wel may swych a lady
   godes moder be.[33]

This is of course a highly sophisticated use of the repetitive style, for which "I syng of a myden" has been justly admired.[34] To speak of it as primarily a feature of folksong and only secondarily as a feature of the carol or the lyric seems to me a mistake. It is more likely, I think, that this is a widespread characteristic of all those songs, whatever their modern classification, which preceded and accompanied the birth of the popular ballad. This is confirmed by the fact that such repetitions can be found in all categories of songs in the Sloane manuscript, which is indeed a remarkable showcase of stylistic traits destined to influence the popular ballad at several key points in the course of its development. To look at the problem in any other way is to rely excessively on the existence of hypothetical texts.

One further point about the significance of the Sloane carols for balladry needs to be made. In his discussion of the carol as a dance song, Greene postulates separate origins for the internal and external refrains,

33. Sloane No. xxv; Brown, *Religious Lyrics of the Fifteenth Century*, p. 119. For the thirteenth-century source of this song, see Brown (ed.), *English Lyrics of the Thirteenth Century* (Oxford, 1932), p. 55.

34. An excellent analysis, with references to earlier studies, is Stephen Manning, "I Syng of a Myden," *PMLA*, LXXV (1960), 8–12.

attributing the former to the ballad and the latter (also called the burden) to the carol.[35] Much as I admire the judiciousness of his analysis, I must point out that his discussion seems to neglect the chronological factor: first there were carols and then later came the ballads. As Greene points out, refrain ballads of whatever type are a minority in the Child canon, and although internal refrains are more common in ballads, other types, including the typical carol burden, do occur.[36] My conclusion from all this, as mentioned briefly in the preceding chapter, is that the refrains which are an important feature of early ballads are the heritage of a pre-existing folksong tradition.[37] There is no evidence to suggest that from some earlier time ballads existed in a set form (e.g., with internal refrain) for which we lack earlier examples simply because they happen not to have been written down. A theory of ballad origins must begin with an examination of early collections like the Sloane songbook.

It is not my purpose here to go into the question of ballad origins. In contrast to Greene's theory of the internal refrain as a ballad feature, however, I would like merely to suggest that the origin of the internal refrain should be first sought in the carols themselves, as in the following example from Sloane (XLVIII), also included in Greene's collection (180B):

REFRAIN: M and A and R and I
    Syngyn I wyl a newe song.
1 It wern foure letterys of purposy
 M and A, R and I,
 Tho wern letteris of Mary,
  of hom al our joye sprong.

2 On the mownt of Caluory,
 With M and A, R and I,
 There he betyn his bryte body,
  With schorges that wern bothe scharp and long.

3 Our swete Lady stod hym by,
 With M and A and R and I;

---

35. *The Early English Carols*, introduction, esp. pp. xlviii–lvi.

36. In fact the earliest example of a ballad refrain (excluding Child 115 as ambiguous) is "Captain Car, or, Edom o Gordon" (178), the A version of which in a sixteenth-century MS has an external refrain or burden. See Greene, *The Early English Carols*, p. lii.

37. I am using the phrase "folksong tradition" in the inclusive sense, as mentioned in chapter i above, rather than postulating the folk-art dichotomy so often assumed.

Che wept water with here ey,
   And alwey the blod folwyd among.

4 God that sit aboue the sky,
   With M and A, R and I;
   Saue now al this cumpany,
     And send vs joye and blysse ammong.[38]

It will be noted that the second line in each stanza serves in fact as a refrain, and, although the fourth line varies, the fact that it rhymes throughout the carol (sprong, long, among, ammong) is but one step removed from the kind of variable refrain line which we have found in the earliest extant ballad with internal refrain, "The Fair Flower of Northumberland" (9).

We are now in a position to evaluate Child's selection of the two songs (xxxv and xliv) in the Sloane manuscript for inclusion in his collection of popular ballads. Concerning the riddle song (xxix) little need be said, since Child merely quotes it in the introduction to "Captain Wedderburn's Courtship" (46) and does not give it the status of an actual ballad. Here I will only suggest that he might well have made similar mention of "I have a gentil cook" (xxvi) in his introduction to "The Grey Cock" (248). This piece is undoubtedly related to the folksong which served as the basis of "The Grey Cock" ballad, itself an eighteenth-century creation.

Even a casual reading of the Sloane collection reveals that Child's choice of "St. Stephen and Herod" (22) is open to question. If we suppose that he canonized it because of its narrative, we must admit that many other songs in this manuscript—in fact most of them—have an equally strong narrative line. If we think he chose it because of its meter or its incremental repetition, we must recognize that other pieces would have been equally good examples of these things. My only explanation is that he chose this song for the sake of the "delightful little legend" of St. Stephen which it contains. But I do not mean this as a criticism. On the contrary it is fortunate that Child included this song, not only for its own sake, but also because it is representative of that body of folksong which was of such great importance in the shaping of the ballad tradition.

38. For evidences of oral transmission see Greene's notes to this song (*The Early English Carols*, p. 390) and compare the Sloane text with the other version printed by Greene (180A) from Bodleian MS English Poet.e.l. Other songs in the Sloane MS could profitably be studied in this way.

2. The folksong tradition   41

Concerning the one crucial selection, "Robin and Gandeleyn" (115), it is difficult to speak with assurance. Why is it uniquely written in the manuscript without division into lines or stanzas? Is the so-called refrain line, "Robynn lyth in grene wode bowndyn," which precedes and follows the text, in fact a refrain? Is it a Robin Hood ballad or not? I find myself unable to answer these questions.[39] It is possible that "Robin and Gandeleyn" is the first of the popular ballads.

The religious songs

Discussion of the traditional religious songs and carols will be confined to those found in the Child canon, plus a few others that have come to the attention of scholars since the time of Child. The earliest of these are "The Maid and the Palmer" (21), found in the Percy manuscript (ca. 1650); "St. Stephen and Herod" (22), already mentioned as one of the songs in the Sloane manuscript of the first half of the fifteenth century; "Judas" (23), from a thirteenth-century manuscript in the library of Trinity College, Cambridge; and the "Corpus Christi" carol found in a sixteenth-century manuscript in Balliol College, Oxford.[40] Of the songs recovered in more recent times "The Cherry-Tree Carol" (54), "The Carnal and the Crane" (55), and "The Holy Well," the last not included by Child, first appear in William Sandys' *Christmas Carols, Ancient and Modern* (London, 1833); one other piece in the Child collection, "Dives and Lazarus" (56), was printed in Joshua Sylvester's *A Garland of Christmas Carols* (London, 1861); and finally there is "The Bitter Withy," first printed in full by Frank Sidgwick in *Notes and Queries* in 1905.[41]

As I have already suggested, the "stability" of the religious songs has apparently been so great that the date of recovery of versions seems less significant than is the case with ballads. Not only do we find carols surviving for more than four hundred years,[42] but also in several texts archaic phrases persist, no longer understood, as can be seen in such fossils as "I wish" for "ywys" in "Sweet Jesus"; the "three jolly jerdins" and "upling scorn and downling scorn," whatever these may mean, in "The Bitter

---

39. Child says that "Robin and Gandeleyn" is not a Robin Hood ballad, though the basis for this judgment is not made clear.

40. All are in Child, *ESPB*, except "Corpus Christi," which is found in the commonplace book of Richard Hill, Balliol College, Oxford MS 354, described by Greene, *The Early English Carols*, pp.

339 f., and in greater detail in *MÆ*, XXIX (1960), 21 n.

41. Several of these seem to be based on earlier broadsides, and a stanza of "The Bitter Withy" was printed in *N&Q*, 4th ser., I (1868), 53.

42. See Greene, "The Traditional Survival of Two Medieval Carols."

Withy"; and "upon one good Saint Stephen" for "on a good set steven," meaning "in a good firm voice" in "The Holy Well."[43] But even without these linguistic evidences of antiquity, the textual history of a carol like "Corpus Christi" that exists in both early and late versions reveals a stability of form and resistance to change without parallel in the ballad tradition.[44]

When we examine the earlier group of songs mentioned above, it is difficult to find much evidence that will throw light on later developments. "Judas" is of course by all odds the earliest, but we cannot be sure that it is a song at all.[45] Or, even if it was, then like "St. Stephen and Herod" it seems not to have lasted long, for there are no known modern versions. The one song in this group that connects significantly with ballad tradition is "The Maid and the Palmer" (21), a biblical song which relates, with apocryphal additions, an encounter at the well between Jesus and the woman of Samaria (John 4:6–26). This piece is of interest for the present study not only because it is still another example of an interlaced refrain similar to that of "The Three Ravens" (26) but also because it seems to have served as inspiration for the creation of an early refrain ballad already mentioned, "The Cruel Mother" (20).

As was the case with "John Dory" (284) mentioned above, "The Maid and the Palmer" appears to be completely dominated by the melodic setting, as is evident in the stanza form (21A1):

1 The maid shee went to the well to washe
  Lillumwham, lillumwham!
The mayd shee went to the well to washe,
  Whatt then? what then?
The maid shee went to the well to washe,
  Dew ffell of her lilly white fleshe.
   Grandam boy, grandam boy, heye!
Leg a derry, leg a merry, mett, mer, whoope, whir!
  Driuance, larumben, grandam boy, heye!

43. Greene comments on "I wish" in "Sweet Jesus" as a sign "that the carol has been subjected to popular oral tradition" (*ibid.*, p. 230). A similar phenomenon is evident in the riddle songs, as mentioned above ("woman was" becoming "woman's wish" and then "woman's voice"). All of these examples suggest an extremely stable and enduring oral tradition. They are not unrelated to the experience of the present-day caroler who sings "Round John Virgin" for "round yon Virgin" in "Silent Night."

44. See *ibid.*, pp 223 ff.

45. One of my students, William L. Mensel, in an unpublished study of the English texts of the manuscript containing "Judas" (Trinity College, Cambridge MS 323, f.34), regards the narrative of "Judas" as similar in movement to that of two other texts in the same manuscript, the "Life of St. Margaret" (f.20) and "Journey of the Three Kings" (f.35).

Nevertheless, this song has a substantial narrative developed in its fifteen stanzas. While the maid is washing, an old palmer (Jesus) comes and asks her for a drink of water. When she makes excuses, the palmer chides her by saying that if he were her lover she would give him a drink, which leads her to swear that she has no lover. To this the palmer replies (21A8–10):

> 8 Saies 'Peace, ffaire mayd, you are fforsworne!
>   Nine children you have borne.
>
> 9 'Three were buryed vnder thy bed's head,
>   Other three vnder thy brewing leade.
>
> 10 'Other three on yon play greene;
>   Count, maid, and there be 9.'

About the year 1686 appeared "The Duke's Daughter's Cruelty, or, The Wonderful Apparition of two Infants who she murtherd and buried in a Forrest for to hide her Shame."[46] Although perhaps based on some actual crime, this ballad seems to be inspired to some extent by "The Maid and the Palmer." After giving birth to illegitimate children, she kills and buries them (20O9–11):

> 9 She dug a grave, it was long and deep,
>   And there she laid them in to sleep.
>
> 10 The coldest earth it was their bed,
>   The green grass was their coverlid.
>
> 11 As she was a going by her father's hall,
>   She see three children a playing at ball.[47]

46. Child, *ESPB*, II, 500–501. For date see Ewald Flugel, "Zur Chronologie der englischen Balladen," *Anglia*, XXI (1899), 339.

47. The picture of a forlorn mother burying her babe(s) may have been inspired by a version of "The Famous Flower of Serving-men" (106), like the one communicated to Percy by the Dean of Derry (Child, *ESPB*, II, 429a). Between stanzas 10 and 11 of the broadside quoted occurs a stanza which Child relegates to a footnote with this comment (V, 501): "*After 10 is introduced, absurdly, this stanza, derived from* 'The Famous Flower of Serving-Men:'
    She cut her hair, changed her name
From Fair Elinor to Sweet William." The presence of this couplet in the earliest version of "The Cruel Mother" is probably not without significance. Both versions of Child 20 found in the Percy papers have the mother give birth to *two* babes, and both agree in reporting *three* babes, one royally arrayed and two naked, playing ball near her father's hall. Although there is no explanation given for this (but see 20N8), perhaps we are to suppose that the two resurrected babes are joined by the Christ child (see Dan. 3:24–25), whose fondness for playing at the ball is at least as old as the "Childhood of Jesus" (MS Addit. 31042, l. 672) and is preserved in the opening stanza of "The Bitter Withy." Granted the principle of stability of occasion already mentioned (see chap. ii, n. 1, above), this feature of "The Cruel Mother" might be regarded as confirmation of the existence of "The Bitter Withy" in 1686, were it not for the fact that playing at the ball is such a common occurrence.

In "The Maid and the Palmer" the third group of three children are buried "on yon play greene"; in "The Cruel Mother," the dead children have returned as revenants and are playing ball undoubtedly "on yon play greene" of the earlier text. This is a master stroke of ballad creation.[48]

When we turn to the later group of religious songs it is interesting to note that although a piece like "Dives and Lazarus" (56) is based strictly on the canonical Gospel (Luke 16:19–31), several important texts contain stories derived ultimately from the Apocryphal "Infancy" Gospels of the Middle Ages. Since the time of the Reformation, of course, the distinction between canonical and apocryphal materials has been made more sharply than was true before the sixteenth century, and it is therefore difficult to imagine conditions appropriate for the creation of songs based on the Apocrypha in a post-medieval setting. Nor is there in these songs any suggestion of antiquarian reconstruction. What has been said in general of the antiquity of the religious songs and carols applies with particular force to the infancy songs. They are pieces of stained glass from a beautiful window, the over-all design of which has faded from memory.

Legendary materials like the Infancy Gospels were intimately associated with the canonical Scriptures in the Middle Ages, not merely to satisfy an obvious human interest and curiosity, but also to accentuate the main contours of biblical narrative, and, utilizing the medieval system of harmonistics, to give the common man a panoramic view of the Bible and its major themes. The story of Seth is perhaps one of the best illustrations of the harmonistic function of biblical legends.[49] When Adam feels that he must soon die, he sends his good son Seth (an obvious replacement for Abel) to paradise to inquire about the oil of mercy promised to mankind. At the gates of paradise the angel permits Seth to look inside, where he sees a great dead tree in the midst of the garden. A serpent is coiled around this tree, while at its roots, deep in the ground, Seth sees the soul of his dead brother, Abel, and in the top of the tree he sees a babe wrapped in swaddling clothes. That child, says the angel, will provide the oil of mercy which is promised to mankind. From this graphic beginning the legend develops an elaborate symbolic foreshadowing of New Testament developments, including the doctrine of the Trinity, but the point to emphasize here is that in one highly visual image of the tree

48. There is a penance theme in the earliest version of "The Cruel Mother," stanzas 21–22, echoing the penance assigned the maid by the palmer (21A12–15), and this is even more evident in certain later versions of "The Cruel Mother,"

notably 20 I, J, K, L, and the version from Findlay's MSS printed by Child, V, 211 f.

49. See Esther Quinn, *The Quest of Seth* (Chicago, 1962).

this legend skilfully conveys the central biblical theme of the redemption. The technique is that of St. Paul (I Cor. 15:22): "For as in Adam all die, even so in Christ shall all be made alive."

On a more humble and popular level, this is the rationale of vernacular narratives such as the northern *Childhood of Jesus,* preserved in a British Museum manuscript of the fifteenth century.[50] Although this text is concerned, literally, with the period from the birth to the manhood of Christ, it contains not only popular motifs and folklore but also numerous consciously developed foretastes of what is to come in Jesus' life. Here we meet with Barabbas and his son (!) Dismas (the name assigned in the Apocryphal Gospels to the penitent thief); Judas, who shows evil inclinations even as a boy; Sir Kayface (=Caiaphas) the schoolmaster; and, finally, the playmates of Jesus whose general hostility toward him foreshadows the attitude of the crowd at the trial, with its cry of "Crucify him!" By the use of his divine power, Jesus often takes vengeance on his playmates in a manner that suggests the author is simply indulging in irresponsible wish fulfilment. Since Jesus must eventually pay the supreme price to redeem mankind, let him at least have a little earthy revenge before the time comes when he must take a more lofty point of view. But just to be on the safe side, the author causes Jesus to heal and revive the victims of his childish wrath, usually in response to the intervention of the Virgin Mary.

The stanza form of the *Childhood of Jesus* is normally twelve four-foot lines rhyming *ababababcdcd*, and if we think in terms of quatrains this metrical system is not unlike that of the songs in the Sloane manuscript rhyming *abab*. Lines 13–28 of the *Childhood*, in fact, if divided into quatrains, are somewhat suggestive of an Epiphany carol:

> 1 When Jhesu was of Marie borne—
> Thare blyssede myghte that birthe be—
> Thre kynges come knelande hym by-forne
> And made hyme homage alle three.
>
> 2 Kyng Herode thoghte and þer-to had sworne
> Jhesu dede that he wolde see.
> Marie wolde noghte hir sone ware lorne:
> Owte of contre thane gane scho flie.

50. MS Addit. 31042, printed in *Archiv*, LXXIV (1885), 327–339. The Childhood stories can be seen in their larger harmonistic setting in Richard Morris (ed.), *Cursor Mundi* (EETS, O.S. 57, 59, 62, 66, 68 [London, 1874–1878]). This remarkable poem is extremely valuable for its presentation of the medieval world-picture; it is usually dated *ca.* 1300.

3 Fro hir fomene scho flede that daye
  Owte of hir kythe thare mene hire knewe,
  And bad a mane that he scholde saye
  Scho went thare forthe whene thaie sewe.

4 And whene the Jewes thare forthe come,
  Corne alle newe Þe fande to schere—
  For full faste thay gane eke anone,
  To looke if Þat thay thayme myghte oughte dere.[51]

This is not to assert that the above text was sung, but merely that it was admirably suited for adaptation during the fifteenth century when so many new religious songs were being composed.

Several motifs appearing in "The Carnal and the Crane" (55) can be found near the beginning of the *Childhood of Jesus*. Besides the Epiphany theme and the episode of the sowing and harvesting in one day, a miracle reminiscent of one of the "impossible tasks" in the riddle songs (2B13; cf. 55, st. 19), we find the adoration of the beasts (ll. 29–36):

Forthir-mare thane es Joseph gane
In the wildirnes by a bryme.
Marye sawe lebardes full many ane
And other bestis full grete and gryme.
Thane saide Marie: "we be alle slayne,
Allas, thies wayes waxes alle dyme!"
Bot Jhesu blissede those bestis ilkane:
And lesse and mare thay lowttede hyme.

This finds its counterpart in "The Carnal and the Crane":

14 And when they came to Egypt's land,
    Amongst those fierce wild beasts,
  Mary, she being weary,
    Must needs sit down to rest.

15 'Come sit thee down,' says Jesus,
    'Come sit thee down by me,
  And thou shalt see how these wild beasts
    Do come and worship me.'

The adoration of the beasts is of course designed to fulfil the messianic

51. *Archiv*, LXXIV (1885), 327. Compare the typical Epiphany carol in Sloane MS, No. XXXII (Greene 123B), though the meter differs. For similar rhyme pattern (*abab*) compare Sloane I, XL, XLI, LI, LXXI.

2. The folksong tradition   47

prophecy of Isaiah (11:6): "The wolf also shall dwell with the lamb, and the leopard shall lie down with the kid; and the calf and the young lion and the fatling together; and a little child shall lead them."[52]

Perhaps the most familiar apocryphal episode is that preserved in "The Cherry-Tree Carol" (54), the miracle of the tree bowing down to permit the Virgin to gather cherries. In the *Childhood of Jesus* this incident occurs during the flight into Egypt. Mary is weary from travel and from the heat of the desert sun, and Joseph helps her to sit down under a tall tree to rest. The Christ child overhears his mother wishing for some of the fruit of the tree (ll. 77–88):

> Whene Mary thus hade made hir mane,
> Hire sone wiste whate was his wille;
> Of that froyte fulle gude wane
> He gaffe hire ynoghe, and that was skille:
> Jhesu thane spake to the tree anone:
> "Lowte downe, he sayde, my modir vn-tille,
> Tille scho and Joseph bathe hafe tane
> Of thy froyte alle that thay wille."
> The tree lawe to thaire fete gane folde,
> Tille thay hade tane alle Þat Þay hade tithte.
> And whene thay hade tane alle Þat Þay wolde,
> Als Jhesu it bade it stode agayne vppe-righte.

In "The Cherry-Tree Carol," on the other hand, this episode forms a part of the courtship of Joseph and Mary, the moment when Joseph first learns that she is with child, and the unborn babe speaks from his mother's womb (54A6–7):

> O then bespoke the babe,
> within his mother's womb:
> 'Bow down then the tallest tree,
> for my mother to have some.'
> Then bowed down the highest tree
> unto his mother's hand;
> Then she cried, See, Joseph,
> I have cherries at command.

The removal of this story from its place in the flight into Egypt sequence

---

52. In the medieval view Christ's ful-filment of Isaiah's prophecy is also a re-turn to the golden age before the Fall, as described for example in *Cursor Mundi*, ll. 683–698.

is a striking development, showing an ingenuity that is scarcely attributable to folk "re-creation."[53] The setting is no longer the desert but an orchard (garden); Mary's desire for the fruit (cherries) is not from weariness or heat, but rather it is the desire of any expectant mother; and Joseph's angry response to Mary's request (54A5),

O then bespoke Joseph
    with words most unkind:
'Let him pluck thee a cherry
    that brought thee with child.'

provides a dramatic cue for the intervention of the true Father speaking through the unborn Son, commanding the tree to bow down. The one slightly awkward development here is the Child's prophecies concerning himself. These are of course traditional, but the shifted setting requires either that the child prophesy from his mother's womb, as he does in some later versions,[54] or that he be born and subsequently prophesy, as is the case in the earliest version (54A9–10):

Then Mary plucked a cherry,
    as red as the blood,
Then Mary went home
    with her heavy load.

Then Mary took her babe,
    and sat him on her knee.
Saying, my dear son, tell me
    what this world will be.

But the most significant point is that the new setting of the cherry-tree incident necessarily makes this piece a Christmas or Nativity carol, and hence not unnaturally there appears a third solution to the problem, namely, versions of "The Cherry-Tree Carol" (like 54B) in which an angel takes the place of the infant and delivers the prophecies for him. It may be that

53. The transfer of the story to a nativity setting is already accomplished in the fifteenth-century *Ludus Coventrae*. See *English Nativity Plays*, ed. Hemingway, (Yale Studies in English, XXXVIII), p. 102.

54. In a Library of Congress version, AAFS Album 14, sung in 1946 by Mrs. Maud Long at Hot Springs, N. C., Joseph takes Mary on his knee (compare Child 54A10 quoted below) but addresses the unborn child, "Pray tell me, little baby, when your birthday shall be," to which the child replies with a prediction of his birth. In the earlier versions, however, the babe is born and sitting on Mary's knee when he predicts his own death and resurrection. The secular adaptation of this can be seen in the mother-son dialogues of "Edward" (13), "The Twa Brothers" (49), and "Lizie Wan" (51). The sun and the moon that shall rise together at the resurrection (54A12) are variously described as meeting on yon hill (51B17) or dancing on the green (49D20) to provide the slayer's paraphrase for "neuer."

this particular set of stanzas (54B9–18) can be considered a separate song under the title "Joseph and the Angel," but its presence in texts of "The Cherry-Tree Carol" is no accident.

A final observation needs to be made concerning the harmonistic function of the cherry-tree miracle in the larger biblical context mentioned above. This can be seen when we compare the incident just considered with a dramatization of the temptation of Eve in the fourteenth-century Cornish drama, *Origo Mundi*:[55]

EVE: I am perplexed, thinking
        What I may do
    Through plucking the apple,
        For fear of there being guile in thee.

DEVIL: Pluck it at my peril;
        Without delay, quickly be done,
    And also cause thy husband
        That he eat from it.

EVE: Bend down the tree toward the ground,
        That I may reach them.

DEVIL: I will, but come quietly,
        Pluck it and go thy way.

Eve then takes the fruit and gives some to Adam, and the drama of the Fall then develops according to the familiar biblical narrative. But the point has been made: the bowing trees of the Old and New Testaments are graphic reminders of the Fall and redemption. A fragment of this harmonic system is preserved in "The Cherry-Tree Carol."[56]

55. The only edition presently available is that of Edwin Norris, *The Ancient Cornish Drama* (2 vols.; Oxford, 1859). The original Cornish text of the passage quoted is *Origo Mundi*, ll. 193–204 (Norris, I, 14–16):

EUA: Ameys of ow predyry
    pan-dra allaf the wruthyl
an avel orth y dyrry
    rag ovn genes bones gyl
DEMON: torre yn ov feryl vy
    heb hokye fast haue ydo
hag inweth gvra theth worty
    may tebro ef annotho
EUA: Stop an wethen troghan dor
    may hyllyf aga hethes
DEMON: my a ra saw dus yn clor
    torre ha ke the-gerthes

The text and translation differ from Norris occasionally since I am quoting from a new edition of the *Origo Mundi* by Phyllis Pier Harris (Ph.D. dissertation, University of Washington, 1964). For an examination of the problem of dating this text and references to other studies, see David C. Fowler, "The Date of the Cornish *Ordinalia*," *MS*, XXIII (1961), 91–125.

56. Other examples of biblical and legendary harmonistics can be found in the *Childhood of Jesus*. The final disposition of the Tree of Life, with imagery from Ps. 1 (ll. 89–112) is essentially biblical, while the episode of the sawing of the plank (ll. 810–833) comes from the legend of Seth.

The apocryphal *Childhood of Jesus* contains another episode or series of episodes which served as the basis for two recently recovered carols, "The Bitter Withy" and "The Holy Well."[57] As has already been mentioned, there are several incidents that illustrate the hostility of Jesus' playmates, foreshadowing the antagonism of the mob later on at the trial and crucifixion. Judas, for example, is struck dead by Jesus for breaking up some dams he had made in a little stream but is saved from this fate by Mary, who persuades her son to bring him back to life. At her request Jesus revives him but warns his mother prophetically that Judas will live to betray him (*Childhood*, ll. 149–192). On another occasion some children ask Jesus to go play and leap with them on some hills. The outcome is that all the children, except for Jesus' special playmate Osepe, fall down and are killed. The reason for this is not entirely clear, but Jesus offers the following explanation to Osepe (ll. 288–289):

"Why wenys þou, Osepe, þay felle so sare?
For þay wend alle to be my pere."

Whatever this statement may mean in context (one thinks whimsically of the motivation of God in Gen. 3:22), it seems very likely that these lines are the basis of the superior attitude of the children in both "The Bitter Withy" and "The Holy Well" when Jesus asks if he may play with them. In the former the children reply scornfully:

"Oh, we are lords' and ladies' sons,
    Born in bower or in hall,
And you are but some poor maid's child
    Born'd in an ox's stall."[58]

In "The Holy Well" the response is the same:

But they made answer to him, 'No:'
    They were lords' and ladies' sons;
And he, the meanest of them all,
    Was but a maiden's child, born in an ox's stall.[59]

57. In the discussion of "The Holy Well" and "The Bitter Withy" which follows I am often indebted to two students, Janet Graves and Kathleen Vlach, whose research on these two carols has been very helpful and illuminating. Both texts are conveniently reprinted in Leach, *The Ballad Book*, pp. 689–691. Previous important and related studies are G. H. Gerould, "The Ballad of the Bitter Withy," *PMLA*, XXIII (1908), 141–167;

Phillips Barry, "The Bridge of Sunbeams," *JAF*, XXVII (1914), 77–89; and Batho, "The Life of Christ in the Ballads."

58. The text of "The Bitter Withy" quoted here (st. 4) is that given by Frank Sidgwick in *N&Q*, 10th ser., IV (July 29, 1905), 84.

59. Stanza 5 of the Sandys version of "The Holy Well" as reprinted by Gerould, "The Ballad of the Bitter Withy," 164–165.

2. The folksong tradition   51

Up to this point the two carols are remarkably similar. In both texts Jesus asks permission of Mary to go play (in "The Bitter Withy," specifically to play ball) and is rebuffed by the children. But the subsequent divergence of the two is striking. In "The Bitter Withy" Jesus gets revenge by enticing his playmates to follow him over the water on a bridge which he fashions out of sunbeams, and they of course fall and drown. In response to the not unreasonable criticism of the dead children's mothers, Mary punishes Jesus by giving him three slashes with the withy switch. In "The Holy Well," however, when Jesus is rejected by his playmates, he returns weeping to tell his mother what happened. But when Mary indignantly proposes that Jesus take revenge he piously rejects the idea (sts. 12–13):

'Sweet Jesus, go down to younder town
    As far as the Holy Well,
And take away those sinful souls,
    And dip them deep in hell.'

'Nay, nay,' sweet Jesus said,
    'Nay, nay, that may not be,
For there are too many sinful souls,
    Crying out for the help of me.'

In view of the uncertainty surrounding the nature of the game or other activity of the children it is difficult to say exactly where in the *Childhood of Jesus* the source of these songs may be found. The emphasis on the well as the setting in "The Holy Well" carol suggests a possible connection with the episode in which, in another clash with his hostile playmates, Jesus miraculously restores his water pot, shattered by a child named Akere after Jesus had managed to beat the other children in a race to obtain water from the well (ll. 328–363).[60] But it seems likely that both carols are at least partly based on a later incident in the *Childhood* (ll. 472–520) where Jesus, in a game of "follow the leader," entices the children to sit with him on a sunbeam, with the result that they fall to the ground and are seriously injured. The whole community is aroused at this, and Mary is displeased (ll. 505–512):

Mary lykede it fulle ille,
And sayde: "Dere sone, this foly late þou cesse!

---

60. For an interesting discussion of both carols in relation to the well episode, see the article on "The Bitter Withy" by Anne G. Gilchrist and Lucy E. Broadwood in *Journal of the Folk-Song Society,* IV, 38–45.

I pray the, if it be thi wille,
Thou late vs somewhare lyfe in peese.

"Thou sees thies Jewes wille vs spille:
Swete sone, nowe for my prayere
Late thayme ryse, if it be thi wille!"
And thane he blyssede thayme þat þer were.

This follows the pattern we have already seen to be characteristic of these incidents: after the intervention of Mary, Jesus restores his fallen play-mates. In this case, however, a particular point is made of Mary's dis-pleasure, and it is but one further step to introduce corporal punishment and the withy legend.

The most striking feature of "The Holy Well" is its reversal of the characterization of the child and his mother, causing Mary to seek revenge, and Jesus to act as a restraining influence. The immediate and obvious explanation is that "The Holy Well" is a post-Reformation version of "The Bitter Withy." It is possible, however, that a basis for Mary's apparent vindictiveness can be found in the *Childhood* itself.[61] It will be recalled that when Jesus restores Judas to life, he warns Mary that this same boy, when grown, will betray him to death (ll. 189–192). Although his mother says nothing in response to this, on two subsequent occasions she seems almost to retract her pleas for mercy. The first is in response to Jesus' prophetic description, after restoring Sir Kayface to life, of what this man would do to him at some future time (ll. 260–263):

"Modire, one mee he salle halde mote
And do bete my body alle bare,
So þat a flye sall nott mowe sette hir fote
Neuer nowrewhare one my body for sare."

On hearing this prophecy Mary is overcome with sorrow (ll. 264–267):

And for thase wordes hir liste noghte synge,
Swilke sorowe one hir dere sone to see.
"The thare not," scho said, "late hym so lange lyffynge,
My dere sone, 3if thi wille it be."

On another occasion Jesus prophesies that the very children who are his playmates will one day crucify him, and again Mary is grieved (ll. 569–572):

61. I am indebted to my student, Mrs. Graves, for this suggestion. See Janet M. Graves, " 'The Holy Well': A Medieval Religious Ballad," *WF*, XXVI (1967), 13–26.

Whene scho that herde, hir liste no sange,
That þay hir dere sone so solde spille.
"The thare noghte late þame lefe so lange,
My dere sone, if it be thi wille."

Obviously Mary's sympathy for the children disappears when it is made known to her that they will crucify her son. Perhaps some such attitude underlies the characterization of the vindictive Virgin of "The Holy Well."[62]

From what has been said thus far it should be evident that the *Childhood of Jesus* (or a similar compilation) is an important source of the carols, and that these carols are of considerable antiquity, in spite of the lateness of recovery of texts like "The Bitter Withy" (1905). Moreover, although it is not possible always to speak confidently of sources, there are other evidences of a common ground for religious song and the *Childhood*. In a very popular Nativity carol, for example, the miracle of the virgin birth is explained by means of a well-known metaphor (Greene 21A4):

As the son shynyth thorow the glas,
So Jhesu in her body was:
To serue hym he geve vs grace,
O lux beata Trinitas.[63]

In the *Childhood* Joseph and Mary are questioned by the Jews about the parentage of their son, and they answer briefly and truthfully. But Jesus himself then offers the following amplification (ll. 432–435):

And Jhesu to thayme ansuerde righte thenne:
"Als sonne that schynes thorowe the glasse,
With-ine my modire with-owttene weme,
And scho a maydene never-the-lesse."

It is entirely possible, I believe, that there were other religious songs in tradition based on the Apocryphal Infancy Gospels which have not survived. Such a statement of course is not subject to verification, but I would like to conclude this discussion of the *Childhood* by referring to one possible instance of its influence on the popular ballad.

62. If the above interpretation of "The Holy Well" is correct, then this carol must stand as independent of "The Bitter Withy" and of equal antiquity. Their basic similarity would then account for contamination of the two in modern times.

63. See Greene's note to this carol in *The Early English Carols*, p. 357, for other occurrences of this figure for the Virgin's conception.

"The Lord of Lorn and the False Steward" (271) is first found in the Percy folio manuscript (ca. 1650), but a ballad with that title was entered in the stationer's register as early as 1580. This piece in turn is based on an earlier romance, *Roswall and Lillian.*[64] The romance is a variant of the story-type usually called "The Fair Unknown." Young Roswall is sent abroad by his father to reside with the King of Bealm, in the company of a trusted steward. The steward proves false, however, and represents himself as the nobleman, while the child's identity is not known. Yet Roswall becomes a favorite at the court, and he and the King's daughter Lillian fall in love. The usual tournament follows, Roswall is the victor, the evil steward is discovered and hanged, and the lovers are happily married.

The particular incident in this story of interest for our present purpose occurs at the very beginning, where motivation is provided for the departure of young Roswall from his home. In the romance we are told that Roswall, having overheard the piteous complaint of three lords confined in his father's prison, secretly enabled these lords to escape (the same lords who were to help him later in the tournament). His father, not knowing who had done this, swore that the culprit should die. When the truth is made known, Roswall's mother pleads with her husband to forgive the child, but he responds (ll. 131–138):

> "That may not be, madam!" he said,
> "For I a faithfull vow have made,
> That, as soon as I may him see,
> My own two hands his bane shall be.
> Therefore I pray you, day and night,
> To keep him well out of my sight,
> Till I send him to some countrie,
> Where he may safely keeped be."[65]

Thus, in the romance Roswall leaves home under the cloud of his father's wrath.

The case is quite different in the ballad. Here we are told that the Lord of Lorn sent his only son to school, where it soon became evident that the boy was unusually gifted (271A2–5):

> Learning did soe proceed with that child,
>   I tell you all in veretie,

64. See Child, *ESPB*, V, 42 ff.; Oscar Lengert, "Die Schottische Romanze 'Roswall and Lillian,'" *Englische Studien*, XVI (1892), 321–356.

65. Lengert, "Die Schottische Romanze 'Roswall and Lillian,'" pp. 327 f. I am quoting from the longer of the two versions (Edinburgh, 1663).

2. The folksong tradition   55

He learned more vpon one day
    Then other children did on three.

And then bespake the schoole-master,
    Vnto the Lord of Learne said hee,
I thinke thou be some stranger borne,
    For the holy gost remaines with thee.

He said, I am noe stranger borne,
    Forsooth, master, I tell it to thee;
It is a gift of Almighty God
    Which he hath given vnto mee.

The schoole-master turned him round about,
    His angry mind he thought to asswage,
For the child cold answer him so quicklie,
    And was of soe tender yeere of age.[66]

Apparently the schoolmaster's anger was not easily assuaged, for in the next stanza we are informed that the child took leave of his schoolfellows and went home, where he informed his father of his newly recognized ability (271A9–10):

'Good tydings, father, I haue you brought,
    Good tydings I hope it is to thee;
The booke is not in all Scottlande
    But I can read it before your eye.'

A ioyed man his father was,
    Euen the worthy Lord of Learne:
'Thou shalt goe into France, my child,
    The speeches of all strange lands to learne.'

Thus instead of departing under a cloud, the ballad hero leaves with his proud father's blessing in order to take the continental tour, so to speak, and thus further his education.

While it is likely that this fundamental change in the beginning of the story was inspired by a later school episode in *Roswall and Lillian*,[67] there is not enough detail in the romance itself to account for the rather specific characterization of both the schoolmaster and the child. But there

66. The two versions of the ballad have almost identical versions of the school episode except for one added stanza in the broadside text (271B10).

67. *Ibid.*, p. 333: *Roswall and Lillian*, A version, lines 299–314, and, with interesting variants, the D version, lines 119–126. Another interesting school episode can be found in "The Child of Bristowe," lines 37 ff., as printed in W. Carew Hazlitt, *Remains of the Early Popular Poetry of England*, I (1864), 110–131.

is no need to look for a romance original of this incident. Whatever its immediate origin, it is undoubtedly derived ultimately from one of the school episodes found in the Infancy Gospels.

In the *Childhood of Jesus*, on the advice of Sir Levy, Sir Kayface, and all the masters of the community, Mary and Joseph send Jesus to school, where it soon becomes evident that he is a child of exceptional ability. One of the devices used to demonstrate this in the poem, interestingly enough, is the riddle. When the dyer in Jericho asks Jesus "whare was thou borne & whaa Þe gatte?" the child replies (ll. 625–628):

"In Þe burgh," sayd Jhesu, "of Bedleme
Of a Maydene was I borne;
I hafe awnntes and nane eme,
My ffadire standis me by-forne."

In the school episode under consideration, Jesus confounds the schoolmaster by asking him "what es my thoghte," a question reminiscent of "King John and the Bishop" (45). The schoolmaster, Kayface, replies (ll. 218–220):

"By hym Þat alle this werlde has wroghte,
I wiste neuer by nyghte ne daye
What thou thynkes in thi thoghte."

In the intellectual competition that follows Jesus confounds his listeners with a brilliant exposition of the Law and a riddling description of himself. Kayface, apparently enraged, smites Jesus on the head.

Later on, because of the hostility of the community, the Holy Family is forced to move to Nazareth, where Jesus is once more sent to school, this time to a master Rabyne. Again the child asks questions that the schoolmaster is unable to answer (ll. 454–455):

And for he ne couthe saye hym, he changide chere
And for schame he was nere schent

This is a less violent response than that of Kayface, and hence closer to that of the schoolmaster in "The Lord of Lorn" ballad. Even more to the point, master Rabyne has a theory about the source of the child's wisdom, and he discusses this with Jesus (ll. 460–471):

Bot maister Rabyne his resons felde,
Said: "Dauid Þe prophete fonde in his lare
Þat intill a maydene meke and milde

The haly gaste fra heuene solde fare,
And aftirwarde scho solde bere a childe,
Clene maydene, als scho was are.
If it ne ware thi werkes wilde,
I monde wene that thou it ware."
He ansuerde: "Als Habraham said by-forne,
Wiete thou wele that it es I.
Thurghe Adame synne þat ware forlorne,
With my blode I salle thaym by."

This conversation is of course epitomized in "The Lord of Lorn and the False Steward" (ll. 271A3–4):

And then bespake the schoole-master,
   Vnto the Lord of Learne said hee,
I thinke thou be some stranger borne,
   For the holy gost remaines with thee.

He said, I am noe stranger borne,
   Forsooth, master, I tell it to thee;
It is a gift of Almighty God
   Which he hath given vnto mee.[68]

If, as seems likely, this ballad was composed during the reign of Henry VIII (1509–1547),[69] it may be that the Reformation was not yet sufficiently advanced to have done away with the use of the Infancy Gospels in religious teaching. On the other hand, a possibility remains that the school episode in "The Lord of Lorn and the False Steward" is derived from a popular religious song or carol based on the *Childhood of Jesus*.

The "Corpus Christi" carol

REFRAIN: Lully, lulley; lully, lulley;
   The fawcon hath born my mak away.

1 He bare hym vp, he bare hym down;
  He bare hym into an orchard brown.

2 In that orchard ther was an hall,
  That was hangid with purpill and pall.

68. In the B version the schoolmaster calls the boy an "easterling" rather than a "stranger." How either of these words can account for the presence of the Holy Ghost in the child is not clear. Could "easterling" mean a child born on Easter and hence spiritually gifted above the average? The shorter version of *Roswall and Lillian* reads (ll. 123–126):

He learned fast; the master knew
That he had been at schools enew.
The moon had scarcely changed a horn
Till he suspect'd him a noble born.

69. See Child, *ESPB*, V, 42.*

3 And in that hall ther was a bede;
  Hit was hangid with gold so rede.

4 And yn that bed ther lythe a knyght,
  His wowndes bledyng day and nyght.

5 By that bedes side ther kneleth a may,
  And she wepeth both nyght and day.

6 And by that beddes side ther stondith a ston,
  'Corpus Christi' wretyn theron.

This fascinating and mysterious carol, known variously as "Corpus Christi" and "Over Yonder's a Park," has been studied and analyzed perhaps more than any of the songs considered in the present chapter. The earliest known version, quoted above, is found in the commonplace book of Richard Hill, of the early sixteenth century.[70] But it has also been recovered in modern times. The B version in Greene's *Early English Carols* comes from North Staffordshire in 1862; C is from Derbyshire (1908); and D is first printed by James Hogg from the recitation of his mother in 1807.[71]

The best-known and most frequently cited interpretation of "Corpus Christi" is that of Miss Gilchrist, who understands it to be based on the imagery of the Grail legends of the Middle Ages. Joseph of Arimathea, the Grail custodian, carried it to Avalon, which is frequently identified with Glastonbury and is described in the carol as an "orchard brown." Next the hall is the Grail castle, and the bed on which lies the bleeding knight is the couch of the wounded fisher King. The weeping "may" is the damsel who serves the Grail, and the stone by the bed is the paten of the Eucharist. Thus far we have Miss Gilchrist's interpretation of the earliest version, the A text. In B, a hound appears at the bed's foot licking the knight's blood, perhaps representing Joseph of Arimathea, whose blossoming thorn at Glastonbury is also introduced in the version; but the weeping "may" of the A text has evidently been misunderstood, for she is here replaced by the kneeling Virgin. It would then follow from Miss Gilchrist's theory that later versions of the carol depart still further from

70. Balliol College, Oxford MS 354; see n. 40, p. 42, above. Four versions are printed in Greene, *The Early English Carols*, No. 322A–D; and for a recent study with convenient reference to previous work see Greene, "The Meaning of the Corpus Christi Carol," *MÆ*, XXIX (1960), 10–21.
71. See Greene, "The Meaning of the Corpus Christi Carol," pp. 10–11, where the four texts are listed and reference is made to a version by Niles. Greene was apparently not aware of another (American) version printed in the *JEFDSS*, IV (1942), 122 f. This last version is also a Christmas carol. It was obtained by Miss E. K. Wells in North Carolina and was brought to England in 1936.

its original meaning. The Derbyshire version, for example, is changed into a Christmas carol by virtue of its final stanza (C6):

> Over that bed the moon shines bright,
> Denoting our Saviour was born this night.

And a similar corruption would need to be assumed in the more recent North Carolina version (1936), with its refrain,

> Sing May, Queen May, Sing Mary.
> Sing all good men for the new born baby.[72]

and its startlingly different description of the bleeding knight (st. 6):

> On that bed a young Lord sleeps,
> His wounds are sick and see he weeps.

Having had for some time a deep interest in the Grail legends, I came to Miss Gilchrist's interpretation of "Corpus Christi" with complete sympathy, hoping it might be so. Yet I cannot believe that it is, nor do I think that subsequent criticism has provided a satisfactory substitute for the Grail theory. Hence to conclude the present chapter I would like to offer an interpretation of the carol not previously suggested.[73]

In one sense the "Corpus Christi" carol contains only the simplest and most readily identifiable imagery. Its basic figure is the Christ-knight metaphor, very popular in the Middle Ages,[74] which perhaps finds its most effective expression in the fourteenth-century alliterative poem, *Piers the Plowman,* as in the following description of Christ's triumphal entry into Jerusalem:

> One semblable to the Samaritan, and some-del to Piers the Plowman,
> Barfote on an asse bakke, botelees cam prykye,
> Wyth-oute spores other spere, spakliche he loked,
> As is the kynde of a kny3te that cometh to be dubbed,
> To geten hem gylte spores or galoches ycouped.
> Thanne was Faith in a fenestre and cryde 'a! *fili Dauid!'*
> As doth an heraude of armes whan auntrous cometh to iustes.
> Olde Iuwes of Ierusalem for Ioye their songen,
> *Benedictus qui venit in nomine domini.*[75]

72. *JEFDSS,* p. 122 f.
73. For much of what follows I am indebted to a student, James Turnette, whose study of "Corpus Christi" successfully challenges, I think, the current theories as to its meaning, and provides the best explanation that I have encountered for the A version refrain. Also valuable is the discussion by Batho, "The Life of Christ in the Ballads," esp. pp. 93–96.

74. See Sister Marie d. L. Le May, *The Allegory of the Christ Knight in English Literature* (Washington, D.C., 1932).

75. Skeat (ed.), *Piers the Plowman,* I, 520 (B text passus XVIII, 10–17).

The carol has of course its own elaboration of the chivalric imagery: the splendid hall, the ornate bed with the knight lying therein, and even the faithful hound of the Staffordshire version are a part of this aristocratic setting.

Placed strategically in the midst of the chivalric scene are certain unmistakable, traditional Christian signs and symbols. In the A version our only explicit reference is the phrase "corpus christi" written on the stone, thus clearly identifying the knight as Christ. This is really all that is needed, for we then know that the kneeling "may" is the Virgin, and we recognize the scene as a *Pietà*. The later texts, however, uniformly underscore this identification so that no mistake is possible. The blossoming thorn, for example, was symbolic of Jesus and his power over sin (the thorns which were Adam's heritage), although this figure is usually associated with his birth, as in the following first stanza of an Epiphany carol (Greene 123A1):

> Ther ys a blossum sprong of a thorn
> To saue mankynd that was forlorne,
> As the profettes sayd beforne;
> Deo Patri sit gloria.

More specifically connected with the crucifixion is the water and blood motif found in the Derbyshire version (C4):

> Under that bed there runs a flood,
> The one half runs water, the other runs blood.

This is of course symbolic of the water of baptism and the blood atonement, based on the description in the Gospel of the piercing of Christ's side (John 19:34). None of these added symbols contradicts the meaning of the A version; they simply reinforce it.

One feature of "Corpus Christi" which has been explained as an unfortunate aberration is the tendency of the later versions to become associated with Christmas. But perhaps it is not necessary to regard this as an aberration. The first line of refrain or burden in the A text, in fact, suggests that the song was originally conceived as a "lullaby" carol, traditionally associated with Christmas from time immemorial:

> Lully, lulley; lully, lulley.

The failure of critics to perceive this is perhaps due in part to an inadequate appreciation of the nature of the "figurative imagination," that way of thinking so characteristic of the Middle Ages which is attributable to the typological method of studying the Bible.[76] By this means, for example, events in the life of Christ could be telescoped into a single lyric moment expressing both the love of the Virgin for her child and a prophetic meditation on the sufferings he must later undergo, as expressed in the following passage from a lullaby carol (Greene 148A4–9):

'Lullay, lullay, lytil chyld, myn owyn dere fode;
How xalt thou sufferin be naylid on the rode?'
   So blyssid be the tyme.

'Lullay, lullay, lytil chyld, myn owyn dere smerte
How xalt thou sufferin the scharp spere to thi herte?'
   So blyssid be the tyme.

'Lullay, lullay, lytyl child; I synge al for thi sake;
Many on is the scharpe schour to thi body is schape.'
   So blyssid be the tyme.

'Lullay, lullay, lytyl child; fayre happis the befalle;
How xalt thou sufferin to drynke ezyll and galle?'
   So blyssid be the tyme.

'Lullay, lullay, lytil chyld; I synge al beforn;
How xalt thou sufferin the scharp garlong of thorn?'
   So blyssid be the tyme.

'Lullay, lullay, lytil chyld; qwy wepy thou so sore?
And art thou bothin God and man, quat woldyst thou be more?'
   So blyssid be the tyme.

In the light of this lyrical technique, therefore, we see that the *Pietà* in "Corpus Christi" is envisioned prophetically by the Virgin, and the refrain reminds us that this all takes place while she is rocking the Christ child. The second line of the refrain ("The fawcon hath born my mak away") is a chivalric metaphor referring to the death on the cross, and as such it beautifully balances the lullaby refrain preceding it. That the crucified is here called the Virgin's "make" is quite understandable when we remember the love imagery taken from the *Song of Solomon* and applied to the Virgin and Christ as in this stanza from another lullaby carol (Greene 145, st. 3):

76. See Erich Auerbach, "Figura," English trans. in *Scenes from the Drama of European Literature* (New York, 1959), pp. 11–76. Miss Batho likewise, though she considered "Corpus Christi" a poem of the entombment, has an appreciation of "the mystical standpoint" ("The Life of Christ in the Ballads," p. 95).

To hys modyr gen he seye,
'For this mylke me must deye;
It ys my kynd therwith to playe,
My swet modyr, peramowr.'[77]

The telescoping of history, the juxtaposing of present and future, and the sudden allegorical relevance of imagery from the *Song of Solomon* constitute eloquent testimony to the power of the figurative imagination, and one is therefore not surprised to find in a single carol of the Annunciation the entire sweep of events from the opening description of Mary as an expectant mother (Greene 242, st. 1),

Mary moder, meke and mylde,
Fro schame and synne that ye vs schyllde,
For gret on grownd ye gon with childe,
　　Gabriele nuncio.

through the birth (2), crucifixion (3), resurrection (4), and, finally, the ascension of the Virgin herself (5).

In the light of the above remarks, a final point can be made about the relationship between the "Corpus Christi" carol and "The Three Ravens" (26). These two songs have been quite rightly linked together in discussions by earlier critics, but the nature of the connection has not been very clearly stated. The most perceptive and responsible suggestion comes from B. H. Bronson, who sees "The Three Ravens" as the secular antecedent of which the "Corpus Christi" carol is a "pious adaptation."[78]

It is possible that Bronson has based his remarks on the consensus of earlier scholarship without giving particular thought to the question of religious or secular priority, but in any case I can only record my belief that "Corpus Christi" came first and "The Three Ravens" came afterward. Although twentieth-century scholars have generally regarded the Middle Ages as bursting with a secular vitality which at times, regrettably, is subjected to "pious adaptation," insincere but somehow needful, there are fortunately signs that we are overcoming this limited view of the medieval spirit, at least as it is reflected in the art and literature of that period.[79] As far as the folksong tradition is concerned, a mere glance

77. In discussing the quest of the Virgin motif associated with the crucifixion, Miss Batho calls attention to the influence of the *Song of Solomon* in the elaboration of this quest ("The Life of Christ in the Ballads," p. 90).

78. Bronson, *The Traditional Tunes of the Child Ballads*, I, 308.

79. See D. W. Robertson, Jr., *Preface to Chaucer* (Princeton, 1962), esp. chap. i.

at the Sloane manuscript discussed above will reveal that its songs are nearly all vital and impressive compositions, whether they are concerned with amorous love, satire, or religious meditation or praise. Indeed my conclusion is that the greatest dedication and artistic skill has gone into the religious pieces, and that these creations entered a living folksong tradition which preserved them devoutly for many centuries. I do not believe it is overstating the case at all to say that "The Three Ravens" is a beautiful song precisely because it is a secularized, chivalric *Pietà*.[80] And, as we shall have occasion to observe, the closer one studies the popular ballad, the more evident becomes its debt, both collectively and in individual ballads, to the religious folksong tradition.

---

80. No difficulty is seen in the humanizing of the devil in "Riddles Wisely Expounded;" but scholars have been apparently reluctant to see this same tendency at work in the transition from "Corpus Christi" to "The Three Ravens."

3. Rymes of Robyn Hood

The early ballads of the greenwood about Robin Hood and other outlaws are very important for understanding the evolution of balladry. In the first place these ballads became the most popular and enduring creation of the minstrel muse in the fifteenth and sixteenth centuries, and as such had a strong formative influence, as we shall see, in the shaping of new ballads in the seventeenth and eighteenth centuries. In the latter period, especially, the Robin Hood texts were pilfered frequently to supply the commonplace stanzas needed in the composition of completely new eighteenth-century ballad mosaics unrelated to the Robin Hood tradition.

Of even greater importance for our present purpose is the fact that this minstrelsy of the greenwood provides our earliest examples of that narrative symmetry mentioned briefly in the first chapter, which played such an important role in the early history of the ballads. In considering the outlaw ballads in the present chapter, therefore, it will be well to take note of the kinds of narrative structure to be found in these texts in order to see in better perspective the subsequent evolution of narrative form in the ballad.

Before turning to the analysis of specific ballads, it is necessary to consider briefly whether or not we are to suppose that these early outlaw narratives were actually sung. Let me hasten to say that I do not raise this question out of any perverse desire to prove that they were not ballads. On the contrary, I believe that without the impetus of the Robin Hood repertoire the popular ballad would never have come into being. Hence I am completely in accord with those who support the inclusion of these texts in the Child canon. Yet it has been my observation that students of the ballad have tended to avoid this question, with serious consequences for study of the development of balladry. If anything has obscured ballad origins more than the old communalist-individualist controversy, it has been the failure of scholars to search for that elusive but historically precise moment in time when the recited narratives of late medieval minstrelsy began to be sung.[1] To see the importance of this, it

1. For the history of controversy over ballad origins, see esp. the early chapters of Wilgus, *Anglo-American Folksong Scholarship since 1898.*

is only necessary to realize that the earliest Robin Hood texts were probably not songs, but "rymes."

The case in support of recitation of the early Robin Hood narratives has been presented convincingly by E. K. Chambers in the *Oxford History of English Literature* and therefore need not be repeated here in detail.[2] But since Chambers' views seem to have been largely ignored, a brief recapitulation of his main thesis will not be out of place.[3]

Although the distinction between narrative and lyric poetry has always been difficult to make, it is possible to recognize in fifteenth-century England a body of lyric poetry composed in distinctive stanza forms often with a refrain and a group of narrative poems frequently in couplet or septenar meters. Of the latter type there are a few historical poems, numerous popular edifying narratives such as *The Childe of Bristowe*, comic and satirical pieces, poems on the theme of the King and the Subject, represented in the Child collection, as we shall see, by "King Edward the Fourth and a Tanner of Tamworth" (273), and of course the Robin Hood narratives.

Early references to Robin Hood are rather ambiguous with respect to the question of singing versus recitation, since words like "sing," "song," or "cantitare" may refer to a form of delivery which we would call "chanting" in order to distinguish it from the kind of "singing" associated with the lyric or folksong tradition.[4] Thus in *Dives and Pauper* (*ca.* 1410) mention is made of "a tale or a song of robyn hode," and Walter Bower (*ca.* 1450), in a passage added to the *Scotichronicon* speaking of the currency of exploits of Robin Hood and Little John in *romanciis, mimos, et bardanos*, uses the words *cantitare delectantur* as well as *recitantur*. In the latter half of the fifteenth century we find in *How the Plowman*

---

2. E. K. Chambers, *English Literature at the Close of the Middle Ages* (Oxford, 1945), chap. iii, "Popular Narrative Poetry and the Ballad," pp. 122–184. Chambers' chapter on the carol and the fifteenth-century lyric (pp. 66–121) is also valuable for anyone interested in the folksong tradition as discussed above in chapter ii of the present study.

3. W. E. Simeone, "The May Games and the Robin Hood Legend," *JAF*, LXIV (1951), 265–274, refers to the familiar passage in the B text of *Piers the Plowman* (passus V, ll. 400–401) and remarks: "Written about 1377, these lines suggest that some kind of Robin Hood songs were then on everyone's lips, and intimate that the 'rymes' of Robin Hood

must have originated at least fifty to one hundred years prior to the recording of Sloth's boast" (p. 266). Maurice Keen, *The Outlaws of Medieval Legend* (Toronto, 1961), speaks in passing of "the humble minstrels who sang the outlaw ballads" (p. 156). I do not find that the question has ever been debated.

4. Geoffrey Chaucer, addressing his "litel bok" of *Troilus and Criseyde*, prays that it will be understood, "red wherso thow be, or elles songe" (V, 1797). For other examples of this usage, see H. H. Carter, *A Dictionary of Middle English Musical Terms*, ed. George B. Gerhard (Bloomington, Ind., 1961): Singen, *vb.* A. III (p. 440).

Lerned his Pater Noster the line, "They songe goynge home warde a Gest of Robyn Hode," and in a burlesque we hear of a sow that "harpyd Robyn Hode."[5]

A similar ambiguity of terms is evident in the early Robin Hood tales, as represented by "A Gest of Robyn Hode" (117), "Robin Hood and Guy of Gisborne" (118), "Robin Hood and the Monk" (119), and "Robin Hood and the Potter" (121). For example, "The Monk" is called a "talkyng" (119, st. 90), and various typical transitions suggest spoken delivery, as in "Now speke we of Roben Hode" (121, st. 80), "Let vs leaue talking of Litle Iohn" (118, st. 21); but the sixth fytte of the *Gest* begins with "Lythe and lysten, gentylmen, and herkyn to your songe" (117, st. 317). Nevertheless, Chambers concludes, I think rightly, that "what we have to do with is not sung but recited minstrelsy, a talking, a speaking."[6]

That we have to do here with recited minstrelsy is suggested especially by the widespread occurrence in the Robin Hood tales of the seasonal *incipit* (118, 119, 121), the "Lythe and lysten" formula, and, notably in the *Gest* (117), the division into fyttes. Add to these the conventional narrative transitions, pious conclusions, and frequent direct address to the audience, and it becomes difficult to suppose that these texts have anything in common with the sung ballads of the later period, except in the sense that the latter "inherited the tradition of medieval popular minstrelsy."[7] Chambers' conclusion in this matter is best summarized in the following words (p. 148):

> Certainly many ballads, possibly most ballads, have at some time been sung. But not all ballads. One of our earliest English ballads, *Robin Hood and the Monk*, has already been noted above as a "talking." And this may well be the best description of other long minstrel ballads, even if they were given in a chanting tone, and perhaps with some musical accompaniment.

Although this conclusion is of necessity somewhat hypothetical, it is the best statement I know of regarding the minstrel ballads in the Child canon.[8]

5. Chambers, *English Literature at the Close of the Middle Ages*, pp. 130–131. Child, *ESPB*, III, 41, refers to a passage in Major's *Historia Maioris Britaniae* (1521) which reports that the deeds of Robin Hood are known all over England *in cantibus*.

6. Chambers, *English Literature at the Close of the Middle Ages*, p. 137.

7. *Ibid.*, p. 141.

8. To some extent I think the sheer length of minstrel narratives militated against their adaptation to the rounded tunes of folksong. The problem is illustrated in some of the longer ballads sung for example by Ewan MacColl in the

In his subsequent discussion of the early ballads Chambers eliminates, correctly I believe, "Judas" (23) and "St. Stephen and Herod" (22) as not ballads, properly speaking. He also excludes "Robyn and Gandeleyn" (115), though I am doubtful about his conjecture that this grim narrative of the greenwood "was probably meant to be sung at a Christmas feast" (pp. 131, 153). Efforts to see ballads flourishing as early as the twelfth century on the dubious evidence of "Sir Aldinger" (59), not to mention "Queen Eleanor's Confession" (156), are rightly condemned. After surveying the field Chambers concludes that even in the sixteenth century there was as yet no great development of ballads of the "Child" type (p. 157). To this I can only add that if by ballads of the "Child" type he means especially the lyrical narratives of the eighteenth century, then the statement is certainly accurate.

To what Chambers has to say about minstrelsy I would append my belief that the folksong tradition as defined in chapter ii above had already come into contact with minstrelsy in the fifteenth century and that this development is perhaps attested in "Robyn and Gandeleyn" (115), which may be our first known popular ballad in the sense of a narrative sung to a rounded melody rather than a chant. If this is correct, it seems likely that the use of traditional tunes as settings for minstrel narratives in the sixteenth century was probably more widespread than Chambers seems willing to allow.

Since we are concerned in this chapter especially with the Robin Hood ballads it will be well at this point to consider a further bit of evidence suggesting that some of these texts may have been sung at an earlier date. I refer to a passage in an early sixteenth-century interlude attributed to John Rastell (ca. 1475–1536), entitled *The Nature of the Four Elements*.[9] This is a didactic, allegorical drama in which basic lessons in philosophy, cosmography, and morality are set forth in dialogue form with occasional intervals of comic relief. During one such comic sequence Sensuall Appetyte is sent to fetch minstrels (here meaning "instrumentalists") who will provide music for a dance, while Humanyté and Yng-

Riverside recordings of the *English and Scottish Popular Ballads* (Riverside RLP 12–621 ff., ed. Kenneth S. Goldstein). In most cases MacColl knew the tune and a few stanzas from tradition, but he sings a very full and lengthy version from written sources. In listening to some of the longer narratives as MacColl sings them I get the feeling that his tune was never meant to "carry" that many stanzas.

9. Halliwell (ed.), *The Interlude of the Four Elements*; also in the *Tudor Facsimile Texts*, "The Nature of the Four Elements," ed. John S. Farmer (London, 1908). It is referred to by Child, *ESPB*, III, 42, and is discussed in a recent and impressive book by John Hollander, *The Untuning of the Sky* (Princeton, 1961), pp. 99–101.

noraunce are left by themselves. The following dialogue then takes place:[10]

HU. Now yf that Sensuall Appetyte can fynd
  Any good mynstrelles after hys mynd,
  Dowt not we shall have good sport.

YNG. And so shall we have for a suerté:
  But what shall we do now, tell me,
  The meane whyle for our comfort.

HU. Then let us some lusty balet syng.

YNG. Nay, syr, by the Hevyn Kyng!
  For me thynkyth it servyth for no thyng,
  All suche pevysh prykyeryd song!

HU. Pes, man, pryksong may not be dispysyd,
  For therwith God is well plesyd,
  Honowryd, praysyd and servyd
  In the churche oft tymes among.

YNG. Is God well pleasyd? trowst thou therby?
  Nay, nay, for there is no reason why,
  For it is not as good to say playnly,
  Gyf me a spade,
  As gyf me a spa, ve, va, ve, va, ve, vade?
  But yf thou wylt have a song that is good,
  I have one of Robyn Hode,
  The best that ever was made.

HU. Then, a feleshyp, let us here it.

YNG. But there is a bordon, thou must bere it,
  Or ellys it wyll not be.

HU. Than begyn and care not to . . .[11]
  Downe, downe, downe, &c.

YNG. Robyn Hode in Barnysdale stode,
  And lent hym tyl a mapyll thystyll;
  Than cam our lady and swete saynt Andrewe.
  Slepyst thou, wakyst thou, Geffrey Coke?
  A c. wynter the water was depe.
  I can not tell you how brode.
  He toke a gose nek in his hande,

10. Halliwell (ed.), *The Interlude of the Four Elements*, pp. 50–51.
11. See Farmer (ed.), "The Nature of the Four Elements," sig. E8ʳ The corner of the page is torn away, but very little is lost; perhaps one or two words.

And over the water he went.
He start up to a thystell top,
And cut hym downe a holyn clobe.
He stroke the wren betwene the hornys,
That fyre sprange out of the pygges tayle.
Jak boy, is thy bowe i-broke?
Or hath any man done the wryguldy wrage?
He plukkyd muskyllys out of a wyllowe,
And put them into his sachell!
Wylkyn was an archer good,
And well coude handell a spade;
He toke his bend bowe in his hand,
And set hym downe by the fyre:
He toke with hym lx. bowes and ten,
A pese of befe, another of baken.
Of all the byrdes in mery Englond,
So merely pypys the mery botell!

This fascinating passage contains several matters of interest to the ballad historian. Not the least of these is Humanyté's proposal that they "some lusty balet syng." Here we have perhaps the earliest reference to a "balet" as being sung, although it is evident that "balet" here is identified with "prykyeryd song," that is, composed music written down for singing, usually in parts.[12] Significantly, it is Yngnoraunce who scoffs at this kind of singing and proposes instead a *good* song, namely, Robin Hood. This fits the general pattern of pejorative references to folksong in the sixteenth century, if we remember the word "balet" in this passage retains its favorable, artistic connotations, not as yet having been appropriated in common usage to refer to broadside productions.[13]

The song being parodied is "Robyn Hode in Barnysdale Stode," a lost text referred to elsewhere in Nicholas Udall's translation of *Erasmi Apothegmata* (1542), although it might be more accurate to say that the author is satirizing a type of Robin Hood song rather than any particular one.[14] But the important thing to observe is that the piece is definitely a

12. Hollander, *The Untuning of the Sky*, p. 101. It is perhaps for this reason that Friedman (*The Ballad Revival*, p. 44) dates the movement of the "balets" toward popular song "from about 1510," though the date of Rastell's *Interlude* is probably closer to 1520.

13. See Friedman, *The Ballad Revival*, pp. 35–44.

14. Furnivall, *Robert Laneham's Letter*, pp. li–lii. The "song" is replete with ministrel commonplaces used bathetically, e.g., see "Slepyst thou, wakyst thou . . ." and the parallels cited by Child in the introduction to "Old Robin of Portingale" (80), *ESPB*, II, 240.

song, with a "burden," which Humanyté is instructed to bear: "Downe, downe, downe, &c." In Child's collection this refrain is a very common one in the Robin Hood ballads, but not earlier than the middle of the seventeenth century, as in "Robin Hood and the Butcher" (122B). Its appearance in Rastell's parody is the earliest instance I know of a connection between the "downe, downe" refrain and a Robin Hood text.

Although the evidence just considered points to an early date for the beginning of sung ballads, this should not be allowed to obscure the fact that most of the early outlaw texts we are considering are clear examples of late medieval minstrelsy rather than songs. Even "Adam Bell, Clim of the Clough, and William of Cloudesly" (116), which first appears in the second quarter of the sixteenth century, has unmistakable features of the late metrical romances. It has the seasonal *incipit,* and the minstrel addresses his audience in the customary manner (116, st. 5):

> Now lith and lysten, gentylmen,
>> And that of myrthes loueth to here.

Furthermore one recognizes certain commonplace lines, "as lyght as lefe on lynde" (st. 94^2), the alliterative poetic diction of "the kynges bowmen buske them blyue" (st. 144^1), and the characteristic division into "fyttes" (st. 51):

> To Caerlel went these good yemen,
>> In a mery mornyng of Maye:
> Her is a fyt of Cloudesli,
>> And another is for to saye.

There are also frequently stanzas rhyming *abab* (note especially sts. 79–86), and even one instance of a five-line stanza rhyming *abcbc* (st. 74):

> Than Clowdysle cast hys eyen asyde,
>> And sawe hys bretheren stande,
> At a corner of the market-place,
>> With theyr good bowes bent in theyr hand,
> Redy the iustyce for to chase.

With these characteristic features of minstrelsy so prominent in the relatively late "Adam Bell," it is not surprising to find them in such abundance in the earliest Robin Hood ballads, to which we must now turn.

"A Gest of Robyn Hode" (117)

It is often remarked that "A Gest of Robin Hood" is made up of a group of separate Robin Hood ballads "stitched" or "strung" together. To some extent this may simply echo Child's theory that it is "A popular epic composed from several ballads" and "A three-ply web" of adventures.[15] But I suspect that theoretical considerations are not entirely absent, and that the form of this remarkable narrative is being interpreted in such a way as to establish the early existence of popular Robin Hood ballads. That earlier metrical narratives of Robin Hood existed may well be true; but to say that "A Gest of Robin Hood" is merely a stringing together of such tales is unfortunate, since it fails to recognize the poem's remarkable unity and above all its narrative symmetry.

The narrative symmetry of the early minstrel ballads is not something unique, but rather it is a phenomenon often found in various forms of narrative art, from medieval romance to the modern novel.[16] One thinks immediately of the formal repetitions of a folktale like "Kulhwch and Olwen," which give the Welsh story a rather rigid symmetrical form. But the use of patterned repetitions in narrative structure is by no means confined to folk tradition; it can be found, admittedly in highly sophisticated form, in the work of such gifted narrators as Chrétien de Troyes and Chaucer.

One of the greatest poems of the twelfth century was Chrétien's *Perceval*, the first Grail narrative and the model for numerous later romances of the Arthurian cycle in both France and England.[17] It chronicles the career of Perceval from his rustic home in the forest of Wales to the moment of his success as a knight of King Arthur's court, and concludes his story at a hermitage in the forest where the young hero learns to submit his worldly ambition to a higher, spiritual authority.[18] The poem has a remarkable symmetry which reinforces its religious theme. It begins in spring, moves through the "winter" of Perceval's worldly

15. Hodgart, *The Ballads*, p. 72; Child, *ESPB*, III, 49 f.

16. See E. K. Brown, *Rhythm in the Novel* (Toronto, 1950).

17. Alfons Hilka (ed.), *Der Percevalroman* (Halle, 1932); William Roach (ed.), *Le Roman de Perceval ou Le Conte du Graal* ("Textes Litteraires Français" [Geneva, 1956]). The complete text is translated by Robert W. Linker, *The Story of the Grail* (Chapel Hill, N.C., 1960); a translation of the Perceval adventures is available in R. S. Loomis and L. H. Loomis, *Medieval Romances* ("Modern Library No. 133" [New York, 1957]), pp. 8–87.

18. For an interpretation of the poem in relation to its religious theme, see David C. Fowler, *Prowess and Charity in the Perceval of Chrétien de Troyes* (Seattle, 1959). Other studies are listed in *ibid.*, pp. 79–81. More recent interpretations are Urban T. Holmes, Jr., and Sister M. Amelia Klenke, *Chrétien, Troyes, and the Grail* (Chapel Hill, N.C., 1959); and Helen Adolf, *Visio Pacis: Holy City and Grail* (University Park, Pa., 1960).

prestige and acclaim, and returns to springtime (Easter) in the hermitage, the scene of the hero's spiritual rebirth. The contrast between the spirituality of Perceval and the worldliness of Gauvain is underscored by parallel adventures in the other world, Perceval at the Grail castle and Gauvain at Escavalon. The parallel lameness of Perceval's father and the fisher king point toward an identification of the two. Finally, similar incidents at the beginning and end of the narrative dramatize a change in the hero's values. When the story opens in the forest of Wales, Perceval meets a group of knights, magnificently clad in armor, and this experience leads him to seek knighthood at Arthur's court. At the end of the story, in the forest near the hermitage, he meets a group of knights and ladies barefoot and in ragged clothes (because it is Good Friday), and on their advice he is led to seek spiritual counsel at the hermitage.

The example of *Perceval* shows that in the hands of a skilled poet like Chrétien narrative repetition rarely means identical recurrence. Instead there is usually some dramatic change designed to introduce by contrast a new increment of meaning, as when the knights first appear to Perceval in shining armor, then in rags. Readers of Chaucer will recall a similar skilled use of repetitions to produce an admirable narrative symmetry in "The Knight's Tale," the relevance of which to Chaucer's theme has been well described by Charles Muscatine.[19]

The fact that there has been little discussion of narrative symmetry in the ballads is perhaps due to the notion that the latter are lacking in art and therefore cannot be supposed to possess features in common with the poetry of a Chrétien or a Chaucer. But as I have tried to suggest, the "new minstrelsy" which we are considering is patterned after medieval romance, and it can be expected to reflect its motifs and narrative structure. Hence it is not surprising, and probably not coincidental, that "A Gest of Robin Hode" displays the kind of narrative symmetry that we normally associate with medieval romance.

"A Gest of Robyn Hode" begins in the Arthurian manner. Robin Hood, the most courteous of outlaws, refuses to eat until he has some "vnkouth gest." He sends Little John and two other outlaws to find someone, and they return with a poor knight, Sir Richard at the Lee, who dines with Robin Hood and tells of his misfortune and his debt of four hundred pounds, owed to the abbot of Saint Mary's. Robin lends him the money on the security of Our Lady (sts. 1–81).

The poor knight, Sir Richard, finds the abbot at dinner and first

19. "Form, Texture, and Meaning in   (1950), 911–929.
Chaucer's *Knight's Tale*," *PMLA*, LXV

pleads for an extension of time, but is cruelly refused. He then pays the debt to the consternation of the abbot and sets out to return to Robin Hood his money (sts. 82–143). Meanwhile, Little John secretly takes service with the hated sheriff of Nottingham. One day, after quarreling with the sheriff's butler, who refused to serve him any dinner, John makes friends with the cook (after fighting him to a draw), and the two of them join Robin in the greenwood, bringing with them much of the sheriff's silverware and a considerable amount of money. The sheriff, meanwhile, is in the forest hunting, and Little John tricks him into an ambush, with the result that he is forced to have dinner and spend the night with Robin Hood and the outlaw gang before being allowed to return to Nottingham (sts. 144–204).

In the greenwood Robin Hood refuses to dine until he has sent Little John and two other outlaws to find some uncouth guest. They return with a monk of Saint Mary's abbey, who dines with the outlaws and then is forced to surrender his money. Robin sends the monk on his way and says that Our Lady has discharged the knight's debt; when Sir Richard returns to the greenwood and attempts to repay the outlaw, Robin will take nothing (sts. 205–280).

When Robin Hood and his men come to Nottingham to participate in an archery contest, the sheriff tries to capture them but they escape and are given protection by their friend Sir Richard (sts. 281–316). The frustrated sheriff seeks the help of King Edward and furthermore captures the knight with a view to executing him quickly. But Sir Richard's wife appeals to Robin, who rescues the knight and kills the sheriff (sts. 317–353).

At last the King arrives with the intention of capturing Robin Hood, and, disguised as an abbot, he is stopped by the gang and forced to dine on his own deer before he is recognized by the outlaws, who ask forgiveness. The King grants them a pardon, on condition that Robin Hood and his men will come into the King's service (sts. 354–417). For sport the King and his men are clothed in Lincoln green and all return happily to Nottingham. Robin Hood is unhappy in the King's household, and after little more than a year he returns to the greenwood and never again enters the King's service. Eventually he is treacherously slain by the prioress of Kyrkesly (sts. 418–456).

Even this brief summary of the plot of "A Gest of Robyn Hode" indicates the central theme and its relationship to the sequence of events. Robin Hood is a courteous outlaw, with a passion for justice, who therefore hates the exploiting, greedy monks of Saint Mary's and the treacherous sheriff of Nottingham, but who loves good knights like Sir Richard and is unfailingly loyal to his king.

It will be noted that one of the most frequent events in the "Gest" is a dinner. This is perhaps understandable as a form of wish fulfilment with considerable appeal to a popular audience of the poor and needy, but it serves in this poem primarily as an occasion for the testing of character. Robin Hood has dinner with the knight, the sheriff, the monk, and the King, which is to say nearly all of the major figures in the story, and each time, in various ways, the dinner provides an opportunity for some kind of test or disclosure. Even Sir Richard's interview at Saint Mary's takes place while the abbot is having his dinner. It is possible, I suppose, to assume that the various Robin Hood ballads "stitched together" to form the "Gest" all simply happened to contain these commonplace eating episodes. But this assumption should not be allowed to obscure the fact that our author has used these scenes with great skill to dramatize the courtesy of Robin Hood's friends and the avarice and cruelty of his enemies.

Instances of the courtesy of Robin Hood and his companions are to be found almost from the very beginning of the poem. Little John is quite correct in his first approach to the knight, Sir Richard at the Lee (sts. 243–244):

> Litell Johnn was full curteyes,
>   And sette hym on his kne:
> 'Welcom be ye, gentyll knyght,
>   Welcom ar ye to me.
>
> 'Welcom be thou to grene wode,
>   Hende knyght and fre;
> My maister hath abiden you fastinge,
>   Syr, al these oures thre.'

Robin is equally courteous in receiving the knight, and their conversation throughout the meal could be taken as a model of courtly behavior (sts. 29–31):

> They brought hym to the lodge-dore;
>   Whan Robyn hym gan see,
> Full curtesly dyd of his hode
>   And sette hym on his knee.

'Welcome, sir knight,' than sayde Robyn,
    'Welcome art thou to me;
I haue abyden you fastinge sir,
    All these ouris thre.'

Than answered the gentyll knight,
    With wordes fayre and fre;
'God the saue, goode Robyn,
    And all thy fayre meyne.'

This scene contrasts sharply with that which takes place in the dining hall of the abbey where Sir Richard comes to plead for an extension of time for repaying his loan (sts. 102–103):

Lordes were to mete isette
    In that abbotes hall;
The knyght went forth and kneled downe,
    And salued them grete and small.

'Do gladly, syr abbot,' sayd the knyght,
    'I am come to holde my day:'
The fyrst word the abbot spake,
    'Hast thou brought my pay?'

The knight pleads vainly for mercy in turn to the high justice, the sheriff, and again to the abbot, who villainously tells him to "spede the out of my hall." The good knight at last loses patience (st. 115):

Vp then stode that gentyll knyght,
    To the abbot sayd he,
'To suffre a knyght to knele so longe,
    Thou canst no curteysye.'

When the knight suddenly confronts the abbot and his men with the money for payment of the loan, he also points the moral (st. 121):

'Haue here thi golde, sir abbot,' saide the knight,
    'Which that thou lentest me;
Had thou ben curtes at my comynge,
    Rewarded shuldest thou haue be.'

At this news the abbot seems to have lost his appetite (st. 122):

The abbot sat styll, and ete no more,
    For all his ryall fare;
He cast his hede on his shulder,
    And fast began to stare.

76

In a subsequent dinner scene less satiric than comic, the sheriff of Nottingham, faced with the necessity of eating a meal with his own stolen silverware, suffers a similar loss of appetite (st. 191):

Sone he was to souper sette,
    And served well with silver white,
And when the sherif sawe his vessell,
    For sorowe he myght nat ete.

By far the most elaborate repetition of the dinner scene is that involving the monk in the fourth fytte, which is closely modeled after Robin's dinner with the knight in the first fytte. This is one of our best illustrations of the minstrel's technique, for it has enough close repetition to show how such a device could serve as a memory aid, while at the same time there is enough significant variation to dramatize an important contrast between the knight and the monk. Whole passages are repeated: stanzas 17–20, telling how Little John, Uruch, and William Scarlok go in search of a dinner guest, are repeated almost exactly in stanzas 208–212, with the exception of one stanza (211) in which Little John girds on a sword.[20] Then the passages diverge at that point where the dinner guests arrive (sts. 21, 213):

But as they loked in to Bernysdale
    Bi a derne strete,
Than came a knyght ridinghe;
    Full sone they gan hym mete.

. . . .

But as they loked in Bernysdale,
    By the hye waye,
Than were they ware of two blacke monkes,
    Eche on a good palferay.

Even the slight variations here point a contrast. The knight takes a side-street, the monks ride (proudly? apprehensively?) on the highway; he rides alone "in symple aray" (st. 23^2), while the monks ride each on a good palfrey in the company of fifty men (st. 216).

Our attitude toward the monk is determined somewhat by the be-

20. The girding on of the sword in stanza 211 of the "Gest" is added deliberately, I think, to foreshadow the hostility and threat of violence implicit in the meeting of the outlaws with the monk and his party. A similar function can be assigned to stanza 245, in which Robin warns the monk that he will lose his money if he is lying about the amount.

haviour of the outlaws toward him. Whereas Little John had been very
courteous to the knight, he speaks sharply to the monk when he orders
him to have dinner with his master. But there is likewise a contrast in the
reply of the guests (sts. 26, 221):

'Who is thy maister?' sayde the knyght;
    Johnn sayde, Robyn Hode;
'He is a gode yoman,' sayde the knyght,
    'Of hym I haue herde moche gode.'

    . . . .

'Who is your mayster?' sayd the monke;
    Lytell Johan sayd, Robyn Hode;
'He is a stronge thefe,' sayd the monke,
    'Of hym herd I neuer good.'

Like the knight before him, the monk is brought to the outlaws'
lodge, but unlike Sir Richard he fails the test of courtesy (sts. 226–227):

Robyn dyde adowne his hode,
    The monke whan that he se;
The monke was not so curteyse,
    His hode then let he be.

'He is a chorle, mayster, by dere worthy God,'
    Than sayd Lytell Johan:
'Thereof no force,' sayd Robyn,
    'For curteysy can he none.'

But perhaps the most skilful use of repetition here is in the passage describing the outlaws' search of their guest's personal effects (sts. 39–43,
243–248). A basic contrast is of course seen in the fact that the knight
tells the truth when asked how much money he has, whereas the monk
lies. The one extra stanza in the repeated passage, however, warns the
monk that he will lose his money if he is lying (st. 245), and the outcome
of the search points a dramatic contrast between the knight and the
monk (sts. 42–43, 247–248):

Lyttell Johnn sprede downe hys mantell
    Full fayre vpon the grounde,
And there he fonde in the knyghtes cofer
    But euen halfe a pounde.

78

Littell Johnn let it lye full styll,
     And went to hys maysteer full lowe;
'What tidynges, Johnn?' sayde Robyn;
     'Sir, the knyght is true inowe.'

·   ·   ·   ·   ·   ·   ·   ·   ·   ·   ·   ·

Lytell Johan spred his mantell downe,
     As he had done before,
And he tolde out of the monkes male
     Eyght hondred pounde and more.

Lytell Johan let it lye full styll,
     And went to his mayster in hast;
'Syr,' he sayd, 'the monke is trewe ynowe,
     Our Lady hath doubled your cast.'

John's leisurely obeisance in the first passage is in contrast with his haste in the second, and a nice distinction in the meanings of "true" is implied. The knight spoke the truth; the monk is a "true" messenger of Our Lady—he has brought the money—which is indeed a courteous interpretation of the monk's duplicity.

From what has been said of the narrative symmetry employed by the poet it should be evident that "A Gest of Robyn Hode" is the work of a skilled artist, and that the stitching that binds the various episodes together is more significant than the assumed vestigial remains of earlier Robin Hood ballads. That the repetitions we have examined occurred independently in earlier ballads and then converged accidentally to reinforce the poet's theme is extremely unlikely; but if on the other hand it is supposed that the poet changed the form of the ballads which he strung together so as to achieve a narrative symmetry, then this supposition merely implies that his poem utilizes earlier narrative sources, a fact which has long been known.[21] Hence it is not really possible to speak of sources for the poem *in ballad form*. All this leads me, in the absence of other evidence, to the conclusion that the separate Robin Hood ballads often supposed to be the sources of the poem actually did not come into being until well after 1400, which is the date usually assigned to "A Gest of Robyn Hode." Reluctant as I am to say so, it may nevertheless be true

21. Child refers to the resemblances between stories of Robin Hood and Fulk Fitz Warine in *ESPB*, III, 43; the indebtedness of Robin Hood to earlier outlaw narratives is one of the main themes of Keen, *The Outlaws of Medieval Legend.*

that "Robin Hood's Death" (120), for example, was inspired by stanzas 451–456 of the "Gest."[22]

"Robin Hood and the Monk" (119) and "Robin Hood and the Potter" (121)

The "talking" of the monk and Robin Hood (119, st. 90) is the earliest of the Robin Hood pieces and is preserved in a Cambridge manuscript of about 1450.[23] This manuscript, to judge from its contents, seems to have served primarily as a priest's source book. The first group of texts now in the manuscript (it is defective at the beginning) starts with John Mirk's *Instructions for Parish Priests*, a manual containing materials for use in preparing sermons.[24] Then follow *The ABC of Aristotle*, an alphabetized series of maxims; a table of diverse months of the year, with weather predictions; a Latin *oratio* against thieves and robbers (!), *contra fures et latrones*; *Passio Domini*, which is a version of *The Northern Passion*;[25] and finally two moralistic pieces, one entitled *Memento Homo* and the other a treatise on the seven deadly sins.

A second group of texts in the Cambridge manuscript is made up primarily of short metrical narratives, both serious and comic, but usually with some moral theme expressed or satirically implied. This group includes *The Unnatural Daughter*, the story of a girl who finally obtains the forgiveness of God after a sinful life; *King Edward and the Shepherd*; a humorous narrative type identified by Chambers as "The King and the Subject," discussed below in connection with the Child ballad "King Edward the Fourth and a Tanner of Tamworth" (273);[26] *The Clerk and the Nightingale*, a courtly love debate on the worth of womankind;[27] the

22. *Ibid.*, p. 112, in discussing the death of Robin Hood as given in the "Gest," refers to the two independent ballad versions as representing an earlier tradition, in spite of the fact that they appear first in the seventeenth and eighteenth centuries: "But the survival of two other ballads, which seem to be of individual origin and tell the same story of the death of the outlaw chief, prove that this is another tale tacked on artificially as a finale." The rest of his interpretation, though presented with great ingenuity and persuasiveness (pp. 112–115), is dependent on the unproved assumption that the ballads are "of individual origin."

23. Cambridge University Library MS Ff. 5.48. The contents of this MS are listed in Hartshorne, *Ancient Metrical Tales*, pp. x–xviii. Of the twenty-seven pieces listed, Hartshorne prints seven, mostly from this MS: "A Tale of King Edward and the Shepherd," pp. 35–80; "A Ballad" (on a feast), pp. 145–150; "A Tale of the Unnatural Daughter," pp. 151–164; "The Mourning of the Hare," pp. 165–168; "A Tale of a Father and his Son," pp. 169–178; "A Tale of Robin Hood," pp. 179–197; and "The Tale of the Basyn," pp. 198–208.

24. E. Peacock (ed.), *Myrc's Duties of a Parish Priest* (EETS, O.S. 31 [London, 1868]).

25. F. A. Foster (ed.), *The Northern Passion* (EETS, O.S. 145, 147 [London, 1912, 1913]).

26. Child, *ESPB*, V, 71–72; Chambers, *English Literature at the Close of the Middle Ages*, p. 128.

27. Printed as No. 179, "The Clerk and the Nightingale, I" in R. H. Robbins, *Secular Lyrics of the XIVth and XVth Centuries* (Oxford, 1952), pp. 172–176.

bawdy *Tale of the Basyn,* a fabliau; *The Turnament of Tottenham,* a skilled burlesque of chivalry; some prognostications; and another moralistic metrical narrative emphasizing the evil consequences of adultery and the blessings of marital fidelity, *A Father and his Son.*[28]

A third, more explicitly didactic group of pieces in this manuscript contains a considerable variety of literary forms. There are several poems of or to the Virgin; a set of "prophetick rules"; excerpts from the *South English Legendary;*[29] a *Short Metrical Chronicle of England* through the reign of Edward I; a satirical lament entitled *The Mourning of the Hare;* more seasonal predictions (in prose); and two satirical rhyming pieces, one on an incontinent priest, the other describing a magnificent feast.

A final group of three metrical tales concludes this enumeration of the contents of the Cambridge manuscript: one is *A Lady Who Buried the Host;* another *Thomas of Erceldoune,* the romance on which the ballad "Thomas Rymer" (37) is based; and, last of all, "Robin Hood and the Monk" (119).

As has been already suggested, the common denominator of this seeming miscellany is the interest of the priestly compiler. If we recognize the seriousness of his didactic purpose, while at the same time we avoid the modern tendency to construct an overly solemn image of the priesthood, then it is possible, I think, to see in this compilation an effort to provide materials for the entertainment and instruction of a popular audience. The man behind this collection may well have been one of that class of minstrel that the author of *Piers the Plowman* praises for having "holy writ ay in his mouth," as opposed to those children of Judas whom he calls "japers and janglers."[30]

In the context of this manuscript collection "Robin Hood and the Monk" is readily recognizable as a purely entertaining tale like *King Edward and the Shepherd.* I can only suppose that Child chose the one and not the other because "Robin Hood and the Monk" is composed in the quatrain form destined to be the regular ballad stanza, whereas *King Edward and the Shepherd* has a twelve-line stanza *aabccbddbeeb.* The difficulties which Child faced in defining the limits of the ballad canon

28. Title used by Chambers, *English Literature at the Close of the Middle Ages,* p. 125. Other titles sometimes found for this piece are *The Adulterous Falmouth Squire* and *Against Breaking of Wedlock.*

29. C. Horstmann, (ed.), *The Early South English Legendary* (EETS, O.S. 87 [London, 1887]).

30. Skeat (ed.), *Piers the Plowman.* For a full and valuable discussion of the min-strel references and their significance see E. Talbot Donaldson, *Piers Plowman: The C-Text and Its Poet* (New Haven, 1949), pp. 136–155. Two other important studies cited by Donaldson are K. J. Holzknecht, *Literary Patronage in the Middle Ages* (Philadelphia, 1923), and H. S. Bennett, "The Author and His Public in the Fourteenth and Fifteenth Centuries," *E&S,* XXIII (1937), 7–24.

at the point of origin were so great that I am not at all inclined to be critical of the choices which he actually made; but in re-enacting his choice here I wish merely to point out what frequently seems to be lost sight of, namely, that the fact of Child's selection of "Robin Hood and the Monk" from the Cambridge manuscript does not in itself mean that this piece must be regarded as a sung ballad. All the manuscript evidence suggests that it is a "talkyng," no different in this respect from the other pieces in the collection than the "talkyng" of A Father and his Son:

> Man for thy myschif thou the amend
>> And to my talkyng thou take gode hede
> Ffro vij dedly synnes thou the defende
>> The lest of alle is for to drede.[31]

The piety of this opening stanza is essentially not unlike the piety of the conclusion of "Robin Hood and the Monk" (119, st. 90):

> Thus endys the talkyng of the munke
>> And Robyn Hode i-wysse;
> God, Þat is euer a crowned kyng,
>> Bryng vs all to his blisse!

Although the tale of "Robin Hood and the Monk" lacks the narrative symmetry we found in the "Gest," it does have some good examples of incremental repetition, and it is interesting to note that this latter feature often appears in conjunction with the stylized epithets of late medieval romance ("Þou prowde schereff") and the diction of alliterative poetry ("Buske Þe and make Þe bowne"), as in the following (119, sts. 21–22):

> 'Rise vp,' he seid, 'Þou prowde schereff,
>> Buske Þe and make Þe bowne;
> I haue spyed Þe kynggis felon,
>> Ffor sothe he is in Þis town.

> 'I haue spyed Þe false felon,
>> As he stondis at his masse;
> Hit is long of Þe,' seide Þe munke,
>> 'And euer he fro vs passe.'

This is a particularly interesting example because it shows so well the lingering technique of later balladry beginning to emerge in a context of late medieval minstrelsy. Other instances of artful repetition help to pro-

31. Hartshorne, *Ancient Metrical Tales,* p. 169.

vide dramatic emphasis at crucial moments in the narrative. Such is the effect of repetitions in the account of the slaying of the monk and his page (sts. 47–48, 52), the reconciliation of Robin Hood and Little John (sts. 77–80), and above all the speech of the King at the end, in which the theme of the tale is given in a richly elaborated series of repetitions, full of promise for the future of ballad style (sts. 85–89):

'Litul John has begyled vs bothe,
     And þat full wel I se;
Or ellis þe schereff of Notyngham
     Hye hongut shulde he be.
'I made hem ȝemen of þe crowne,
     And gaf hem fee with my hond;
I gaf hem grith,' seid oure kyng,
     'Thorowout all mery Inglond.
'I gaf theym grith,' þen seid oure kyng;
     'I say, so mot I the,
Ffor sothe soch a ȝeman as he is on
     In all Inglond ar not thre.
'He is trew to his maister,' seid our kyng;
     'I sey, be swete Seynt John,
He louys better Robyn Hode
     Then he dose vs ychon.
'Robyn Hode is euer bond to hym,
     Bothe in strete and stalle;
Speke no more of this mater,' seid oure kyng,
     'But John has begyled vs alle.'

The other early Robin Hood ballad under consideration is "Robin Hood and the Potter" (121), preserved in a manuscript of about 1500.[32] This date is late enough that one might suppose it to have been a sung ballad, but I can find nothing that points in this direction. Furthermore this text lacks both the narrative symmetry of the "Gest" and the functional repetitions we have just seen in the preceding ballad. Just a trace of the minstrel's division of the story into fyttes remains (121, st. 30):

Tho Roben droffe on hes wey,
     So merey ower the londe:
Her es more, and affter ys to saye,
     The best ys beheynde.

32. Cambridge University Library MS   Ee.4.35.

Perhaps confirming this indication of minstrel technique is the fact that several stanzas rhyme *abab*.[33]

The Cambridge manuscript in which "Robin Hood and the Potter" is preserved resembles to some extent the manuscript containing "Robin Hood and the Monk" discussed earlier in this chapter. Both MSS have the didactic narratives, *A Father and his Son* and *A Lady Who Buried the Host*, and both MSS include a treatise against the seven deadly sins. Whereas the earlier volume has a version of *King Edward and The Shepherd*, the later collection has another piece on the theme of the King and the Subject entitled *The King and the Barker*, a text which Child prints as Appendix I to "King Edward the Fourth and a Tanner of Tamworth" (273). It is interesting to note that this piece is printed in an appendix even though it is apparently in couplet or quatrain form. Did Child think that "Robin Hood and the Potter" was a sung ballad but that "The King and the Barker" was not? It is difficult to say. The two pieces stand side by side in the same manuscript with no visible means of demonstrating that one is a ballad and the other a metrical narrative. But surely we need no longer hesitate to affirm that both "The Potter" and "The Barker" are products of the minstrel tradition. They were recited and not sung.

If the above conclusion is correct, then there is no real evidence to suggest that "Robin Hood and the Monk" and "Robin Hood and the Potter" were ever sung. But the case is far otherwise for "The King and the Barker," the history of which will conclude this chapter, thus providing a convenient transition from the recited tales of the late medieval period to the beginnings of authentic narrative song in the new minstrelsy of the sixteenth century.

"King Edward the Fourth and a Tanner of Tamworth" (273)

The three texts to be considered here are "The King and the Barker" (Cambridge MS, *ca.* 1500), "A . . . Historie, betweene King Edward the Fourth and a Tanner of Tamworth" (London: John Danter, 1596), and "King Edward the Fourth and a Tanner of Tamworth" (late seventeenth-century broadsides). "The Barker" is printed as Appendix I in Child, the "Historie" as Appendix II, and "King Edward" as the ballad itself (273).[34] Child's use of an appendix to distinguish the first two of these texts from the third coincides significantly with my belief that the first

---

33. Stanzas rhyming *abab* are 1, 9–10, 35, 37, 45, 51, 53, 60, 62.

34. A third appendix in Child contains "King Henry II and the Miller of Mans-field," *ESPB*, V, 84–87; but this is an analogue rather than another version of "King Edward."

two texts are metrical tales, whereas the third is, as we know, a ballad sung "to an excellent new tune."[35] Unlike the Robin Hood pieces considered above, therefore, these three texts provide us with the rare opportunity of observing the transformation of a minstrel narrative into a popular ballad.

In order to perceive the excellence of "The King and the Barker," we must first recognize that the text has come down to us with certain "omissions, transpositions, and other faults" to which Child calls attention.[36] Indeed there is one textual problem in particular that seriously affects the narrative. It will be recalled that the king meets the barker while on a hunt and, without revealing his identity, persuades him to ride with him on the way to Drayton Basset. At this point (in the text as we have it) Lord Basset appears with his men and they all fall on their knees, thus revealing to the barker that his companion is none other than the king (sts. 30–33). And yet, although we are told that the barker feared he would be hanged and was so terrified that he forgot to remove his hood, nevertheless as Child remarks "the conviction that 'this' is the king seems to make no difference in the tanner's bearing."[37] During the comic hunting episode that follows, in which the two men trade horses and the barker is thrown by the king's steed, no mention is made of Lord Basset and his men, and the barker's casual tone of address to the king (st. 53) contrasts sharply with his earlier terror.

When we recall, however, that in both the "Historie" (sts. 48–51) and "King Edward" (sts. 31–34) Lord Basset and his men do not appear until the end of the story, where revelation of the king's identity is appropriately climactic, then it seems likely that this order of events was probably followed in the supposed original of "The King and the Barker." In fact I am convinced that stanzas 30–33 of "The Barker," which describe the meeting with Lord Basset, should be inserted between stanzas 54 and 55 in order to restore the original narrative sequence.[38] Hence the following discussion of the text assumes this rearrangement of stanzas.

35. *ESPB*, V, 77.
36. *ESPB*, V, 78. "The King and the Barker" certainly seems to have been transcribed from memory. Compare the remarks of Miss Cornelius on the MS version of "King John and the Bishop" in "A New Text of an Old Ballad."
37. *ESPB*, V, 78. Since the tanner's fear is made so explicit in stanzas 30–33, it might be more accurate to say that knowing the king's identity made no difference in the tanner's *subsequent* bearing.

38. Evidence supporting this supposed shift in the text of "The Barker" can be seen in the repetition more or less without change of the line "Thos they reyd together talkyng" (st. 30) at the point where I believe the recognition scene should be inserted (before st. 55). If one of these narrative transition stanzas originally belonged after stanza 29 and before stanza 34, then we have all the conditions necessary to explain the trick of memory which caused the error to occur.

The main theme of "The King and the Barker" is the conversion of the rude barker from an attitude of hostility toward the king to one of friendliness, a theme which in itself supports the relocation of stanzas suggested above. The winning of the peasant's friendship is much more meaningful if he is unaware of the king's identity, since the revelation of the truth would inhibit the naturalness of their relationship, as it in fact does in stanzas 31–33. In the development of the conversion theme the comedy of contrast between the high and low estates of the two men is skilfully exploited. The king is unfailingly polite while maneuvering the barker into accompanying him, and the barker repeatedly insults the king or displays the limitations of his worldly knowledge (e.g., "cowhides are dear").

The most effective exploitation of the contrasting estates can be seen in the narrator's use of the cowhides, which are "planted" early in the story (st. 4) and referred to frequently throughout. The barker is seated on the hides while riding his horse, and he refuses to part with them for any reason. After they swap horses during the hunt, it is these same cowhides that frighten the king's horse, causing him to throw the barker. As a final flourish, at the end of the story, the king gives the barker a hundred shillings "to mend his cowhides."

The narrative style of "The King and the Barker" is not unlike that of the early Robin Hood tales considered above. Although structural symmetry such as is found in the "Gest of Robyn Hode" does not occur, a few stanzas are repeated, as when the king promises to intercede on the barker's behalf (sts. 9, 23),[39] and an occasional phrase or line ("Thos they reyd together talkyng," sts. 30, 55) is repeated in order to underscore narrative transitions.

Perhaps the most striking stylistic feature in the text is the use of incremental repetition in the comic climax to the hunting episode. The repeated lines suggest the waves of laughter emitted by the king when the tanner is thrown from the horse (sts. 46–48):

With a stombellyng as he rode,
    Þe tanner downe he cast;
The kyng lowhe and had god game,
    and seyde, Ser, Þou rydst to ffast.

39. The king's promise to intercede helps prepare for the later meeting with Lord Basset. It is worth mentioning also that "The Barker" preserves a motif that does not survive in the later versions, namely, the king's effort while incognito to learn what is the common opinion of Lord Basset among his subjects.

The kyng lowhe and had god game,
    and sware be Sent John,
Seche another horsman
    say Y neuere none.

Owre kyng lowhe and had god bord,
    and sware be Sent Jame,
Y most nedys lawhe,
    and thow were mey dame.

We have had occasion to observe this repetitive style not only in the Robin Hood tales but also in "Robyn and Gandeleyn" (115) and the carols and lyrics of the Sloane manuscript. As in the examples previously cited, its use here is artful rather than popular. Not only does it express stylistically the king's laughter, the passage also conveys that spirit of camaraderie which is the means whereby the "conversion" of the barker is effected in the succeeding stanzas (sts. 49–54). The unpretentious but skilful narrative technique of "The King and the Barker" is an excellent example of that late medieval minstrelsy which was to contribute so much to the development of the popular ballad.

The "Historie," first published in 1596, is in one way simply a metrically polished version of "The Barker," almost exactly the same length (fifty-six stanzas instead of fifty-seven), and having the same general theme—the conversion of the tanner from an attitude of scorn to one of respect for the king. But there are some interesting changes in the narrative. Perhaps the most fundamental one is in the hunting episode, where the temporary swapping of horses is converted into a horse trade, which becomes the center of interest, so that the tanner's wild ride is no longer the main event and is in fact disposed of in a single quatrain (st. 39). Replacing the intrinsic comedy of the tanner's ride is a slapstick description of the tanner's efforts to mount the king's horse (sts. 33–38), a passage showing a professional awareness of the tried and true formulas for popular success rather than a genuine comic sense.

Characterizations are considerably changed in the "Historie." Whereas in "The Barker" the king had been ironically polite (st. 9), in the "Historie" he becomes mildly didactic (st. 10), while the tanner's scornful rejection of the king's offer of a dinner in "The Barker" (st. 18) takes on a certain irony in the later text (st. 13). Above all, the basis of the tanner's conversion is no longer the camaraderie of the hunt but rather his admiration of the king's skill as a horse trader (st. 45):

'Dost thou loue to keepe gold?' quoth the tanner,
    the king answered and said, Ye;
'Then I would thou were my neere kinsman,
    for I thinke thou wilt thriue and thee.'

This is clearly a new and more sophisticated explanation of the tanner's respect for the king.

Turning to stylistic matters, we find that the most striking feature of "The Barker," its use of incremental repetition in the comic climax (sts. 46–48), is not preserved in the "Historie" at all. "Abide, good fellow . . . ye make ouer great hast" is all the king says when the tanner falls from the horse. Nevertheless, an interesting new stylistic feature does appear in the later text, namely, a narrative symmetry in the horse-trading episode (sts. 23–46), the most important incident in the entire story.

The symmetry of the horse-trading episode is made possible by the fact that there are two trades. The tanner first drives a hard bargain before exchanging horses with the king, and then, after the tanner is thrown, the king drives an even harder bargain before agreeing to swap horses again. The bargaining formula that opens the first scene (st. 26) is repeated in the second (st. 41) with scarcely a single change in phrasing, but the variations in the subsequent stanzas emphasize the king's superior trading ability. The conclusion of the first trade is described as follows (sts. 30–32):

'What boot will you haue?' then said our king,
    'tell me now in this tide;'
'Neuer a single pennie,' quoth the tanner,
    'but a noble of gold so red.'

'Why, there is your noble,' said our king,
    'well paid looke that you be;'
'I would haue sworne on a book,' quoth the tanner,
    'thou hadst not one pennie.'

Now hath the king the tanner's mare,
    she is nothing faire, fat nor round,
And the tanner hath the king's good steede,
    the saddle is worth fortie pound.

The corresponding stanzas describing the second trade reveal significant variations (sts. 42, 43, 46):

'What boote wilt thou haue?' quoth the tanner,
    'tell me in this stound;

'Neuer a groat nor pennie,' said our king,
    'but of thy gold twentie pound.'

'Nay, here is thy noble,' quoth the tanner again,
    'and Christ's blessing and mine;
'Yea, here is twentie good groats more,
    goe drinke them at the wine.'

. . . .

Now hath the tanner Brocke, his mare,
    and vnder him his good cowhide,
Our noble king his horse againe,
    which was a well faire steede.

This use of stanzaic repetitions to bring out a contrast is very similar to what we have seen, for example, in the first and fourth fyttes of "A Gest of Robyn Hode" (117). But there is an interesting difference. Whereas in the "Gest" the narrative symmetry extends through a hundred or more stanzas, in the "Historie" it is confined to an episode of twenty-four stanzas. The technique of medieval romance narrative is thus being readied for use in the popular ballad. But we have not yet crossed the threshold into balladry. The "Historie" must be regarded as belonging in the category of metrical narrative, not yet sung to a rounded tune, but, for all that, "verie pleasant and merrie to read."[40]

The ballad of "King Edward the Fourth and a Tanner of Tamworth" (273) reduces the length of the story by about one-third (from fifty-six to thirty-nine stanzas), omitting the king's request to become the tanner's apprentice ("Historie," sts. 19–22) and other comic byplay such as the haggling that takes place during the horse trade (sts. 27–29, 44–45). It preserves the symmetry of the bargaining episode (273, sts. 17–19, 28–30), but in doing so loses the functional quality of the "Historie" by blurring some of its contrasts. The king's superior bargaining power, for example, brought out so well in the "Historie," is lacking in the unvaried repetition of the ballad (sts. 18, 29):

'What boot wilt thou ask?' then said our king,
    'what boot dost thou ask on this ground?'
'No pence nor half-pence,' said the tanner,
    'but a noble in gold so round.'

. . . .

40. *ESPB*, V, 83.

'What boot will you ask?' quoth the tanner,
    'What boot will you ask on this ground?'
'No pence nor half-pence,' said our king,
    'but a noble in gold so round.'

This tendency toward a rigid repetition without significant variation is a very interesting development. Are we witnessing the influence of rounded melodies on a minstrel narrative? Whatever the explanation, the result is a wearing away of the sharp edges of characterization we have found in the earlier texts. The extra money which the tanner subsequently offers the king in the ballad is unexplained, and the tanner is thus invested with an unmotivated generosity.

Another new development in "King Edward," perhaps even more significant for the future of balladry, is the tendency toward a multiplication of formulaic stanzas which are repeated with variations designed to underscore stages of plot development. To some extent one can see this type of formulaic stanza growing out of symmetrical narrative, as when the double occurrence of a bargaining stanza in the "Historie" (sts. 26, 41) becomes tripled in the ballad (sts. 17, 20, 28):

'But if you needs with me will change,
    As change full well may ye,
By the faith of my body,' quoth the tanner,
    'I look to have boot of thee.'

    . . . .

'But if so be we needs must change,
    as change thou must abide,
Though thou hast gotten Brock my mare,
    Thou shalt not have my cow-hide.'

    . . . .

'But if that we needs now must change,
    as change that well we mought,
I'le swear to you plain, if you have your mare,
    I look to have some boot.'

Another instance of formulaic repetition appears in the ballad, however, which is entirely independent of structural symmetry in the earlier versions. It will be recalled that the tanner's hostile attitude toward the king is dramatized several times in the course of the story. First he scornfully refuses to direct him to Drayton Basset ("Historie," st. 11), next he hints somewhat fearfully that the king is an outlaw (st. 15), and finally

90

he comes out flatly and accuses the king of being a thief (st. 49). The relationship of these three stanzas to one another in the "Historie," however, is purely thematic; there are no studied repetitions to emphasize their function (sts. 11, 15, 49):

'Go play the great jauel!' quoth the tanner,
    'I hold thee out of thy wit;
All day haue I ridden on Brocke, my mare,
    and I am fasting yet.'

  . · . · . · . · . · . · .

'What art thou, good fellow?' quoth the tanner,
    'of thee I am in great feare,
For the clothes that thou wearest on thy back
    are not for a lord to weare.'

  . · . · . · . · . · . · .

'Now out alas!' quoth the tanner,
    'that euer I saw this tide;
Thou art a strong thiefe, yonder be thy fellowes,
    will haue my mare and my cowhide.'

In the ballad, on the other hand, the tanner's hostile attitude has become somewhat stylized, as can be seen in the following stanzas (273, sts. 8, 12, 32):

'Away, with a vengeance,' quoth the tanner,
    'I hold thee out of thy wit.
For all this day have I ridden and gone,
    And I am fasting yet.'

  . · . · . · . · . · . · .

'Away, with a vengeance,' quoth the tanner,
    'of thee I stand in fear;
The aparrell thou wearst on thy back
    May seem a good lord to wear.'

  . · . · . · . · . · . · .

'Away, with a vengeance,' quoth the tanner,
    'with thee I'le no longer abide;
Thou art a strong thief, yonder be thy fellows,
    they will steal away my cow-hide.'

Here we see a typical development marking the transition from minstrelsy to the sung ballad. It is but one step removed from what we find in the *Ever Green* version of "Johnie Armstrong," where the king's rejection of

Johnie is repeated five times in the course of the ballad without the slightest verbal variation (169C8):

'Away, away thou traytor strang!
    Out of my sicht thou mayst sune be!
I grantit nevir a traytors lyfe,
    And now I'll not begin with thee.'

A final point needs to be made about the evolution of stanza form as illustrated by the texts we have been considering. The stanzaic irregularities of "The Barker" suggest that it may have been originally composed in couplets, which are converted into quatrains in the "Historie" and "King Edward," as can be seen in a comparison of parallel stanzas ("Barker," st. 3; "Historie," st. 3; "King Edward," st. 2):

As he rode, he houer-
    toke yn the wey
A tannar off Dantre,
    yn a queynte araye.
   . . . .

But as our king on his way rode forth,
    by eight a clocke of the day,
He was ware of a tanner of mery Tamworth,
    was in a quaint aray.
   . . . .

Our king he would a hunting ride,
    by eight a clock of the day,
And well was he ware of a bold tanner,
    came riding on the way.

One of the most interesting features of the development of stanza form, however, as mentioned above in chapter 1, is the way in which the "weak" line of late medieval minstrelsy is transformed into a source of stylistic strength in the popular ballad by functioning as the repeat line in incremental repetition. In this connection it is perhaps significant that whereas "weak" or "tag" lines occur in "The Barker" and are very frequent in the "Historie,"[41] they disappear completely from the ballad. In the few cases where parallel stanzas are preserved we can actually see the transforma-

41. The following stanzas contain examples of the weak line: "The Barker," 9, 23, 30, 40; "Historie," 7, 10, 25, 27, 30, 34, 42, 50, 53. The ballad retains one familiar tag in stanza 4: "under this trusty tree," although even here the meaning seems more specific than is usual (see "Historie," st. 7).

tion from weak line to incremental repetition, as in the following two examples:

"Historie," st. 30:	'What boot will you haue?' then said our king, 'tell me now in this tide;
The ballad, st. 18:	'What boot wilt thou ask?' then said our king, 'what boot dost thou ask on this ground?'
"Historie," st. 42:	'What boote wilt thou haue?' quoth the tanner, 'tell me in this stound;'
The ballad, st. 29:	'What boot will you ask?' quoth the tanner, 'What boot will you ask on this ground?'

Of course the increments in the above illustration are mere padding and do not add significantly to the meaning of the passage, but they nevertheless signalize the beginnings of a technique destined to be used with great skill in eighteenth-century ballads.

The textual history of "King Edward the Fourth and a Tanner of Tamworth" has provided us with a unique opportunity to observe the evolution of the popular ballad from its beginnings in late medieval minstrelsy to its emergence in ballad form in the seventeenth century. As a result we are now in possession of criteria which can be used to advantage in the next chapter, where it will frequently be necessary to attempt to distinguish between late instances of minstrel narrative and our earliest examples of the popular ballad.

4. The new minstrelsy

In the preceding chapter it was suggested that the "rymes of Robyn Hood" and other tales of the greenwood such as "Adam Bell" and "The King and the Barker" were metrical narratives more closely related to medieval romance than to balladry. We are now ready, in the present chapter, to consider that great creative period of the sixteenth and seventeenth centuries when the short metrical tale merged with the folksong tradition to produce for the first time on a large scale authentic ballads sung to rounded tunes. Although these ballads often resemble the earlier "rymes" in style and narrative structure, they show important new features, as we have observed in "King Edward the Fourth and a Tanner of Tamworth" (273), which are at least in part attributable to the influence of their melodic setting, and which are very important for the future of the popular ballads. In order to emphasize this positive achievement of the sixteenth and seventeenth centuries, I refer to the ballads of this period collectively as "the new minstrelsy."[1]

Many of the ballads to be considered in the present chapter are those on historical subjects which Child placed immediately following the Robin Hood section. It should be pointed out that these historical ballads seem to be arranged by Child approximately in the order of presumed date of composition rather than the date of appearance of earliest versions. Hence "Sir Hugh, or, the Jew's Daughter" (155) is first in the series because the story belongs to the thirteenth century, whereas the ballad itself first appears in Percy's *Reliques* (1765) more than five hundred years after the date of the entry in the Annals of Waverly (1255).[2] The events in "Gude Wallace" (157) are assigned to the year 1298, but the earliest known version of the ballad appears in a chapbook of about 1745. The plan of the present history of balladry, therefore, requires that "Sir Hugh," "Gude Wallace," and others in this category be considered later on in the appropriate section of this study dealing with ballads of the eighteenth century.

The ballads of the new minstrelsy can be divided into three groups

---

1. To put it another way, I use the title "the new minstrelsy" to avoid suggesting that these ballads are "the mere detritus of the romances." See Friedman, *The Ballad Revival*, p. 20.
2. *ESPB*, III, 235.

for convenience in the following discussion. First to be considered are those historical ballads (whatever may be the date of events celebrated in them) which have been preserved in manuscripts of the sixteenth century. Second are those found for the most part in seventeenth-century broadsides, garlands, or other printed collections. The third and final group, to which a separate chapter must be devoted, consists of those ballads that appear first in the Percy folio manuscript (ca. 1650). To some extent it is of course arbitrary to categorize the texts in this way. The Percy folio manuscript in particular has a great variety of pieces, ranging from metrical romance to ballad, and extending chronologically (speaking of date of composition) from perhaps the fourteenth to the seventeenth century. But as long as we remain alert to the possibility of such variety within a single collection, there should be no difficulty and the benefits should be considerable. For it is only by considering these texts in the approximate order of their appearance that we can hope to trace the evolution of ballad style.[3]

The first group of ballads to be considered as examples of the new minstrelsy are those preserved in manuscript copies of the sixteenth century. They are "The Battle of Otterburn" (161), "The Hunting of the Cheviot" (162), "Sir Andrew Barton" (167), "Flodden Field" (168), and "Captain Car, or, Edom o Gordon" (178). Before looking at these texts directly, however, it will be helpful to consider the state of the minstrel profession in the sixteenth century, and this can best be done, I think, by examining some of the manuscript evidence. It would not be feasible to analyze the contents of all the manuscripts containing versions of the five ballads mentioned above, nor are all of them equally valuable for this purpose.[4] But it will be well to consider at least one of these, namely, the Bodleian Library MS Ashmole 48, dated 1557–1565, which contains the earliest known version of "The Hunting of the Cheviot" (162), a ballad celebrating English and Scottish heroism at the battle of Otterburn in 1388.[5]

3. Certain ballads in sixteenth-century manuscripts are found also in the Percy folio MS: "The Hunting of the Cheviot" (162), "Sir Andrew Barton" (167), and "Captain Car, or, Edom o Gordon" (178). Ballads that occur first in the Percy MS will be considered in the next chapter.

4. The York MS of "Sir Andrew Barton" (ESPB, IV, 502 ff.) was originally part of a "ballad book," but this one ballad is the only piece that survives.

5. For a valuable review of the contents of this MS, including an estimate of its date, see Hyder E. Rollins, "Concerning Bodleian MS. Ashmole 48," MLN, XXXIV (1919), 340–351. The portion of this chapter dealing with MS Ashmole 48 originally took the form of a paper entitled "A Sixteenth Century Minstrel's Book," read before the California Folklore Society meeting at the University of California, Los Angeles, on April 9, 1965.

MS Ashmole 48

Thomas Wright edited the Ashmole manuscript for the Roxburghe Club (London, 1860), giving it the title *Songs and Ballads, with Other Short Poems, Chiefly of the Reign of Philip and Mary*. It is not clear exactly which of the items in his edition Wright would classify as "ballads," but in any case we know that of the seventy-six pieces in the manuscript, only one was included by Child in the ballad canon, namely, "The Hunting of the Cheviot" (162).

A little over half of the texts in MS Ashmole are attributed to specific authors, including Richard Sheale, Henry Spooner, Thomas Watertoune, Henry Lord Morley, Thomas Lord Vaux, John Wallys, Oliver Currant and John Fielding, William Elderton, John Manton, and William Case. As this list indicates, the customary anonymity of medieval collections is now largely a thing of the past. Of the men mentioned above, William Elderton will be familiar to students of the ballad as the author of a broadside which Child printed as an appendix to "King James and Brown" (180), and Richard Sheale will be remembered as the reputed author of "The Hunting of the Cheviot" (162).[6] In his preface Wright goes so far as to conclude that "this most curious collection of poems was made by Richard Sheale, and that the greater part of it is in his handwriting."[7] On the other hand, Child is uncompromising in his rejection of Sheale's authorship of "The Hunting of the Cheviot," and more recently H. E. Rollins has concluded that someone other than Sheale compiled the MS from printed broadsides.[8] In spite of the various views that have been expressed, no one has directly analyzed the contents of the MS for the purpose of deducing its nature or purpose. Is it a mere commonplace book, as Rollins thought, or could it be the repertoire of a minstrel like Richard Sheale? With this question in mind let us briefly consider the kinds of "songs and ballads" it contains.

The texts in the Ashmole manuscript are predominantly didactic, as can be seen in the following approximate groupings: thirty-three are concerned with moral and religious counsel, twenty are satirical, fifteen are amorous, and eight belong roughly in the narrative category. Many

6. Child, *ESPB*, III, 445–456, 303. Hyder E. Rollins, "William Elderton, Elizabethan Actor and Ballad-Writer," *SP*, XVII (1920), 199–245, esp. 225–227. A. B. Friedman, "A New Version of 'Musselburgh Field,'" *JAF*, LXVI (1953), 74–77, esp. 76–77.

7. Wright, *Songs and Ballads*, p. vii.
8. Child says (*ESPB*, III, 303): "This ballad was of course part of his (Sheale's) stock as minstrel; the supposition that he was the author is preposterous in the extreme." See also Rollins, "Concerning Bodleian MS. Ashmole 48," pp. 349–351.

of these are reminiscent of songs in the Sloane MS discussed above in chapter ii. Perhaps the main difference between the two collections is that whereas nearly all of the Sloane texts seem designed for singing, some of those in Ashmole are intended for reading or recitation.

There is a great variety of poetic forms represented in the Ashmole MS. More than two-thirds are in stanzas, of which the largest single type is what Friedman helpfully calls the "pseudo-ballade," having an eight-line stanza usually rhyming *ababbcbc*, with the last line (or two lines) often employed as a refrain.[9] Most of the remainder, about twenty in all, are written in long or short couplets. "The Hunting of the Cheviot" is in long couplets, though Child of course prints these in the more familiar ballad quatrain.

A comparison of the opening lines of texts in this MS with the examples from fifteenth-century minstrelsy considered in the preceding chapter reveals some interesting differences. No longer do we find the "Lythe and listin, gentilmen" formula of late metrical romance; instead the narrator or singer in many of the poems and songs shows an increasing literary consciousness and uses miscellaneous forms of direct address to the audience alternating with a *chanson d'aventure* type of introduction. Several of the pseudo-ballades having moral themes obviously indebted to *Piers the Plowman* and its sequence, for example, use a conventional dream vision opening: "As I lay of lat musynge in my bede" (xx), "Of late as I layde me to reste uppone my bede" (xxvi), and "As I lay slombrynge in manner of a trans" (xxvii). A few poems affect a disarming, intimate relationship with the listener, as in the opening line of an amorous and playful text, "My frynd, the lyf I lead at all . . . " (xiv), whereas others speak directly and rhetorically as in an antifeminist poem: "O cruell damys" and "o lovars all" (xxi).

Another type of opening formula is the familiar citation of an "auctoritee" in the medieval manner, familiar for example to readers of Chaucer. Thus we have "In historyes off olde to rede" (xvii), "In Bocas an Guydo I rede and fynde" (xlix), and "I rede howe that the marbell stone" (lix). At first glance this might seem far removed from the popular style we are accustomed to associate with balladry. Yet it is actually quite similar to such citations as we find in "The Battle of Otterburn" (161A35):

9. Friedman, *The Ballad Revival*, pp.   35–44.

4. The new minstrelsy   97

But nyne thowzand, ther was no moo,
   The cronykle wyll not layne:
Forty thowsande of Skottes and fowre
   That day fowght them agayne.

In this sense the "auctoritee" formula of the Ashmole poems is no different from what we find in contemporary ballads.

Although it might be argued that most of the formulas thus far cited are stock phrases that do not establish the Ashmole MS as a minstrel's book, there are a few which do seem to me to point in this direction. Surely these *chanson d'aventure* formulas are suggestive of the itinerant minstrel: "My jornay lat as I dyd take" (xxix), "This indars day, as I cane pas" (xxxvi, st. 2), "Wanderyng on my way, as I was wont for to wende" (xxxvii). Such opening lines, in fact, are precisely the same kind of thing as the first line of "Crow and Pie" (111), "Throughe a forest as I can ryde," which Child calls a "minstrel-ballad."[10] Furthermore the one Child ballad in our MS, "The Hunting of the Cheviot," shows an affinity with the minstrel tradition in its customary division of the narrative into "fyttes" (162A24):

That day, that day, that dredfull day!
   the first fit here I fynde;
And youe wyll here any mor a the hountynge
   a the Chyviat,
     yet ys ther mor behynde.

But even granted occasional formulas from minstrelsy in certain texts, one might still argue that the vast majority of selections in the Ashmole MS are art songs and poems having nothing whatsoever to do with the minstrel profession. Such indeed seems to be the argument implied by Rollins when he remarks that "A minstrel of Sheale's type could not possibly have sung more than two or three of the pieces contained in the MS."[11] In my opinion this conclusion is based on too narrow a conception of the minstrel's repertoire, and, if I am not mistaken, it seems to regard him exclusively as a singer. Moreover, there is other evidence of minstrelsy where one might least expect to find it, namely, in those pieces that seem to be poems unrelated to popular tradition. One of the texts belonging in the "amorous" category, for example, is a clever and courtly

10. *ESPB*, II, 478. Child seems to have included "Crow and Pie" mainly because it contains an early example of the name-

request, stanzas 13–14.
11. Rollins, "Concerning Bodleian MS. Ashmole 48," p. 350.

poem in praise of a lady, yet less than half-way through the author pauses in his extravagant description (xxiii):

> Thus of here fewtre ys disskripcion,
> But yete of hure I have note all donne;
> Of my darlynge this ys the furste fyte,
> And ye pleas ye shall hear more of hite.

Then there follow more than a hundred lines in praise of his "darlynge." A different kind of evidence of minstrelsy can be seen in the opening formula of the satirical pseudo-ballade by John Wallys on the fickleness of wives: "Good awdience, harken to me in this cace" (xxxviii).

The examples of the minstrel style cited above, be it noted, are exclusive of those pieces signed by the name of Richard Sheale in the MS. But these texts, as is generally admitted, certainly do belong in the minstrel repertoire: they are "The Hunting of the Cheviot" (viii); a moral poem in praise of good works (xviii); a rhymed narrative in which Sheale relates how he was robbed of a large sum of money (xlvi); a short metrical expression of thanks for dinner (xlviii); and an elegy on the death of Lady Margaret, Countess of Derby (lvi). All of these pieces (except xlviii) are in the long couplet form characteristic of "The Hunting of the Cheviot." Number xlvi in particular offers glimpses of the life and hard times of a minstrel in its opening lines: *200497*

> O God, what a world ys this now to se!
> Ther ys no man content with his degre.
> I can cum in no company, be nyght nor be day,
> But all men lacke mony, me thinkes I her them say;
> Whiche thinges for to hear makys myn ears weary,
> For withowt mony men cannot be myrry.
> For wher the have no mony in store,
> Ytes tyme for the mynstrell to gete owt ath dore.

Since he is going to tell about the robbery and make an appeal for funds, this opening of course is a clever device to undercut by anticipation the grumbling of his audience in response to the forthcoming appeal. Sheale then goes on to describe how the robbery adversely affected his ability as a minstrel:

> After my robbery my memory was so decayde,
> That I colde neathar syng nore talke, my wyttes wer so dismayde;
> My awdacitie was gone, and all my myrry tawke.

4. The new minstrelsy   99

Ther ys sum hear have sene me as myrry as a hawke;
But nowe I am so trublyde with phansis in my mynde,
That I cannote play the myrry knave accordyng to my kynde.

The above lines certainly suggest that a minstrel such as Sheale, who
was probably in the service of the Earl of Derby,[12] was expected to "talke"
as well as "syng" and "play the myrry knave." And in fact several of the
shorter pieces in the Ashmole MS provide precisely the kind of material
that would be useful to Sheale in his role as general entertainer, as can
be seen in the following example of gnomic wit (LXXI):

Theare be three things doe well agree,
The church, the court, and destinie;
For none will ought to other leave.
The church from live and dead doth reave;
The court takes both the righte and wronge;
And Death doth take the weake and stronge.

Three things are unsatiable, priests, monckes, and the sea.
Presbiteri, fratres, et mare, numquam satiantur, etc.
        Preists, women, and the sea.

The notes following the six-line poem evidently serve as a reminder of
variations on this theme. Numbers LXIX–LXXIII in the MS seem to be
examples of such bouquets of wit—what might be called the minstrel's
"patter."

In arguing against Wright's conjecture that the Ashmole MS was
Sheale's own work, Rollins exclaims: "Imagine him singing poems by
Lord Surrey and George Gascoigne!"[13] But there is no need, as we have
seen, to assume that the minstrel confined himself to singing. Even more
to the point, we should not jump to the conclusion that a poem was
never sung. As Rollins himself has shown, number LIX is the MS sung
"to the tune of lusty gallant" was suggested by the poem "That length of
time consumeth all thinges" in *Tottel's Miscellany* (1557),[14] and numerous other "poems" in the collection were clearly meant to be sung.
Even where no tune is indicated, it is reasonable to suppose, for example, that John Wallys' wedding piece "Our Jocky sal have our Jenny"
(XXXVI) was sung and perhaps even danced. Evidence collected by
Rollins from the Stationer's Register suggests also that numbers XVI,

12. Wright, *Songs and Ballads*, pp. iii, vii.
13. Rollins, "Concerning Bodleian MS. Ashmole 48," p. 350, referring to Nos. xxx and LXXV in the MS.
14. *Ibid.*, p. 346.

100

XXII, XXX, XXXII, and LVIII were sung, even though there is no evidence of this in the text. And it is difficult to avoid the conclusion that number LXIV, though it lacks the expected tune designation, is a narrative song. It tells the story of the judgment of Solomon in six-line stanzas which frequently have a refrain in the last two lines. I quote the two opening stanzas:

Wysdom woold I wyshe to have,
    As Salamon requyred,
When God appoynted hym to crave
    Whatsoever hys hart desyred.
Whereuppon, very well,
Salamon in Israell.

In every dowbt and jeoperdy
    When justyce cam to delynge,
Cowld serche and shyfte by subtylty
    Of every pak and pealynge.
Whereuppon, very well,
Salamon in Israell.

Of all the various kinds of poems and songs in the Ashmole MS, one of the most interesting and significant is numbered LXIII, which tells the story of Troilus and Criseyde in seventeen quatrain stanzas rhyming *abab*. The first three stanzas read as follows:

When Troylus dwelt in Troy towne,
    A man of nobell fame a,
He schorned all that loved the lyne
    That longd to merry game a.

He thowght his hart so overthwart,
    His wysdom was so suer a,
That nature could not frame by art
    A bewty hym to lure a.

Tyll at the last he cam to churche
    Where Cressyd sat and prayed a,
Whose lookes gave Troylus such a lurche,
    Hys hart was all dysmayde a.

The story is obviously drawn from Chaucer's poem, but it concentrates on the consummation of the love affair at Pandarus' house. At the moment when Troilus kneels beside Criseyde's bed the author inserts a stanza which is in part based on the poem, but which epitomizes Criseyde's half-pretended womanly reserve in an amusingly popular way:

> But, humbly kneelynge on hys knee,
>   With syghes dyd love unfolde a;
> Her nyght gowne then delyvered she
>   To keepe hym from the colde a.[15]

In short, this is a characteristic narrative re-creation of the sort often undertaken by minstrels in the sixteenth century. That the "ballad" of Troilus and Criseyde was sung should be evident from the stanza form (reminiscent of "John Dory"), but the matter is put beyond dispute by the heading which appears in the MS just before the first stanza: "To the tune of Fayne woold I fynd sum pretty thynge to geeve unto my lady."

I conclude, with Thomas Wright, that the Ashmole MS is a minstrel's book, probably compiled by Richard Sheale, and that its contents tell us much about the professional minstrel's repertoire. I stress the adjective *professional* here, using it to refer to those who were retained by aristocrats like the Earl of Derby, because the term "minstrel" can be applied to various kinds of musicians and other entertainers in the sixteenth century, thus making it difficult to authenticate any conclusion about the minstrel profession in general. Yet I think what we have deduced from our MS can also be applied to some extent to the humbler grade of itinerant gleeman described, for example, by George Puttenham in *The Arte of English Poesie*, who warns against glutting the ear with too much rhyme.

> vnlesse it be in small & popular Musickes song by these *Cantabanqui* vpon benches and barrels heads where they haue none other audience then boys or countrey fellowes that passe by them in the streete, or else by blind harpers or such like tauerne minstrels that giue a fit of mirth for a groat, & their matters being for the most part stories of old time, as the tale of Sir *Topas*, the reportes of *Beuis* of *Southampton*, *Guy* of *Warwicke*, *Adam Bell* and *Clymme* of the *Clough* & such other old Romances or historicall rimes, made purposely for recreation of the common people at Christmasse diners & brideales, and in tauernes & alehouses and such other places of base resort, also they be vsed in Carols and

---

15. See *Troilus and Criseyde*, III, 883 ff. It is possible that the nightgown comes from a misunderstanding or variant reading of Chaucer's "quysshen" (cushion) (III, 964).

102

rounds and such light or lasciuious Poemes, which are commonly more commodiously vttered by these buffons or vices in playes then by any other person.[16]

What we see here is in fact that conjunction of late metrical romances and the folksong tradition described above in chapter i. It is in the kind of repertoire described by Puttenham that the popular ballad had its origin.

Our inferences about Richard Sheale and the minstrel profession are supported by a vivid account of a minstrel in action provided by Robert Laneham in his letter to a friend, in which he describes the entertainments at Kenilworth Castle on the occasion of Queen Elizabeth's visit there in July, 1575.[17] Laneham writes often with a reckless exuberance, and hence his descriptions must be read with caution. Yet his portrait of the minstrel seems authentic, and it is therefore of particular interest for our purposes to observe that he seems to regard him as an archaic figure. This can be seen in the opening lines of his account:

> Mary, syr, I must tell yoo: Az all endeuoour waz too mooue mirth & pastime (az I tolld ye): eeuen so a ridiculoous deuise of an auncient minstrell & hiz song waz prepared to haue been prof-fered, if meet time & place had been foound for it. Ons in a woorshipfull company, whear, full appointed, he recoounted his matter in sort az it shoould haue been vttred, I chaunsed too be: what I noted, heer thus I tel yoo: A parson very meet seemed he for the purpoze, of a xlv. yeers olld, apparelled partly as he woold himself.[18]

Laneham goes on to describe him in great detail, no doubt with tongue in cheek, down to the "pair of pumps on hiz feet, with a cross cut at the toze for cornz: not nu indeede, yet cleanly blakt with soot, & shining az a shoring horn." Nor does he neglect "hiz harp in good grace dependaunt before him" and his "wreast," or hammer, for tuning the harp, "tyed to a green lace, and hanging by."

The minstrel launches into a comic monologue, which Laneham re-cords at length, praising the local produce of Islington and expounding like a herald the "auncient armez" of the "woorshipfull village of Isling-ton." Laneham tells us that he spoke this comic routine "az one that waz

16. George Puttenham, *The Arte of English Poesie*, ed. Willcock and Walker (Cambridge, 1936), pp. 83–84.

17. Furnivall, *Robert Laneham's Letter*, pp. 36–42.
18. *Ibid.*, p. 36.

wel schoold, & coold hiz lesson parfit withoout booke too aunswear at full, if question wear askt hym." At the conclusion, when the minstrel "seemde to gape after a praiz for hiz *Beauparlar*," a member of the company (no doubt by prearrangement) arose and delivered a mock refutation of the minstrel's interpretation of the "arms" of Islington. At this the minstrel affected an injured air, until the company with fair words restored his good spirits. Whereupon he made ready to sing a song:

> Appeerez then a fresh, in hiz ful formalitee, with a louely loock: after three loly cooursiez, cleered his vois with a hem and a reach, and spat oout withal, wiped hiz lips with the hollo of his hand, for fyling hiz napkin, tempered a string or too with his wreast: and after a littl warbling on hiz harp for a prelude, came foorth with a sollem song, warraunted for story oout of King Arthurz acts, the first booke and 26. chapter, whearof I gate a copy, and that iz this.

Laneham then quotes six rime royal stanzas constituting the first fytte, or *primus passus* of the minstrel's song, of which the first two stanzas can serve as an illustration:

> So it befell vpon a Penticost day,
> When King Arthur at Camelot kept coourt rial,
> With hiz cumly Queen, dame Gaynoour the gay,
> And many bolld Barrons sitting in hall,
> Ladies apparaild in purpl and pall,
> When herauds in hukes herried full by,
> "Largess! Largess! cheualiers treshardy!"

> A doouty Dwarf too the vppermost deas
> Right peartly gan prik, and, kneeling on knee,
> With steeuen full stoout amids all the preas,
> Said "hail, syr king! God thee saue and see!
> King Ryens of Northgalez greeteth well thee,
> And bids that thy beard anon thou him send,
> Or els from thy iawz he will it of rend."

What we have deduced about Richard Sheale from the Ashmole MS accords well with the description of Laneham's minstrel. Both of them are general entertainers, they talk as well as sing, and apparently they have a comic routine or patter prepared for use on appropriate occasions. We know little of the Islington minstrel's repertoire, of course, but his

Arthurian song is precisely the counterpart of Sheale's "Troilus and Criseyde," and both confirm Puttenham's "old Romances or historicall rimes."

It might perhaps be argued that while sixteenth-century minstrelsy is an interesting object of study, it is nevertheless irrelevant to the history of the popular ballad, which should not be confused with late metrical romances set to music. But it would be a serious mistake, I think, to suppose that while professional minstrels were singing of Arthur and Troilus in the halls of Kenilworth and perhaps the taverns of Tamworth, some nameless folksinger in the hinterlands was singing "Fair Annie" (62) and "The Lass of Roch Royal" (76). This is unlikely in the extreme. If the latter two existed at all as ballads in the sixteenth century (and on this point evidence is lacking), it is probable that they would be in the minstrel repertoire and would be similar in form to the sung romances we have seen to be characteristic of this period, "Fair Annie" perhaps in the form of an epitomized "Patient Griselda," and "The Lass of Roch Royal" as an accused queen romance.[19]

The role of minstrels in the formative period of balladry has been largely ignored and requires further study. But it is already evident, I believe, that in matters of both style and repertoire they contributed much to the development of the popular ballad. Furthermore, as we shall have occasion to observe later, the so-called mixture of romances and ballads in the Percy folio MS ceases to be a problem when the genetic relationship of minstrelsy and balladry is correctly understood.

Before turning to the five ballads preserved in sixteenth-century MSS, there is one final point about the Ashmole MS that requires consideration. What is the significance of the presence of "The Hunting of the Cheviot" in this MS? Was it simply copied from an early printed broadside, as Rollins believes, or was it transcribed from the recitation or the memory of a minstrel like Richard Sheale? If the ballad was actually a part of Sheale's repertoire, did he merely acquire it from someone, or did he himself compose it? It is impossible, of course, to provide certain answers to these questions at present. But there are a few features of the Ashmole MS that may point the way toward a future solution.

As we have seen, more than two-thirds of the selections in the Ashmole MS are in stanza form, mostly of the pseudo-ballade type. In light of this

19. Friedman, *The Ballad Revival*, p. 47, quotes Charles Cotton: "We in the country do not scorn, Our walls with ballads to adorn Of Patient Grizell, and the Lord of Lorne." For indications of the Accused Queen story type in "The Lass of Roch Royal" (76), see chapter vii, below.

it is perhaps significant that of the five pieces written in long couplets (VIII, XVIII, XIX, XLVI, LVI), including "The Hunting of the Cheviot," four are signed with the name of Richard Sheale.[20] His one composition in a different form is the brief thanks for a dinner written in short couplets (XLVIII). From this one might conclude that Sheale's favorite vehicle was the long couplet, and that he was therefore the author of the ballad to which he signed his name. But I prefer to read the MS evidence as suggesting that the ballad was inherited by the minstrel, perhaps from a predecessor, and that by signing his name he was merely claiming it as his own property. My conclusion from the metrical evidence would be that Sheale used "The Hunting of the Cheviot" as a model for his own compositions, which are clearly inferior to it. The nearest he comes to showing talent as a minstrel composer is in the elegy on the death of the Countess of Derby (LVI), where an occasional example of professional technique can be found:

> Nowe ys this noble lady dede,
> whome all the world dyd love;
> She never hurte man, woman, nor childe,
> I dar well say and prove.
>
> She never hurte non off her men,
> in worde nor yete in dede,
> But was glade allway for them to speake
> such tym as the had nede.[21]

There is one other way to view the significance of the inclusion of "The Hunting of the Cheviot" in the Ashmole MS, and that is its relevance to the family interest and pride of Sheale's patrons and employers. However much Sheale may have cherished the ballad for its own sake, he must also have been conscious of the appeal it would undoubtedly have to the aristocratic northern families that he visited in his professional wanderings. In this connection it is interesting to look at the brief poem of thirty-five lines (number LI) in short couplets which, although it is unsigned, is very similar in form and content to the unsigned poem of

---

20. The one item in long couplets not signed by Richard Sheale is No. XIX, which is identified by Rollins ("Concerning Bodleian MS. Ashmole 48," p. 343) with the anonymous "Description of an ungodly worlde" in *Tottel's Miscellany.*

21. Wright, *Songs and Ballads,* p. 180, where the text is printed in couplets following the MS. I use the quatrain form in conformity with Child's practice because it makes more visible the techniques already discussed. In the passage quoted, uninspired as it is, we can observe the use of incremental repetition ("She never hurte," etc.) and the weak line ("in worde nor yete in dede").

thanks for a dinner (number XLVIII) which we know is Sheale's from internal evidence. Whether or not number LI is actually by Sheale, its presence in the Ashmole MS along with "The Hunting of the Cheviot" is no accident, as can be seen, I believe, in the opening lines:

Within in the northe contre
Many noblemen ther be;
Ye shall well understande,
Ther ys the yerle off Westmorland,
The quynes lyffeteanant,
A noble man and a valyante.
Then ther ys the yerle off Combarlande,
And the yerle off Northomberlande,
And ser Harry Perse his brothar,
As good a man as anothar;
He ys and hardy knyght,
And hath ofte put the Skottes to flyght.

The poem then goes on to mention "my lord Ivars" and "my lord Dacars," coupled with a warning to the Scots that "northarne men wyll fight." Others mentioned are "ser Harry Leye" and "ser Rychard Lye," and the piece concludes as follows:

All thes well I do knowe;
Yet ys ther many moo,
The which I cannot nam,
Thar be men of mickle fame.
God save the yerle off Shrowesbyrry!

If this is not the work of Sheale, still it must surely be the composition of some wandering minstrel intent upon pleasing aristocratic families, primarily those of the northern counties.

This review of the contents of the Ashmole MS has told us a good deal about the minstrel profession, its repertoire, and its role in the creation of ballads out of the materials of late metrical romances. In apprehending the larger function of the minstrels as a general entertainer we have learned to expect a great variety both of substance and of poetic forms in his performances, and we are also more conscious of his talking as well as his singing function. Likewise we have found the theory of ballad origins sketched in earlier chapters supported by the conjunction in the minstrel repertoire of "old Romances" from the medieval period and "Carols and rounds" of the folksong tradition. Letting the above in-

ferences and conclusions serve as a background, therefore, we may now
turn to the analysis of particular examples of "the new minstrelsy."

Ballads in sixteenth-century manuscripts

Of the five ballads preserved in manuscripts of the sixteenth century,
the first two are "The Battle of Otterburn" (161) and "The Hunting of
the Cheviot" (162).[22] We need to consider these two ballads together, not
only because they appear to describe the same event, but also because
the relationship between the two has never been satisfactorily explained.
That Child regarded "The Battle of Otterburn" as the earlier ballad is
evident from the lower number he assigned to it, though he admits that
the grammatical forms of "Cheviot" are older than those found in "Otterburn." After pointing out the resemblances between the two texts, Child
gives his opinion as follows:

> The differences in the story of the two ballads, though not
> trivial, are still not so material as to forbid us to hold that both may
> be founded upon the same occurrence, the Hunting of the Cheviot
> being of course the later version, and following in part its own
> tradition, though repeating some portions of the older ballad.[23]

Although Child never really explains why he thought that "The Hunting of the Cheviot" was "of course" the later version, his view seems never
to have been seriously questioned.[24]

It is generally agreed that from a literary point of view "The Hunting
of the Cheviot" is the better ballad and that its language is more archaic
than that of "Otterburn." To this I would merely add that "Cheviot" is
in fact the earlier and "Otterburn" the later ballad. Believing firmly that
"it would be against the nature of things that there should not have been
a ballad as early as 1400,"[25] Child undoubtedly attributed the greater his-

22. The analysis of these two ballads
which follows first appeared as "'The
Hunting of the Cheviot' and 'The Battle
of Otterburn'" in *WF*, XXV (1966),
165–171.

23. *ESPB*, III, 304.

24. The most thorough study since
Child is Karl Nessler, *Geschichte der Bal-
lade "Chevy Chase"* (Berlin, 1911). D. S.
Bland has published two notes, "'Mac-
beth' and 'The Battle of Otterburn,'"
N&Q, CXCIV (1949), 335 f., and "The
Evolution of 'Chevy Chase' and 'The

Battle of Otterburn,'" *N&Q*, CXCVI
(1951), 160 f. Friedman says, in *The
Viking Book of Folk Ballads*, p. 276, that
"Otterburn" is the older ballad and "tells
the story with reasonable accuracy;" but
he adds that "Cheviot," in addition to
being later, "follows local legend and
partisan traditions rather than the chronicles and warps history badly in order to
glorify the English, especially the House
of Percy."

25. *ESPB*, III, 293.

torical accuracy of "Otterburn" to an oral tradition going back almost to the time of the battle (1388). But while this is indeed a possibility, it seems more reasonable, in view of the linguistic evidence, to suppose that "Otterburn" owes its historical accuracy to written records ("The cronycle wyll not layne," 161A35), and that the more unhistorical ballad is in this case the earlier.

Not only is "The Hunting of the Cheviot" earlier, but it is also, I believe, the source of "The Battle of Otterburn." That the two are related is put beyond dispute by the presence in both of stanzas that "correspond," as Child phrases it.[26] The dramatic encounter in battle between Percy and Douglas is thus described in the earlier ballad (162A31):

At last the Duglas and the Perse met,
　　lyk to captayns of myght and of mayne;
The swapte togethar tylle the both swat,
　　with swordes that wear of fyn myllan.

And in "Otterburn" we read (161A50):

The Perssy and the Dowglas mette,
　　That ether of other was fayne;
They swapped together whyll that the swette,
　　Wyth swordes of fyne collayne.

Later on the ferocity of the battle is generally described in an excellent stanza common to both ballads. I quote first from "Cheviot" (162A47):

Ther was neuer a freake wone foot wolde fle,
　　but still in stour dyd stand,
Heawyng on yche othar, whylle the myghte dre,
　　with many a balfull brande.

The same stanza occurs in "Otterburn" (161A58):

Ther was no freke that ther wolde flye,
　　But styffely in stowre can stond,
Ychone hewyng on other whyll they myght drye,
　　Wyth many a bayllefull bronde.

Perhaps it could be argued that stanzas like the one just quoted, and like the later stanza about the widows coming to the battlefield (162A57

26. *ESPB*, III, 304.

and 161A67), are floating commonplaces, part of the minstrel's stock in trade, and hence are not evidence of a direct connection between the two ballads. The same cannot be said, however, of the following stanza which occurs in the passage naming those slain in battle (162A56):

> Ser Charls a Murre in that place,
>   that neuer a foot wolde fle;
> Ser Hewe Maxwelle, a lorde he was,
>   with the Doglas dyd he dey.

Here is the same stanza in "Otterburn" (161A61):

> Syr Charlles Morrey in that place,
>   That never a fote wold flee;
> Syr Hewe Maxwell, a lorde he was,
>   Wyth the Dowglas dyd he dye.

Evidence like this supports the conclusion that the two ballads are definitely related.

The nature of this relationship will be apparent when we realize that "Cheviot" tends to favor Douglas and is probably of Scottish origin, while "Otterburn" extolls Percy and hence is definitely English in its outlook. This can best be seen in a direct comparison of the two ballads, keeping in mind that we are looking, not for evidence of historical knowledge, but for indications of the slant given to events and the qualities assigned to the two major personalities, Percy and Douglas.

In "Cheviot" Percy is represented as the aggressor, expressing his determination to hunt in the Cheviot hills in such a way as to make it an obvious and swaggering challenge to Douglas (162A1–9). In "Otterburn," on the other hand, it is Douglas who issues the challenge by burning Northumberland, to which Percy gallantly responds in a scene which displays Percy's dignity and courtliness to advantage (161A11–17). Here our sympathies are obviously meant to be with Percy, not Douglas.

Immediately before the battle, each ballad uses the device of describing the approaching forces from the enemy's viewpoint.[27] Thus in "Cheviot" a squire of Northumberland sees Douglas and his men, whose columns are impressively described (162A10–12). The squire then tells his English comrades (I assume) to prepare for battle, in words full of awe and wonder at the spectacle of the approaching Scots (162A13):

27. Adopting the enemy's viewpoint is a device used effectively in the apocryphal Gospel of Nicodemus, where the devil's point of view is used to describe the approach of Christ in the "Harrowing of Hell."

'Leave of the brytlyng of the dear,' he sayd,
   'and to your boys lock ye tayk good hede;
For neuer sithe ye wear on your mothars borne
   had ye neuer so mickle nede.'

In "Otterburn," on the other hand, it is a Scottish knight who spies the approach of the "noble Percy" and informs Douglas of the fact with a similar tone of excitement and wonder in his words (161A21–22):

He prycked to hys pavyleon-dore,
   As faste as he myght ronne;
'Awaken, Dowglas,' cryed the knyght,
   'For hys love that syttes in trone.

'Awaken, Dowglas,' cryed the knyght,
   'For thow maste waken wyth wynne;
Yender haue I spyed the prowde Perssye,
   And seven stondardes wyth hym.'

Douglas answers proudly and summons his men (161A23–28), but we are clearly meant to feel a patriotic excitement at the approach of the English forces and Percy's seven standards.

The exchange of words between Percy and Douglas before the battle provides the opportunity for another interesting and illuminating comparison of the two ballads. In "Cheviot" the heroic initiative is clearly with Douglas. It is Douglas who challenges Percy's right to hunt, Douglas who speaks the noble line "one of us shall die" (162A17), and Douglas who proposes a single combat between the two leaders. Percy of course comes in on cue, saying that he will hunt in spite of the Scots and agreeing eagerly to the single combat, but the poet obviously wants us to admire Douglas more than Percy. The exchange is in fact so one-sided that the author, whose partiality never overrides his poetic judgment, restores the balance between the English and Scottish viewpoints with the dramatic refusal of the English squire, Wytharyngton, to stand idle while his captain fights (162A22–23).

When we look at the corresponding passage in "Otterburn" the picture we have of the two leaders is quite different. Here it is Percy, not Douglas, who does the challenging, Percy who speaks the noble line "one of us shall die" (161A30), and Percy who makes the heroic gesture (corresponding to Douglas' single combat offer) of dismounting and driving away his horse so as to make flight impossible. A more complete reversal of roles here is scarcely imaginable. Douglas of course answers Percy "with great words," but there is little else he can do. Percy clearly has the initiative. To this the author of "Otterburn" adds another episode designed to dramatize Percy's heroism, namely, the incident in which Percy refuses to wait for reinforcements promised by his father (161A36–44). This underscores his courage and daring in view of the twenty-to-one odds boasted by Douglas in rather unheroic fashion (161A31).

The actual fight between Percy and Douglas as described in the two ballads shows the same contrasting viewpoints we have observed in earlier episodes. In "Cheviot" Douglas seems on the point of overpowering his opponent, but he is so greatly impressed by Percy's fighting ability that he offers him an earl's wages if he will yield (162A33–34):

'Yelde the, Perse,' sayde the Doglas,
    'and i feth I shalle the brynge
Wher thowe shalte haue a yerls wagis
    of Jamy our Skottish kynge.

'Thoue shalte haue thy ransom fre,
    I hight the hear this thinge;
For the manfullyste man yet art thowe
    that euer I conqueryd in filde fighttynge.'

Percy of course refuses to yield, but at this crucial juncture an arrow pierces Douglas, so that we never learn what might have been the outcome of the contest between the two men. Douglas dies heroically urging his men to fight on, and Percy magnanimously pays tribute to him in the justly famous lines (162A38–39):

The Perse leanyde on his brande,
    and sawe the Duglas de;
He tooke the dede mane by the hande,
    and sayd, Wo ys me for the!

'To haue savyde thy lyffe, I wolde haue partyde with
    my landes for years thre,
For a better man, of hart nare of hande,
    was nat in all the north contre.'

Admirable as is the balance of heroic virtues here achieved, it is important to note that the poet's partiality toward Douglas is never absent for a moment. In spite of his magnanimity, Percy serves mainly as a means of extolling Douglas. Furthermore, when he has performed this function Percy is then slain, contrary to historical fact, by the Scottish

112

knight Sir Hugh Montgomery (162A40–46). Whatever the chronicles might say, Douglas' death had to be avenged.

On the other hand, in "Otterburn" the situation is quite different. To be sure, Douglas does indeed call on Percy to yield, but without the generosity and admiration for his opponent expressed in the earlier ballad. Instead he merely says that he deduces from the quality of his armor that Percy is a man of high rank. As before Percy refuses to yield, and the two men resume fighting. But this time it is made clear that Percy himself overcomes and slays Douglas (161A55–56):

> The Perssy was a man of strength,
> I tell yow in thys stounde;
> He smote the Dowglas at the swordes length
> That he felle to the growynde.
>
> The sworde was scharpe, and sore can byte,
> I tell yow in sertayne;
> To the harte he cowde hym smyte,
> Thus was the Dowglas slayne.

Thus ends the account of the fight in "Otterburn." Gone are the heroic last words of Douglas, the magnanimous tribute of Percy, and the unhistorical slaying of Percy by Montgomery. There follows merely a general description of the battle and thereafter a roll call of the slain on both sides. The capture of Percy by the Scots, which is historically accurate, is merely alluded to in the concluding stanzas, since to dwell on this would detract from the glorification of Percy and the English which is the main purpose of the "Otterburn" ballad.

In view of the contrast between the two ballads it is difficult to understand how modern scholars can speak of "Cheviot" as distorting history to glorify the English, when precisely the opposite seems to be true. But there is one passage near the end of the ballad which perhaps explains this interpretation. I refer to stanzas describing the reaction of the kings of Scotland and England to news of the battle (162A59–64). King James mourns the death of Douglas, commenting that there is not another captain like him in all Scotland. The English King, Henry IV, on the other hand, pointedly remarks that although he has a hundred captains as good as Percy, he will nevertheless avenge his death, which he then proceeds to do in the battle of Homildon. But as Child remarks, this battle was fought fourteen years after Otterburn; moreover, "the occasion of Homildon was really another incursion on the part of the Scots, and the same Percy was in command of the English who in the ballad meets his death

4. The new minstrelsy   113

at Otterburn."[28] Surely, as Child implies, this is a distortion of history designed to favor the English, or more specifically, I might add, to favor those northern families praised in the Ashmole MS who "hath ofte put the Skottes to flyght" (LI). But it is important to remember that the death of Percy depicted in the ballad takes liberties with history for precisely the opposite reason.[29]

The contradictory nature of the historical evidence in "The Hunting of the Cheviot" leads me to conclude that the stanzas giving the reaction of the English and Scottish kings are a late interpolation. None of the "borrowed" stanzas in the later "Otterburn" ballad come from this passage, in spite of the fact that its English bias would have fitted quite harmoniously into "Otterburn." Hence I conclude that "Cheviot" in its original form probably ended with stanza 58, or at least that stanzas 59–65 were not a part of the original.

Possible confirmation of the theory that stanzas 59–65 were a later addition to "Cheviot" can be seen in the metrical form of the ballad. More than half of the sixty-eight stanzas of the text as printed by Child have the rhyme scheme *abab*, and I suspect that this was its original metrical form, before the eroding effect of oral transmission perhaps obliterated some of the rhymes, especially in lines one and three.[30] Furthermore, in light of the relationship between the two ballads proposed above, it is interesting to note that of the seventy stanzas of "Otterburn" only twelve rhyme *abab*, and four of these are the stanzas "borrowed" from "Cheviot." This is precisely what we might expect if, as I have suggested, "Otterburn" is the later ballad, and hence that much farther removed from the original metrical form.[31] But it is especially interesting in the present connection to observe that the *abab* stanzas in "Cheviot" cease abruptly after stanza 58, the point at which the supposed interpolated passage begins. While this in itself might not be conclusive, it nevertheless fits in well with the inferences we have already drawn about the Scottish viewpoint of the original ballad.

The next historical ballad in the group presently under discussion is

28. *ESPB*, III, 304.

29. It is possible, I suppose, to argue that mere ignorance is responsible for unhistorical details in the ballad, but I believe the characterization of Percy and Douglas argues that history is being manipulated.

30. Stanzas of 162A with *abab* rhymes are 4–8, 11, 14–16, 19, 21, 23, 26–31, 35, 38, 40, 42–44, 46–47, 49–50, 52–58. Those without this rhyme scheme tend to be metrically irregular. To the above list should perhaps be added stanza 12, assuming lines one and three rhyme guid/Twyde ("guid" for "good"). See stanza 26, where Scottish "wouche" rhymes with "yenoughe." Stanzas of 161A with *abab* rhymes (excluding stanzas common to both) are 1, 7, 15, 33, 48, 54–56.

31. "Otterburn" also introduces an occasional stanza with a line having internal rhyme: 161A2, 40–41, 48.

"Sir Andrew Barton" (167), based on events of the year 1511, and preserved in a sixteenth-century MS in York Minster Library.[32] Child did not know of this version while preparing the materials for the third volume of his edition, and therefore it appears among the additions and corrections in the fourth volume. Child's A version is taken from the Percy folio MS and his B version from a seventeenth-century broadside. In its broadside form "Sir Andrew Barton" was sung to the tune of "Come follow my love." It is an excellent ballad and a worthy example of the new minstrelsy of the sixteenth century.

The story told in both the York and Percy MSS is essentially the same. In response to an appeal from London merchants, King Henry sends Lord Charles Howard to capture Andrew Barton, a Scottish pirate whose robbing of merchant ships in the Channel was making trade with the Continent unprofitable. Howard chooses a good gunner, Peter Simond, and a noble bowman, William Horsley, to head up his crew. While sailing in search of Barton, Howard is fortunate enough to encounter Harry Hunt, a former prisoner of the pirate, who agrees to lead the English to the enemy. The battle is fierce, but it is finally decided by the skill of the English archer, Horsley, who prevents the Scots from releasing the "beams" on their mainmast. The value of these "beams," though not made clear in the ballad, was evidently such that if they could have been dropped they would have virtually assured victory for the Scottish crew. The archer Horsley, however, shoots down the men who attempt to climb the mast, including finally Barton himself. An English victory is thus assured, but the famous words of the dying Sir Andrew are the climax of the ballad (167York68–69):

'Feight, maisters!' said Sir Andrewe Barton,
    'I'se a lettle hurt, but I ame not slayne;
I'le lie me downe and bleede a whill,
    I'le risse and feight with yowe agayne.

'Yet feare noe English dogges,' said Sir Andrewe Barton,
    'Nore fore there force stand ye in noe awe;
Stick stifeley to Sir Andrewe Barton,
    Feight till ye heare my whisstill blowe.'

The York MS text of "Sir Andrew Barton" is some fifty years earlier than the Percy folio version, and in light of this fact it is interesting to note a few differences between the two which suggest that the York

32. *ESPB*, IV, 502–507.

version preserves certain original features of reportorial style. In the description of the meeting at sea between Lord Howard and Harry Hunt, for example, which is lacking in the Percy text, we can see the kind of vivid, pictorial representation usually associated with an eyewitness account (167York19):

> When he sawe the lion of England out blaisse,
> The streemers and the roose about his eye,
> Full soonne he let his toppe-saill fall;
> That was a tooken of curtissie.

There is a tendency for such sharpness of detail to be worn down or eliminated both in the Percy folio and broadside versions of the ballad. This can be seen especially where an original stanza is preserved in later versions but is changed in the course of transmission. An example is the stanza describing the first glimpse that Lord Howard has of Sir Andrew Barton in the light of dawn (167York38):

> A larborde, wher Sir Andrewe laye,
> They saide he tould his gold in the light;
> 'Nowe, by my faith,' saide my lord Charlles Howwarde,
> 'I se yonne Scootte, a worthe wight!'

Here is the same stanza in the Percy MS (167A36):

> And the hache-bord where Sir Andrew lay
> Is hached with gold deerlye dight:
> 'Now by my ffaith,' sais Charles, my lord Haward,
> 'Then yonder Scott is a worthye wight!'

And again in the Douce broadside (167B32):

> The lord then swore a mighty oath,
> 'Now by the heavens that be of might,
> By faith, believe me, and by troth,
> I think he is a worthy knight.'

Thus in the York version we are given a vivid picture of Sir Andrew, counting his ill-gotten gold boldly in the light of day.[33] Like every warrior at the moment of battle, Howard cries out in admiration mingled with eager anticipation of the fight, a cry which is at least as old as the words of Cyrus in Xenophon's *Anabasis*: "I see the man!"[34] The contrast in the

33. Notice the use of "they said" in 167York38, 57. These could be construed as references to eyewitness informants.
34. *Anabasis*, Book I, chap. viii.

116

Percy text is considerable, where Howard's admiration is presumably stimulated by the sight of Barton's expensive hatch boards which are decorated with gold. In this we see not only a blurring of the original sharp picture, but also we can detect a drift toward the commonplace descriptions of later balladry, in which all ships are destined to have masts of beaten gold. Finally, of course, the broadside removes all traces of the original scene, and Lord Howard is reduced to swearing a mighty oath and expressing a motiveless admiration for Barton.

Like some of the rhymes of Robin Hood considered in the preceding chapter, "Sir Andrew Barton" contains interesting examples of narrative symmetry. In the York MS this symmetry is partly verbal and partly a matter of narrative structure. In the Percy version, interestingly enough, the symmetry is made explicitly verbal throughout, as can be seen in a comparison of the two texts in the passage describing Howard's selection of his chief gunner and archer (167York11–16). By far the most important symmetrical passage, however, is the one describing the shooting down of the two men on Barton's ship who climbed the mast for the purpose of releasing the beams against the English (167York55–60):

'Come hether quick, thou Girdon goode,
    And come thou hether at my call,
Fore heare I may noe longer staye;
    Goe up and let my beames down fall.'

Then he swarmd up the maine-mast-tree,
    With mickell might and all his maine;
Then Horsley with a broode-headed arrowe
    Stroke then Girdon throughe the weame.

And he fell backe to the hatches againe,
    And in that wound full sore did bleed;
The blood that ran soe fast from hime,
    They said it was the Girdon's deed.

'Come hether, thow James Hamelton,
    Thowe my sister's sonne, I have noe moe;
I'le give the five hundreth pound,' he saide,
    'Ife thowe wilt toe the topsaille goe.'

Then he swarmd up the mayn-mast-tree,
    With mickell might and all his mayne;
Then Horsley with a broode-arrowe-head
    Tooke him in at the buttuke of the utuer beame.

4. The new minstrelsy   117

Yet frome the tre he would not parte,
 But up in haist he did prossed;
Then Horsley with anotheir arrowe
 Strooke then Hamelton throughe the heade.

With this compare the same passage in the Percy folio MS (167A52–57):

'Come hither to me, thou Gourden good,
 And be thou readye att my call,
And I will giue thee three hundred pound
 If thou wilt lett my beames downe ffal.'

With that hee swarued the maine-mast tree,
 Soe did he itt with might and maine;
Horseley, with a bearing arrow,
 Stroke the Gourden through the braine.

And he ffell into the haches againe,
 And sore of this wound that he did bleed;
Then word went throug Sir Andrews men,
 That the Gourden hee was dead.

'Come hither to me, Iames Hambliton,
 Thou art my sisters sonne, I haue no more;
I will giue thee six hundred pound
 If thou will lett my beames downe ffall.'

With that hee swarued the maine-mast tree,
 Soe did hee itt with might and maine;
Horseley, with another broad arrow,
 Strake the yeaman through the braine.

That hee ffell downe to the haches againe;
 Sore of his wound that hee did bleed;
Couetousness getts no gaine,
 Itt is verry true, as the Welchman sayd.

The tendency of the Percy folio version to regularize the symmetry and make it verbally explicit is evident in the above passage. Whereas in York only Hamilton is offered money, in Percy both receive offers, Gordon three and Hamilton six hundred pounds. Especially noteworthy is the difference in over-all correspondence of the two attempts to climb the mast. In the York MS Gordon is shot once and falls to the hatches, while Hamilton is first wounded, keeps climbing, and is finally shot through the

118

head by a second arrow. There is, in other words, an increment, a progression in the action pointing toward the climactic effort of Sir Andrew himself. But in the Percy text this increment is erased; Hamilton is shot once and falls to the hatches as had Gordon before him.[35] This means of course a gain in explicit symmetry but a loss in subtlety of dramatic development of the narrative.

It is tempting to suppose that the drift from implicit to explicit narrative symmetry noted above is due to the influence of a rounded melody on the minstrel narrative. But in this case it is difficult to be sure because we cannot certainly know whether the text was sung, either in the York or the Percy version. In fact the reportorial style of the York text suggests a metrical, non-musical composition of the early Robin Hood type, and at least one transitional line, reminiscent of "Robin Hood and Guy of Gisborne" (118, st. 21), suggests that "Sir Andrew Barton" was originally designed to be recited rather than sung (167York37): "Now will we leave talkinge of Harry Hunt . . . ." But these stylistic features are not so evident in the Percy text, and therefore since we know the ballad was sung in the seventeenth century it may be that Percy's folio MS preserves the sung ballad in a relatively early form, before it was "retrenched and marred" by those who prepared it for "the vulgar press."[36]

The ballad of "Flodden Field" (168) first appears in Thomas Deloney's *Jack of Newbery* (1597) and is a rather slight, boastful song celebrating the famous English victory over the Scots in 1513. More important for our present purpose is the piece included by Child under number 168 as an appendix, likewise entitled "Flodden Field," which is printed from the Percy folio MS but which is also found in a Harleian MS of the second half of the sixteenth century.[37] Unlike the ballad, this "poem," as Child calls it, has as its setting the King's headquarters at Tournay in France, where news of the victory at Flodden is brought to him. The center of narrative interest is a report of the English victory sent to the King by the Earl of Surrey falsely attributing cowardice to the men of Lancashire and Cheshire, followers of the Earl of Derby (Stanley), who himself is with the King in France. Here is Child's description of the piece:[38]

> This poem, a history in the ballad style, was composed to vindicate the behavior of Lancashire and Cheshire at Flodden, and to glorify the Stanleys; in the accomplishment of which objects it

35. The last two lines of 167A57 break the parallelism and constitute an irrelevant proverbial filler. In the broadside version the symmetry noted above is almost totally lacking (167B11-14, 43–47).
36. *ESPB*, III, 334.
37. *ESPB*, III, 353 ff.
38. *ESPB*, III, 354.

becomes incumbent upon the minstrel to expose the malice of the Earl of Surrey, to whom he imputes the "wrong writing" which caused such heart-burning.

It is interesting that Child calls the "Flodden Field" poem a "history in the ballad style" composed by a minstrel. For although this piece certainly lacks the heroic character of "The Hunting of the Cheviot" and the drama of "Sir Andrew Barton," in narrative style it closely resembles the technique of the new minstrelsy which we are considering. The opening stanza, for example, contains a formula typical of the short metrical narrative:

Now let vss talke of the Mount of Flodden,
Fforsooth such is our chance,
And let vs tell what tydings the Earle of Surrey
Sent to our king into France.

But perhaps the most distinctive feature of this text is its use of a long series of "farewell" stanzas in which the Earl of Derby, thinking his men have been slain or captured at Flodden, bids them a sad farewell. I quote only the last three stanzas in the series (168App45–47):

'Ffarwell Christopher Savage, the wighte!
Well I know that thou are slaine;
For whiles thy life wold last to fight,
Thou wold neuer besids the plaine.

'Ffarwell Dutton, and Sir Dane!
You haue beene euer trew to mee;
Ffarwell the Baron of Kinderton!
Beside the feild thou wold not flee.

'Ffarwell Ffitton of Gawsworth!
Either thou art taken or slaine;
Doubtelesse while thy life wold last,
Thou wold neuer beside the plaine.'

After this the Earl of Shrewsbury tries to comfort him, but without success. Derby goes on to bid farewell to his house and lands (168App51–54):

'Farwell Lancaster, that litle towne!
Farwell now for euer and aye!
Many pore men may pray for my soule
When they lye weeping in the lane.

120

'Ffarwell Latham, that bright bower!
    Nine towers thou beares on hye,
And other nine thou beares on the outer walls;
    Within thee may be lodged kings three.

'Ffarwell Knowsley, that litle tower
    Vnderneth the holtes soe hore!
Euer when I thinke on that bright bower,
    Wite me not though my hart be sore.

'Ffarwell Tocstaffe, that trustye parke,
    And the fayre riuer that runes there beside,
There I was wont to chase the hinde and hart!
    Now therin will I neuer abide.'

The first of the "farewell" passages quoted above, in which the Earl
mourns the supposed loss of his man, seems modeled in part on the epic
motif of the list of men killed in battle, as we find it for example in "The
Hunting of the Cheviot" (162A56):

Ser Charls a Murre in that place,
    that neuer a foot wolde fle;
Ser Hewe Maxwelle, a lorde he was,
    with the Doglas dyd he dey.

But the second series of farewells shows that the author was also adapting
a motif found elsewhere in the minstrel repertoire. A good illustration of
this can be seen in one of the songs (number LXVIII) of the Ashmole MS
discussed earlier in this chapter. I quote two stanzas from the middle
of this song:

Fare well haukynge and huntynge bothe;
    Fare well game, solace, and gle;
Fare well, my ladye, fayre of face,
    I wene I wyll the never more se.
      I so sycke, make my bed, I will dye nowe.

Fare well, castell, towne, and tower;
    Fare well, gardene that ys gren;
Fare well, hale, chambere, and bowre
    For I may not byde wheare I have bene.
      I so sycke, make my bed, I wyll dye nowe.[39]

39. Wright, *Songs and Ballads*, pp. 205 f.

While this kind of device can perhaps be dismissed as a conventional "exile" formula, it is an important feature of the new minstrelsy that is revived later in "Johnie Armstrong" (169C29–31), "Jock O the Side" (187A20–24), and other ballads, notably "Lord Maxwell's Last Goodnight" (195), which consists almost entirely of stanzas using the "farewell" motif.

A final example of the minstrel technique in the "Flodden Field" poem is the narrative symmetry used in describing the King's response, first to the false message sent by the Earl of Surrey (168App8–9):

> Then bespake our comlye king,
> Said, Who did fight and who did flee?
> And who bore him best of the Mount of Fflodden?
> And who was false, and who was true to me?

> 'Lancashire and Cheshire,' sayd the messenger,
> 'Cleane they be fled and gone;
> There was nere a man that longd to the Erle of Darby
> That durst looke his enemyes vpon.'

Later on, when the real messenger arrives from the queen, the truth is brought out in the following parallel stanzas (168App89–90):

> Then bespake our comlye prince,
> Saiinge, Who did fight and who did flee?
> And who bare them best of the Mount of Fflodden?
> And who is false, and who is true to mee?

> 'Lancashire and Cheshire,' said the messenger,
> 'They haue done the deed with their hand;
> Had not the Erle of Derbye beene to thee true,
> In great aduenture had beene all England.'

The first of these two stanzas is of course repeated almost verbatim, while the variations introduced in the second underscore the contrast between the two reports. This technique is quite similar to that discussed above in "Sir Andrew Barton" (167), where parallelism is used to dramatize the turning point of the sea battle, the attempt of Sir Andrew to release the beams.

Compared to "The Hunting of the Cheviot," "Sir Andrew Barton," and other such ballads, "Flodden Field" is indeed an inferior composition, and its subject, the injustice done to the Earl of Derby, is certainly lacking in universality. Yet although Child was perhaps right to relegate it to an appendix, he was also well advised to include it in his edition, for this "poem" is a valuable illustration of the influence of the new minstrelsy on the development of ballad style.

The last of the ballads presently under consideration is "Captain Car, or, Edom o Gordon" (178), preserved in a late sixteenth-century British Museum MS, Cotton Vespasian A.xxv, a very interesting volume containing more than fifty songs and "ballets."[40] Of particular significance for the evolution of balladry which we are tracing is the fact that "Captain Car" is the first ballad in the minstrel tradition (leaving aside "Robyn and Gandeleyn") having a refrain (178A1):

It befell at Martynmas,
    When wether waxed colde,
Captaine Care said to his men,
    We must go take a holde.

Syck, sike, and to-towe sike,
    And sike and like to die;
The sikest nighte that euer I abode,
    God lord haue mercy on me!

To some extent the poetic diction of the earlier minstrel narratives is preserved, as in "Busk and bowne, my mery men all" (178A25), but there are some interesting stylistic innovations, and the stanzas tend to conform more closely to the prevailing metrical pattern of the ballad quatrain (4-3-4-3). Stanzas rhyming *abab*, fairly common in the minstrel tradition, are totally lacking here, and the ballad is less than half as long (thirty stanzas) as any other in this group.

The narrative structure of "Captain Car" lacks that symmetry which we have often observed in minstrel ballads, but instead it seems to rely on the unilateral repetition, with variations, of certain key stanzas like the following (178A14, 18, 29):

'I desire of Captaine Care,
    And all his bloddye band,
That he would saue my eldest sonne,
    The eare of all my lande.'

    . . . .

---

40. See R. Boddeker, "Englische Lieder und Balladen aus dem 16. Jahrhundert," *Jahrbuch fur romanische und englische Sprache und Literatur*, N.F. II (1875), 81–105, 210–239, 347–367; concluded in III (1876), 92–129.

'Fye vpon the, Captayne Care,
   And all thy bloddy bande!
For thou haste slayne my eldest sonne,
   The ayre of all my land.'

. . . .

'Fye vpon the, Captaine Care,
   And all thy blody bande!
Thou haste slayne my lady gay,
   More wurth then all thy lande.'

Instead of a parallelism of incident, as in "Sir Andrew Barton," what we have here is a parallelism of choric comment, the first two stanzas spoken by the wife, and the last by Lord Hamilton when he learns of the murder.

In light of the characteristics described above, we may conclude that the ballad of "Captain Car" illustrates an important new development taking place in the late sixteenth century. Whereas in the earlier period metrical tales for the most part were being adapted or set to music, "Captain Car" *was composed to fit a known melody.* Herein lies the explanation, I believe, for the rather striking innovations of style, meter, and narrative structure which we have observed in this remarkable ballad.

Ballads in seventeenth-century broadsides and garlands

Before turning to the Percy folio manuscript we need to consider briefly ten ballads that first appear in broadsides and garlands of the seventeenth century. Three of these are based on historical events of the sixteenth century and were probably composed near the time of the events described: "The Death of Queen Jane" (170), "Musselburgh Field" (172), and "King James and Brown" (180). Three others were composed in the seventeenth century by known authors and are conscious ballad imitations: "The Famous Flower of Serving-Men" (106) and "Robin Hood's Golden Prize" (147) are both by Lawrence Price, while "A True Tale of Robin Hood" (154) is by Martin Parker.[41] Three more in this group are outlaw ballads: "Johnie Armstrong" (169), "Hughie Grame" (191), and "Geordie" (209). Finally there is "Queen Eleanor's Confession" (156) which, for want of a better term, we may call an "antiquarian" ballad of the late seventeenth century. These ten ballads provide an interesting contrast to the sixteenth-century group just considered. With the possible

---

41. Rollins, "William Elderton," p. 227,   n. 69; *ESPB*, III, 227.

exception of "Johnie Armstrong," not one of them could be called a minstrel ballad.

To some extent the shortage of new minstrel ballads in the seventeenth century can be explained by the fact that the minstrel profession suffered a sharp decline during this period. But it is equally important, I believe, to realize that as the creative role of the minstrel deteriorated, a new kind of balladmaker was taking his place, namely, the composer of "ballets" for the popular press. Perhaps the best-known of these literary composers is William Elderton, author of the broadside which Child prints as an appendix to "King James and Brown" (180), a ballad which is itself preserved in the Percy folio MS. Although Child says nothing about the relationship of Elderton's broadside to the ballad, a more recent critic, Rollins, has a definite opinion: "But Elderton's authorship is indisputable: the ballad is his work, toned and improved by tradition."[42]

A recently discovered text of "Musselburgh Field" (172) has led Friedman, who is somewhat more cautious than Rollins, to suggest that this ballad, also preserved in the Percy folio MS, may have stemmed originally from an early broadside version:[43]

> "Musselburgh Field" and "Bishoppe and Browne" stand at nearly the same distance from their respective originals; it would be hard to say which has been traditionalized or adapted the less; yet Child canonized "Musselburgh Field" and summarily rejected the other. One begins to wonder whether Child would not also have rejected "Musselburgh Field" if he had known of the drollery text, writing the ballad off as an "imperfect and incorrect copy" of an ancient broadside.

The third in this group of ballads of broadside origin is "The Death of Queen Jane" (170). This is the most interesting case because, unlike the other two, this ballad has remained in tradition to the present day and is very popular in America.[44] The actual death of Jane Seymour occurred on October 12, 1537, while the first evidence of a song on the subject appears in the Stationers' Registers for the year 1560. "The Doleful Death of Queen Jane" is printed in the *Crowne Garland of Golden Roses* (1612) and numerous times thereafter.[45] But Child did not include

42. Rollins, "William Elderton," p. 227.
43. Friedman, "A New Version of 'Musselburgh Field,'" p. 77.
44. Tristram P. Coffin, *The British Tra-*ditional Ballad in North America* (rev. ed.; Philadelphia, 1963), pp. 113–114.
45. *ESPB*, III, 372.

this in his edition, even as an appendix, probably because its style is so clearly untraditional, as can be seen in the opening stanza:

When as King Henry rul'd this Land,
He had a Queen I understand;
Lord Seymour's Daughter fair and bright,
King Henry's Comfort and Delight:
Yet Death, by his remorsless Pow'r,
Did blast the Bloom of this sweet Flow'r:
 O mourn, mourn, mourn, fair Ladies;
 Jane your Queen, the Flower of England's dead.[46]

No one, I think, would contend that this piece is of popular origin. Yet it would be a mistake to suppose that there is no connection between it and the popular ballad which emerges in the eighteenth century. Indeed Nygard has recently argued plausibly that this "wretched poem," first printed in the *Crowne Garland*, is the source of the popular ballad, and he compares it with two modern, highly lyrical versions, one from Scotland and one from North Carolina, and concludes: "The broadside is clearly the beginning; the ballad has moved in the direction of the impersonal, the nameless, the unlocalized, and the archetypal."[47]

Although the minstrel tradition is undoubtedly the primary source of momentum in the evolution of balladry, the opinions expressed by Rollins, Friedman, and Nygard confirm my own belief that certain of the popular ballads have a literary origin. Of course not many of these show the striking lyrical development of "The Death of Queen Jane":

Well, Jane was in labor for Six days or more;
 She grieved and she grieved and she grieved her heart sore.
She sent for Prince Henry, Prince Henry came o'er;
 Said, "The red rose of England shall flourish no more."[48]

But it is helpful to see in examples of this kind the power of oral tradition in transforming an artificial literary production into an authentic ballad, and it augurs well for the future of ballad scholarship that this is being recognized as a possibility in such pieces as "King James and Brown," "Musselburgh Field," and "The Death of Queen Jane." To quote

46. I quote from *A Collection of Old Ballads* (anon.) (London, 1723), II, 118.
47. Nygard, "Ballads and the Middle Ages," p. 95.
48. *Ibid.* See Archive of American Folk Song, Library of Congress recording LC 1487, AAFS 104B, for a version of the "Death of Queen Jane" sung with banjo by Bascom Lamar Lunsford at Swannanoa, N. C., 1946.

Nygard once more: "If a tendency in the accretional understanding of the ballads is discernible, it is that ballads are mistakenly identified in an inclusive way with the late Middle Ages. That process by which they came into being, the shaping effect of oral transmission, was lasting and markedly present in later times."[49]

The ballads by Lawrence Price and Martin Parker are also of literary origin, but they differ from the group just considered in that they appear to be conscious imitations or adaptations. The opening stanza of Price's "The Famous Flower of Serving-Men" (106) is immediately recognizable as non-popular:

You beautious ladies, great and small,
I write unto you one and all,
Whereby that you may understand
What I have suffered in this land.

Yet certain conventions of seventeenth-century balladry are imitated (106, sts. 24–25):

'What news, what news, old man?' quod he;
'What news hast thou to tell to me?'
'Brave news,' the old man he did say;
'Sweet William is a lady gay.'

'If this be true thou tellest me
I'le make thee a lord of high degree;
But if thy words do prove a lye,
Thou shalt be hanged up presently.'

The second of these two stanzas is of course quite similar to the famous stanzas in "Little Musgrave and Lady Barnard" (81A11–12) which are parodied in Fletcher's *Monsieur Thomas*.[50] Price's other ballad, "Robin Hood's Golden Prize" (147), is an amusing imitation of the minstrelsy of the greenwood, but in style and meter it is far removed from the "rymes" of Robin Hood discussed in chapter iii above. The same can be said of Martin Parker's "True Tale of Robin Hood" (154). In view of the great popularity of the Robin Hood ballads, it is not at all surprising to find such imitations beginning to appear. More were destined to be composed in this and the following century.

The popularity of Robin Hood should not be allowed to obscure a

49. Nygard, "Ballads and the Middle Ages," p. 95.

50. *ESPB*, II, 243.

small but interesting group of outlaw ballads of a different type. While Robin Hood continued to harbor the illusion that the King of England was his vindicator and would recognize the rightness of his cause, a new kind of outlaw, less romantic than his predecessor, was learning that this was not the case, and that any outlaw who surrendered to the king could expect to incur the full penalty of the law. The struggle against the corrupt power of the Church had been won; England and Scotland were moving uneasily but surely toward political union; the noble and patriotic outlaw was becoming an archaic figure. This is the fate of "Johnie Armstrong" (169).

As was mentioned briefly in chapter i above, "Johnie Armstrong" is especially interesting for structural developments that are evident in a comparison of the *Wit Restord* version of 1658 (169A) and the *Ever Green* version obtained from oral tradition and printed by Ramsay in 1724 (169C). The earlier text has the diction and meter, slightly regularized, of a minstrel ballad and indeed seems to draw on "Sir Andrew Barton" (167), as in Johnie's exhortation to his men (169A16):

> Saying, Fight on, my merry men all,
>   And see that none of you be taine;
> For I will stand by and bleed but awhile,
>   And then will I come and fight againe.

The description of the outlaws' fight for freedom (169A14),

> Then, God wott, faire Eddenburrough rose,
>   And so besett poore Ionne rounde,
> That fowerscore and tenn of Ionnes best men
>   Lay gasping all upon the ground.

perhaps owes something to "The Hunting of the Cheviot" (162B29),

> They closed full fast on euerye side,
>   noe slacknes there was found,
> But many a gallant gentleman
>   lay gasping on the ground.

but this may be a commonplace description of battle, since it does not occur in the earliest version of "Cheviot" (162A28).

Although there are enough verbal correspondences between the early and late versions of "Johnie Armstrong" to attest a genetic relationship, the *Ever Green* text is dramatically different from its ancestor, both in form and content. The echoes of earlier minstrelsy are gone, the description of the outlaws' fight for freedom is in fact eliminated completely, and, most important, nearly the entire ballad (twenty-four out of thirty-three stanzas) is occupied with the speeches of Johnie and the king. Most of these speeches consist of offers of gifts expressed in patterned stanzas followed by a stanza expressing the king's refusal, repeated without verbal variation after each offer (169C17–18):

'Grant me my lyfe, my liege, my king,
    And a brave gift I'll gie to thee;
All betwene heir and Newcastle town
    Sall pay thair yeirly rent to thee.'

'Away, away, thou traytor, strang!
    Out of my sicht thou mayst sune be!
I grantit nevir a traytors lyfe,
    And now I'll not begin with thee.'

If the assumption of a genetic relationship between versions is correct, this is a remarkable instance of a ballad being sung into symmetry.

The latter part of the *Ever Green* text of "Johnie Armstrong" devotes several stanzas to the expression of Johnie's disillusionment, to an exchange of taunts between Johnie and the king, and, finally, to Johnie's leave-taking as expressed in the "farewell" formula (169C31):

'Farweil, my bonny Gilnock-Hall,
    Whair on Esk-syde thou standest stout!
Gif I had lived but seven yeirs mair,
    I wald haif gilt thee round about.'

Interestingly enough, this last feature of "Johnie Armstrong" influences the development of the "criminals' goodnights," a later type of ballad,[51] of which the "George Stoole" broadside (209App) is a representative seventeenth-century example. The ballad of "Geordie" (209) illustrates the eighteenth-century tendency to provide a happy ending. That "Johnie Armstrong" was perhaps considered the archetype of the condemned outlaw, a pathetic figure, can be seen in the concluding stanza of one other seventeenth-century outlaw ballad, "Hughie Grame" (191A23):

'Here, Johnny Armstrong, take thou my sword,
    That is made of the mettle so fine,
And when thou comst to the border-side,
    Remember the death of Sir Hugh of the Grime.'

51. Grouped together in Friedman, *The*   232.
Viking Book of Folk Ballads, pp. 218–

Among the ballads examined in the present chapter, two have been especially useful for illustrating stages in the evolution of the new minstrelsy. "Captain Car" (178), with its refrain stanza and its choric repetitions, marks the point at which minstrel ballads were probably first composed to fit a known melody. "Johnie Armstrong," in the *Ever Green* version, offers an interesting example of the shaping effect of oral tradition in its thoroughgoing verbal parallelism. As ballads were increasingly sung to rounded tunes in the seventeenth century, however, it is only reasonable to anticipate the development of new ballads modeled directly on the diction, meter, and verbal parallelism of those older ballads that had been, like "Johnie Armstrong," sung into symmetry. Such a ballad, I believe, is "Queen Eleanor's Confession" (156), which appears first in a broadside of about 1685. In this somewhat antiquarian ballad a confessional scene is used, allowing Queen Eleanor to confess her sins unwittingly to King Henry and the Earl Marshall, both disguised as friars (156A10–13):

'The first vile thing that ere I did
    I will to you unfold;
Earl Martial had my maidenhead,
    Underneath this cloath of gold.'

'That is a vile sin,' then said the king,
    'God may forgive it thee!'
'Amen! Amen!' quoth Earl Martial,
    With a heavy heart then spoke he.

'The next vile thing that ere I did
    To you I'll not deny;
I made a box of poyson strong,
    To poyson King Henry.'

'That is a vile sin,' then said the King,
    'God may forgive it thee!'
'Amen! Amen!' quoth Earl Martial,
    'And I wish it so may be.'

It might perhaps be maintained that this is merely a late version of a metrical tale showing the same shaping effect of oral transmission that we have observed in "Johnie Armstrong." On the other hand, in "Queen Eleanor" the whole narrative idea is built around the confessional scene, and the verbal parallelism seems to me intrinsic rather than develop-

130

mental. I conclude that "Queen Eleanor's Confession" is an early example of a narrative song composed in imitation of the symmetrical structure that orally transmitted ballads were beginning to achieve. Hence it anticipates, as we shall see, important features of eighteenth-century ballad composition. But to pursue these developments now would be to get ahead of the story, for we have yet to consider the most important of all seventeenth-century ballad collections: the Percy folio MS.

5. The Percy folio manuscript

The most important single document relative to the history of balladry is undoubtedly the large folio-size manuscript found by the clergyman Thomas Percy in the mid-eighteenth century. Inside the cover of this MS Percy wrote the following note giving the circumstances of his discovery:

> This very curious Old Manuscript in its present mutilated state, but unbound and sadly torn &c., I rescued from destruction, and begged at the hands of my worthy friend Humphrey Pitt Esq., then living at Shiffnal in Shropshire, afterwards of Priorslee, near that town; who died very lately at Bath (viz. in Summer 1769). I saw it lying dirty on the floor under a Bureau in yᵉ Parlour: being used by the Maids to light the fire.[1]

Although this discovery probably gave Percy the idea of publishing a collection of ballads, his *Reliques of Ancient English Poetry* (1765) included a mere fraction of the contents of the folio MS. There is evidence that he planned separate publication of the romances, a most important group of texts not adequately represented in the *Reliques*,[2] but this project did not materialize. Hence the great wealth of the folio MS was not known to scholars until it was published by Hales and Furnivall in 1867–1868.

Nearly two hundred texts, including fragments, are contained in the more than five hundred pages of the MS. There are some seventeen romances, twenty-four metrical "histories," forty-five Child ballads, and more than a hundred miscellaneous songs, including lyrics and satirical pieces. The MS seems to have been compiled about 1650 from various sources, primarily written but also perhaps from oral tradition. There is some evidence, mainly toward the end of the volume, that the compiler may have used printed sources, notably Thomas Deloney's *Strange Histories* and *The Garland of Good Will*.

To some extent Percy's MS can be called a commonplace book like

---

1. J. W. Hales and F. J. Furnivall (eds.), *Bishop Percy's Folio Manuscript* (3 vols.; London, 1867–1868), I, lxiv.

2. Falconer, (ed.) *Percy-Hailes Correspondence*, pp. 54 f.

the *Shirburn Ballads.*[3] Even more to the point, it resembles the minstrel book of Richard Sheale (Ashmole 48), discussed in the preceding chapter, in its miscellaneous collection of moral, satirical, amorous, and narrative songs. It is unique among the MSS we have considered, however, in the large number of romances and popular ballads that it contains. To argue that this is a minstrel's book like Sheale's would be a mistake. Yet it seems reasonable to suppose that minstrelsy provided the rationale for this collection. In the middle of the seventeenth century, at precisely that time when minstrelsy was dying, someone gathered the surviving materials of this tradition into a collection obviously greater than a single minstrel's repertoire, but patterned after one nevertheless. Far from reflecting an indiscriminate antiquarianism, the late medieval romances in this volume reveal the compiler's awareness that these were the very foundation of the minstrel's art. The large number of ballads is also significant: by the mid-seventeenth century this type of narrative song had become one of the most popular genres in the minstrel's repertoire. The Percy folio MS both illuminates the early history of ballad style and marks the end of the period of minstrel influence on the evolution of balladry.

Romances

Of the several types of romances preserved in the folio MS, one of the most characteristic is a group of sixteenth-century abridgments of famous medieval romances. "Sir Lancelot of Dulake" (MS, p. 36) is an epitome in ballad stanza of the Tarquin episode in Sir Thomas Malory's *Morte Darthur*, no doubt taken from the original published in Deloney's *Garland of Good Will*. "Kinge Arthurs Death" (MS, p. 178), also in ballad stanza, summarizes the most famous events of Malory's last book, allowing Arthur himself to be the narrator in Part I, with a separate, third-person narrative of the last battle in Part II. One of the most popular non-Arthurian romances of the Middle Ages, *Guy of Warwick*, is represented by no less than three pieces: "Guye and Amarant" (MS, p. 232), "Guy and Phillis" (p. 254), and "Guy and Colebrande" (p. 349). The first of these is written (by Samuel Rowlands) in a six-line stanza rhyming *ababcc*, and the second, a fragment, is in the ballad stanza; but the third is an authentic metrical romance in the Thopas stanza (*aabccb*), composed probably in the fifteenth century. With the exception of the last-

3. Friedman, *The Ballad Revival*, p. 30.

named, all of these romances fit into the category of minstrelsy discussed in the preceding chapter: we are reminded of Richard Sheale's metrical epitome of "Troilus and Criseyde" and the Arthurian song of Robert Laneham's minstrel at Kenilworth in 1575.

Two other late abridgments of medieval romances, in rhyming couplets, are "The Emperour and the Childe" (MS, p. 314), which is a brief summary of *Valentine and Orsin*, and "The Squier" (MS, p. 444), perhaps that abridgment of *The Squire of Low Degree* licensed to John Kyng in 1560.[4] In any case, both of these texts belong almost certainly to the sixteenth century. Although not in ballad form, they are both of ballad length, written in what would be the equivalent of about forty-five ballad stanzas.

Of the five romances mentioned above "The Squier" best illustrates the influence of this genre on balladry. The young man of low station who obtains the hand of a lord's or king's daughter is of course a motif very popular in the ballads, notably "Tom Potts" (Child 109), which is in the folio MS (p. 409). Similarly "The Lord of Lorn" (Child 271), also in the folio MS (p. 73), has a hero who disguises himself as a servant and in this capacity wins the love of a king's daughter.[5] More important for the history of ballad style is the fact that "The Squier" contains a wealth of those characteristics found in the later ballads, as can be seen, for example, in the frequent use of incremental repetition (ll. 9–14):

> Such a service he cold him gett,
> he serued the Kings daughter in her seate;
> such a service he was put in,
> he serued the Kings daughter with bread & wine;
> he serued this Lady att table and Chesse
> till hee had woone her loue to his.

When the king learns of the affair he locks up the squire and delivers to his daughter a disfigured corpse, letting her believe that this is her slain lover. She embalms the body and keeps it by her bed, mourning for her lost love, as she thinks, though she tries to conceal the cause of her grief from her father. When the king asks her why she mourns, she replies (ll. 117–126):

4. Hales and Furnivall, *Bishop Percy's Folio Manuscript*, III, 263.
5. "The Lord of Lorn" (271) is based on the late medieval romance *Roswall and Lillian*, as mentioned in chapter ii; it is also discussed farther on in the present chapter. Later ballads with a similar theme are "Richie Story" (232) and "The Kitchie-Boy" (252).

"Father," shee sais, "as I doe see,
itt is ffor no man in Christentye.
Father," shee sayes, "as I doe thriue,
itt is ffor noe man this day aliue;
ffor yesterday I lost my kniffe;
much rather had I haue lost my liffe!"
"My daughter," he sayes, "if itt be but a blade,
I can gett another as good made."
"Father," shee sais, "there is neuer a smith but one
that can smith you such a one."

This same figure used as an evasion of the truth occurs in "Leesome Brand" (Child 15), and in even more elaborate form in "Sheath and Knife" (Child 16).

That "The Squier" stands midway between romance and ballad is perhaps best illustrated in the heroine's vow of chastity. In *The Squire of Low Degree*[6] the king tries to cheer up his daughter by promising her all sorts of wealth and entertainment in a long and extravagant rhetorical passage (ll. 739–852), to which the girl replies simply (ll. 853–854):

"Gramercy, father, so mote I the,
For all these thinges lyketh not me."

Later, the king overhears his daughter's vow (ll. 939 ff.):

"And, squyer, for the love of the,
Fy on this worldes vanyte!
Farewell golde, pure and fyne;
Farewell velvet, and satyne . . . .
Nowe wyll I take the mantell and the rynge,
And become an ancresse in my lyvynge:
And yet I am a mayden for thee,
And for all the men in Chrystente . . . ."

When she completes her vow, the king, now satisfied that his daughter will remain steadfast in her love, informs her that the squire is still alive and the happy conclusion follows.

Several interesting new developments occur in the shorter sixteenth-century version. In the first place the long passage containing the king's extravagant promises has been broken up into a series of exchanges between father and daughter (ll. 127–148):

6. Joseph Ritson (ed.), *Ancient Engléish Metrical Romanceës* (London, 1802), III, 145–192.

"Daughter," hee sais, "to-morrow I will a hunting ffare,
& thou shalt ryde vppon thy chaire,
& thou shalt stand in such a place
& see 30 harts come all in a chase."
"Father," shee sayes, "godamercy,
but all this will not comfort me."
"Daughter," he sais, "thou shalt sitt att thy meate,
& see the ffishes in the ffloud leape."
"Father," shee sais, "godamercy,
but all this will not comfort mee."
"Thy sheetes they shall be of they Lawne,
thy blankets of the ffine ffustyan."
"Father," shee sais, &c.
"& to thy bed I will thee bring,
many torchers faire burninge."
"Father," shee sais, &c.
"If thou cannott sleepe, nor rest take,
thou shalt haue Minstrells with thee to wake."
"Father," shee sais, &c.

This ballad-like use of dialogue we have already had occasion to observe in the *Ever Green* version of "Johnie Armstrong" (169C), even including the use of "&c" to indicate the repetition of stanzas. There is no certain evidence that "The Squier" was sung; but the form of the text itself strongly suggests that it was.

In "The Squier" the girl's vow is of course much briefer than that given in the romance (ll. 109–112):

"Squier," shee sais, "now ffor thy sake
I will neuer weare no clothing but blacke.
Squier," shee sais, "Ile neuer looke att other thing,
nor neuer weare mantle nor ringe."

Note that the anchoress' vow has been misunderstood, so that the mantle and ring are now rejected as part of a general vow of austerities, such as we find, for example, in the ballad of "Clerk Saunders" (69A20–22):

'O Sanders, I'le do for your sake
    What other ladys would na thoule;
When seven years is come and gone,
    There's near a shoe go on my sole.

136

'O Sanders, I'le do for your sake
    What other ladies would think mare;
When seven years is come an gone,
    Ther's nere a comb go in my hair.

'O Sanders, I'le do for your sake
    What other ladies would think lack;
When seven years is come an gone,
    I'le wear nought but dowy black.'

This ballad will be considered in detail in the next chapter, but it is interesting to note in passing that, like the heroine of "The Squier," May Margret in "Clerk Saunders" refuses her father's efforts to comfort her (69A24–26). One cannot read the late metrical romances of the folio MS without being impressed by the accuracy of Hodgart's speculation:

> There may have been an intermediate stage, in the re-shaping of courtly romances into a popular form, which the ballad makers (in this case, probably minstrels) would then popularize still further. The Percy Folio MS. has several romances of this kind, already half-way to becoming ballads . . . .[7]

This "intermediate stage" is dramatically evident in "The Squier," both in its incremental style and its adaptation of romance commonplaces and motifs.

A second group of romances in the folio MS consists of those which are copies, in whole or in part, of authentic medieval romances known from other sources. These are "Sir Lambewell" (MS, p. 60), "Merline" (p. 145), "Sir Triamore" (p. 210), "Sir Eglamore" (p. 295), "Libius Disconius" (p. 317), and "Sir Degree" (p. 371). All of these are metrical romances in the Thopas stanza except "Merline" and "Sir Degree," which are in couplets; in all of them the art of the late medieval minstrel is evident. Although these romances are not so closely related to balladry as the first group discussed above, they are nevertheless important antecedents of the ballad tradition. "Sir Eglamore," as Bronson has shown,[8] is the ultimate ancestor of the modern forms of "Sir Lionel" (Child 18).

"Sir Triamore," though it does not survive in ballad form, contains

---

7. Hodgart, *The Ballads*, p. 77. As an example of the intermediate stage Hodgart mentions "The Grene Knight" (folio MS, p. 203), but he does not develop his idea any further.
8. Bronson, *The Traditional Tunes of the Child Ballads*, I, 265 f.

features that are influential in later balladry. When Triamore, for example, cuts off Burlong's legs at the knee (ll. 1492–1494),

> Burlong on his stumpes stood
> as a man that was nye wood,
>   & fought wonderous hard.

one is reminded of the similar berserk heroism of Witherington in the ballad of "Chevy Chase" (162B50).[9]

A more striking anticipation of a ballad motif in "Sir Triamore" occurs near the beginning of the romance, when the exiled Queen Margaret, expectant mother of Triamore, is attacked by the evil steward Marrock and his men. The Queen's guardian, Sir Roger, bravely opposes the attackers, enabling the Queen to hide from them, but he is finally overpowered and killed. When the men are gone, the sorrowful Queen returns to the scene only to find the knight Sir Roger slain, with his faithful greyhound lying at his feet (ll. 361–372):

> "Alas," shee said, "that I was borne!
> my trew knight that I haue lorne,
>   they haue him there slaine!"
> full pitteouslye shee mad her moane,
> & said, "now must I goe alone!"
>   the grey-hound shee wold haue had full faine;
> the hound still by his Master did lye,
> he licked his wounds, & did whine & crye.
>   this to see the Queene had paine,
> & said, "Sir Roger, this hast thou for me!
> alas that it shold euer bee!"
>   her hayre shee tare in twayne.

The Queen then prepares to leave (ll. 379–390):

> Right on the ground there as he lay dead,
> shee kist him or shee from him yead.
>   god wott her hart was sore!
> what for sorrow & dread,
> fast away shee can her speeded,
>   shee wist not wither nor where.

9. Child lists other examples of this in   *ESPB*, III, 306.

138

The good grayhound for waile & woe
from the Knight hee wold not goe,
  but Lay & licked his wound;
he waite to haue healed them againe,
& therto he did his paine:
  loe, such loue is in a hound!

This scene is of course similar to that found in "The Three Ravens" (26), where the fidelity of hawk, hound, and lady is given supreme lyrical expression. It is sufficient here to point out that the basic chivalric setting for this lyric was ready to hand in the minstrel's repertoire. "Sir Triamore" is in no final sense the source of "The Three Ravens," for, as we have seen, the genesis of the latter is a complex affair related to religious folksong. Yet the pathetic tableau in "Sir Triamore" helps to explain how the chivalric and religious traditions could combine to produce the secular *Pietà* of "The Three Ravens."

In addition to the ballad entitled "The Marriage of Sir Gawain" (Child 31), the Percy folio MS contains three unique Gawain romances. "The Turke and Gowin" (MS, p. 38) and "The Grene Knight" (p. 203), both in the Thopas stanza, are later variations of the fourteenth-century alliterative poem, *Sir Gawain and the Green Knight*. "The Carle of Carlile" (MS, p. 448), is a recasting of an early fifteenth-century romance, *Syre Gawene and the Carle of Carelyle*. All three of these poems, in one way or another, shed light on the relationship of ballads and romances.

The journey to the otherworld in "The Turk and Gowin" is similar to that in the romance of *Thomas of Ersseldoune*, which is the basis of the ballad "Thomas Rymer" (37). Like Thomas, Sir Gawain is led into a hill (ll. 65-71):

He led Sir Gawaine to a hill soe plaine;
the earth opened & closed againe,
  then Gawaine was adread;
the Merke was comen & the light is gone;
thundering, lightning, snow & raine,
  thereof enough they had.

The experience of Thomas is similar, even if lacking the dramatic variations of weather:

Scho ledde hym in at Eldone hill,
  vndir-nethe a derne lee,

Whare it was dirke as mydnyght myrke,
   And euer Þe water till his knee.

The montenans of dayes three,
   He herd bot swoghynge of Þe flode;
At Þe laste he sayde, Full wa es mee!
   Almaste I dye, for fawte of fode.[10]

When they reach their destination Gawain finds, again like Thomas, delicious food which he is cautioned not to eat (ll. 83–88):

A Bord was spred within that place,
all manner of meates & drinkes there was
   for groomes that might it againe:
Sir Gawaine wold haue fallen to that fare,
the turke bad him leaue for care;
   then waxt he vnfaine.

But whereas Thomas is warned that plucking the fruit will send him to hell, the Turk gives Gawain no reason for the prohibition, and in fact fetches him some harmless food to appease his hunger. The symbolism of *Thomas of Ersseldoune* has become mere magic in "The Carle of Carlile."

"The Grene Knight" is simply a minstrel's shortened and simplified version of the better-known and more artful alliterative poem of the fourteenth century. Its main value in connection with the ballads is its representative quality. No piece in the folio MS is more typical of late medieval minstrelsy. It has the typical "fillers" which Chaucer satirized so effectively in the *Tale of Sir Thopas,* and which we have observed especially in the Robin Hood ballads: "I tell withouten scorne," "I tell you this tale for true," and "vnder the greenwood tree." Its stylized descriptions are foretastes of what is to be thought of later as typical ballad diction (ll. 277–282):

When he rode ouer the Mold
his geere glisterd as gold
   by the way as he rode;
many furleys he there did see,
fowles by the water did flee,
   by brimes & bankes soe broad.

The language of "The Carle of Carlile" finds its echo in later balladry, as can be seen in this description of the monstrous carl (ll. 185–188):

10. *ESPB,* I, 327, sts. 30–31.

His ffingars were like to teddar stakes,
& his hands like breads that wiues bake;
50 Cubitts he was in height;
Lord, he was a Lothesome wight!

The gothic ugliness of the carl is echoed in the description of the giantess
in "King Henry" (32, st. 6):

Her teeth was a' like teather stakes,
  Her nose like club or mell;
An I ken naething she 'peard to be,
  But the fiend that wons in hell.

The most significant feature of "The Carle of Carlile," however, is the
way in which its narrative structure reinforces the thematic emphasis
on Gawain's courtesy by the use of parallelism. When Gawain, Kay, and
the bishop arrive at the carl's gate, Gawain's patience and courtesy is
contrasted with Kay's impatience and boorishness. The politeness of
Gawain's request for shelter (ll. 139–146) is emphasized by the porter's
repeating it to the carl word for word (ll. 161–168), and by the carl's
prompt welcome. Gawain's superiority over both Kay and the bishop
is illustrated dramatically by the stable episode. During dinner Kay suddenly decides to go look after his horse, and when he reaches the stable
he drives the carl's horse out, leaving his own animal to enjoy the corn
and hay. The carl suddenly appears and gives Kay a hard blow for
striking his horse. When Kay returns, the bishop goes out to the stable
and the scene is repeated in virtually the same language, thus underscoring the parallelism. At last, when the bishop returns, Gawain goes out
and finds the carl's foal beside his, but instead of driving him away, he
takes his mantle and covers the animal with it. The carl is watching and
thanks Gawain for his courtesy. The moral is carefully pointed at the
end of each episode. After the carl hits the bishop, for example, the latter
protests (ll. 267–272):

"Mercy!" said the Bishopp, "I am a clarke!
somewhatt I can of christs werke."
He saith, "by the Clergye I sett nothing,
nor yett by thy Miter nor by thy ringe.
It ffiteth a clarke to be curteous & ffree,
by the conning of his clergy."

We have already seen this criticism of churchmen in "A Gest of Robyn
Hode" (117, sts. 226–227):

Robyn dyde adowne his hode,
    The monke whan that he se;
The monke was not so curteyse,
    His hode then let he be.

'He is a chorle, mayster, by dere worthy God,'
    Than sayd Lytell Johan:
'Thereof no force,' sayd Robyn,
    'For curteysy can he none.'

But the significant point to note here is not so much the similarity of theme but rather the fact that both romance and ballad use the same technique of structural parallelism to implement the theme of courtesy.

The last to be considered, but easily the best of the romances in the folio MS is "Eger and Grime."[11] This is a truly remarkable work, in that although it is a late fifteenth-century composite of romance common-places, it is told with such freshness and (one might say) with such un-medieval realism that it has attracted considerable critical attention. What has not yet been sufficiently recognized, however, is the extent to which "Eger and Grime," particularly in the folio version, illustrates the narrative technique of late medieval minstrelsy.[12]

Eger and Grime are close friends, sworn to help each other in time of need. Eger loved the king's daughter, Winglayne, a proud lady who scorned any man who had ever been defeated. Eger won many honors on the field of battle to please his lady but at last was defeated by the warrior Gray Steel, who shamed him forever by cutting off his little finger as a sign of defeat. When Eger returned home sorely wounded, Grime under-took to avenge his friend and restore him to the good graces of Winglayne by disguising himself as Eger in the battle with Gray Steel. Follow-ing Eger's directions, Grime first comes to the home of Lillias, the beautiful lady who had saved Eger by her skill in dressing his wounds. She receives Grime hospitably and encourages him to take vengeance on Gray Steel. The next day Grime engages Gray Steel in an epic fight and finally kills him, cutting off his right hand as a token of victory. Before returning home triumphantly as Eger, he and Lillias are formally

11. James R. Caldwell (ed.), *Eger and Grime* ("Harvard Studies in Comparative Literature," Vol. IX [Cambridge, 1933]). See also Mabel Van Duzee, *A Medieval Romance of Friendship: Eger and Grime* (New York, 1963).

12. Caldwell prints the Percy and the Huntington-Laing versions of *Eger and Grime* in parallel text form. The Hunting-ton-Laing version is almost twice as long as the Percy text and lacks the narrative technique of minstrelsy evident in the Percy version.

betrothed. The deceiving of Winglayne is successful, and Eger is congratulated by all for the victory over Gray Steel. Then Eger marries Winglayne, and Grime marries Lillias.

It has already been suggested by Child that there may be a relationship between "Eger and Grime" and two ballads found in the folio MS: "Sir Cawline" (61) and "Sir Lionel" (18). Although Child tries to keep alive the possibility of an independent ballad origin, particularly for "Sir Cawline," it seems more likely that Caldwell is right when he observes: "Obviously the ballads are to be regarded as having borrowed from the romance rather than as having contributed to it."[13] Another ballad of friendship and love which may owe something to "Eger and Grime" is that remarkable piece, also preserved in the folio MS, "Will Stewart and John" (107).

As Caldwell has shown, the printed edition of "Eger and Grime," contrary to earlier opinion, is closest to the original form of the romance, while the Percy folio version is a much later (and shorter) reworking of the story. What scholars have failed to observe, however, is that whereas the printed edition is a straightforward literary narrative, the folio text contains numerous examples of that structural parallelism which we have seen to be characteristic of the narrative art of the new minstrelsy. It should be remarked in passing that this phenomenon occurs too often in the folio MS to be the accidental result of miscellaneous collecting and is in fact confirmation of the belief expressed earlier that this MS is essentially a reflection of the minstrel's repertoire.

An opportunity for the development of parallelism in "Eger and Grime" exists near the beginning of the story by virtue of the fact that the wounded Eger gives Grime a detailed account of his adventure, some of the details of which are repeated in the subsequent adventure of Grime. Thus there are two descriptions of Lillias, one by Eger in telling how she dressed his wounds (ll. 215–218), and a second description when Grime visits her before the battle with Gray Steel (ll. 793–796). The wording of these two passages is virtually identical. I quote the first only:

Shee was cladd in scarlett redd,
& all of fresh gold shone her heade,
her rud was red as rose in raine,
a fairer creature was neuer seene.

13. Caldwell, *Eger and Grime*, p. 62.

After Lillias had treated Eger's wounds he was brought to a bed and went to sleep to the sound of music (ll. 263–272):

> The Ladye fayre of Hew & hyde,
> shee sate downe by the bedside;
> shee laid a souter vpon her knee,
> theron shee plaid full loue somlye,
> & yett for all her sweet playinge,
> oftimes shee had full still mourninge;
> & her 2 maydens sweetlye sange,
> & oft the weeped, & their hands wrange;
> but I heard neuer soe sweet playinge,
> & euer amongst, soe sore siking.

At this point we are not told why Lillias and her maids were mourning. The explanation is given, however, in the parallel passage describing Grime's visit with the lady before the fight with Gray Steel. After serving him a rich supper, Lillias conducts him to bed (ll. 851–864):

> The Ladye louesome of hew and hyde
> sett her downe by his bed side,
> shee layd a sowter vpon her knee,
> & theron shee playd full loue somlye,
> & her 2 mayds full sweetlye sang,
> & euer they wept, & range their hands.
> Then spake Gryme to that Ladye fayre:
> "Of one thing, Madam, I haue great Marueile,
> for I heard neuer soe sweet playinge,
> & ofentetimes soe sore weepinge."
> Shee commanded her sowter to be taken her froe,
> & sore shee wrange her hands 2:
> "Sir," shee sayd, "I must neuer be weele
> till I be auenged on Sir Gray Steele . . . ."

The parallelism here serves to build suspense until the mysterious mourning is explained in such a way as to inject an added element of passion into the forthcoming conflict. It is interesting to note, further, that Lillias' explanation of the feud between her family and Gray Steel (ll. 869–886) is anticipated almost word for word by the knight whom Grime meets on the road (ll. 737–754). The only changes in wording are those necessitated by the change in speakers. This repetition serves to heighten the

144

fearsomeness of Gray Steel, thus underscoring the danger confronting Grime, as can be seen in the two lines following the conclusion of the knight's remarks (ll. 755–756):

> For all the words he spake in that time,
> nothing it feared the Knight Sir Grime.

A final example of parallelism occurs near the end of the story in connection with arrangements for the marriage of the two heroes. When Grime returns to Lillias after his victory over Gray Steel, the girl's father, Earl Gares, invites him to stay for dinner (ll. 1251–1260):

> The Erle tooke Gryme by the hand,
> to the pallace the yode Leadand;
> a rich dinner ther men might see,
> of Meate & drinke was great plentye;
> the certaine sooth if I shold say,
> he was meate fellow for the Ladye gay.
> & when the dinner was all done,
> the Erle tooke Grime into a chamber soone,
> & spurred him gentlye,
> "Sir, beene you marryed in your countrye?"

Grime assures the Earl that he is not married and that he loves Lillias "too well to forsake" her. The marriage date is then set, and Grime returns to the kingdom of Beame to complete his mission on behalf of Eger. The impersonation is carried out successfully, and a reconciliation between Eger and Winglayne is effected. Grime maintains the initiative in bringing the lovers together and in arranging the marriage by consultation with Winglayne's father, Earl Bragas (ll. 1371–1383):

> Gryme tooke him by the hand,
> to the palace the yode Leadand:
> a rich dinner there men might see,
> Meate & drinke there was plentye;—
> certaine sooth if I shold say,
> he was meate fellow with the Ladye gay;—
> & when the Dinner was all done,
> Grime tooke the Erle to councell soone;
> "as my Lord Egar is the Knight
> that winneth the worshipp in euery fight,
> & if hee shall haue your daughter free,

att your owne will I haue gotten him to bee;
I read anon that it were done."

Thus in the two passages quoted, identical descriptions of a banquet are followed by discussion of arrangements for a marriage.

The narrative symmetry in the Percy folio version of "Eger and Grime" is not achieved without some loss of coherence, as Caldwell points out in the introduction to his edition:

> Again, in P 1371–1376 the reconciliation between Eger and Winglayne is brought about merely by seating them side by side at a banquet. In HL (2507–2520) Winglayne arranges a splendid procession of her maidens to welcome Sir Eger home from the hunt, and before the whole company she kneels to ask his forgiveness.[14]

But this fails to account for that narrative symmetry which is a unique feature of the folio text (not occurring in the printed editions at all) and which is of great significance for our present purpose in understanding the evolution of balladry. MacEdward Leach has observed:

> Ballads are a thing of growth; in their earliest forms many, but certainly not all, of the ballads probably told stories as detailed as any conventional narrative; but as they are re-created by the folk, the slow elements and the undramatic elements are dropped and only the hard core of tension remains—the moment of drama.[15]

"Eger and Grime" is of course not a ballad; it is a romance. But in the Percy folio MS version it has taken one important step in the direction of balladry, not indeed through re-creation by the folk, but rather through a deliberate structural change attributable to the narrative art of the minstrel.

Histories

There are some two dozen pieces in the folio MS on historical subjects, and they tend to fall into two main categories. One is what might be called the short rhymed history, usually of fairly late date, sixteenth or early seventeenth century. The other category comprises metrical histories of relatively early date, belonging to the minstrel tradition.

14. *Ibid.*, p. 24.   15. Leach, *The Ballad Book*, p. 3.

The earliest of the miscellaneous rhymed histories (omitting the fragmentary "Siege of Roune") is probably the "Earles of Chester" (MS, p. 105), a sixteenth-century stanzaic life of the Earls Randle II and Randle III of Chester, who lived in the twelfth and thirteenth centuries. Others are "Cales Voyage" (p. 234), a satirical piece on relations with Spain written perhaps in 1630; "Agincourte Battell" (p. 241), which may profitably be compared with the later ballad "King Henry Fifth's Conquest of France" (Child 164); "Herefford and Norfolke" (p. 265), largely an exile's "farewell"; "Buckingam Betrayd by Banister" (p. 270), one of several pieces on this theme; "White Rose and Red" (p. 288), a dull recital of the Tudor line; and "Leofricus" (p. 507), a metrical version of the Lady Godiva story. Most of the remaining historical works are bunched together near the end of the MS (pp. 414 ff., 490 ff.) and are obviously taken from printed sources, primarily Thomas Deloney's *Strange Histories* and *Garland of Good Will*. Although, as Friedman has shown, these compositions are part of the context in which balladry must be viewed, they do not contribute much to the evolution of ballad style, with which we are now concerned.

Of particular interest in connection with balladry are the minstrel histories, one of which, "Flodden Field" (MS, p. 117), has already been considered in the preceding chapter as an example of the new minstrelsy. This same basic type of historical narrative is further represented by "Scotish Feilde" (p. 79), "Bosworth Feilde" (p. 434), and "Ladye Bessiye" (p. 464). The first of these is composed in alliterative long lines and the other two in rhyming quatrains. Like "Flodden Field," all of them contain much praise of the courage and loyalty of the Stanleys. I suspect that we have here a group of compositions made and preserved by minstrels in the employ of the Stanley household. To this group probably belongs "Death and Life" (MS, p. 384), a remarkably fine alliterative poem of the first half of the fifteenth century.[16]

In spite of its alliterative form, "Scotish Feilde" has affinities with early ballads like "Chevy Chase" (162) which occasionally make effective use of alliteration in addition to rhyme. This relationship is especially evident in descriptions of battle scenes. A typical passage in "Scotish Feilde" is the following (ll. 327–329):

16. See J. H. Hanford and J. M. Steadman (eds.), *Death and Liffe*, in SP, XV (1918), 223–294. The editors discuss the date of the poem on pp. 229–232. As pure speculation I will mention the possibility that *Death and Liffe* may have served as literary model and inspiration for the author of "Scotish Feilde," a self-conscious and late example of alliterative poetry.

Theire was swinging out of swords, and swapping of headds;
We blanked them with bills through all their bright armor,
That all the dale dunned of their derfe strokes.

With this compare a similar battle scene in the "Chevy Chase" ballad
(162A30):

Thorowe ryche male and myneyeple,
    many sterne the strocke done streght;
Many a freyke that was fulle fre,
    there vndar foot dyd lyght.

The list of wounded and slain is likewise a common feature of poem and
ballad. "Scotish Feilde" has such a list immediately following the first
clash of the two armies (ll. 344–348):

The barne of Kinderton full keenly was killed them beside,
soe was Hauforde, I you hett, that was a hend sweere,
Full-show full fell was fallen to the ground,
Christopher Sauage was downe cast that kere might he neuer,
& of Lancashire, John Laurence, god haue mercy on their soules!

This kind of list with brief characterizations of the men interspersed is
of course well known in "Chevy Chase" (162A52–56). And the courage
of the men in "Scotish Feilde" (ll. 349–350),

These frekes wold neuer flee, for noe feare that cold happen,
But were killed lik Conquerors in their Kings service,

finds its counterpart in "Chevy Chase" (162A47):

There was neuer a freake wone foot wolde fle,
    but still in stour dyd stand,
Heawyng on yche othar, whylle the myghte dre,
    with many a balfull brande.

The victory of Henry VII over Richard III at the battle of Bosworth
Field in 1485 is the subject of "Bosworth Feilde" and "Ladye Bessiye."
These two poems are closely related, and Child is very likely correct in
suggesting that the passages they have in common belonged originally to
"Ladye Bessiye," which is certainly the more lively and original of the
two.[17] But both pieces are full of the conventional motifs found in the
minstrelsy of battle. In "Bosworth Feilde," for example, we find the tra-

17. *ESPB*, III, 331 f.

ditional roll call of heroes (ll. 225–336), the "farewell" of Lord Strange when he is condemned, as he thinks, to die (ll. 505–536), and a list of the slain (ll. 605–632), including one Thriball, whose heroism when his legs were hewn off reminds us of Witherington in "Chevy Chase."

"Ladye Bessiye" tells essentially the same story as "Bosworth Feilde," except that, as the title indicates, the princess Elizabeth, destined to be Henry's queen, is the heroine from beginning to end. Thus it is somewhat startling to find the conventional list of heroes put in the mouth of Lady Bessie and used as a part of her argument to persuade her father to lead the revolt against Richard. Yet this is in accord with the author's thesis, namely, that Richard's overthrow was caused by a girl's desire for her beloved. As Sir John Savage remarks, on hearing the news (ll. 413–414): "Womens witt is wonder to heare!/ my vnckle is turned by your Bessye!"

Some of the langauge of "Ladye Bessiye" is destined to become identified with ballad diction. Such is the case, for example, in the loyal servant's refusal of a reward from his prince (ll. 789–792):

"I will none of thy gold, Sir Prince,
     nor yett none of thy ffee;
if euery haire of my head were a man,
     with you, Sir Prince, that they shold bee."

This sentiment is of course very common in balladry, if not in life, notably in the form which Child calls the "dower despised" (99A34):

'I'm seeking nane o your gold,' he says,
     'Nor of your silver clear;
I only seek your daughter fair,
     Whose love has cost her dear.'

A commonplace in the form of a battle boast also occurs in "Ladye Bessiye," when Sir William Stanley defies Richard, telling him he will meet him on Bosworth field, and he adds (ll. 877–878):

"such a breakeffast I him hett
     as neuer subiect did to Kinge!"

The same boast occurs in "Bosworth Feilde" (l. 179; cf. 566) and in some of the historical ballads, notably "Musselburgh Field" (172, st. 7) and "The Rising in the North" (175, st. 36).

Like many of the texts in the folio MS, "Ladye Bessiye" employs some of those structural repetitions that are the hallmark of minstrelsy. The

5. The Percy folio manuscript   149

principal device used to introduce these repetitions is the secret letter which the Earl of Derby writes to each of the relatives whose support he will need in the fight with Richard. Bessie herself writes down the message from her father's dictation (ll. 201–212):

> "Father Stanley, now let me see,
>   ffor euery word write shall I."
> "Bessye, make a letter to the Holt
>   there my brother Sir William doth Lye;
> "bidd him bring 7 sad yeomen,
>   all in greene clothes lett them bee,
> & change his Inn in euery towne
>   where before hee was wont to Lye;
> "& lett his fface be towards the benche,[18]
>   lest any man shold him espye;
> & by the 3^d day of May
>   that he come and speake with mee."

The letter is dictated four times in almost identical language, and the faithful retainer Humphrey is sent to the west country to deliver the messages. Further structural repetition is achieved by a detailed account of the delivery of the letters to each of the addressees. This is of particular interest as an early example of the message motif so frequently found in ballads. Humphrey does not, like the ballad messenger, bend his bow and swim at the broken bridges, or slack his shoon and run in the green grass; in fact he is well supplied with money and horses. Yet his mission is exploited skilfully to dramatize the reactions of the men who receive the secret message. When Sir William read the letter, "he stood still in a studiinge" (l. 326); Lord Strange, roused from his bed in the night, looked at the letter and "the teares trickled downe his eye" (l. 374); Sir Edward Stanley and his brother read the message quickly together "and vp they lope, and laught aloude" (l. 396); when Sir John Savage first glanced at the letter, "all blanked was his blee" (l. 412); and finally Humphrey delivers his last letter (ll. 425–428):

> When Sir Gilbert Talbott the lettre looked on,
>   a loude laughter laughed hee:
> "Faire ffall that Lord of hye renowne!
>   to rise and stirr beginneth hee!"

18. Furnivall queries the meaning of this line (*Bishop Percy's Folio Manuscript*, III, 329, n. 3). Perhaps it warns Sir William to keep his head down in company to avoid recognition.

We are still a century away from the earliest known version of "Sir Patrick Spens," but the ground is already being prepared by the humble minstrel for that justly famous stanza (58A4):

> The first line that Sir Patrick red,
> A loud lauch lauched he;
> The next line that Sir Patrick red,
> The teir blinded his ee.

Although not strictly historical, a group of three pieces on the King and Subject theme can perhaps be mentioned here by way of concluding the section on histories in the folio MS. I refer to "King Henry II and the Miller of Mansfield" (MS, p. 235), "John de Reeue" (p. 357), and "The Pore Man and the Kinge" (p. 424). The first of these has already been referred to in connection with the discussion of "King Edward the Fourth and a Tanner of Tamworth" (Child 273). "The Pore Man and the Kinge" is a seventeenth-century composition directed against lawyers, closely resembling a ballad issued by Martin Parker in 1640. But the earliest and easily the best of the King and Subject narratives is "John de Reeue," a minstrel creation in the familiar Thopas stanza of the late metrical romances. Scenes of high comedy such as the arming of John (ll. 593–640) bespeak an author possessing both a knowledge of romance conventions and the skill to parody them successfully. It is very likely that "John de Reeue" directly or indirectly inspired most of the King and Tanner narratives of the fifteenth and sixteenth centuries.

Songs

Well over a hundred "songs," loosely defined, are scattered throughout the Percy folio MS: lyrics, satirical pieces, classical and popular narratives, and songs of moral counsel are some of the subtypes under this general heading. The nineteenth-century editors of the MS, to some extent following the classifications of Bishop Percy, printed forty-two of these songs in a separate volume with the title "Loose and Humorous Songs." But it is well to remember that in the MS they are not set apart, and that in this respect the folio MS resembles earlier collections like the Sloane and Ashmole MSS considered above.

Immediately following "Chevy Chase" and just before "The Grene Knight" is a group of songs (MS, pp. 191–203) including a surprising number of lyrics by seventeenth-century poets. The first of these is "To Althea, from Prison" by Richard Lovelace (1618–1658), the most famous stanza of which is given in a form somewhat different from the text that has been so often anthologized:

Stone walls doe not a prison make,
 nor Iron barrs a cage,
the spotlesse soule and Inocent
 Calls this an hermitage.
If I haue freedome in my loue,
 & in my soule am free,
angells alone that sores aboue
 enioyes such Lybertye!

This is followed by Edmund Waller's "Cloris"; Martin Parker's loyalist song, "The Kinge Enioyes his Rights Againe"; "The Egiptian Quene" and (probably) "Newarke" by John Cleveland; Thomas Carew's "Amongst the Mirtles"; and, finally, George Wither's "Shall I, Wasting in Despair." We are reminded of the fact that Richard Sheale's book (Ashmole 48) contained a large number of songs and poems attributed to specific sixteenth-century authors. It is worth observing, I think, that the close relationship between poet and populace remained firm until at least the beginning of the nineteenth century, when the furtiveness of Wordsworth's desire to see his poems circulated as broadsides signals the end of an era.[19]

There are six songs in the folio MS that may be called primarily satirical. "Bell My Wiffe" (MS, p. 291), "Sittinge Late" (p. 317), and "Are Women Faire" (p. 479) satirize universal human frailties and usually involve the battle of the sexes. These are a part of the tradition represented in the Child canon by such ballads as "Our Goodman" (274) and "Get Up and Bar the Door" (275). Other songs satirize more specific social phenomena. "The Lavinian Shore" (p. 463), once attributed to Shakespeare, purports to be the cry of a huckster selling love, rank, and fame to any who has gold to pay for them. "Come My Dainty Doxeys" (p. 464) pretends with exuberance to praise the gypsy way of life:

Come my dainty doxeys, my dills, my deares!
 we haue neither house nor land,
yet neuer want good cheere;
wee take no care for candle, rents;
wee sleepe, we snort, we snore, in tents.

19. Friedman, *The Ballad Revival*, p. 271. American poets, notably Whitman, Frost, and Sandburg, have also to some extent maintained this close relationship.

It is interesting that the humorous tone of this song fits in well with what has been suggested as the satirical and humorous quality of the original form of "The Gypsy Laddie."[20] Many of the songs in this MS are useful to the student of balladry as reminders of seventeenth-century atmosphere and attitudes. A romantic view of gypsy life in ballads before the eighteenth century would be unlikely, if not impossible.

A final example of satirical song is "To Oxfforde" (p. 464), which supposedly lampoons a visit of James I to the university in 1605:

> To Oxford the King is gone
> with all his pompous grace,
> to vew the sights & see the learning
> of that ffamous place,
> where clownes of the towne—
> clothed in their scarlett gownes—
> gaue the King such a thing
> as passes all imageninge;
> a paire of gloues, to testifye their loues
> which to the King they bore.

The gift of gloves is ridiculed by this delicate suggestion that the Oxford "clownes" are trying to have a love affair with the King. Not content with this touch, the song continues, on a note of rising incredulity, to dwell on the gloves until they are reduced to the absurd:

> They gaue him a payre of gloues
> of stiffe & strong staggs lether;
> I say, a payre of hunting gloues
> to keepe out wind and wheather.

This sophisticated satire is of course to be expected in university circles; it is not the kind of thing that is kept alive in popular tradition.

Several other songs reflect the learning or at least the interests of the university, namely, those that celebrate classical heroes and heroines. There are two songs about those perennial favorites, Dido and Aeneas (MS, pp. 443, 514), one on Hero and Leander (p. 455), and a song in three stanzas epitomizing the story of Troilus and Criseyde. Of these perhaps the most interesting is "Queene Dido" (p. 514), with its depiction of the "grim and pale" ghost of Dido, and the medieval tableau of the death of Aeneas, complete with attendant fiends.

20. See J. A. Knoblock, " 'The Gypsy Laddie' (Child 200): An Unrecognized Child of Medieval Romance," WF, XIX (1960), 35–45.

A piece somewhat difficult to classify is "Marke More Foole," which tells a story set in the time of King Solomon. A rich man loses his purse filled with gold. When a poor man finds it, the owner claims it contained more than the poor man returned to him, and he takes the poor man to be tried before the king. On their way to court they pass a knight and his lady on horseback. The poor man, as it happens, is carrying some sheep-skins which make a noise that frightens the lady's horse. The lady is thrown to the ground and in the fall one of her eyes is pierced by a piece of stubble. Her companion immediately accuses the poor man and joins the rich man on the road to court to press charges. As the party passes near the sea, the poor man, understandably concerned over his predica-ment, suddenly tries to escape his captors by leaping into the water. Unfortunately he lands on two fishermen who happened to be below him in a boat, and his fall breaks the neck of one of them. The other fisher-man, unharmed, joins the group in order to press charges. When Solomon has heard all three complaints he seems at a loss (ll. 85–88):

> The King hee turned him round about,
>   being well aduised of euery thinge.
> Quoth he, "neuer since I can remember,
>   came 3 such matters since I was Kinge."

At this juncture Marke More, the fool, asks Solomon to let him pass judgment on these three cases and the king agrees. Marke then interro-gates the poor man, who tells the truth in each case and confirms it with a witness. Convinced that the poor man is in the right, Marke hands down the following judgments: the rich man must follow the poor man by the heels until they find another such purse full of gold, and when they do the rich man may keep it; since the poor man's wife has two eyes, the knight can trade wives with him; and finally, he rules that the poor man is to be placed in a boat and the fisher is to leap from the cliff on top of him. Needless to say, all three accusers prefer to pay compensation to the poor man rather than accept these judgments.

This remarkable narrative has the spiral structure of an Eastern tale such as can be seen, for example, in "Abu Kasem's Slippers."[21] Speaking of the Fool, the editors of the folio MS observe: "Who was the individual whose acuteness is here celebrated, we cannot precisely state" (III, 127). Without being able to cite a specific source, however, I suspect that "Marke" is Marcolf, that impudent, wise fool of the medieval legend of

21. See Heinrich Zimmer, *The King and the Corpse* (New York, 1948), pp. 9–25.

Solomon and Marcolf.[22] How he found his way into the folio MS I hesitate to conjecture.

In contrast to the retellings of traditional stories just considered are the romantic narrative songs of which "The Nut-Brown Maid" (MS, p. 420) is a prototype. These include "A Jigge" (p. 294), a military version of "The Nut-Brown Maid" which finds its counterpart in the Child ballad "Trooper and Maid" (299), as well as numerous other songs on the same general theme; "The Blind Beggar of Bednall Green" (p. 276), a ballad unaccountably omitted by Child, which survives in tradition in the twentieth century; Elderton's "Marye Aumbree," composed to the tune of the "Bednall" ballad just mentioned and celebrating the military exploits of its fighting heroine; "Ladyes Fall" (p. 268), a domestic tragedy with romantic touches in the "Nut-Brown Maid" tradition; and "Maudline" (p. 481), a bizarre romance of young love and Protestant heroism in the Inquisition in Italy. This seemingly odd collection of songs most closely resembles that group of folio ballads referred to later on in this chapter under the heading of "domestic tragedy."

A final category of songs consists of those containing moral or religious counsel. Here we find a dramatic contrast between the Ashmole MS, in which moral and religious songs were the largest single group (some thirty-three of them), and the folio MS, which has no more than two of this type. In fact the first of these, entitled "Conscience" (p. 243), might better be termed a satire or moral allegory. In it Conscience complains that whereas formerly he was respected in the king's court, Westminster Hall, and throughout society, now he is scorned by all wherever he goes (ll. 60–66):

"Then went I to London, where once I did wonne,
　　but they bade away with me when the knew my name;
'for he will vndoe vs to bye & to sell,'
　　they bade me goe packe me, & hye me for shame,
　　they lought at my raggs, & there had good game;
'this is old threed-bare Conscience that dwelt with St. Peeter;'
　　but they wold not admitt me to be a chimney sweeper.

Conscience tries to take up the cobbler's trade but is whipped out of town. He then visits lawyers, merchants, gentlemen, and husbandmen, and is

---

22. The Latin dialogue is edited by Walter Benary, *Salomon et Marcolfus* (Heidelberg, 1914), but this does not include the story told in "Marke More Foole." See J. D. Bruce, *The Evolution of Arthurian Romance From the Beginnings Down to the Year 1300* (Gottingen, 1923), I, 115, 391.

rejected by all. Even the clergy are unsympathetic. Not until pride is banished will England be blessed. In this highly traditional piece one recognizes easily the influence of *Piers the Plowman*, not only in the conception of a personified Conscience who comes before the king in Westminster Hall, but also in such imaginative passages as the poet's description of the flight of Falseness, Guile, and Liar from the king's constable:

> Thanne Falsnesse for feer fleigh to the freris,
> And Gile doth him to go, agast forto deighe;
> Ac marchauntis mette with hym, and made him abide,
> Besshette hym in here shoppis to shewen here ware,
> Aparailide hym as a prentice the peple to serve.
> Lightliche Lighere lep awey thennes,
> Lurkyng thorugh lanes, to-luggid of manye.
> He was nowhere welcome, for his many talis,
> Overal yhuntid and yhote trusse . . . .[23]

Although "Conscience" is composed in rime royal, it clearly belongs in the allegorical tradition of *Piers the Plowman* and its sequence. Its nearest relative in the folio MS is "Death and Liffe."

The one characteristic song of moral counsel in the MS is "The Fall of Princes," written in the eight-line stanza of Chaucer's "Monk's Tale" (*ababbcbc*) with the same last line repeated at the end of each stanza to underscore the theme of mortality: "ffor heere we be sure to live but a space." It utilizes the *ubi sunt* formula of medieval tragedy, beginning with Adam and (in this case) ending with Henry VIII. In addition to the usual biblical and historical figures, we find a stanza devoted to the heroes of romance (ll. 73–80):

> Where is King Arthur the venturer, with his Knights bold?
>   or Sir Tristeram, that treasure of curtesye?
> or Sir Gawaine the good, with his helmett made of gold?
>   or Sir Lancelott dulake, a Knight of Chiualrye?
> where is King Charlemaine of France, from them wold neuer flee?
>   yett these cold not refuse death with his mace.
> heere you may see, for all the hye degree,
>   that here we beene sure to liue but a litle space.

It is interesting to remember that in the century that elapsed from the

23. T. A. Knott and D. C. Fowler (eds.), *Piers the Plowman: A Critical Edition of the A-Version* (Baltimore, 1952), pp. 81–82 (A text, passus II, ll. 172–180).

time of the Ashmole MS to the Percy MS, texts like this one had almost entirely vanished from the repertoire, and narrative songs and ballads, a small minority in Ashmole, had greatly increased in numbers and importance. The minstrel profession in the mid-seventeenth century had but little space to live, yet, if we rightly assess the folio MS, it was leaving behind a rich store of narrative song.

That the Percy folio MS was compiled during the twilight of minstrelsy in a somewhat nostalgic spirit is difficult to prove, and yet one senses this in reading through its contents. One song in particular, "In Olde Times Paste" (p. 405), seems to sum up this spirit (ll. 1–16):

> In old times past when merry men
> did merry makers make,
> no man did greater matters then
> then Lancelott of Dulake.
> Good Robin hood was liuinge then,
> which now is quite forgott,
> & soe was faire Mayd Marryan,
> a pretty wench, god wott.
> William of cloudeslee did dwell
> amongst the buckes & does,
> Clim of the Cloughe & Adam Bell
> killed venison with their bowes.
> Through the wood these Iollye bowmen went,
> both ouer hill & dale, & dale & dale,
> vp & downe, vpp & downe,
> through many a parke & pale.

The singer goes on to describe the pleasures and pastimes of the good old days and then sadly bids them farewell. Now the world is changed, he says (ll. 53–64):

> More sparinge for a pennye nowe
> then then was for a pound;
> rich men, alas, they know not how
> to keepe ne hawke nor hound.
> All merriments are quite fforgot,
> & bowes are laid aside;
> all is to litle now, god wott,
> to maintaine wordlye pryde.
> Where I began, there will I end,

the old time sure was best;
    vnless that misers quicklye mend,
        old mirth may take his rest.

Surely these are the sentiments of a minstrel, whose livelihood is of course
dependent on the liberality of great lords, whose fortunes in the seventeenth century were rapidly disintegrating under the pressures of social
change. One recalls the similar words of the minstrel Richard Sheale,
written in the Ashmole MS nearly a century earlier:

I can cum in no company, be nyght nor be day,
But all men lacke mony, me thinkes I her them say;
Whiche thinges for to hear makys myn ears weary,
For withowt mony men cannot be myrry.
For wher the have no mony in store,
Yt es tyme for the mynstrell to gete owt ath dore.[24]

But whereas Sheale uttered these words with tongue in cheek, the singer
of old times in the folio MS is recognizing the sad truth that the "old
mirth," minstrelsy, is about to "take his rest."

The ballads

From the nearly two hundred pieces in the Percy folio MS, Child
selected forty-five that he considered "ballads" according to his unspoken
definition. Eighteen of these survive uniquely in this manuscript; twenty-
two appear in their earliest form here, with later versions being recovered
in the eighteenth or nineteenth centuries; two are ballads of which
sixteenth-century copies supply the only other known versions; and three
exist in versions both earlier and later than the text in the folio MS.[25]

No doubt to some extent Child was guided in his selection by the fact
that certain of the ballads survive elsewhere, but, as the above figures
show, this kind of cross-check was frequently not available to him. Another criterion seems to have been the stanza form. Child tended to admit
texts written in the ballad quatrain but excluded those, for example, in
the Thopas stanza. This is what largely determined his choice of romance

24. Wright, *Songs and Ballads*, p. 156.
25. Ballads surviving uniquely in the
folio MS are 29, 30, 31, 48, 60, 61, 80,
108, 118, 159, 165, 166, 171, 174, 175,
176, 177, 180; those having their earliest
version in the folio MS are 7, 18, 21, 59,
63, 67, 81, 83, 107, 109, 120, 122, 123,
124, 140, 142, 145, 158, 172, 187, 267,
271 (of these last 81, 109, 122, 123, 124,

142, 145, 172, 271 survive in other seventeenth-century versions; 7, 63, 81, 83, 120,
140, 158, 187 in the eighteenth century;
and, somewhat dubiously, 18, 21, 59, 67,
107, 267 in the nineteenth century).
Ballads having their latest version in the
folio MS are 116 and 162; and, finally,
those existing in versions both earlier and
later than the folio MS are 45, 167, 178.

ballads, although he by no means admitted everything in quatrain form. At first glance one might suppose that the presence of a refrain would offer a good means of authenticating ballads. But it is a fact sometimes overlooked that only two of the forty-five ballads show refrains, although it is very likely that at least six others had them.[26] One can only conclude in retrospect that Child chose these forty-five ballads with great discrimination.

Leaving aside Child's criteria, it is illuminating to classify the forty-five ballads according to types. Eight are derived from late medieval romance; twelve are historical; ten are outlaw ballads; three are perhaps best designated as love stories and one other as a moral tale; two represent special forms already discussed in connection with the carol and the riddle; and, finally, there is a group of nine ballads which, for lack of a better term, I will refer to as "domestic tragedies."[27] Of particular interest, moreover, is the fact that thirty-six of these are minstrel ballads, while the remaining eleven—the two special forms and the nine "domestic tragedies"—show a significant departure from the traditional style and diction of the new minstrelsy.[28] In other words we have an opportunity, in the folio MS, to observe the beginnings of an important transitional phase in the evolution of balladry. The significance of this will emerge, I trust, in the following discussion of ballads in the folio MS.

One would naturally expect the romance ballads to show the clearest traces of antiquity, but the first of these, "Sir Lionel" (18), is a disap-

26. The two ballads in the folio MS with refrain are 18 and 21. Six others probably had refrains: 45, 120, 122, 142, 172, 178. Concerning the folio version of "Musselburgh Field" (172), Friedman remarks: "Quite possibly the refrain was still being sung at the time the ballad was recorded, only the compiler of the Percy Folio MS, with his usual tendency toward abbreviation, may have regarded it as an unnecessary flourish in a written copy, however vital to the ballad when sung" ("A New Version of 'Musselburgh Field,'" p. 76).

27. Romance ballads: 18, 29, 30, 31, 59, 60, 61, 271; histories: 158, 159, 162, 166, 167, 171, 172, 174, 175, 176, 177, 180; outlaw ballads: 116, 118, 120, 122, 123, 124, 140, 142, 145, 187; love stories: 107, 108, 109; moral tale: 267; special forms: 21 (carol) and 45 (riddle); domestic tragedies: 7, 48, 63, 67, 80, 81, 83, 165, 178.

28. In this connection it is interesting to observe Friedman's conclusion (The Ballad Revival, p. 31): "In all, only a quarter of Child's texts from the Folio

MS appear, on stylistic grounds, to come directly from oral tradition . . . ." He does not specify which ballads these are, but it is perhaps not coincidental that I find eleven "non-minstrel" ballads out of the forty-five in the folio MS: 7, 21, 45, 48, 63, 67, 80, 81, 83, 165, 178. On the other hand, I would hesitate to regard these as ballads from oral tradition in contrast to the minstrel ballads, for I think that the main feature that distinguishes the two groups is a new development in style and narrative structure in the "domestic tragedies" which is attributable to the growing influence of melody on the ballad form. This development was first noted in the preceding chapter in the discussion of "Captain Car" (178). An awareness of the newer ballad style, by the way, seems implicit in a parody in the folio MS entitled "As It befell One Saturday" (p. 92). This parody might profitably be compared with the one in John Rastell's The Nature of the Four Elements, "Robyn Hode in Barnysdale stode," quoted in chapter iii, above.

pointment in this respect. Based on the romance, "Sir Eglamour of Artois" (MS, p. 295), the folio version is composed in quatrains with interlaced refrain in the second and fourth lines (18A1):

Sir Egrabell had sonnes three,
> *Blow thy horne, good hunter*
Sir Lyonell was one of these.
> *As I am a gentle hunter*

No doubt it is the refrain that led Child to put "Sir Lionel" so early (number 18) in the canon, because of his theory that refrains are a sign of antiquity. And yet on the basis of evidence known to Child himself,[29] it seems highly unlikely that the folio version of "Sir Lionel" is older than the reign of Henry VIII. Furthermore, Bronson has clearly demonstrated that a ballad was re-created from the romance, probably in 1615 by Samuel Rowlands, and that modern survivals of the "old Bangum" type, usually considered descendants of the folio version, are actually independent of it.[30] It is to be hoped that demonstrations of this kind will remove some of the mystery surrounding the question of ballad origins. As we have seen in an earlier chapter, the conjunction of minstrelsy and folksong observable in the creation of "Sir Lionel" and its sequence is precisely what can be expected in the creative period of the new minstrelsy.

The three Arthurian ballads, though they are without refrains, do seem to be nearer the romance genre from which they are derived than is "Sir Lionel," and yet at the same time they have certain features recognizable in later balladry. The proud porter of "King Arthur and King Cornwall" (30, sts. 11–19) reminds us of his ancient counterpart in the early twelfth century, "Kulhwch and Olwen," while at the same time he foreshadows the numerous proud young porters of later balladry. In matters of style, it is interesting to find examples of incremental repetition in both "The Boy and the Mantle" (29) and "The Marriage of Sir Gawain" (31). The latter ballad has a particularly effective instance in the stanzas describing Sir Kay's response to the loathly lady (31, sts. 34–35):

Sir Kay beheld this ladys face,
> And looked vppon her swire;
'Whosoeuer kisses this lady,' he sayes,
> 'Of his kisse he stands in feare.'

29. *ESPB*, I, 209.

30. Bronson, *The Traditional Tunes of the Child Ballads*, I, 265 f.

Sir Kay beheld the lady againe,
    And looked vpon her snout;
'Whosoeuer kisses this lady,' he saies,
    'Of his kisse he stands in doubt.'

We have seen this device used, both for serious and comic effect, in such various early pieces as "Robyn and Gandeleyn" (115) and "The King and the Barker" (273AppI).

Three intriguing ballads which Child grouped together are "Sir Aldingar" (59), "King Estmere" (60), and "Sir Cawline" (61). These seem to be significantly related to Scandinavian balladry and, at the same time, they contain vague echoes of common romance themes and motifs. A twelfth-century origin for "Sir Aldingar" has been argued with a view to establishing the antiquity of the ballad tradition, but the independent studies of Taylor and Christophersen seem to militate against such an early date.[31] Although it is impossible to prove, I suspect that all three in this group are formed from earlier metrical romances. It is difficult to base any argument on "King Estmere," since Percy unfortunately tore the leaves containing it out of his folio MS. But as Child himself reluctantly recognized, "Sir Cawline" shows evidence of having been based on a metrical romance, as can be seen, for example, in stanza 11:

'Itt is ffor your loue, ffayre ladye,
    That all this dill I drye;
Ffor if you wold comfort me with a kisse,
Then were I brought ffrom bale to blisse,
    Noe longer here wold I lye.'

The irregularity of this stanza strongly suggests that behind it lies the familiar Thopas stanza of late medieval romance (*aabccb*). " 'Sir Cawline' may possibly be formed upon a romance in stanzas," remarks Child, who hastens to add, "which itself was composed from earlier ballads." No such earlier ballads, of course, are known to exist; the statement is simply one more indication of the desire, by no means limited to Professor Child, to affirm the antiquity of the ballad tradition.

A final example of the romance ballad is "The Lord of Lorn and the

31. Donald S. Taylor, "The Lineage and Birth of Sir Aldingar," *JAF*, LXV (1952), 139–147; Paul Christophersen, *The Ballad of Sir Aldingar* (Oxford, 1952). The latter is a book-length study of considerable merit, but the author has been rightly criticized by Nygard for his "acceptance of the dubious assumption that William of Malmesbury knew the ballad of *Sir Aldingar* in the twelfth century" (Nygard, *The Ballad of Heer Halewijn*, pp. 8 f.).

False Steward" (271), derived ultimately from the late medieval romance of "Roswall and Lillian." This ballad has been referred to in an earlier chapter in connection with its possible indebtedness to the *Childhood of Jesus,* but it is worth a second look, for it is one of the most remarkable examples of a romance ballad in the Child canon. Not only does it have innovations like the schoolmaster episode discussed earlier, but it also exhibits that narrative symmetry which we have come to expect from minstrelsy at its best.

The focal point of interest in "The Lord of Lorn" is of course the disguise of the noble child as Disaware, a serving boy. When the child is forced by the evil steward to assume a new identity, he asks (271A29):

'What must be my name, worthy steward?
   I pray thee now tell it me:'
'Thy name shalbe Pore Disaware,
   To tend sheepe on a lonelye lee.'

By the use of repetition the pathos of the boy's situation is emphasized in the ballad, first when the child goes to live with the shepherd and his wife (271A31–32), and next when the duke's daughter encounters him in the forest (271A50–51):

'Where wast thou borne, thou bonny boy?
   Where or in what countrye?'
'Madam, I was borne in faire Scottland,
   That is so farr beyond the sea.'

'What is thy name, thou bonny boy?
   I pray thee tell it vnto mee;'
'My name,' he sayes, 'is Poore Disaware,
   That tends sheepe on a lonely lee.'

Later, when the evil steward discovers the child standing with the duke and his daughter, he asks him his identity in virtually the same words, changed just enough to convey the threatening tone of his questions (271A61–62):

'Where was thou borne, thou vagabond?
   Where?' he sayd, 'and in what country?'
Says, I was borne in fayre Scotland,
   That is soe far beyond the sea.
'What is thy name, thou vagabond?
   Haue done quicklie, and tell it to me;'

162

'My name,' he sayes, 'is Poore Disaware,
    I tend sheep on the lonelie lee.'

Other narrative elements in the ballad receive a similar emphasis, as in the stable scene where stanza repetitions dramatize the revelation of the boy's identity (271A68–76), and in the two proposals of marriage (A43, 106).

The accent of minstrel style is unmistakable in "The Lord of Lorn," not only in the use of the "weak" line ("I tell you all in veretie," A2[2]), but also in such transitional stanzas as the following (271A36):

Let vs leaue talking of the Lord of Learne,
    And let all such talking goe;
Let vs talke more of the false steward,
    That caused the child all this woe.

At the same time, however, there is a slight indication of post-minstrelsy technique in what might be called self-generating dialogue, in which the answer is a mirror image of the question (271A56–57), a feature destined to become common in eighteenth-century ballads. The broadside version of "The Lord of Lorn" (271B), more compressed than the folio text, loses some of the latter's symmetry but adds some incremental repetition of its own, as can be noted in the stable scene (B45–51). It seems reasonably certain that the folio version is earlier, and that the broadside is moving toward the compressed narrative characteristic of later balladry.

In summary, it can be said that six of the ballads in this group represent authentic survivals of late metrical romances, whereas the other two, "Sir Lionel" and "The Lord of Lorn," illustrate two quite different developments. "Sir Lionel" shows what happens when the narrative structure of minstrelsy is subordinated to the demands of the melody to which the romance is adapted. "The Lord of Lorn" illustrates the achievement of the new minstrelsy, unhampered by melodic restrictions, in transforming late medieval romance into ballad form. Both of these developments were important factors in the evolution of balladry.

Several of the twelve historical ballads in the folio MS have already been considered, and it is therefore unnecessary to deal with these as a group.[32] There are interesting points to be observed, however, in certain of the remaining historical ballads. "The Rose of England" (166) is unique in its allegorical exposition of the Tudor myth, though somewhat reminiscent of the pedestrian stanzaic history in the folio MS entitled

32. Historical ballads discussed earlier are 162, 167, and 180, as well as "Flodden Field" (168App).

"White Rose and Red" (MS, p. 288), where the white rose of York and the red rose of Lancaster are knit in "A true loues knott" (1. 43). It is tempting to suppose that this flower symbolism suggested the ubiquitous rose and brier motif, which appears first in the late seventeenth-century broadside version of "Fair Margaret and Sweet William" (74A). The idea is of course ancient and is to be found in medieval romance, but there is a curious parallelism in the action of the boar (representing Richard III) in "The Rose of England" (166, st. 5),

> Hee tooke the branches of this rose away,
>> And all in sunder did them teare,
> And he buryed them vnder a clodd of clay,
>> Swore they shold neuer bloome nor beare.

and the parish clerk in "Fair Margaret and Sweet William" (74A20):

> There came the clerk of the parish,
>> As you this truth shall hear,
> And by misfortune cut them down,
>> Or they had now been there.

Perhaps even closer to the violence of the boar is Scott's Black Douglas in "Earl Brand" (7B20):

> But bye and rade the Black Douglas,
>> And wow but he was rough!
> For he pulld up the bonny brier,
>> And flang't in St. Mary's Loch.

Most of the ballads in the historical category celebrate incidents and battles that occurred in the sixteenth century, but it is perhaps significant that the three best ballads, "Hugh Spencer" (158), "Durham Field" (159), and "Chevy Chase" (162), appear to have a fourteenth-century setting. These seem to have been conceived with a depth of emotion that the more recent ballads, in spite of their patriotism, somehow lack. There is in "Durham Field," for example, a nostalgia similar to that in the folio song "In Olde Times Paste" (p. 405) referred to earlier in this chapter (159, st. 65):

> Then was welthe and welfare in mery England,
>> Solaces, game, and glee,
> And every man loved other well,
>> And the King loved good yeomanrye.

Ballads of this type, though often sentimental, sound a truer note than those that cheerfully follow the Tudor line.

164

"Hugh Spencer's Feats in France" (158) is unique among the historical ballads in the folio MS by virtue of its survival in oral tradition in the eighteenth and nineteenth centuries. It begins as an excellent minstrel's ballad, with highly functional narrative symmetry in the description of Spencer's choice of horses (158A17–19) and his encounter with the French knight (A23–24, 28–29). It next appears in the eighteenth century in a version sent to Percy by the Duchess dowager of Portland. This version is a fascinating illustration of the shaping influence of melody on a minstrel ballad, as can be seen in these typical stanzas (158B33–34):

'It shall neer be said in England,'
    says Hugh Spencer, he;
'It shall neer be said in England,'
    says Hugh Willoughby;

'It shall neer be said in England,'
    says John of Atherly,
'That a queen of another nation
    eer had her will of we.'

One can almost hear the tune in the words of this version; the rhythm must have been very rapid and emphatic. Something of this same quality is preserved in the Aberdeenshire version collected in 1829 (158C), although the opening stanza of this text suggests it may have borrowed its tune from "Captain Car" (178D1). Nevertheless, "Hugh Spencer," in its seventeenth-, eighteenth-, and nineteenth-century versions, is one of the best ballads in the Child collection for observing the transition from minstrelsy to the popular ballad shaped by melodic influence.

The outlaw ballads were considered as a group in an earlier chapter, and hence several of the ten in the folio MS have already been discussed. "Robin Hood Rescuing Three Squires" (140), however, is an excellent example of the minstrelsy of the greenwood, and in its several versions it provides us with an opportunity to observe the transition to what might be called the baroque minstrelsy of eighteenth-century broadsides. In this ballad Robin plots to rescue an old woman's three sons who are condemned and about to be executed by the sheriff of Nottingham. On his way to the town he exchanges clothes with a poor old man, and thus disguised as a beggar he volunteers to serve as hangman for the three squires. Suddenly he blows his horn, his men rush in, and the squires are rescued before the execution can be carried out.

The folio version (A) is unfortunately defective, but enough of it remains to allow comparison of its narrative structure and technique with that of the eighteenth-century York garland represented by version B. The fragment begins abruptly with Robin's asking the old man to exchange clothes with him (A1–3):

. . . .

> In faith thou shalt haue mine,
> And twenty pound in thy purse,
>   To spend att ale and wine.'

'Though your clothes are of light Lincolne green,
  And mine gray russett and torne,
Yet it doth not you beseeme
  To doe an old man scorne.'

'I scorne thee not, old man,' says Robin,
  'By the faith of my body;
Doe of thy clothes, thou shalt haue mine,
  For it may noe better bee.'

Notice what happens to this straightforward dialogue in the eighteenth-century York garland (B10–12):

'Come change thy apparel with me, old man,
  Come change thy apparel for mine;
Here is forty shillings in good silver,
  Go drink it in beer or wine.'

'O thine apparel is good,' he said,
  'And mine is ragged and torn;
Wherever you go, wherever you ride,
  Laugh neer an old man to scorn.'

'Come change thy apparel with me, old churl,
  Come change thy apparel with mine;
Here are twenty pieces of good broad gold,
  Go feast thy brethren with wine.'

This development of strict parallelism in Robin's conversation with the old man reminds us of the earlier and similar phenomenon in "The King and the Barker." The difference is that the parallelism in "Robin Hood Rescuing Three Squires" is much more fully developed in the early (folio) version and becomes so thoroughgoing in the York garland that it is virtually a new thing. The comedy of Robin donning the old man's rags, for example, is exploited in four parallel stanzas in the folio version

166

(A4–7) and expanded to five in the garland (B13–17), while the narrative transitions, circumstantial and diverse in the folio version, are effected in the garland by the repeated use of a formulaic stanza (B2, 8, 18):

Now Robin Hood is to Nottingham gone,
    With a link a down and a day,
And there he met a silly old woman,
    Was weeping on the way.
      . . . .

Now Robin Hood is to Nottingham gone,
    With a link a down and a day,
And there he met with a silly old palmer,
    Was walking along the highway.
      . . . .

Now Robin Hood is to Nottingham gone,
    With a link a down and a down,
And there he met with the proud sheriff,
    Was walking along the town.

It is this kind of "block" composition by stanzas that is largely a new thing in eighteenth-century balladry. Not only did whole stanzas move from ballad to ballad with great ease, but also devices like the transition formula just quoted were widely imitated, as can be seen in this justly admired stanza from "Sir Patrick Spens" (58A3):

The king has written a braid letter,
    And signed it wi his hand,
And sent it to Sir Patrick Spence,
    Was walking on the sand.

The "rapid jump" of this transition, which Hodgart aptly calls "a classic example of montage," is thus the skilful use of a technique that is characteristic of the baroque minstrelsy of the eighteenth century.[33]

The last of the minstrel ballads in the Percy folio MS are the three love stories, "Will Stewart and John" (107), "Christopher White" (108), and "Tom Potts" (109), and the moral tale of "The Heir of Linne" (267). All are good examples of the minstrel's narrative art, but the best is undoubtedly "Will Stewart and John," which can appropriately serve as our final example of the artistic achievement of the new minstrelsy.

33. Hodgart, *The Ballads*, p. 30. Another excellent example of baroque minstrelsy is "Jock o the Side" (187).

Will Stewart languishes in care-bed for the love of the Earl of Mar's daughter, whom he has never seen. His brother John volunteers to help him win the girl and enters the service of the earl in order to have the opportunity to speak to her on his brother's behalf. The earl's daughter shows interest in Will and tells John to write him a letter. Will is to come meet her at St. Patrick's Church, bringing a hundred of his best men with him. They are to participate in "sixteen games att ball," and if they win over half of them she will "love him more tenderly." When Will receives this letter he leaps out of care-bed and follows her instructions to the letter. At St. Patrick's Church the lovers kiss under the watchful eye of the girl's mother, and Will Stewart and his men compile a percentage of .750 in the summer games. Unfortunately when Will subsequently asks the earl for his daughter's hand, the earl angrily refuses. This sends Will and John home to Argyle Castle, where Will leaps into care-bed. Shortly thereafter Will gets out of bed long enough to attend a parliament in Edinburgh, where he is made an earl, but since he still lacks his love he returns home once more to care-bed. At this point his brother John again offers to help, and, disguising himself as a beggar, he goes to speak to the Earl of Mar's daughter. She sends word by John in a letter for Will to meet her at Martingsdale and bring a hundred of his best men, and they will be married. Will follows instructions and they are married according to plan. Within a year the lady is great with child, and her father is informed of this, but without being told of the marriage. Whereupon a superfluous shotgun wedding is staged for his benefit, and thus the stubborn Earl of Mar is finally brought to give his consent to the marriage.

Perhaps better than any other ballad in the Child canon, "Will Stewart and John" illustrates that narrative symmetry which is characteristic of the new minstrelsy. As the above summary indicates, the wooing of the Earl of Mar's daughter necessitates two journeys on Will's part, one to the summer games and another for the rendezvous at Martingsdale. This fact, together with the two letters of instructions, invites a double parallelism in the narrative which the minstrel author exploits to the full. The girl's first message to Will, for example, is as follows (107, sts. 23–27):

'Bidd him meete me att St. Patricke's Church
    On Sunday after St. Andrew's day;
The fflower of Scotland will be there,
    And then begins our summer's play.

168

'And bidd him bring with him a hundred gunners,
  And rawnke ryders lett them bee,
And lett them bee of the rankest ryders
  That be to be ffound in that countrye.

'They best and worst, and all in like,
  Bidd him cloth them in one liuerye;
And ffor his men, greene is the best,
  And greene now lett their liueryes bee.

'And clothe himselfe in scarlett redd,
  That is soe seemlye ffor to see;
Ffor scarlett is a ffaire coulour,
  And pleasant allwayes in a woman's eye.

'He must play sixteene games att ball,
  Against the men of this countrye,
And if he winn the greater part,
  Then I shall love him more tenderlye.'

Will's journey is then described in such a way as to match these instructions stanza for stanza (sts. 29–32, 37):

Hee mustered together his merry men all,
  Hee mustered them soe louelilye;
He thought hee had had scarson halfe a hundred,
  Then had hee eleuen score and three.

He chose fforth a hundred of the best
  That were to be found in that countrye,
He cladd them all in one coulour,
  And greene i-wis their liueryes bee.

He cladd himselfe in scarlett redd,
  That is soe seemelye ffor to see;
Ffor scarlett is a ffaire coulor,
  And seemlye in a woman's eye.

And then towards Patricke Church he went,
  With all his men in braue array,
To gett a sight, if he might,
  And speake with his lady gay.

<blockquote>
. . . .

Sixteen games were plaid that day there—
   This is the truth as I doe say—
Willie Stewart and his merry men,
   The carryed twelue of them away.
</blockquote>

Prompted by brother John's return visit disguised as a beggar, the lady sends a second message to Will, perfectly parallel to the first, and in virtually the same language, except that she specifies Martingsdale instead of St. Patrick's Church and elopement instead of the summer games (sts. 73–77). The only lapse in this parallelism is the failure of the narrator to specify the green livery of the men and Will's scarlet clothing, pleasant to a woman's eye (sts. 80–82). Thus from beginning to end the progress of the action in "Will Stewart and John" is highlighted by a series of colorful and pageant-like repetitions; the effect is that of a carefully worked out choreography. Furthermore, the various episodes are linked by those delightful transition stanzas that show Will leaping in and out of care-bed as the ups and downs of the narrative require. In this ballad the art of the minstel is revealed at its best.

The last group of nine ballads in the folio MS are put together under the heading "domestic tragedy" not because they have very much in common (beyond what is suggested by this heading) but because they seem to lack many of those features of style and narrative structure which we have found to be associated with minstrelsy. Stated more positively, they seem to represent a new kind of ballad, the kind which was destined to replace minstrelsy in the eighteenth century. As is usual in such cases, however, the ballads in this group exhibit a great variety of characteristics, for in them we see ballad style in an age of transition. That which unites them is their concentration on a moment of violence or high emotion; their diversity arises from the variety of influences from medieval romance, chronicle, and international balladry that give substance and impact to the narrative. The magnetic field which attracted these diverse elements was probably some actual event or deed of violence, as we know to be true in the case of "Sir John Butler" (165) and "Captain Car" (178), but in most cases the actual people and events have been forgotten, and in the ballads character and action have been made to conform to archetypal patterns determined by the selection of narrative features from earlier romance, chronicles, or international balladry. The result is a conflation of motifs which makes these ballads difficult to categorize,

170

unless we perhaps speak of them as "composites." The kind of re-creation of domestic tragedy they contain can also be found in Elizabethan drama, for example, in *Arden of Feversham,* where the scenes on the fog-bound Kentish coast involving a macabre ferryman (IV, ii–iii) give an added dimension to the sordid murder plot by means of the classic stygian setting. In somewhat analogous fashion are the assignation, adultery, and murder themes treated in our ballads of domestic tragedy.

The original form of "Earl Brand" (7) is somewhat of a mystery, since the folio version (which is the earliest) is in quatrains, while some of the nineteenth-century versions are in couplets with refrain and differ considerably in the details of the story. It is therefore especially regrettable that the folio version is a fragment. There is evidence, however, that the ballad was popular in the early seventeenth century,[34] and I suspect that the later ballad of "Johnie Cock" (114) is an adaptation of it to a greenwood setting. Other instances of its influence are difficult to establish because of the lack of a complete early version. Nevertheless, it seems likely that "Earl Brand" became an archetypal domestic tragedy which contributed its share of memorable stanzas to the growing treasury of ballad commonplaces.

"Young Andrew" (48) survives uniquely in the Percy folio MS and offers a sharp contrast to "Earl Brand" in that it seems to have had no influence on other ballads, but is itself a composite of bits and pieces borrowed from others. Child recognized elements of "Lady Isabel and the Elf-Knight" (4) and "The Fair Flower of Northumberland" (9), to which might be added "The Knight and the Shepherd's Daughter" (110) and "Crow and Pie" (111) for the battle of the sexes theme (48, sts. 3–4), and "Earl Brand" for the motif of the seven brethren (48, st. 21). The ending of "Young Andrew" is defective, but it would appear that the villain is slain by a wolf. Child remarks: "Why he was not promptly disposed of, and how the wolf comes into the story, will probably never be known."[35] It may well be, however, that the distinctive wolf ending represents the most prominent feature of the historical incident that prompted this ballad, and that the borrowings were woven together to provide a composite assignation story leading up to the known historical fact of the villain's death. The seven brethren are invoked, for instance, but they never appear, probably because they are simply one of the motifs introduced to provide a prelude to the real-life climax. That ballads

34. *ESPB,* II, 457 n.   35. *ESPB,* I, 432.

have continued to be composed in the manner of "Young Andrew" can be seen in such recent examples as "Naomi Wise" and "The Banks of the Ohio."

So much attention has been paid to the problem of the origin of "Sir Aldingar" (59) that its subsequent history and influence have been largely ignored. Yet it is possible to argue that echoes of this venerable ballad can be detected in "Little Musgrave and Lady Barnard" (81), "Glasgerion" (67), "Old Robin of Portingale" (80), and "Child Maurice" (83), all belonging in the group of domestic tragedies now under discussion and all featuring assignations leading to violence.

It will be recalled that "Sir Aldingar" tells of the attempt by a false steward, Aldingar, to commit adultery with the queen. When she spurns his request, he deceives a poor leper and persuades him to lie in the queen's bed. Quickly then he goes to the king, telling him that the queen has chosen a new love, and offers to show him the proof. The king replies (59A10–11):

'If this be true, thou Aldingar,
    That thou dost tell to me,
Then will I make thee a rich knight
    Both of gold and fee.

'But if it be false, Sir Aldingar,
    That thou doest tell to me,
Then looke for noe other death
    But to be hangd on a tree.
Goe with me,' saide our comly king,
    'This lazar for to see.'

They go to the queen's chamber where they of course find the leper, and the king accuses the queen, who immediately realizes that Sir Aldingar is responsible for the deception. She laments her plight and describes a dream in which a griffin carried her crown away and would have seized and carried her to his nest also, had it not been for a little hawk who slew the griffin and rescued her. She appeals for a knight who will come and fight with Aldingar to maintain the justice of her cause in a trial by combat. Messengers are sent out, and one of them meets a little child, who promises to help the queen, and repeats her dream almost verbatim. On the day when the queen is to be burned, the child appears and challenges the contemptuous Aldingar to fight (59A42):

Saies, The first stroke that's giuen, Sir Aldingar,
    I will giue vnto thee,
And if the second giue thou may,
    Looke then thou spare not mee.

As it turns out, Aldingar is unable to deliver a return stroke, for the child with one blow cuts off both of his legs at the knee (A46):

'A preist, a preist,' says Aldingar,
    'me for to houzle and shriue!
A preist, a preist,' sayes Aldingar,
    'While I am a man liuing a-liue!'

He then proceeds to confess his adulterous desires, the planting of the leper in the queen's bed, and concludes with the medieval equivalent of *crime does not pay*: "Falsing neuer doth well." The last words of his repentance are a request for forgiveness and an appeal to the king to love his wife (A51–52):

'Forgiue, forgiue me, queene, Madam!
    For Christs loue forgiue me!'
'God forgaue his death, Aldingar,
    And freely I forgiue thee.'

'Now take thy wife, thou King Harry,
    And loue her as thou shold;
Thy wiffe shee is as true to thee
    As stone that lies on the castle wall.'

In the ballad of "Little Musgrave" adultery is not merely threatened but accomplished. The two meet at church and quickly disclose their love for each other (81A5):

Quoth she, I have loved thee, Little Musgrave,
    Full long and many a day;
So have I loved you, fair lady,
    Yet never word durst I say.'[36]

They arrange to lie together that night in Lady Barnard's bower, but their conversation is overheard by a little footpage, who hastens to Lord Barnard with the news. Lord Barnard's reply is (81B2–3):

36. It is necessary to resort to the *Wit Restord* version (1658) here since the folio text is defective.

'If it be trew, thou little foote-page,
    This tale thou hast told to mee,
Then all my lands in Bucklesfeildberry
    I'le freely giue to thee.

'But if this be a lye, thou little foot-page,
    This tale thou hast told to mee,
Then on the highest tree in Bucklesfeildberry
    All hanged that thou shalt bee.'

When Lord Barnard confronts the lovers in his wife's bower, he graciously provides Musgrave with a sword and the battle begins (81A23):

The first stroke that Little Musgrave stroke,
    He hurt Lord Barnard sore;
The next stroke that Lord Barnard stroke,
    Little Musgrave nere struck more.

Seeing the death of her lover, Lady Barnard vows to pray for his soul,
something which, she pointedly adds, she will not do for her own husband. This is too much for Lord Barnard (81A26):

He cut her paps from off her brest;
    Great pitty it was to see
That some drops of this ladie's heart's blood
    Ran trickling downe her knee.

But the violence of this deed brings him to his senses and he repents
and praises the lovers (81A27–28):

'Woe worth you, woe worth, my mery men all
    You were nere borne for my good;
Why did you not offer to stay my hand,
    When you see me wax so wood?

'For I have slaine the bravest sir knight
    That ever rode on steed;
So have I done the fairest lady
    That ever did woman's deed.'

This flamboyant tragedy is probably based on some actual event, but a
few traces of the Aldingar pattern are evident, notably the stanzas beginning "If it be trew," etc., the two strokes of the fight, and the repentance stanzas at the end just quoted above. Since "Little Musgrave" was

174

destined to be very popular and influential, one can be deceived into supposing that the connection between it and "Sir Aldingar" is merely due to the sharing of ballad commonplaces. But this view is simply the consequence of the failure of ballad scholars to study the chronological development of balladry. A motif or theme had to be created before it could become common, and stylistic analysis can often reveal whether a particular stanza is indigenous or transplanted, as may be seen in the following examples.

The assignation theme in "Glasgerion" (67) has attracted a number of miscellaneous motifs. The meeting of the would-be lovers is occasioned by the fact that Glasgerion is a skilled harper in the royal court. When he harps before the king's daughter, she praises his skill, and he reveals his love for her (67A4):

'Faire might you fall, lady!' quoth hee;
    'Who taught you now to speake?
I haue loued you, lady, seuen yeere;
    My hart I durst neere breake.'

She then invites him to her bower that night, just as Lady Barnard invited Little Musgrave. But from this point forward the plot of the anticipated lover dominates, and the ballad introduces the deceiving "lither lad" (perhaps a reversal of Barnard's loyal page) who takes his master's place with the king's daughter. The action in general is poorly motivated, and the naïveté of the lad in assuming he will not be found out suggests that "Glasgerion" is a composite ballad on the order of "Young Andrew."

In "Old Robin of Portingale" (80) the adultery theme of "Little Musgrave" is re-created using the January–May situation, the old husband and young wife, best known in Chaucer's "Merchant's Tale." This plot, usually given a comic or satiric turn, in the ballad has a tragic outcome. Old Robin's little foot page overhears the lady plotting with Sir Gyles, the false steward, to kill her husband. He informs Old Robin, who pretends illness and is lying in wait fully armed when the steward and his men come in. The old man kills them all, and when his wife enters, kills her too.

Although "Old Robin" is clearly a composite, it is skilfully put together. The loyalty of the little foot page, who in "Little Musgrave" swims rivers to reach Lord Barnard, is expressed in "Old Robin" by sheer grief (80, st. 8):

He mourned, sikt, and wept full sore;
    I sweare by the holy roode,
The teares he for his master wept
    Were blend water and bloude.

With this stanza compare the following from "Earl Brand" (7F5):

He leaned ore his saddle bow
    To kisse this lady good;
The teares that went them two betweene
    Were blend water and blood.

This is an inspired and just expression of the plight of the two lovers in "Earl Brand"; as an expression of the little foot page's sympathy for his master, the padded imitation in "Old Robin" is excessive and lacking in decorum. Here is a remarkably good example of the way in which stylistic analysis can distinguish between original and borrowed stanzas.

Most of the remainder of "Old Robin" is taken or adapted from "Little Musgrave." This is evident in the old man's response to the foot page's information (80, sts. 13–14):

'If it be true, my little foot-page,
    Ile make thee heyre of all my land.'
'If it be not true, my deare master,
    God let me neuer thye:'
'If it be not true, thou litle foot-page,
    A dead corse shalt thou be.'

The fight between Old Robin and his would-be assassins is of course not a duel, and it is therefore not at all reminiscent of "Little Musgrave." Immediately after the battle, however, the lady enters the room (80, sts. 27–28):

And the first thinge that this ladye stumbled vpon
    Was of Sir Gyles his ffoote;
Sayes, Euer alacke, and woe is me,
    Here lyes my sweete hart-roote!

And the second thing that this ladie stumbled on
    Was of Sir Gyles his head;
Sayes, Euer alacke, and woe is me,
    Heere lyes my true-loue deade!

176

It is tempting to suppose that this particularly gruesome example of incremental repetition owes its inspiration to "Little Musgrave" (81A23):

> The first stroke that Little Musgrave stroke,
>> He hurt Lord Barnard sore;
> The next stroke that Lord Barnard stroke,
>> Little Musgrave nere struck more.

This sort of thing is difficult to prove, but there can be no mistake about the conclusion that follows the lady's discovery of Sir Gyles' body. Here Old Robin equals and then surpasses the vindictive ferocity of Lord Barnard (80, st. 29):

> He cutt the papps beside her brest,
>> And bad her wish her will;
> And he cutt the eares beside her heade,
>> And bade her wish on still.

Immediately Old Robin repents of his violence, although, unlike Lord Barnard, he has no merry men to rebuke for not restraining him (80, st. 30):

> 'Mickle is the mans blood I haue spent,
>> To doe thee and me some good;'
> Says, Euer alacke, my fayre lady,
>> I thinke that I was woode!

Whereupon he makes his foot page his heir, and he himself goes on a pilgrimage to the Holy Land, a conclusion which seems somewhat antiquarian. In putting "Old Robin" ahead of "Little Musgrave" Child may have intended to suggest that it was the earlier ballad.[37] The stylistic evidence indicates, however, that "Little Musgrave" was the model on which the narrative of "Old Robin" was fashioned.

"Child Maurice" (83) is a particularly interesting variation on the assignation theme of "Little Musgrave and Lady Barnard," with perhaps a suggestion or two also drawn from the archetypal "Sir Aldingar" (59). Child Maurice is hunting in the silver wood and sends his little foot page to John Steward's wife with a cryptic message and two tokens, a mantel and a ring. The cryptic message reminds us of the symbolic dream of the

---

37. Child says: "The information given by a page, the reward promised and the alternative punishment threatened him, the savage vengeance taken on the lady and the immediate remorse, are repeated in 'Little Musgrave,' No. 81" (*ESPB*, II, 240).

queen in "Sir Aldingar," especially since, like the dream, it is repeated later on in a functional way to advance the plot. As a matter of fact in "Child Maurice" the foot page repeats the message entirely to the lady, at which time her husband overhears it, and then John Steward repeats the tokens to prove to Child Maurice that he knows about the assignation.

The influence of "Little Musgrave" on this ballad is less obvious than it was in "Old Robin of Portingale," but it is nevertheless present. We do not find, for example, the stanzas beginning "If this be true, thou little tinny page . . ." (81A11), since the truth or falsity of the message delivered by the page is not so crucial as to call for either an inheritance or a hanging. Yet one of these stanzas does seem to be echoed in the words of John Steward's wife (83A16):

'Now peace, now peace, thou litle ffoot-page,
    Ffor Christes sake, I pray thee!
Ffor if my lord heare one of these words,
    Thou must be hanged hye!'

But of course her husband does overhear and goes to the silver wood to seek Child Maurice. When he finds him, he exclaims (83A22):

How now, how now, Child Maurice?
Alacke, how may this bee?

This is certainly a dramatic moment in the ballad, but these lines lack the sharp impact of Lord Barnard's exclamation (81A19):

How now, how now, thou Littell Musgrave,
    Doest thou find my lady sweet?

The fight between John Steward and Child Maurice, though described with less economy than the one between Lord Barnard and Little Musgrave, is nevertheless similar in its incremental technique (83A26–27):

But hee pulled forth a bright browne sword,
    And dryed itt on the grasse,
And soe ffast he smote att Iohn Steward,
    I-wisse he neuer did rest.

Then hee pulled fforth his bright browne sword,
    And dryed itt on his sleeue,
And the ffirst good stroke Iohn Stewart stroke,
    Child Maurice head he did cleeue.

John Steward carries the head back home and offers it to his wife, telling her to embrace and kiss it, "for thou lovedst him better than me." This of course corresponds to the grim and passionate conclusion of "Little Musgrave," when Lady Barnard vows to pray for her lover and not her husband. But suddenly, at this point in "Child Maurice" we are presented with a dramatic revelation (83A30):

But when shee looked on Child Maurice head,
    Shee neuer spake words but three:
'I neuer beare no child but one,
    And you haue slaine him trulye.'

The ballad ends with John Steward's repentance (83A31–32):

Sayes, Wicked be my merrymen all,
    I gaue meate, drinke, and clothe!
But cold they not haue holden me
    When I was in all that wrath!

'Ffor I haue slaine one of the curteousest knights
    That euer bestrode a steed,
Soe haue I done one of the fairest ladyes
    That euer ware womans weede!'

These two stanzas are obviously transplanted from "Little Musgrave," where Lord Barnard's rebuke to the merry men who accompanied him to Buckellsfordbery makes sense. No such preparation for John Steward's merry men exists in the other ballad. The stanza praising Child Maurice and the lady, moreover, seems to ignore the previous dramatic disclosure of their relationship and is in fact verbally quite close to its counterpart in "Little Musgrave." Here we have another example of the way in which a comparative analysis can determine the direction of borrowing.

Concerning "Child Maurice" the editors of the Percy folio MS observe: "For the overpowering vigour of its objective style it may be compared with *Little Musgrave and Lady Barnard*."[38] To this I would merely add my belief that such a comparison suggests itself because "Child Maurice" was inspired by the latter ballad. But it is no mere imitation. The revelation of the child's identity at the end introduces a new dimension of drama into the ballad form. John Home's selection of "Child Maurice" as the basis of his tragedy of *Douglas* (1756) was not an arbitrary choice, and it is probably no accident that dramatic ballads like

38. Hales and Furnivall, *Bishop Percy's Folio Manuscript*, II, 500.

5. The Percy folio manuscript   179

the "Edward" of Percy's *Reliques* (1765) appear in increasing numbers in the eighteenth century.

The one ballad that remains to be discussed in the present chapter, "Child Waters" (63), is difficult to classify, but it is undoubtedly the best in the Percy folio MS. It has affinities with such different literary works as Chaucer's "Clerk's Tale," "The Nut-Brown Maid," "The Knight and Shepherd's Daughter" (110), and "Ladyes Ffall" (in the folio MS, p. 268). Although not technically a tragedy, I would judge that by virtue of its style it belongs with the domestic tragedies just considered rather than with the ballads of the new minstrelsy.

The intensity of emotion in "Child Waters" is of course found in many of the ballads, particularly the eighteenth-century ones, but most of these are much shorter and achieve their emotional effects by compression. The singular excellence of "Child Waters," I believe, is attributable to its emotional intensity combined with a leisurely narrative. There is little leaping, but much lingering. Paired stanzas with extensive and measured parallelism are very common (63A4–5, 6–7, 11–12, etc.), and no less than six stanzas are required to describe the arrival of Ellen and Child Waters at the hall (63A18–23):

'Seest thou not yonder hall, Ellen?
    Of redd gold shine the yates;
There's four and twenty ffayre ladyes,
    The ffairest is my wordlye make.

'Seest thou not yonder hall, Ellen?
    Of redd gold shineth the tower;
There is four and twenty ffaire ladyes,
    The fairest is my paramoure.'

'I doe see the hall now, Child Waters,
    That of redd gold shineth the yates;
God giue good then of your selfe,
    And of your wordlye make!

'I doe see the hall now, Child Waters,
    That of redd gold shineth the tower;
God giue good then of your selfe,
    And of your paramoure!'

There were four and twenty ladyes,
    Were playing att the ball,
And Ellen, was the ffairest ladye,
    Must bring his steed to the stall.

180

There were four and twenty faire ladyes
    Was playing att the chesse;
And Ellen, shee was the ffairest ladye,
    Must bring his horsse to grasse.

After Ellen endures a series of painful humiliations, and in spite of her advanced pregnancy, Child Waters orders her up early in the morning to feed his horse, showing the most scrupulous concern for the animal's diet (63A31–32):

This night and itt droue on affterward
    Till itt was neere the day:
He sayd, Rise vp, my litle ffoote-page,
    And giue my steed corne and hay;
And soe doe thou the good blacke oates,
    That he may carry me the better away.

And vp then rose Ffaire Ellen,
    And gaue his steed corne and hay,
And soe shee did and the good blacke oates,
    That he might carry him the better away.

The most agonizing use of leisurely narration, however, comes near the end. Ellen has fed the horse, and while still in the stable alone she is seized with the pangs of childbirth. The mother of Child Waters hears her groans and calls to him to rise. With perfect objectivity the narrator describes the unfathomable calm of the man as he dresses to go down to the stable (63A35–36):

But vp then rose Child Waters,
    And did on his shirt of silke;
Then he put on his other clothes
    On his body as white as milke.

And when he came to the stable-dore,
    Full still that hee did stand,
That hee might heare now Faire Ellen,
    How shee made her monand.

In a manner that defies analysis, the ballad poet has succeeded in suggesting the godlike, otherworldly character of Child Waters, without which his testing of fair Ellen would be intolerable. As a result of this achievement the ending of the ballad comes, like the restoration of Job's fortunes in the biblical narrative, as a solemn benediction in response to Ellen's lament (63A37–38):

5. The Percy folio manuscript   181

Shee said, Lullaye, my owne deere child!
    Lullabye, deere child, deere!
I wold thy father were a king,
    Thy mother layd on a beere!

'Peace now,' he said, 'good Faire Ellen,
    And be of good cheere, I thee pray,
And the bridall and the churching both,
    They shall bee vpon one day.'

We have now concluded our survey of the romances, histories, songs, and ballads in the Percy folio MS. Although in a sense it is a miscellany, the large corpus of late medieval minstrelsy in the collection is its outstanding feature. The conjunction of romances and ballads in the MS is not the fortuitous result of random collecting, but rather it attests the genetic relationship between these two genres which has been suggested in the present study. By this I do *not* mean that "the ballads as a whole are simply fragments of Romances,"[39] but that romances provided the style and narrative technique that determined the evolution of the popular ballad. Interestingly enough, as we have seen, several stages in this evolution can be observed between the covers of the Percy folio MS.

39. Hodgart, *The Ballads*, p. 77.

6. Revenant ballads

In this chapter we depart temporarily from the strict chronological analysis previously employed in order to consider the revenant ballads, those that depict otherworld figures or in some way relate to the return of the dead from the grave. It is appropriate to discuss these ballads here, since the earliest of them are found in the seventeenth century; but it is also important that they be taken as a group, including those that first appear in later periods, for it is only in this way that the origin, development, and achievement of revenant balladry can be adequately recognized.

Most discussions of the popular ballad make a sharp distinction between the lore of the ballad world and the beliefs of Christianity. Wimberly has even suggested, in his otherwise excellent study entitled *Folklore in the English and Scottish Ballads,* that the best ballads are the most pagan ones:

> Certain conceptions of the Otherworld as portrayed in British balladry are more or less Christian in character. But we should repeat here, what we have already observed from time to time in the preceding chapters, that Christian thought in our popular poetry is on the whole alien and intrusive. Our best ballads are pagan at heart, fully as much so as the traditional songs of Scandinavia, and their religion is as heathen as that of the Helgi lays.[1]

One gets the impression from Wimberly's book that the folk have kept alive a pagan cosmology distinct from Christianity and with a vitality of its own. Obvious Christian elements in the ballads are dismissed as "intrusions." Even so acute a critic as Hodgart seems to accept this view without reservation.[2]

To deny the existence of a body of popular lore about death and the otherworld would be foolish indeed, but I think it is more meaningful and illuminating in studying the ballad to see this folklore as giving popular substance to Christian belief rather than standing in opposition

1. Lowry C. Wimberly, *Folklore in the English and Scottish Ballads* (New York, 1928), p. 401.

2. Hodgart, *The Ballads*, chap. vi, "The Folklore of the Ballads," pp. 114–130.

to it. The folk imagination is entirely free of the ideological perspectives of modern anthropology, and it can therefore operate in perfect harmony with Christian thought. The revenant ballads are a good illustration of this point.

It has been customary, following Wimberly, to regard the bodily revenant of the ballads as a folk concept and the disembodied spirit or ghost as "literary" or "Christian." But Christianity itself is ambiguous on this point. The soul-body dualism of the Greeks is unmistakably present in Christian tradition, but so is the unitary conception of the Jews, as can be seen in the insistence of the Apostle's Creed on a resurrection of the body. Thus in the *Cursor Mundi* the dead that appear portentously at the crucifixion arise literally from their graves and "coomen to toun amonge men," while in the alliterative poem *Piers the Plowman* a "ded bodye" comes out of a deep grave to announce the beginning of a battle between Life and Death (the "Harrowing of Hell") and then sinks back into the earth.[3] This is perfectly consistent with the Jewish emphasis of the Gospels on the bodily resurrection of Jesus and is a common feature of the depiction of the returning dead in medieval literature. The ballad revenant is archaic but not pagan.

Before turning to the revenant ballads themselves it will be helpful first to recognize that the otherworld of balladry, like the revenant himself, is based on Christian beliefs enlarged and expanded by the folk imagination. The evidence for this, however, comes not from oral tradition, but from medieval legend, as can be seen, for example, in "The Turke and Gowin" and "Thomas of Ersseldoune."[4] These late metrical romances both contain the journey under a hill to the otherworld, suggestive of Celtic folk tradition, and in the latter text this is curiously combined with a vision of heaven, paradise, purgatory, and hell. The presence of this unmistakably Christian vision in the medieval romance itself has made it difficult for critics to argue that the same phenomenon in the ballad of "Thomas Rymer" is an intrusion. But in any case such an argument is completely unnecessary. Imaginative extensions of what might be called the orthodox Christian landscape are very common in medieval legend and romance.

A good illustration of the medieval otherworld journey in a Christian

3. Richard Morris (ed.), *Cursor Mundi.* London, 1874–93. 3 vols. (EETS OS nos. 57, 99, 101). Quotation from II, 961, lines 16795 ff. Skeat (ed.), *Piers the Plowman*; quotation from B text, passus XVIII, 62 ff. The same kind of revivifying of dead bodies is depicted in the apocryphal Gospel of Nicodemus.

4. Percy folio MS, pp. 38–46 ("The Turke and Gowin"), and Child, *ESPB*, I, 326-329 ("Thomas of Ersseldoune").

setting is the late metrical tale of *A Father and his Son*.[5] This text is particularly interesting in connection with the ballads since it is found in the Cambridge University Library MS Ff.5.48, which includes "King Edward and the Shepherd" (cf. Child 273), "Robin Hood and the Monk" (119), and "Thomas of Ersseldoune" (cf. Child 37). In it a son is allowed to see his dead father, who had been guilty of adultery and is suffering eternal punishment in hell. By contrast, he is also permitted to see his dead uncle, a good man, enjoying the bliss of paradise. The child is praying by his father's grave when there comes one in a white surplice who privily takes him by the sleeve, offering to lead him to where he can see his father burning in hell:

> He led hym till a cumly hill,
>> The erth opeynd, in thei gede,
> Smoke and fyre ther can out well
>> And mony gests gloyng on glede.

Even more interesting and detailed is the description of paradise. The angel conducts the child to a fair forest:

> He led hym to a fayre erber
>> The ʒatis were of clen cristall
> To his siʒt wer passyng fayre
>> And briʒt as any beriall.

> The wallis semyd of gold briʒt
>> With durris and with toures strong
> They herd vpon the ʒatis on height
>> Mynstralsy and the angel song.

> The pellican and the popyniay
>> The tornor and the turtil trew
> A hundirth thousand vpon hy
>> The nyʒtyngale with notis new.

This is immediately recognizable as a form of the literary garden so popular in medieval poetry.[6] Based on the biblical garden of Genesis with additions from apocrypha like the legend of Seth,[7] this garden with its

5. Hartshorne, *Ancient Metrical Tales*, pp. 169–178.
6. See D. W. Robertson, Jr., "The Doctrine of Charity in Mediaeval Literary Gardens," *Speculum*, XXVI (1951), 24–49. It is of course unlikely that the iconographical significance of these gardens is operable in the metrical romances and ballads. The situation is similar to that of the carols, which preserve fragments of themes from biblical exegesis no longer understood. See chap. ii, above.
7. Quinn, *The Quest of Seth*.

6. Revenant ballads   185

characteristic landscape can be found in the *Roman de la Rose,* Chaucer's *Parliament of Fowls,* the *hortus deliciarum* of *Cursor Mundi, Piers the Plowman, Pearl,* and many other poems and romances of the later Middle Ages.[8] But we need not look so far afield. Precisely the same garden can be found in the "pagan" otherworld of "Thomas of Ersseldoune" (37App 32–33):

> Scho lede hym in-till a faire erbere,
>> Whare frwte was growand gret plentee;
> Pere and appill, bothe ryppe þay were,
>> The date, and als the damasee.
>
> þe fygge, and alsso þe wyneberye,
>> The nyghtgales byggande on þair neste;
> þe papeioyes faste abowte gane flye,
>> And throstylls sange, wolde hafe no reste.

Returning to *A Father and his Son,* we find that the child is next permitted to behold a strange bleeding tree on a green hill. The angel explains the signification of this tree:

> The angel seid this is the tre
>> That god adam the frute forbede
> And therfore dryvon owt was he
>> And in the erth his life he lede.
>
> Ffor in the same place that thou seest hit blede
>> Grew the appull that adam bote
> And that was thorow Evys rede
>> And the deuoll of hell wol I wot.

The angel goes on to explain that the tree bleeds every time a sinner approaches it. This is a remarkable example of the use of an ancient folk motif for didactic purposes, similar in its conception to the scorched footprints of Adam and Eve described in the legend of Seth. But especially interesting in this connection is the parallel passage in "Thomas of Ersseldoune" where Thomas starts to pluck some of the fruit of the garden (37App34–35):

> He pressede to pulle frowte with his hande,
>> Als mane for fude þat was nere faynt;
> Scho sayd, Thomas þou late þame stande,
>> Or ells þe fende the will atteynt.

8. Some relevant comparisons are made in my earlier book, *Piers the Plowman:* *Literary Relations of the A and B Texts,* pp. 66–71.

If þou it plokk, sothely to saye,
    Thi saule gose to þe fyre of helle;
It commes neuer owte or domesdaye,
    Bot þer in payne aye for to duelle.

Concerning this passage Child remarks: "It was not that Thomas was about to pluck fruit from the Forbidden Tree . . . ."[9] But surely this is exactly what he was about to do, and it is no accident that immediately following these stanzas comes the vision of heaven, paradise, purgatory, and hell (sts. 36–41). Thomas Rymer's elfland is clearly a province in the Christian otherworld of the romance.

Keeping in mind the importance of medieval conceptions of the otherworld, we may now turn to a consideration of the ballads themselves. The earliest of the revenant ballads is "Fair Margaret and Sweet William" (74), first alluded to in Beaumont and Fletcher's *Knight of the Burning Pestle* (1611), and preserved in a broadside of the late seventeenth century. Margaret and William are lovers, but for reasons that are not explained William takes another bride, and Margaret dies of grief. On William's wedding night the "spirit" of Margaret comes and stands at William's feet, saying (74A6):

'God give you joy, you two true lovers,
    In bride-bed fast asleep;
Loe I am going to my green grass grave,
    And am in my winding-sheet.'

The following morning, curiously enough, William says nothing about the appearance of Margaret and instead merely tells the bride that he dreamed his bower was full of red swine and his bridebed full of blood. He then rides to fair Margaret's bower, where he is admitted by her seven brothers, and learns that Margaret is dead. In his grief he utters a vow (74A13):

'I'll do more for thee, Margaret,
    Than any of thy kin;
For I will kiss thy pale wan lips,
    Tho a smile I cannot win.'

This is the traditional "vow of austerities" used for example in "The Squier" (Percy MS, p. 444) and "Clerk Saunders" (69A20–22), but here it is combined with the kiss of death motif found in later revenant balladry (77B4):

9. Child, *ESPB*, I, 322 n.

'My mouth it is full cold, Margret
    It has the smell now of the ground;
And if I kiss thy comely mouth,
    Thy life-days will not be long.'

Instead of the customary self-denials, William vows to kiss the dead girl
and thus bring an end to his life. His subsequent remarks about his own
funeral suggest an awareness that his "days will not be long." The ballad
concludes with the rose and brier growing out of the graves, suggesting
the union of the two lovers after death.

It is worth noting that although Margaret is our earliest ballad ghost,
she appears to be a disembodied spirit rather than the bodily revenant
that the studies of Wimberly and others might lead us to expect. But in
light of what has been said above about the ambiguity of the Christian
tradition concerning the dead, this should not be surprising. The coming
of a spirit to announce the death of a loved one can be traced easily and
directly through the Middle Ages back to classical times, as can be seen
in the story of Ceyx and Alcione, first told by Ovid, retold by the French
poet Machaut, and incorporated by Chaucer in one of his earliest poems,
The Book of the Duchess.[10]

As Chaucer tells the story King Ceyx is lost at sea, and his loving
wife Alcione prays to Juno to send her a dream that will inform her
whether her lord is alive or dead. In answer to this prayer Juno sends a
messenger to Morpheus, the god of sleep, with the following instructions:

Sey thus on my half, that he
Go faste into the grete se,
And byd him that, on alle thyng,
He take up Seys body the kyng,
That lyeth ful pale and nothyng rody.
Bid hym crepe into the body,
And doo hit goon to Alcione
The quene, ther she lyeth allone,
And shewe hir shortly, hit ys no nay,
How hit was dreynt thys other day;
And do the body speke ryght soo,
Ryght as hyt was woned to doo
The whiles that hit was alyve.[11]

10. Ovid's *Metamorphoses*, Machaut's
Dit de la Fonteinne Amoureuse; see also
F. N. Robinson (ed.), *Chaucer's Complete Works* (2nd ed.; Boston, 1957),
notes to *The Book of the Duchess*, from
which quotations are taken.
    11. *Book of the Duchess*, pp. 139–151.

The messenger journeys down to the "dark valley" where he finds Morpheus and gives him his orders. The god of sleep follows instructions to the letter:

> Took up the dreynte body sone
> And bar hyt forth to Alcione,
> Hys wif the quene, ther as she lay
> Ryght even a quarter before day,
> And stood ryght at hyr beddes fet,
> And called hir ryght as she het
> By name, and sayde, "My swete wyf,
> Awake! let be your sorwful lyf!
> For in your sorwe there lyth no red.
> For, certes, swete, I nam but ded;
> Ye shul me never on lyve yse."[12]

Although this seems to say that the body of Ceyx is actually taken up and brought to Alcione, I think we are meant to understand that Morpheus assumed the likeness of his body in Alcione's dream, as is confirmed by the fact that he goes on, in Chaucer's poem, to ask her to bury his body, and gives her directions where the body may be found "the see besyde." He then bids her farewell, and "With that hir eyen up she casteth / And saw noght," which I take it means that the apparition vanished. On the third day thereafter Alcione died.

In addition to the mode of representation of the dead in Chaucer's "Ceyx and Alcione," it is important to notice the purpose of the visitation. "Awake! let be your sorwful lyf!" says the ghost, "For in your sorwe there lyth no red." This is of course a major theme in dialogues with departed spirits. Such is the theme of the Middle English alliterative poem, Pearl,[13] just as surely as it is the theme of the ballad of "The Unquiet Grave" (78A7):

> 'The stalk is withered dry, my love,
>   So will our hearts decay;
> So make yourself content, my love,
>   Till God calls you away.'

The fact that the tears of the bereaved disturb the repose of the dead, so often noted as an example of "folklore" in the ballads, is simply a vivid realization of the consolation theme and as such is indistinguishable from

12. Ibid., pp. 195–205.   13. E. V. Gordon (ed.), Pearl (Oxford, 1953).

6. Revenant ballads   189

the common Christian orientation of the elegiac tradition.

In addition to pointing up similarities, the juxtaposition of Chaucer's "Ceyx and Alcione" and "Fair Margaret and Sweet William" serves to call our attention to certain ways in which the ballad deviates from the expected pattern. First, although the visitation is for the purpose of informing William of Margaret's death, the situation is complicated by the fact that the ghost confronts him in the bridebed. As a result, the announcement of the death of the beloved is no longer merely pathetic in its effect, as in Chaucer, but ironic—"God give you joy, you two true lovers"—and William is forced to invent a dream vague enough to avoid offending his bride but ominous enough to justify his immediate departure to Lady Margaret's bower. Because of these developments the consolation theme is lost, and the action concludes with a rather pointless argument between William and the seven brothers over his right to kiss the corpse. All the evidence suggests that a traditional ghostly visitation has in this ballad been modified to serve as a vehicle for a love-triangle plot. The author has done his work skilfully, while at the same time admittedly he has sentimentalized the *memento mori* theme. This is perhaps best illustrated in his variation of the kiss of death motif: "For I will kiss thy pale wan lips,/Tho a smile I cannot win." In these lines authentic grief has been overridden by the demands of the broadside market.

Whatever reservations we may have about the artistry of "Fair Margaret and Sweet William," its influence on subsequent generations of singers and poets seems to have been considerable. Not only does the rose and brier motif spread rapidly in the eighteenth century, as we have seen, to numerous other ballads, but revenant endings are added to such various ballads as "The Twa Sisters" (10N-Q), "The Twa Brothers" (49B-C), "Lord Thomas and Fair Annet" (73E-H), and "Lord Lovel" (75I). Many new ballads are composed. "Proud Lady Margaret" (47) is a gothic reconstruction of the *memento mori* theme using the riddle formula; "The Wife of Usher's Well" (79A) is an imaginative evocation of the revenant experience, to which Scott's followers seem to have added a prologue in "The Clerk's Twa Sons o Owsenford" (72); and "The Brown Girl" (295), a late eighteenth-century composite, provides the inevitable parody as can be seen, for example, in its reversal of the vow of austerities (295A8):

'I'll do as much for my true-love
    As other maidens may;

I'll dance and sing on my love's grave
    A whole twelvemonth and a day.'

As might be expected in the age of Daniel Defoe and "The Apparition of Mrs. Veal" (1706),[14] broadside balladry contributed its share of revenant narratives. "The Suffolk Miracle" (272) is a version of the Spectre Bridegroom story which survives in a Cornish folktale collected in the nineteenth century. But the broadside is scarcely a ballad in the usual sense; as Child remarks, "this piece could not be admitted here on its own merits,"[15] nor does it survive in subsequent oral tradition. Far more interesting is the case of "James Harris (The Daemon Lover)" (243), which begins as a broadside of 1685. James Harris, a seaman, and Jane Reynolds, who lived near Plymouth, were engaged to be married, but he was forced to go to sea before the ceremony could be performed. When news later arrived that Harris died in a foreign land, Jane married a carpenter and had three pretty children. But one night when the carpenter was away a "spirit" came to Jane's window, identified himself as James Harris, her former love, and tempted her to leave her husband and children and go with him to sea (243A27):

When he had told her these fair tales,
    To love him she began,
Because he was in human shape,
    Much like unto a man.

The broadside gives no account of the death at sea of the wife but instead concentrates on the grief and suicide of the carpenter and the pathetic plight of the orphaned children.

What happens to the broadside when it enters the ballad tradition can be seen in the late eighteenth-century "Rambler's Garland" version (243B), which reduces the story to less than half its original length, omits the preliminaries and courtship of the lovers, the voyage and death of the seaman, and begins in the "last act" with the lover speaking to the wife. It retains the temptation stanzas but reduces the domestic tragedy ending of the broadside to a brief expression of sorrow by the carpenter

14. For the "factual" basis of Defoe's account, see Arthur H. Scouten, "An Early Printed Report on the Apparition of Mrs. Veal," *RES*, VI (1955), 259–263.
15. Child, *ESPB*, V, 58. He gives the real reason for including "The Suffolk Miracle" in these words: "I have printed this ballad because, in a blurred, enfeebled, and disfigured shape, it is the representative in England of one of the most remarkable tales and one of the most impressive and beautiful ballads of the European continent" (V, 59).

and, significantly, introduces a short dialogue between the dead lover and the wife at sea, in which she weeps for her little son, followed by a simple announcement that she and the "mariner" were drowned.

What might have remained a simple, rather pedestrian ballad in the "Rambler's Garland" turns to gold in the fifth edition of Sir Walter Scott's *Minstrelsy of the Scottish Border* (1812),[16] where it is called "The Daemon Lover" (243F). It begins like the garland version with the temptation, adding one stanza in which the wife bids a pathetic farewell to her two babes, and then concentrates on the sea journey, omitting the anticlimactic ending of the broadside and garland texts. But the most striking thing is the re-creation of the revenant as the "daemon lover." The girl no longer weeps for her little son but weeps rather when she spies the mariner's cloven foot. The revenant has become a devil, modeled no doubt on the diabolic tempters of medieval romance, like the temptress, for example, who almost seduces Perceval in Malory's *Quest of the Holy Grail*. Perceval is saved at the last moment when he makes a sign of the cross:

> And therewith the pavylon turned up-so-downe and than hit chonged unto a smooke and a blak clowde. And than he drad sore and cryed alowde,
>
> 'Fayre swete Lorde Jesu Cryste, ne lette me nat be shamed, which was nyghe loste had nat Thy good grace bene!'
>
> And than he loked unto her shippe and saw her entir therein, which seyde,
>
> 'Syr Percivale, ye have betrayde me.'
>
> And so she wente with the wynde, rorynge and yellynge, that hit semed all the water brente after her.[17]

This rather flamboyant ending of the romance episode finds its ballad counterpart in the last stanza of "The Daemon Lover" (243F15):

> He strack the tap-mast wi his hand,
> The fore-mast wi his knee,
> And he brake that gallant ship in twain,
> And sank her in the sea.

A more specific romance connection, however, is evident in the preceding two stanzas of the ballad (243F13–14):

16. Evidence of the existence of "The Daemon Lover" appears first in Laidlaw's letter to Scott of January 3, 1803. A half-dozen stanzas are given as sung by Walter Grieve (*ESPB*, IV, 369).

17. Eugène Vinaver (ed.), *The Works of Sir Thomas Malory* (London, 1954), p. 669. (Caxton's Book XIV, chaps. ix–x).

'O what hills are yon, yon pleasant hills,
    That the sun shines sweetly on?'
'O yon are the hills of heaven,' he said,
    'Where you will never win.'

'O whaten a mountain is yon,' she said,
    'All so dreary wi frost and snow?'
'O yon is the mountain of hell,' he cried,
    'Where you and I will go.'

In his discussion of the mountain otherworld Wimberly suggests that the mountain of hell in "The Daemon Lover" is "a creation of the Norse imagination."[18] But surely this vision of heaven and hell in the ballad echoes that passage in *Thomas of Ersseldoune* where the lady shows Thomas the landscape of heaven, paradise, purgatory, and hell. Perhaps it is significant that the only examples of "the mountain otherworld" Wimberly cites are "Thomas Rymer" and "The Daemon Lover." Far from reflecting the "Norse imagination," these mountains belong to medieval vision literature, of which *Thomas of Ersseldoune* is itself an example.[19] It is no accident that "The Daemon Lover" is first found in Scott's *Minstrelsy of the Scottish Border*, and that this ballad is ingeniously recreated with glittering touches from medieval romance.

Undoubtedly the greatest of the revenant ballads is "Clerk Saunders" (69A–77B), preserved in the manuscripts of David Herd in the latter half of the eighteenth century. It is unfortunate that the integrity of this remarkable piece has been violated in Child's edition. Child deemed it necessary—and perhaps it was—to separate the revenant ending from the story proper and form two ballads: the one, "Clerk Saunders" (69), and the other, "Sweet William's Ghost" (77). There were two reasons for this. One was that versions of "Clerk Saunders" existed (including one in Herd's collection) without the revenant ending, and the other was that the revenant ending existed in versions which lacked the preceding story. Does the longer Herd version (69A–77B) represent the complete ballad, and do the separately preserved "Clerk Saunders" and

18. Wimberly, *Folklore in the English and Scottish Ballads*, p. 133.
19. Howard R. Patch, *The Other World According to Descriptions in Medieval Literature* (Cambridge, Mass., 1950), p. 263. The medieval notion of the devil as dwelling in the north country is alluded to in Chaucer's *Canterbury Tales*, "The Friar's Tale," ll. D. 1413 ff.; and in *Piers the Plowman*, C text, passus II, ll. 112 ff. Biblical support for this idea can be found in Isa. 14:13, where Lucifer's seat is located on a mountain: "I will sit also upon the mount of the congregation, in the sides of the north."

"Sweet William's Ghost" merely survive as fragments of it?[20] Was the original ballad "Clerk Saunders," to which a revenant ending was added? Or was "Sweet William's Ghost" the original, with "Clerk Saunders" added to it as a prologue? To try to answer these questions, which Child undoubtedly asked himself, we need to re-examine the text problem in this ballad and also to identify the traditional themes and motifs which it contains.

Clerk Saunders and May Margret are in love, but she resists his suggestion that they lie together before they are married because she fears they will be discovered by her seven brothers. To enable her to swear to her innocence and "save her oath," Saunders suggests that she lift the doorlatch with his sword, so she can say she never let him in; wear a blindfold, so she can say she never saw him; and carry him to her bed, so she can say he never trod her bower floor. Margret agrees to this, but all their precautions are wasted, for that night the seven brothers burst into the room with their torches burning bright and find the lovers asleep in bed. There is a moment of suspense as six of the brothers, in turn, express their sympathy for the couple and refuse to harm them. But the seventh thinks differently: "Altho there wear no a man but me, I bear the brand, I'le gar him die" (69A14). This seventh brother pierces the sleeping Clerk Saunders through and through with the "cold iron" (69A16–18):

Sanders he started, an Margret she lapt,
    Intill his arms whare she lay,
And well and wellsom was the night,
    A wat it was between these twa.

And they lay still, and sleeped sound,
    Untill the day began to daw;
And kindly till him she did say
    'It's time, trew-love, ye wear awa.'

They lay still, and sleeped sound,
    Untill the sun began to shine;
She lookt between her and the wa,
    And dull and heavy was his eeen.

When Margret sees the blood of his fair body and realizes that he is dead, she utters the traditional vow of austerities, climaxed by her resolve to

20. Versions of "Clerk Saunders" by Jamieson, published in 1806 (69F), and Buchan, published in 1828 (69G), have the revenant ending, but both are inferior composites, and both appear after the publication of a form of Herd's version by Scott in 1802.

194

wear "nought but dowy black." Her father offers her consolation, but she refuses to be comforted. In the evening, when all men have gone to bed, Clerk Saunders comes to Margret's window and asks her to return the faith and troth he had given her—evidently referring to a love token, perhaps a ring.[21] Margret asks first for a kiss, but he warns her that his mouth is cold, and if he should kiss her, her days would not be long. Then, with a note of urgency, he asks again for the return of his faith and troth, for, he says, cocks are crowing, and the singing of birds foretells the coming of day. Margret delays him with a question: what becomes of women who die in childbirth? When he assures her that "their beds are made in the heavens high," she gives the ghost back his troth. Saunders thanks her and departs, after promising to return for her "gine ever the dead come for the quick." Then like the grief-stricken bride in the famous Danish ballad *Aage og Else*, Margret follows him back to the grave and asks for room to lie beside him. But Saunders tells her there is no room and warns her that he sleeps among the worms, with no coverlet but cold meal and a winding sheet.[22]

The summary of "Clerk Saunders" just given follows the long version in Herd's MSS. That this version is more reliable than all the others is evident for several reasons. Not only is it the earliest complete form of the story, but it has the added advantage of being a Herd text. Of all eighteenth-century ballad collectors, David Herd was unquestionably the most reliable. He did not tamper with the texts he received, and it is noteworthy that his long version of "Clerk Saunders" (Herd MSS, I, 177 ff.) is in a group of three ballads and two songs not even in Herd's handwriting.[23] This copyist, whoever he was, exhibits an unusual fidelity in transcribing, as can be seen in the line, twice repeated by the ghost: "Cocks are crowing a merry mid-larf." In a note to "mid-larf" Child remarks, "I retain, although I do not understand *larf*." But as has been pointed out, the line undoubtedly means, "Cocks are crowing on merry middle-earth," *middle-earth* being a common early English term meaning the earth, or this

---

21. Love tokens are an important feature of "The Lass of Roch Royal" (76). See the Ocram broadside version, sts. 7–14; also 76A11–16, B12–16, etc.

22. Child takes "meal" to mean "mold, dust, earth" (V, 357), citing 77B14–15 and 96C36. It may be, however, that some kind of meal was used in preparing a body for burial. In *The Knight of the Burning Pestle*, Act V, scene i, Jasper deceives the merchant into thinking he is a ghost. Immediately preceding his entrance occurs the stage direction: "Enter Jasper, with his face mealed."

23. See Hans Hecht (ed.), *Songs from David Herd's Manuscripts* (Edinburgh, 1904), p. 77. In addition to "Clerk Saunders," the other items in this same handwriting are "Young Hunting" (68A), "Fair Mary of Wallington" (91B), and two songs, "Duncan" and "Kenneth." Some minor alterations in Herd's Text of "Clerk Saunders" are listed by Child in his notes (II, 167, 234), but these seem to have no authority.

world. It is unlikely that the transcriber of the ballad understood the term; but the important thing is that he wrote down exactly what his ear heard, a rare accomplishment in eighteenth-century ballad collecting.

The superiority of Herd's long version of "Clerk Saunders" is even clearer when we compare the quite different ways in which various versions of the ballad depict the return of the troth. The Herd text reads as follows (77B9):

> Up she has tain a bright long wand,
>> And she has straked her trouth thereon;
> She has given it him out at the shot-window,
>> Wi many a sad sigh and heavy groan.

Margret evidently has realized that she is in converse with a dead man, and, mindful of the prohibition against touching such a one,[24] she has stretched her troth on a stick out the window to him to avoid the danger of bodily contact. There can be little doubt that this is the original form of the story and that the various readings of the other versions, as Child observes, "are possibly corruptions of the ceremony performed in B" (the Herd text).[25] Ramsay's version (77A) is the earliest, found in the 1740 edition of the *Tea-Table Miscellany*, and it describes the troth return as follows (77A10):

> She stretched out her lilly-white hand,
>> And, for to do her best,
> 'Hae, there's your faith and troth, Willy,
>> God send your soul good rest.'

The second line is obviously a filler for something forgotten or not understood, and Margret's cautious method of returning the troth is simply lost in this account. Other versions, however, depart more radically from the Herd text, as can be seen in the following stanzas from the early nineteenth-century versions of Motherwell, Robertson, and Kinloch:

> She took up her white, white hand,
>> And she struck him in the breast,
> Saying, Have there again your faith and troth,
>> And I wish your soul good rest. (77C14)

24. See John 20:17: "Jesus saith unto her, Touch me not; for I am not yet ascended to my Father."

25. *ESPB*, II, 227. Wimberly suggests that the ceremony involves "return of troth plight by means of giving back a love token" (*Folklore in the English and Scottish Ballads*, p. 260), but he does not discuss the prohibition against touching the revenant.

Then she has taen a silver key,
    Gien him three times on the breast;
Says, There's your faith and troth, Willie,
    I hope your soul will rest. (77D13)

Then Margret took her milk-white hand,
    And smoothd it on his breast;
'Tak your faith and troth, William,
    God send your soul good rest!' (77E14)

Having Margret strike him in the breast, as in the first example, is of course a flagrant violation of the prohibition against touching the dead man. By using a key, as in the second instance, she perhaps avoids bodily contact, but the ceremony, so far as I know, has no traditional significance. The third stanza quoted, in which the girl "smoothd" her hand on his breast, is of interest in connection with a comment by Gummere. "As for the wand upon which Margaret 'strokes' her troth," he says, "it seems not unlikely that we are dealing with a confused survival of the common method by which savages and even European peasants get rid of a disease by rubbing the affected part upon a stick, a tree, or what not."[26] This seems to rely excessively on folklore as a means of illuminating the text. Surely all three of the above variations originate in a misunderstanding of the original dialect word "straked," meaning "stretched," in the line "she has straked her trouth thereon." In the first two stanzas quoted the verb is understood to mean "struck," and in the third to mean "stroked," that is, "smoothd." To these may be added a fourth "gothick" variation of the troth ceremony in a stanza which Scott obtained from James Hogg (77G1):

'But plait a wand o bonny birk,
    And lay it on my breast,
And shed a tear upon my grave,
    And wish my saul gude rest.

The obvious antiquarianism of this and the other variations is readily evident, and we may safely conclude that Herd's manuscript gives us the "Clerk Saunders" ballad in its most authentic and reliable form, as far as the text itself is concerned.

No single source is known for the story of "Clerk Saunders," but many

26. Francis B. Gummere, *Old English Ballads* (Boston, 1894), p. 349. Quoted by Wimberly, *Folklore in the English and Scottish Ballads*, p. 259.

elements in it are to be found in European balladry, as Child has shown.[27] What has not been adequately recognized, I believe, is the extent to which the ballad is a composite of themes and motifs from medieval romance. The basic plot involves a temptation scene, common enough in the romances, which puts the lovers in a compromising situation in order to test them. Thus in Sir Thomas Malory's tale of *Sir Gareth of Orkeney*, Gareth and Lyonesse, who are actually engaged to be married, arrange a secret meeting one night in order to "abate their lustys secretly:"

> And so there was ordayned grete cowchis and thereon fethir beddis, and there he leyde hym downe to slepe. And within a whyle came dame Lyonesse wrapped in a mantell furred with ermyne, and leyde hir downe by the sydys of sir Gareth. And therewithall he began to clyppe hir and to kysse hir.
>
> And therewithall he loked before hym and sawe an armed knyght with many lyghtes aboute hym, and this knyght had a long gysarne in his honde and made a grymme countenaunce to smyte him.[28]

Gareth survives this encounter with nothing worse than a penitential wound in the thigh,[29] and he beheads the armed intruder, who, however, returns to interrupt a second tryst of the lovers, his head marvelously restored in the manner of the Green Knight. This is but one of many episodes in romance testing the virtue of the hero, in which the fires of lust assail him like a conquering army on the "perilous bed."[30] From Gareth and Lyonesse to "Little Musgrave and Lady Barnard" (81), the confrontation of sleeping lovers with the sword has been a popular theme, providing as it does a lurid juxtaposition of life and death, love and hate.

The particular concern of Margret to save her oath reflects another interest of medieval romance associated with the temptations of courtly lovers. One is reminded of "the ordeal by iron" episode in the story of Tristan and Iseult.[31] King Mark is persuaded to test his queen, Iseult, by having her swear that she has been faithful to him and authenticating

27. *ESPB*, II, 156–158.

28. Vinaver (ed.), *The Works of Sir Thomas Malory*, p. 247.

29. See *ibid.*, p. 670, where Percivale's self-inflicted thigh wound is a rebuke to lust.

30. The trial of the "perilous bed" is endured by two of Chrétien's heroes, Lancelot and Gauvain, in the *Chevalier de la Charette* and *Conte del Graal*. The fiery lances in the Lancelot episode are understood to represent the fires of lust by Robertson, *Preface to Chaucer*, p. 478.

31. Conveniently available in an Anchor book, *The Romance of Tristan and Iseult* as retold by Joseph Bedier (New York, 1945), pp. 116–122. This is a free summary of the episode as given in an anonymous Tristan fragment found in MSS of Béroul.

the oath by picking up a red-hot iron in her bare hand. When the party arrives at Malpas, where the oath is to be administered, it is necessary for Iseult to cross the river. By prearrangement, her lover Tristan is waiting there disguised as a beggar, and Iseult as if by chance orders him to carry her across the river in his arms. When she takes the oath, Iseult swears that she has never been in the arms of anyone except King Mark—and that poor beggar who, as everyone saw, carried her over the stream. The queen then picks up the hot iron, carries it a few paces, and throws it down, showing her hands to the crowd. They are unharmed by the iron. Thus she has "saved her oath." God, it seems, is *courtois* to ladies in distress. This is the most felicitous use of the saved oath theme in medieval romance. There are of course many imitations of the basic idea, one of which is undoubtedly provided by our ballad.[32]

The presence of seven brothers in "Clerk Saunders" suggests a possible connection with an abduction narrative like that of "Earl Brand," first preserved in the Percy folio MS (7F). The early text is fragmentary, but in later versions the hero kills the brothers one by one until the last brother comes up from behind and gives him a deadly wound. This corresponds very closely to the sequential use of the seven brothers in the slaying of Clerk Saunders, though of course there is nothing in "Earl Brand" to match the revenant ending of the other ballad. It is, however, a fascinating if enigmatic fact that seven brothers do appear in the early and influential revenant ballad, "Fair Margaret and Sweet William" (74A), which was considered earlier in this chapter. In this ballad, as we have seen, the brothers do little more than quarrel briefly with William over his right to kiss the dead Margaret. One has the feeling that these brothers, relatively useless here, are vestigial survivals from an earlier form of the story. If their sister were not already dead, their swords would be drawn in defense of her honor. But in "Fair Margaret and Sweet William" there is no need for them to act, even out of revenge; William obligingly dies for sorrow. This kind of cultivation of sentiment contrasts strongly with the tone of "Clerk Saunders," suggesting to me that the latter ballad, though first recovered in the eighteenth century, represents an earlier form of narrative than that preserved in "Fair Margaret and Sweet William."

Further evidence of the antiquity of "Clerk Saunders" can be seen in

32. In Chrétien's *Chevalier de la Charette*, Lancelot swears that Kay has not slept with the Queen, when it is he himself who has done so. Since what he swears is the truth, Lancelot is able to defeat Meleagant's challenge and thus "save his oath."

Margret's vow of austerities, coupled with a refusal to be comforted by her father, which we have already observed in the preceding chapter to be related to a similar vow in the late medieval romance, *The Squire of Low Degree.* But all of the themes and motifs thus far considered relate to the first part of the ballad. What is the origin of the revenant narrative with which the ballad concludes? Most scholars seem to have been satisfied with Wimberly's suggestion that the ballad ghost is derived from the superstitions and practices of a secular folk tradition. It seems to me, however, that the antecedents of the revenant in "Clerk Saunders," like other elements of the ballad, can be found in medieval romance.

Among the more powerful instruments of the medieval pulpit were the stories of punishment of sin in purgatory or hell-fire, and in these stories the informant was usually a ghost returned from the grave. The most famous example of this type is *The Trental of Gregory,* English metrical versions of which date from the early fourteenth century. The story of the *Trental* is summarized by Hulbert as follows:

> The mother of a certain pope had a great reputation for sanctity; secretly, however, she lived in adultery and moreover had slain her two children. After her death she appeared in torment to her son. She told him that she would be saved if a trental of masses (for which she gave directions) were said for her. The pope had the masses said, and at the end of the year she appeared to him in so radiant a form that he supposed her to be the Virgin. The poem ends with some fifty lines discussing the proper methods of performing the trental.[33]

This is of course the type of story that operated so effectively to promote the establishment of chantries for souls of the wealthy in the late Middle Ages and led astray many a parish priest, who, unlike Chaucer's good parson,

> leet his sheep encombred in the myre
> and ran to Londoun unto Seinte Poules
> To seken hym a chaunterie for soules.[34]

In addition to encouraging the congregation to make provision for masses to be sung for the dead, however, these "trental" stories were often severely moralistic in their graphic depiction of tortures of the

33. James R. Hulbert, "The Sources of St. Erkenwald and the Trental of Gregory," *MP*, XVI (1919), 485–493, quotation from 490.

34. *Canterbury Tales*, Prologue, ll. 508–510.

damned. The *Gesta Romanorum*, for instance, paints a horrible picture of a lecherous couple, who are boiled in a caldron, "till the fleshe was sothyn fro the bone."[35] The bones are then removed from the caldron and placed beside it, the man and woman once more spring to life, and immediately they are plunged again into the caldron. The process is repeated *ad infinitum*.

But there are also stories in the *Gesta Romanorum* that stress eternal rewards rather than punishments. There is the case of the monk, Robert, for example, who successfully prayed his two brethren out of purgatory and is himself rewarded, through their intercession, with the promise of eternal life without the customary purgatorial suffering. When the time comes for Robert to die, the two brethren for whom he had prayed appear as ghosts to escort him to heaven:

> It felle on a nyght, that a monke aftir matyns was in the chaptoure house, and loked oute at a wyndowe, and sawe ii monkes sitting on a graue, and cladde in monkes wede, and eythere of hem had a tabernacle tapre brennyng in his hande; and he mervayled gretly what this myght be.

He then fetches the abbot, who asks them who they are, and they tell him the purpose of their visit. The abbot hastens to see about Robert and discovers that he is dead. When he returns to the grave, the two monks are gone, having fulfilled their mission and taken Robert to heaven. "For it is written, 'he that prayeth for anothere, laboreth for hym self, for to come to the blisse of heuyn.' "[36]

Popular as these homiletic stories were, it is not surprising that they find their way into late medieval romance. In the *Awntyrs of Arthure at the Terne Wathelyne*,[37] a fourteenth-century alliterative poem, the ghost of Guinevere's mother appears to Gawain and the queen as they are resting from the hunt under a laurel tree. The apparition is in the likeness of Lucifer and glides to Guinevere; yelling and groaning and sorely sighing she identifies herself to her daughter. Guinevere is frightened, but Gawain comforts her and says he will speak with this spirit to see if he may abate the pains of its body, which was bare and black to the bone and covered with toads and serpents. Gawain, like Lady Else in the Danish ballad,

35. Sidney J. H. Herrtage (ed.), *The Early English Versions of the Gesta Romanorum* (EETS, E. S. 33 [London, 1879]). Quotation is from p. 385.
36. *Ibid.*, p. 382.

37. F. J. Amours (ed.), *Scottish Alliterative Poems* ("Scottish Text Society, Vol. 21" [Edinburgh, 1897]), pp. 116–171.

6. Revenant ballads   201

conjures the ghost in the name of Christ to speak. "Welcome, Guinevere," says the ghost, "thou worthy one. See how doleful death has dressed thy mother! My countenance was once redder than a rose in the rain, my features like the lily, lovely to see; and now I am a grisly ghost, and grimly I groan, lighted with Lucifer in a low pit. Thus am I like unto Lucifer, take witness by me: for all your fresh features, now muse on this mirror, for both king and emperor, thus shall you be."[38] The ghost continues for several stanzas to develop this theme, which is familiarly epitomized in graveyard inscriptions beginning, "As you are now, so once was I; as I am now, so you shall be."

When the ghost has finished speaking, Guinevere promises that masses shall be said for her mother's soul, so as to free her from torment. But before the apparition can depart, Guinevere asks it some questions, which are obligingly answered. What grieves God the most? Pride. What deeds must I do to come to bliss? Alms deeds. Gawain likewise questions the ghost: How shall we fare who live by fighting? Your king (Arthur) is at the height of his power, but Fortune's wheel will turn, and he shall be brought low, together with all the knights of the Round Table. After this grim prophecy, the ghost departs.

In his chapter on the ballad ghost, Wimberly stresses the objectivity and corporeity of the revenant in contrast to the literary notion of a discarnate soul.[39] In medieval romance, however, as we can see in the *Awntyrs of Arthure*, this dichotomy is not so clear. The ghost "glides" in, thus suggesting a disembodied state, but much is made of the loathsome appearance of her tormented body, which is objectively present in the sense at least that both Guinevere and Gawain can see it. Of more immediate interest for our present purposes, however, is the fact that the ghost can be questioned, and evidently it has prophetic powers. We are immediately reminded of Margret's questioning of Clerk Saunders in the ballad: What comes of women who die in labor? Their beds are made in the heavens high. After this Margret gives Saunders back his troth, and he departs.

One further example of late medieval narrative involving return of the dead is *The Childe of Bristowe*, a short metrical tale composed in the Thopas stanza (*aabccb*).[40] Although various forms of the tale exist,

38. *Ibid.*, "Awntyrs of Arthure," ll. 159–169. For the continuation of the *memento mori* theme in folksong and balladry see the excellent article by Anne G. Gilchrist, "'Death and the Lady' in English Balladry," *JEFDSS*, IV (1941), 37–48.

39. *Folklore in the English and Scottish Ballads*, pp. 226 ff.

40. W. Carew Hazlitt (ed.), *Remains of the Early Popular Poetry of England* (London, 1864), I, 110–131. Referred to by Child, *ESPB*, II, 512; Wimberly, *Folklore in the English and Scottish Ballads*, p. 259. Another version of the story, "The Merchant and his Son," is in Hazlitt, pp. 132–152.

this particular version is especially useful here because it is a good example of fifteenth-century minstrelsy which, as we have seen, plays such an important part in the beginnings of the popular ballad. Typical are these lines near the beginning which make the usual appeal of the minstrel for the attention of the audience (ll. 7–12):

> The beste song that ever was made
> ys not worth a lekys blade,
> but men wol tende ther-tille;
> therfor y pray yow in this place
> of your talkying that ye be pes
> yf it be your wille.

A certain wealthy and unscrupulous man has a son who becomes apprenticed to a merchant in Bristow. When the father lies on his deathbed, he requires his son to be his executor, and the son, worried about the state of his unscrupulous parent's soul, in turn requires his father to come back fourteen days after his death to the same chamber where he had died. "I charge you," says the child, "that you appear, that I may see your soul here, whether it be saved or damned, and that you do me no harm, you, nor none that shall come with you."

When his father is dead and buried, the child gives alms freely, does deeds of charity, and has thirty trentals of masses said for his father's soul. When the two weeks have passed, as the boy sits praying, his father's soul appears before him burning like a coal, and the devil leads him by the neck in a burning chain. The father tells his son that he will burn like this for a hundred years unless his ill-gotten gains are restored to the people he robbed in his lifetime. Having reported the state of his soul and thus fulfilled what had been required of him, the father then asks for the return of his troth (ll. 263–264): "gef me my trouthe; y were ago: for til than my soule is lore." But the child refuses, saying (ll. 265–270):

> Nay, fader, that shal not be,
> in better plite y wol yow se,
> yf God wol gef me grace;
> but ye shal me your trouthe plighte,
> this same day fourtenyht
> ye shal appere in this place.

Having spent all his father's wealth in almsgiving and masses, the child next borrows money and makes restitution to all those he can find who had been harmed by his father. When all of the borrowed funds are exhausted, at the end of another two weeks, he returns to the chamber where his father died and awaits the appearance of the ghost.

As the child sits praying, once more the spirit appears to him in the same form, except that the chain is removed from his neck, and his body, though black, no longer burns as before. When the child asks after the state of his soul, the father reports some improvement but explains that he is still in pain because of the tithes and offerings which he withheld from the church. Having made his report, he once more wishes to leave (ll. 373–376):

> Therfor, sone, y pray the
> gef me my trouthe y left with the,
> and let me wynde my way.

But the child refuses and requires the spirit to come again in a fortnight. This time the boy is forced to sell himself in servitude to his master to raise the necessary money for paying the tithes and offerings. At last he has completed this task, and the money is gone. But alas, at this moment he meets a poor man whom his father had robbed, who has not yet been reimbursed. Having no more money, the child nevertheless responds nobly (ll. 448–453):

> Off his clothes he gan take,
> and putt hem on the pore manis bake,
> chargyng for hys fader to pray.
> hosen and shon he gave hym tho;
> in sherte and breche he gan go;
> he had no clothes gay.

When the two weeks are passed, the son at last sees his father's bright soul as a naked child in the company of angels. The soul confirms that it has won salvation and once again asks for the return of the troth. The boy freely returns it and requests his father's blessing. After bestowing a blessing on his son, the father goes to bliss "with moche joye and angelis."

In spite of its obvious didactic cast, *The Childe of Bristowe* illustrates how thorough is the interpenetration of Christian doctrine and folk belief. Far from existing in isolation from religion, folklore regarding the dead was freely employed in medieval times to give shape and form to the ethical teachings of the church regarding the hereafter. It was this fact, rather than a supposed latent hostility to religion, that has kept these folk traditions alive. Numerous illustrations of this could be drawn from the tale we have just considered. In connection with the child's giving his clothes and his "hosen and shon" to the poor man, for instance, one thinks of these moving lines from "The Lyk-wake Dirge:"

When thou from hence doest pass away
    Every night and awle
To whinny-moor thou comest at last
    And Christ receive thy sawle.

If ever thou gave either hosen or shun
    Every night and awle,
Sitt thee down and putt them on
    And Christ receive thy sawle.

But if hosen nor shoon thou never gave nean
    Every night and awle,
The whinnies shall prick thee to the bare beane
    And Christ receive thy sawle.[41]

Like *The Child of Bristowe*, this moving lament combines the doctrine of charitable giving with popular conceptions of the soul's journey after death, across the "whinny-moor" and (in later stanzas) the "brig o dread."[42]

The most important feature of *The Child of Bristowe* for our present purpose, however, is its use of the troth-return motif. As in "Clerk Saunders" we are not told precisely what form the troth takes, but only that after the father's third request the child says, "Have your trouthe. . . fre." It may be in this instance that a mere verbal release is implied, but the principle of assent is the same in both the romance and the ballad. When the ghost obtains this assent, he departs.

Thus we may conclude, I think, that the revenant portion of "Clerk Saunders," like the rest of the ballad, owes much to medieval romance tradition in the questioning of the ghost, the troth-return, and the *memento mori* ending. It is likewise true that folk beliefs like the kiss of death and the departure of the dead at cockcrow are used to advantage. Over and above these things, however, is the fact that "Clerk Saunders" is a great imaginative realization of the revenant theme, making it all the more regrettable that it is split in two in Child's edition. This unfortunate

41. Quoted from Leach, *The Ballad Book*, p. 6. The "whinny-moor" is the furze-covered field or wasteland over which the dead must journey to the other-world.

42. See Wimberly, *Folklore in the English and Scottish Ballads*, pp. 110–114, for discussion of the "brig o dread."

division has made it difficult for the reader to understand how carefully and artfully the two parts of Herd's long version are united. When Margret questions the ghost about the fate of women who die in childbirth, for example, she does not do so out of idle curiosity.[43] Having slept with her lover in the bower and having been left, as a result of his violent death, in a world largely indifferent to her fate, it is pathetically appropriate that she ask her lover's ghost what is to become of her when she perhaps will have to face alone the unknown terrors of childbirth. The ghost's gentle reply is given in a beautiful stanza:

> Their beds are made in the heavens high,
>> Down at the foot of our good Lord's knee,
> Well set about wi gilly-flowers,
>> A wat sweet company for to see.

One is here reminded of the Middle English vision poem, *Pearl*, in which the maiden who is in paradise speaks across the water to the dreamer, teaching him about death and eternal life, and urging him to accept his mortal condition. Yet at the end of the poem the dreamer foolishly seeks to wade across the water to join the maiden in the celestial city, which wakens him, of course, from his dream. So in "Clerk Saunders," when the ghost departs, Margret wishes to go with him in spite of her sure knowledge of his condition. This is the ballad's emotional equivalent to the dreamer's effort to cross the water barrier in *Pearl*. The ghost's grim reminder of human mortality therefore provides a fitting conclusion. Solidly traditional, as we have seen, but touched with the magic of poetic genius, "Clerk Saunders" is the finest example of revenant balladry in English.

---

43. In Ramsay's *Tea-Table Miscellany* version (77A), the question is replaced by a condition for return of the troth; she will not return it until he weds her with a ring. This is surely a secondary development. As "The Awntyrs of Arthure" shows, the ghost as oracle and an answerer of questions is traditional. I agree with Child that "mere curiosity does not sort well with this very seriously conceived ballad" (*ESPB*, II, 227), with reference to the Motherwell, Robertson, Kinloch, and Jamieson versions (77C, D, E, F), but I would add that these are late elaborations of the original childbed question in Herd's version (77B6).

7. The eighteenth century

Before turning, as we shall, to Bishop Percy, David Herd, and Mrs. Brown of Falkland as the three major sources of eighteenth-century balladry, it is necessary in the present chapter to consider representative examples of those ballads which appeared from time to time during the century in miscellaneous collections, songbooks, broadsides, and garlands. The importance of these collections, their rationale and popularity have been dealt with in A. B. Friedman's excellent book, *The Ballad Revival*.[1] Without overlooking the insights made possible by Friedman's study, our attention must now be directed to the ballads themselves, especially those few which, in the early eighteenth century, illustrate the remarkable changes then taking place, as we have seen (chapter i above), in the structure of the ballad.

Published collections of ballads and songs in the first half of the eighteenth century were not numerous, and those that did appear contained few of the Child ballads. Allan Ramsay's *The Ever Green* (Edinburgh, 1724) included only "Johnie Armstrong" (69C), "copied from a Gentleman's Mouth of the Name of Armstrang, who is 6th generation from this John."[2] *A Collection of Old Ballads* (3 vols.; London, 1723–1725) contained six Child ballads of the type popularized in seventeenth-century broadsides.[3] Ramsay's songbook, *The Tea-Table Miscellany* (4 vols.; Edinburgh, 1723–1737), consisted primarily of songs, both popular and literary, but also included more than a half-dozen ballads or related lyrics: "Sweet William's Ghost" (77A), "Bonny Barbara Allan" (84A), "The Bonny Earl of Murray" (181A), "The Gypsy Laddie" (200A), "Rare Willie Drowned in Yarrow" (215A), as well as "The Gaberlunyie-Man" (279App) and "Waly, Waly, Gin Love Be Bony" (204 Intro).

The strong lyric emphasis of the ballads in Ramsay's *Tea-Table Miscellany* illustrates that impact of melody on narrative structure mentioned in the first chapter, which marks the evolution of balladry in the early eighteenth century. In fact "The Bonny Earl of Murray" and "Rare Willie Drowned in Yarrow" are both threnodies in which lyrical expression of

---

1. Friedman, *The Ballad Revival*, pp. 114 ff.

2. Quoted in *ibid.*, p. 137.

3. The ballads are Child 73, 106, 156, 167, 272, 288. See Friedman, *The Ballad Revival*, pp. 146 ff.

grief far overshadows the narrative element. Even "Bonny Barbara Allan" and "The Gypsy Laddie" are not only brief—nine and ten stanzas each— but also highly lyrical, and their style is marked by incremental repetition, a feature of increasing importance in eighteenth-century balladry.

Indeed the *Tea-Table* ballads have much in common stylistically. Compare, for example, the vow of the lord's wife in "The Gypsy Laddie" (200A4),

> 'Yestreen I lay in a well-made bed,
>> And my good lord beside me;
> This night I'll ly in a tenant's barn,
>> Whatever shall betide me.'

with the lament of the heroine of "Rare Willie Drowned in Yarrow" (215A2),

> 'Yestreen I made my bed fu brade,
>> The night I'll make it narrow,
> For a' the live-long winter's night
>> I lie twin'd of my marrow.'

which in turn is not unlike the last stanza of Ramsay's "Bonny Barbara Allan" (84A9):

> 'O mother, mother, make my bed!
>> O make it saft and narrow!
> Since my love died for me today,
>> I'll die for him to-morrow.'

These rhetorical configurations seem rather closely related and testify to an intimate community in which the existing repertoire was used freely but with decorum in the creation and re-creation of ballads. At the same time, a storehouse of commonplace stanzas was gradually accumulating, as can be seen in the recurrence of the "Gypsy Laddie" stanza quoted above in later ballads such as "The Beggar-Laddie" (280B13) and "Trooper and Maid" (299A11).[4]

In addition to having a common rhetorical heritage, the *Tea-Table* ballads illustrate the renewed popularity of incremental repetition, as exemplified in "The Gypsy Laddie" (200A6–7),

> I'll go to bed to my Johny Faa,
>> I'll go to bed to my deary;

4. It is possible that "The Gypsy Laddie" influenced the development of a whole series of Scottish abduction ballads, represented by Child Nos. 222–228; esp. compare 200A3 with 227, sts. 19–21.

For I vow and I swear, by what past yestreen,
    That my lord shall nae mair come near me.

I'll make a hap to my Johnny Faa,
    And I'll make a hap to my deary;
And he's get a' the coat gaes round,
    And my lord shall nae mair come near me.'

and in "The Bonny Earl of Murray" (181A3–5):

He was a braw gallant,
    And he rid at the ring;
And the bonny Earl of Murray,
    Oh he might have been a king!

He was a braw gallant,
    And he playd at the ba;
And the bonny Earl of Murray
    Was the flower amang them a'.

He was a braw gallant,
    And he playd at the glove;
And the bonny Earl of Murray,
    Oh he was the Queen's love!

Although we have seen this very effective technique operating in earlier ballads, as for example in the Percy folio MS version of "Child Waters" (63A), the re-emergence of incremental repetition as a major feature of eighteenth-century balladry is a striking phenomenon attributable in part at least to the increasing importance of melody in the determination of narrative structure. After three hundred years of evolution, the ballad has come full circle and once again draws strength from the folksong tradition. The technique of "The Bonny Earl of Murray" is essentially the same as that of "St. Stephen and Herod," "Robyn and Gandeleyn," and "I Sing of a Maiden."

A quite different collection of songs and ballads is Elizabeth Cochrane's manuscript, a privately owned songbook which seems not to have come to the attention of ballad collectors until the time of Sir Walter Scott.[5] This MS has not been published in full, but it contains four ballads which were first printed in Child's edition: "Gil Brenton" (5E), "The

5. Child informs us that a copy of Elizabeth Cochrane's version of "John of Hazelgreen" (293A) is found "in a folio volume at Abbotsford labelled Miscel- lanies, article 43, having been transcribed by C. K. Sharpe for Sir W. Scott . . . " (*ESPB*, V, 159). The manuscript is now in the Harvard Library.

Lass of Roch Royal" (76A), "Robin Hood and the Bishop of Hereford" (144B), and "John of Hazelgreen" (293A). Child remarks: "The date of the MS., though this is perhaps not determinable, has been put as early as 1730."[6]

Although the number of ballads in this manuscript is disappointingly small, the pieces Child included in his edition seem to be authentic examples of texts from oral tradition in Scotland. In view of what we have seen to be the strong lyrical emphasis of the *Tea-Table* collection it is interesting to note that in the Cochrane songbook "John of Hazelgreen," with its eight-line stanzas, the two parts of which are linked by echoing or repeated lines, is one of the best examples of the shaping influence of folksong in the eighteenth century (293A1):

> Into a sweet May morning,
>   As the sun clearly shone,
> I heard a propper damsell
>   Making a heavy moan;
> Making a heavy moan,
>   I marvelled what she did mean
> And it was for a gentleman,
>   Sir John of Hasillgreen.

As in the version of "Hugh Spencer's Feats in France" (158B), already mentioned in chapter v, the impress of melody on the form of "John of Hazelgreen" is readily apparent. At the same time, the presence of "Robin Hood and the Bishop of Hereford" in the songbook testifies to the preservation in oral tradition of an earlier type of broadside ballad. It is perhaps significant, however, that this version is shorter by nearly half than the Garland text and is, as Child remarks, "very likely only an imperfect remembrance of a broadside."[7] Most important of all of Elizabeth Cochrane's ballads is undoubtedly "The Lass of Roch Royal," which will be discussed later in this chapter. For the present we may turn to "Gil Brenton," a ballad which fortunately survives also in Herd's *Ancient and Modern Scots Songs* (1769) and in manuscripts of Mrs. Brown of Falkland (1783), thus making possible a comparison of the songbook version with independent versions from two of the most reputable sources of ballads in the eighteenth century.

In the songbook version of "Gil Brenton" (5E) the hero, whose name

6. *ESPB*, III, 193. My hunch, based on an analysis of its version of "The Lass of Roch Royal" (76A), is that the Elizabeth Cochrane MS is somewhat later than 1730. How much later I hesitate to say.
7. *ESPB*, III, 193.

210

in this text is Lord Benwall, has gone hunting and while walking alone he meets with a young lady whom he detains all night. When they part in the morning he gives her a pair of gloves and a gay gold ring. Lord Benwall next goes wooing and marries the youngest of seven ladies. As they are journeying toward his home, the bride moans, but when questioned she refuses to explain her sadness. Having reached Lord Benwall's home, the bride is seized by labor pains while they are at supper. When questioned this time she confesses to the groom that she is with child. Lord Benwall calls her a common whore, but his mother (apparently) tells him to go cheer up his merry men while she hears a further explanation from the bride regarding her condition. The girl explains that once when she was walking alone a lord met her and detained her all night, after which he gave her a pair of gloves and a gay gold ring. She offers to show these tokens to the mother, who in turn goes and challenges her son to produce the ring she had given him. Lord Benwall confesses that he gave the ring to a lady whom he now wishes, somewhat belatedly, he might have in his bower, whereupon his mother triumphantly announces that he now has in his home that very lady. When the heir is born, Benwall's name is found written on his breastbone. Overjoyed, Lord Benwall orders his lady clothed in silk and his young son fed with milk.

Like all the other versions of "Gil Brenton," the songbook text has close affinities, as Child has shown, with Scandinavian balladry,[8] and it has a quatrain form with interlaced refrain reminiscent of "Sir Lionel" (18A), one of the Percy folio ballads considered in chapter v. Here is the first stanza of the songbook version (5E1):

> Lord Benwall he's a hunting gone;
> > Hey down, etc.
> He's taken with him all his merry men.
> > Hey, etc.

Even more significant, perhaps, as a sign of the ballad's antiquity is the presence in the songbook version of structural symmetry and functional repetitions which we have seen to be characteristic of late medieval minstrelsy. The first eight stanzas, for example, reveal a studious parallelism. "Lord Benwall he's a hunting gone" begins the seduction episode of four stanzas, followed by "Lord Benwall he's a wooing gone," a second episode of four stanzas relating his selection of a bride. This parallel skilfully

8. *ESPB*, I, 62–67.

suggests a connection between the two episodes (the young lady is the same in both) without actually revealing what it is.

Another effective use of narrative symmetry can be seen in the repeated questioning of the girl by Lord Benwall, first on the homeward journey, and again at supper in his home. "What aileth my dearest and dayly flower?" he asks; "What ails my dear, to make such moan?" To each of his solicitous inquiries she responds negatively, leaving unexplained the reason for her grief. But when he repeats his question word for word at supper, the pains that seize her compel a truthful answer: "I am with child, and it's not to thee, And oh and alas, what shall I doe!" Thus the drama of this revelation is underscored by the repetition of the groom's question on two separate occasions.

Finally it should be noted that the stanza pattern of the seduction episode at the beginning of the ballad is repeated very effectively in the girl's explanation of her condition to the mother. Here is the earlier passage describing the seduction (5E2–4):

As he was walking late alone,
He spyed a lady both brisk and young.

He keeped her so long and long,
From the evening late till the morning came.

All that he gave her at their parting
Was a pair of gloves and a gay gold ring.

With this compare the girl's later description of the same event (5E20–22):

'As I was walking once late alone,
I spy'd a lord, both brisk and young.

'He keeped me so long and long,
From the evening late till the morning came.

'All that he gave me at our parting
Was a pair of gloves and a gay gold ring.'

The repetition here serves to reveal to the listener the identity of the seduced lady and the bride, for which preparation has been so effectively made in the parallelism of the "hunting" and "wooing" episodes at the beginning. The plot of "Gil Brenton" is unusually complex for a ballad, but the structural symmetry of the songbook version preserves for us a narrative that is clear and dramatic in its development.

The Herd text of "Gil Brenton" (5G) is similar to that of Elizabeth

Cochrane's MS, but in some ways it is inferior to it. Much of the structural symmetry we have observed has been eroded away, and the parallelism that remains is more mechanical than functional. The opening account of the seduction is omitted completely, with the resultant loss not only of the symmetry of the "hunting" and "wooing" episodes, but also of the parallelism in the bride's account of the seduction later on. Contamination of Herd's text with a version of "The Cruel Brother" (11)[9] has had a particularly disruptive effect on the repetition of questions leading to the bride's admission that she is with child. The questioner in the first instance is no longer Lord Bothwell (as he is called here) but "the foremost man," to whom the bride surprisingly confesses that her grief is owing to her forthcoming marriage. In a passage of descriptive pageantry peculiar to Herd's text, the sounding of a horn in the greenwood next announces the wedding party's arrival to Lord Bothwell's mother, who orders the servants to prepare the bed and the wedding supper (5G9–13).

The loss of parallelism in the sequence of questions addressed to the bride may be explained in part by the fact that on the homeward journey she is questioned by "the foremost man," whereas at the wedding supper she is questioned by Lord Bothwell himself. And yet, curiously enough, the existence of this parallelism at an earlier stage in the history of "Gil Brenton" can be inferred from a further disruption of the Herd text at this point. What seems to have happened is that the two stanzas containing solicitous questions originally directed to the bride on the homeward journey were divided, the first set of questions now being asked by the foremost man (5G6), "O lady, sits your saddle awry, Or is your steed for you owre high?" and the second set by her husband (5G15): "Or does the wind blow in your glove? Or runs your mind on another love?" This transposition shows the singer's consciousness of a parallelism in the two passages, but it is of course a parallelism not evident to us without an awareness of the form of the text prior to this disruption. That the change is indeed a disruption rather than merely a "variation" is evident when we consider how inappropriate it seems for the groom to ask the bride if the wind is blowing in her glove while they are presumably seated at the dinner table in his home.

In the revelation of the bride's condition and the groom's response, the Herd text resembles the songbook version, but, perhaps in part because of the loss of parallelism already mentioned, it adds explanatory and transitional stanzas preparing the listener for the conversation be-

9. Herd's 5G5 is reminiscent of "The Cruel Brother" fragment (11H), also in Herd, and is perhaps even closer to the Kinloch text (11B12).

tween the bride and the groom's mother (G19–21). The ending is very similar to that of the songbook, though it lacks the stanzas identifying the child as Lord Benwall's son and heir. In spite of my complete respect for Herd, it seems to me that his text of "Gil Brenton" is clearly inferior to the version in Elizabeth Cochrane's MS.

The first thing to notice about Mrs. Brown's version of "Gil Brenton" (5A) is its length. Her seventy-four stanzas more than double the length of the songbook and Herd texts, which are thirty-two and thirty-three stanzas, respectively. But before considering the nature of her additions, it is important to realize that the basic elements of the narrative remain unchanged in this version, and that in its structure it is closer to Herd than it is to the songbook. Like Herd's, Mrs. Brown's version lacks a preliminary seduction episode, thus eliminating the structural symmetry and functional repetitions of the songbook, and it begins by relating how Gil Brenton "sent oer the fame" and "woo'd a wife an brought her hame." As is indicated by this opening stanza, Gil Brenton seems not to have accompanied his bride on her journey to his home, and she is therefore questioned by Sweet Willy, a widow's son, who seems to be Mrs. Brown's realization of Herd's "foremost man."

Some of Mrs. Brown's innovations in "Gil Brenton" are decorative, as in the description of the sevenscore ships that came with her (A2–5). More important are the introduction of the chastity test (A15–26), with the consequent substitution of a maid in the bridal bed reminiscent of Brangwain's role in the romance of Tristan and Iseult;[10] the shifting of the episode in which the bride's condition is revealed from the dinner table to the bridal chamber (A27–32); and the use of a miraculous talking bed to reveal the fraudulent substitution of the maid and the pregnancy of the bride. In a few transitional passages Mrs. Brown seems close to the songbook version,[11] but more often she expands the narrative with great freedom. The bride's account of the seduction in particular is highly elaborated (A41–60), suggesting a fairy encounter similar to that related in "Tam Lin" (Child 39); and to the gay gold ring of the songbook text are added not only Herd's lock of yellow hair (G25) but also such other tokens as black beads and a little penknife. As we shall see in a later chapter, these changes, particularly the ones incorporating

10. Child cites the Tristan parallel and adds (I, 67): "Grundtvig truly remarks that a borrowing by the romance from the popular ballad is as probable a supposition as the converse; and that, even should we grant the name of the hero of the ballad to be a reminiscence of that of Isold's attendant (e.g. Brangwill of Brangwain), nothing follows as to the priority of the romance in respect to this passage."

11. Compare 5A36 with 5E19.

romance themes like the chastity test, the marvelous bed, and the fairy encounter, are typical of the ballads of Mrs. Brown. Here we need only observe that the excellence of her version of "Gil Brenton," which is undeniable, points an interesting contrast with the songbook text. Mrs. Brown's version has a richer texture and is, in short, more "literary"; the songbook text, on the other hand, has a narrative structure more characteristic of traditional balladry.

Although our attention has been centered, naturally enough, on collections like Ramsay's *Tea-Table Miscellany* and Elizabeth Cochrane's songbook, it is well to remember that more ballads were circulated in broadsides, chapbooks, and garlands than in any other form during the eighteenth century. Even the *Tea-Table Miscellany*, as Friedman remarks, was simply an expansion of small pamphlets of *Scots Songs* which Ramsay had been issuing since 1718.[12] In the remainder of the present chapter, therefore, we will consider a few ballads that may be regarded as representative of the eighteenth-century broadside tradition.

One of the earliest of the eighteenth-century broadsides is "Bewick and Graham" (211), which survives in a form perhaps as early as 1720. While drinking wine, the fathers of Bewick and Graham quarrel over which son is the better man, with the result that the two young men, who are sworn brothers, are compelled to fight to the death. Graham finally gives Bewick an awkward stroke and, seeing that his friend is dying, he runs upon his own sword and kills himself.

The narrative in "Bewick and Graham" is well constructed and uses functional repetitions reminiscent of the minstrelsy technique considered in earlier chapters. Thus Graham's father, for example, repeats to his son almost word for word both the insult delivered by Bewick and his own reply (211, sts. 12–13):

'He said thou was bad, and calld thee a lad,
    And bully to his son cannot be;
For his son Bewick can both write and read,
    And sure I am that cannot thee.

'I put thee to school, but thou would not learn,
    I bought thee books, but thou would not read;
But my blessing thou's never have
    Till I see with Bewick thou can save thy head.'

In like manner the father's challenge is repeated to his son as a means

12. *The Ballad Revival*, pp. 140 f.

of forcing him into the quarrel with Bewick (211, sts. 15, 17), and the entire conversation between Bewick and Graham before the duel is filled with echoes and repetitions (211, sts. 28–37). Particularly effective are the parallel descriptions of the action of the two young men as they prepare to fight. Bewick, the scholar, is first described (211, st. 38):

> He flang his cloak from off his shoulders,
>> His psalm-book out of his hand flang he,
> He clapd his hand upon the hedge,
>> And oer lap he right wantonly.

Graham, who is fully armed, is moved by this exhibition of courage and nobly refuses to fight until he has removed his armor (211, st. 41):

> He flang his jack from off his back,
>> His steel cap from his head flang he;
> He's taken his sword into his hand,
>> He's tyed his horse unto a tree.

The close parallelism of these two stanzas sharpens the *clericus-miles* contrast between the two men and is a technique we have often observed in the metrical tales and romances of late medieval minstrelsy. It was perhaps these survivals of the minstrel's art that led Child, who admired "Bewick and Graham" very much, to conjecture that "there was an older and better copy of this ballad than those which are extant."[13]

Although the technique of "Bewick and Graham" is archaic, the ballad has other features that mark it as a product of the eighteenth century. Its use of a stanza imported from a seventeenth-century Robin Hood garland, for example, is indicative of the movement in this period toward the establishment of a treasury of commonplace stanzas;[14] and the frequent employment of incremental repetition accords well with the re-emergence of this phenomenon which we have noted in the more lyrical ballads of *The Tea-Table Miscellany*.[15]

Our concentration on stylistic developments, however, should not blind us to significant changes in the minstrel's choice of subject and theme. To follow the evolution of balladry through a succession of heroes such as Percy and Douglas, Sir Andrew Barton, and Johnie Armstrong is to descend the ladder of social significance. In the early eighteenth century the art of the minstrel, for reasons already discussed, was no longer

---

13. *ESPB*, IV, 145. For another characteristic minstrel device, see 211, st. 24, and note its resemblance to 118, st. 21.

14. Compare 211, st. 22, with 123B9.
15. Examples of repetition are in 211, sts. 9–12, 21–23, 49–50.

able to express great national aspirations as in the past and was therefore reduced to the celebration of local events and deeds of violence such as we find in "Bewick and Graham." But the admirable structure of this ballad provides a significant example of baroque minstrelsy of the eighteenth century.

That the minstrel's art survived in the latter half of the century is evident in "The Duke of Gordon's Daughter" (237), the earliest copies of which are dated about 1775. The duke's daughter Jean goes to Aberdeen with her two sisters where she falls in love with Captain Ogilvie. But the duke opposes the marriage, and Ogilvie is stripped of his command. The couple suffer many hardships wandering for three years in the Highland hills, during which time the girl gives birth to three children. Yet when at last in desperation they come to Castle Gordon, Jean is welcomed, but Ogilvie is scorned and forced to go overseas as a soldier. While abroad he is called back to inherit his late brother's estate and becomes the Earl of Northumberland. This time when he comes to Castle Gordon he is welcomed and offered gold and silver. But he refuses all money, saying that he has come only to fetch bonny Jean and his young family.

Although "The Duke of Gordon's Daughter" is quite obviously a late ballad, it nevertheless has traces of an earlier structure, particularly in its use of functional repetitions to mark the main divisions of the narrative and to serve as a commentary on the action. The contrast in the reception of Captain Ogilvie before and after he has received his inheritance provides the best example (237, sts. 21–22, 27–28):

When she came to Castle Gordon,
    And down upon the green,
The porter gave out a loud shout,
    'O yonder comes Lady Jean!'

'O you are welcome, bonny Jeany Gordon,
    You are dear welcome to me;
You are welcome, dear Jeany Gordon,
    But away with your Captain Ogilvie.'

    . . . .

He soon came to Castle Gordon,
    And down upon the green;
The porter gave out with a loud shout,
    'Here comes Captain Ogilvie!'

'You're welcome, pretty Captain Ogilvie,
    Your fortune's advanced I hear;

No stranger can come unto my gates
   That I do love so dear.'

Unusual as it is to find this device in a ballad of such recent origin, it is perhaps even more surprising to note a survival of the old "weak" line of the minstrel stanza repeated in the first and third stanzas quoted above, "and down upon the green," reminding us of a line from the Robin Hood ballads: "under the greenwood tree."

But in spite of these traces of an earlier style, "The Duke of Gordon's Daughter" unquestionably belongs in the mainstream of eighteenth-century balladry. Whether this is true because it reflects the traits of other ballads of the period or because its popularity encouraged imitation is difficult to say. Nevertheless, in its style can be heard echoes or fore-tastes of such various ballads as "The Daemon Lover" (243F), "Mary Hamilton" (173A), and "Sir Patrick Spence" (58A).[16] Although it is largely free of the commonplace stanzas that were then so popular, hints of these can be seen in the Duke's order to "Go saddle me the black horse" (237, st. 4) and in the "dower despised" stanza beginning "I'll have none of your gold or silver" (237, st. 31). In spite of its baroque style and its medley of motifs, however, "The Duke of Gordon's Daughter" has an integrity of its own and can serve as an excellent illustration of late broadside balladry at its best.

Our final example of a broadside ballad is "The Lass of Roch Royal" (Child 76),[17] perhaps most famous for its so-called "shoe my foot" stanzas, in which the forlorn heroine asks such pathetic questions as these (76D1):

"O wha will shoe my fu fair foot?
   An wha will glove my han?
And wha will lace my middle gimp
   Wi the new made London ban?"

In spite of the popularity of these stanzas, however (they are found in an impressive number of ballads and songs), little study has been devoted to the earliest ballad in which they appear. The purpose of the following analysis, therefore, is to define the type of narrative represented by "The Lass of Roch Royal" in its earliest known versions, and, as a consequence, to restore the Lass to her rightful position as an Accused Queen, a status

16. Compare 243F10 and 237, st. 5; 173A1 and 237, st. 3; 58A3 and 237, st. 10.

17. Child, *ESPB*, II, 213–226; III, 510–512; IV, 471–474; V, 225, 294. The following discussion was originally published as "An Accused Queen in 'The Lass of Roch Royal' (Child 76)," *JAF*, LXXI (1958), 553–563.

which (as we shall see), if not comfortable, is at least not without considerable prestige. To this it need only be added that before we can attempt to distinguish and define the basic narrative structure of the ballad, we will have to examine in some detail the versions given in Child's collection. But this is no mere prerequisite. The convolutions of the texts of "The Lass" constitute a fascinating episode in the history of balladry.

"The Lass of Ocram," probably our earliest text, is a broadside dating from about the middle of the eighteenth century. It was reprinted by Child in his additions and corrections (III, 510–511). Whether or not it is actually the earliest in point of time, it clearly lacks that infiltration by elements from other ballads which is so characteristic of most versions of "The Lass" (and which, in my opinion, eventually destroyed the ballad; but more of this later). The story in this "Ocram" version runs as follows.

The Lass of Ocram is sailing all alone in a rich ship when she meets a proud merchant man. She identifies herself to him (stanza 4 is somewhat corrupt), saying that she is in search of Lord Gregory. The merchant man apparently recognizes her and directs her to "yonder island." She asks at the gate to be let in, but Gregory's mother, speaking as if she were Gregory, demands that she name three tokens which the lovers had exchanged. The lass mentions linen, rings, and her maidenhead, suggesting reproachfully in the process that the value of the various tokens is symbolic of their love relationship. She says, for example, of the rings (st. 12):

> For mine was of the beaten gold,
>   And yours was of block-tin;
> And mine was true love without,
>   And yours all false within.

But as soon as she has accused Gregory of stealing her maidenhead, the mother tells her to be gone, "Or else in the deep seas / You and your babe shall fall." Whereupon the girl asks who will shoe her bonny feet, etc., concluding with "who's to be father of my child / If Lord Gregory is none?" The mother's answer is: let your own family (brother, sister, mother, father) take care of you, and "let God be father of your child, / For Lord Gregory is none." Meanwhile it is apparent that Lord Gregory has been asleep inside all during this conversation; and, when he finally awakens, he tells his mother that he has dreamed he saw the Lass of Ocram floating on the flood. (That she is "floating on the flood" in his dream is our only hint that the lass may be dead.) His mother advises him to lie still and rest, for, she says, the maid passed by here not half an hour ago. Lord Gregory then curses her for not waking him and declares his heart will break for the Lass of Ocram.

The language of this version is polished and regularized; certain stylistic features ("Begone, you base creature!") have the unmistakable stamp of the broadside; and the last stanza (23) is certainly a typical eighteenth-century contribution:

> I will go down into some silent grove,
>> My sad moan for to make;
> It is for the Lass of Ocram
>> My poor heart now will break.

But the ballad has its integrity. There is compression, dramatic understatement, and a carefully contrived climax. Sentimentality is skirted: incremental repetition gives an almost ritual tone to the dialogue but is not prolonged so as to detract from the emotional intensity of the situation. The high point of pathos comes in the "shoe my foot" stanzas (16–17), and a dramatic climax is achieved in the delicate ambiguity of stanza 21, in which the mother is comforting Gregory about his dream:

> Lie still, my dearest son,
>> And take thy sweet rest;
> It is not half an hour ago,
>> The maid passd this place.

We accept her tenderness toward her son as genuine; but although lines 3 and 4 are intended (for Gregory's ears) as reassuring evidence that nothing is wrong with the girl, these innocent-sounding lines carry the whole weight of the mother's hatred. Gregory's curse in the next stanza provides the final resolution by revealing that his mother's "love" has destroyed him, as well as the girl. All in all, this version, while of course not great poetry, should rank high among traditional ballads.[18]

18. It is difficult to understand such aberrations of judgment as the one expressed by W. E. Henley and T. F. Henderson, editors of *The Poetry of Robert Burns* (London, n.d.), in a note on Burns's "Lord Gregory" (III, 455): "Of the several sets of this ballad, the most corrupt and the worst deboshed is *The Lass of Ocram*, in the Roxburghe Collection." I can only explain this as a rather violent reaction to those stylistic features typical of broadsides which, as I have pointed out, can be observed here and there in the "Ocram" version. Perhaps if its language had had a Scottish flavor, the ballad would not have seemed to the editors to be so "deboshed" (Scottish for "debauched"). As a matter of fact, rhymes such as "alone," "main" (st. 3) suggest a possible Scottish origin for the broadside version.

The version of "The Lass of Roch Royal" in Elizabeth Cochrane's songbook (Child A), like the "Ocram" text just discussed, belongs to the first half of the eighteenth century. As the story begins, Isabell of Rochroyall dreams about her love, Gregory. The dream, whatever it was (we are not told), impels her to go seek her beloved. She orders a steed saddled, and after riding a mile or so she meets a "companie" raking over the lea. She is questioned by the company as follows (A6):

> "O whether is this the first young may,
>   That lighted and gaed in;
> Or is this the second young may,
>   That neer the sun shined on;
> Or is this Fair Isabell of Roch Royall,
>   Banisht from kyth and kin?"

Concerning this stanza Child remarks (II, 214): "She meets a company, who ask her questions about a first and a second young may, which *she* seems to understand, but which are not made intelligible to us." This encounter, of course, corresponds to the meeting of the lass and the proud merchant man in the "Ocram" version (sts. 3 and 4). Unfortunately this passage, because of the corruption, can be of little help in elucidating the questions put by the company in A, which we are now considering.[19] But I do not think that these questions are totally unintelligible. "Are you the young maid," they ask, "that visits Gregory openly during the day? Or are you the one that slips in to see him at night? Or are you the one [i.e., Isabell of Rochroyall] that he got into trouble?" Understanding the questions in this way, it is immediately apparent (1) that Gregory is (at least allegedly) a ladies' man, (2) that the three maids represent steps up (or down) the ladder to his affections, and (3) that Isabell's plight is well known. But what motivates the company to ask such questions? On the assumption that they recognize her as Isabell, which seems likely in

19. It seems to me that there is a stanza missing between lines 3 and 4 of the fourth stanza of "Ocram," caused by the printer's eye skipping from "said he" to "said she" as follows:

> "Thou fairest of all creatures
>   Under the heavens," [said he],
> "   .   .   .   .
>   .   .   .   .?"
> "   .   .   .   .
>   .   .   .   ." said she,
> "I am the Lass of Ocram,
>   Seeking for Lord Gregory."

It is of course impossible to say just exactly what the proud merchant man asks the girl, but I suspect it was something like this: "Are you the fairest of all creatures under the heavens," said he, "Or are you the lass of Ocram, seeking Lord Gregory?" And she replies: "No I am not the fairest of all creatures under the heavens," said she, "I am the lass of Ocram," etc. Cf. Child F5–6, where the "ranke robers" ask the girl: "Now whether are ye the Queen herself? / For so ye weel micht bee . . . ," and she replies, "O I am neither the Queen . . . , / Nor sick I seem to be . . . ."

context, the most that can be said is that they do not appear to be favorably disposed toward the girl. Of course ballad conventions ought also to be recognized: this "company" has a function to perform.

But to continue the story as it is given in A. After Isabell identifies herself, she is directed by the company to Gregory's castle, where she tries to gain entry. The dialogue which ensues between Isabell and Gregory's mother has a startling twist. The mother, speaking as Gregory, asks for the usual tokens. But after Isabell has mentioned rings and smocks (she omits maidenhead), the mother drops all pretense and says (A17): "Love Gregory, he is not at home, / But he is to the sea; / If you have any word to him, / I pray you leav't with me." Whereupon the girl asks who will shoe her bonny foot, etc., and who will be the bairn's father. The mother then volunteers, surprisingly, that she will shoe her bonny foot, etc., but that there is none to be the bairn's father till Gregory comes home. And to this the girl strangely replies (A22): "I'll set my foot on the ship-board, / God send me wind and more! / For there's never a woman shall bear a son / Shall make my heart so sore." Whatever this may mean (that she is determined to sail in search of Gregory? that she suspects deception?), she evidently departs without accepting the mother's apparent offer of assistance.[20] Gregory then dreams that he hears the lass knocking at the door, and, when he wakes and mentions this, his mother tells him she has just left. He leaves his mother with execrations and orders his steed saddled. After riding a mile or so he meets Isabell's comely corpse, raking over the lea. He slits the winding sheet, kisses the corpse, and leaves instructions for two funerals. Birk and brier spring out of their graves.

The above version (Child A) is found in Elizabeth Cochrane's songbook, which, like the broadside, cannot be dated with precision. But this does not really matter. They are probably of about the same date. In any case the analysis given reveals that, unlike the broadside, the songbook version has absorbed elements from other ballads. This fact alone establishes the genealogical priority of the broadside, which lacks the tenacious birk and brier found in so many of the romantic ballads (e.g., Child 73, 74, 75, 84, 85).

The diction of the songbook version reflects more clearly than the

20. Child (II, 214) argues that the scene shifts after A17, that the lass returns home, and that it is her own family that offers to shoe her foot, etc. Child understands the line "Banisht from kyth and kin" to mean physical separation, not alienation. This is dubious, to say the least. But then in addition we must assume, if we accept Child's view, that the lass, having made the trip home, and having received offers of assistance from her family, decides after all to sail again in search of Gregory.

broadside what we have come to think of as typical ballad style. " 'Gar sadle me the black,' he says,/'Gar sadle me the broun . . . ,'" etc. But the narrative structure is certainly inferior and reveals a first stage in the degeneration of the ballad. A passion for parallelism is evident in the text. Since, in the intrusive funereal ending, Gregory rode his steed, Isabell must do likewise in the opening section: " 'Gar sadle me the black,' she says,/'Gar sadle me the broun . . . .'" Since Gregory had a dream about Isabell, she must have a dream about him. Thus parallelism is achieved in the ballad, but only at the expense of the sea journey, and the substitution of a vague "companie" (who, like the corpse, come raking over the lea) for the broadside's proud merchant man. We are left only with Isabell's rather pointless statement (A22) that she will set her foot on the shipboard to remind us that an element of fundamental importance—the sea journey—is missing from this version.

In Herd's version (Child B), dated 1776, the "shoe my foot" stanzas are removed from their dramatically appropriate position in the dialogue and placed at the beginning, where they now apparently become rhetorical questions uttered by the lass and addressed to the babe itself (already born? The babe is not mentioned directly again, but is perhaps indicated in B18). In response to these questions someone (her sister?) replies that members of her own family (father, mither, brither) will shoe the babe's bonny feet, etc., and concludes (B4):

> Mysel will kame his bonny head,
>> With a tabean brirben kame;
> And the Lord will be the bairn's father,
>> Till Love Gregory come hame.

Nevertheless, in spite of this comforting assurance, the lass sails away in a rich ship to seek Love Gregory. Soon she meets a "rude rover," who asks her (B8):

> O whether is thou the Queen hersel,
>> Or ane o her maries three?
> Or is thou the lass of Lochroyan,
>> Seeking Love Gregory?

She identifies herself as the latter, and the rover points out a "bonny bower" where he says she will find Love Gregory. The lass then tirls at the pin, demanding entry, and, in spite of the apparent loyalty of her family (B1–4), announces that she is "Banisht frae a' my kin" (B11). There follows the usual dialogue with mention of tokens (rings and maidenhead), except that the conversation ends abruptly, obviously because of the fact that the "shoe my foot" stanzas have been removed and placed at the beginning of the ballad. After naming the tokens, the lass again demands entry and presumably receives no reply (B18–19):

> Then she has turned her round about:
>   "Well, since that it be sae,
> Let never woman that has born a son
>   Hae a heart sae full of wae.
>
> "Take down, take down that mast o gould,
>   Set up a mast of tree;
> For it dinna become a forsaken lady
>   To sail so royallie."

Next we have Love Gregory telling his mother the dream, and she responds as usual. He curses her and orders his steed (" 'Gar saddle to me the black,' he said,/'Gar saddle to me the brown . . .,' " etc.); he rides out to meet the corpse, kisses her rosy lips, and then stabs himself to death. There is no mention of birk and brier.

The shifting of the "shoe my foot" stanzas to the beginning in this version from Herd marks a second stage in the disintegration of the ballad. Not only does this shift rob the lass-mother dialogue of its high point of pathos, but it exposes the "shoe my foot" stanzas to the danger of easy detachment from the rest of the ballad. This is, of course, what actually happens later on. We have a few ballads that lack these stanzas (76C, G), and many that consist of little else than "shoe my foot" (J, plus scores of other ballads and songs). In spite of the intrusion of the funereal ending in this version, the important sea journey is retained; but, because of the new attitude of the lass's family, her sudden departure on the bonny ship is so poorly motivated as to seem useless and arbitrary. One positive feature of Herd's text is significant: for the first time it is suggested (B1–4, 18) that the child is already born.

The fortunes of our ballad (if not of the lass herself) take a turn for the better in the two versions obtained from Mrs. Brown of Falkland. The first of these (Child D) was obtained in 1783. Anny of Roch-royal asks who will shoe her foot, etc., and we are told that her family (father, mother, sister, brother) take on this responsibility, but that the king of heaven must father her child. Nevertheless, at her wish, her father gives her a bonny ship, and, with her young son in her arms, she sails away. There is no mention of an encounter at sea with anyone. After barely a month she arrives at her truelove's door (D8):

224

The night was dark, an the win blew caul,
    An her love was fast asleep,
An the bairn that was in her twa arms
    Fu sair began to weep.

The "fa'se mither" responds and, when Anny identifies herself and "your young son," the mother calls her a witch, warlock, or mermaid. She demands tokens. Anny names napkins and rings, and concludes (D18):

Sae open the door now, Love Gregor,
    An open it wi speed,
Or your young son that is in my arms
    For cauld will soon be dead.

Then the mother (still speaking as Gregory) replies (D19): "I ha gotten another fair love, / Sae ye may hye you hame." Weeping, the lass returns to the ship. Meanwhile, Gregory tells his mother of a dream he had: Anny stood mourning at his door, but none would let her in. His mother tells the truth but in such a way as to excuse herself (D24):

O there was a woman stood at the door,
    Wi a bairn intill her arms,
But I woud na let her within the bowr,
    For fear she had done you harm.

Taking his mother at her word and hence not cursing her, Gregor quickly rushes to the strand, sees the departing ship, and calls aloud to Anny, but to no avail. Then a storm comes up suddenly, and the ship is rent in twain. Anny floats toward the shore, and Gregor wades out to bring in her body. He kisses her lips, mourning over her till sundown, when he dies.

From the summary just given, it should be apparent that Mrs. Brown has taken the poor narrative structure of Herd and made the best of it.[21] Like Herd, she has the "shoe my foot" stanzas at the beginning, but the resulting gap in the dialogue is now filled by the pathetic presence of the weeping child in the lass's arms. (The suggestion for this perhaps came from Herd, B1–4, 18, where, as we have seen, the presence of the child is implied.) Like Herd, Mrs. Brown represents the family as sympa-

21. In making observations of this kind, I do not imply that Mrs. Brown sat at her desk with a copy of Herd and worked out her versions. All I am saying is that the structure of the ballad she knew was evidently close to that represented by Herd's text.

thetic, but she eliminates all statements to the effect that the lass is "Banisht frae a' my kin" (B11) and suggests that the girl wishes (in spite of the comforts offered by her family) to be with Gregor at all costs (D5). Like Herd, Mrs. Brown has the love-death ending, but she abandons Gregory's ridiculous ride from town to town in search of a girl who has just departed on shipboard, and in its place she presents us with a skilfully wrought (if somewhat melodramatic) description of death at sea.

Mrs. Brown's second version (Child E), obtained in 1800, has essentially the same excellent qualities as those of her first. Of course there are differences of emphasis and motivation, and the ballad undergoes some compression, but though a detailed comparison would be interesting, both in itself and in what it reveals about Mrs. Brown,[22] it would be of limited value for our present purpose.

The remaining versions of "The Lass of Roch Royal" are either purely derivative or fragmentary. The text which Child lists as having been communicated to Scott by Major Hutton in 1802 is a diffuse conflation of Herd and Mrs. Brown (B and E) with a few touches from other sources. A text circulating in the first quarter of the nineteenth century and recorded in Pitcairn's MSS (Child C) reveals the final stage in the disintegration of the ballad. It has all the structural faults of Herd's version (Child B), but, in addition, it lacks the "shoe my foot" stanzas; and the questions posed (in B8) by the "rude rover" ("O whether is thou the Queen hersel, / Or ane o her maries three?" etc.) are now (strangely) asked by Gregory's mother, who has hitherto shown no inclination to flatter the lass. The ending falters between Mrs. Brown's picture of death at sea and the intrusive corpse encounter, complete with thorn and brier. Buchan's version (Child G), recorded in 1828, breaks off at stanza 17 with the naming of the tokens (and also lacks the "shoe my foot" stanzas). It is indebted to Mrs. Brown (through Scott), but it is perhaps most noteworthy for its introduction of a carpenter to build the ship. This text, however, accuses itself in the opening line: "It fell on a Wodensday . . ."[23] The rest (Child F, H, I, J, K) are fragments. The nine stanzas from Ireland (H) are interesting as an illustration of the development of a burden and as evidence that a form of the original "Ocram" version

22. See B. H. Bronson, "Mrs. Brown and the Ballad," *California Folklore Quarterly*, IV (1945), 129–140.

23. In *Last Leaves of Traditional Ballads . . . Collected . . . by the Late Gavin Greig* (Aberdeen, 1925), pp. xix–xxxv, the editor, A. Keith, presents an eloquent, and, it seems to me, partly convincing defense of Peter Buchan as a collector. But Buchan's version of "The Lass of Roch Royal" is not one of his strong points.

("Aughrim" in H) had survived independently as late as 1830. James Joyce employs a fragment of an Irish version in his short story "The Dead."[24]

In the preceding analysis we have witnessed the decline and fall of a ballad. "This ballad," says MacEdward Leach, "is rather rare in spite of the fact that it is a moving and tragic story."[25] How did it happen? The admirable narrative structure of the "Ocram" version was dealt a severe blow with the infiltration of the commonplace love-death and the graves spread over with birk and brier. A second blow came when the "shoe my foot" stanzas were removed from their dramatically appropriate position in the lass-mother dialogue and placed at the beginning—the laudable but unartistic purpose of which was to make the family sympathetic. The ballad enjoyed a temporary rebirth in Mrs. Brown but then sank finally into oblivion, detaching and leaving behind as its heritage the multitude of "shoe my foot" stanzas which are to be found in so many different ballads to this day.

Having surveyed the horizontal development of our ballad (what happened to it in the course of transmission), we are now in a position to look at it vertically, that is, to distinguish and define those elements which are fairly constant up to the time of its disintegration. This can be done quickly. And when it is done, we will finally be in a position to ask the question which is, after all, the main concern of the present discussion: What is the type of narrative represented by this ballad? Who is the Lass of Roch Royal?

On the basis of the foregoing analysis of the ballad, the following pattern emerges as representative of the basic narrative structure. A lass is sailing alone at sea on a rich ship when she meets a proud merchant man ("companie," A; "rude rover," B; "rank robers, and a' their companie," F; "rank rever, and a' his companie," Scott MS). He asks her a threefold question which may be taken alternatively as insulting or flattering, and the lass responds by identifying herself, explaining that she is banished from all her kin and is in search of her truelove. He then directs her to a nearby island ("castle," A; "bower," B; "tower," F). She approaches her truelove's door (with her young son in her arms, B [?], C, D-E, G, H; uttering a spell-breaking incantation, F, Scott MS), and asks to come in. Unknown to her lover, who is asleep, his mother answers the door and speaks for him to the lass. The mother demands tokens of their love as

24. I am indebted to my colleague Donald S. Taylor for calling this to my attention.

25. *The Ballad Book*, p. 253.

proof of her identity (after having first called the lass a witch, warlock, or mermaid, D-E, G; a false thief, C). The girl mentions various tokens, the most prominent of which is a ring, and concludes by referring to the loss of her maidenhead. The mother tells her to get out (threatens her with drowning at sea, "Ocram" version and E; says Gregory is not at home, A; says "I [Gregor] hae gotten another fair love," D; pretends not to believe her identity, Scott MS). Whereupon the lass asks who will shoe her bonny foot, etc., and who will be father of her child. The mother, still speaking as the truelove, replies (with sarcasm), let your family take care of you, and (with irony) let God be father of your child. (Of course after the shifting of the "shoe my foot" stanzas to the beginning, members of the family unhesitatingly assume their responsibilities, and the father-hood of God is devoutly intended; but this is a secondary development.) Faced with the finality of what she takes to be her truelove's cruel words, the lass returns to her ship (with her babe in her arms, A [?], B [?], C, D-E) and sails away (implied in "Ocram" and B; explicit in A, C, D-E, Scott MS). Meanwhile, her truelove awakens and relates a dream in which he saw the lass floating on the foam (heard her at the gate, A, B, D; saw her dead at his feet, E). His mother tells him to lie still and sleep, for the maid passed this place less than a half-hour ago—hence the dream can have no sinister significance. (No other version preserves this touch; it appears only in "Ocram." In the others: the mother says with apparent unconcern that the lass was here, but is gone now, A, B; the lass was here, but I wouldn't let her in for fear she might harm you, D; the lass was here, but—ominously—I certainly didn't let her in, E.)[26] The lover then curses his mother and mourns the loss of the girl, who, he presumes, is drowned at sea.[27]

Thus we can now clearly visualize our heroine: she is banished from kith and kin to sail alone on the sea; after finally coming to land she is rebuffed (as she thinks) by her truelove through the machinations of his malevolent mother and is therefore mercilessly driven, with her young babe in her arms, back once more to her ship to sail the seas in peril of her life. It should, I think, be fairly obvious by now that this girl is none other than the Accused Queen, renowned heroine of medieval folktale and romance, who is perhaps best known in Constance, the virtuous lady

26. Total disintegration of the mother's personality occurs in C, where she unceremoniously awakens Gregory (there is no dream), addresses him as "fause gudeson," and calls the lass a "limmer" (hussy).

27. The endings are so various, and in some cases so obviously secondary, that it seems inadvisable to designate any one of them as "original."

of the "Man of Law's Tale" in Chaucer's *Canterbury Tales*.[28]

The basic outline of this story (using Chaucer's version as a model) is as follows. Constance, daughter of the Roman Emperor and famous for her virtue, is affianced to the Sultan of Syria, who has agreed to give up idolatry and become a Christian. The sultan's mother, however, secretly resenting her son's abandonment of his religion, stages a great feast when Constance arrives, in which all the apostates to Christianity are slaughtered. Constance survives the massacre but is placed alone on a well-provisioned ship which sails rudderless on the sea. Years later the ship lands in Northumbria, where Constance is sheltered by a friendly constable and his wife, whom she converts to Christianity. Shortly, however, her tranquility is disturbed by the first of a series of accusations. A young knight, whose overtures have been rejected by Constance, attempts revenge by killing the friendly constable's wife and laying the bloody knife by Constance's side. The constable arrives on the scene, together with his lord, King Alla of Northumbria, and the young knight presses his accusation of murder. King Alla has great pity for the lovely but forlorn Constance and, suspecting the young knight of bearing false witness, orders him to swear on a British book of the Evangelists that his accusation is true. The young knight does this, but as soon as he speaks a hand smites him down in the presence of all, and a voice accuses him of slandering a daughter of Holy Church. This miracle results in the conversion of King Alla and his followers, and the king himself marries Constance. Her trials, however, are not over yet. The king begets a child on her but is compelled to go to war in Scotland and is therefore absent when the child (a boy) is born. A messenger, hastily dispatched with the good news, stops overnight at the castle of King Alla's mother, who, it seems, resents the fact that her son has married "so strange a creature." After getting the messenger drunk, she substitutes for the letter he is carrying one which declares that Constance has been delivered of a monster and that Constance herself must be an "elf." To this message the king replies, in effect, God's will be done; take care of my wife and child. But once again his mother intercepts the letter, replacing it with one which orders the constable to put Constance (and her young son) back on board the ship which had brought her to Northumbria and to shove her off, never to return. A weeping throng watches her departure. Again

28. The whole tradition of the Accused Queen is analyzed in an admirable study by Margaret Schlauch, *Chaucer's Con-* *stance and Accused Queens* (New York, 1927).

she sails aimlessly for years on the sea. At one point in her travels the ship stands in toward a heathen land, opposite a castle, from which emerges a recreant steward, who boards the ship with the purpose of ravishing our heroine. As he is struggling with her, however, he suddenly falls overboard and is drowned. Constance thereupon resumes her maritime journey. The rest of the story is not important for our purposes. It is concerned with the eventual reunion of King Alla and Constance (and her father the emperor) in Rome, where the recognition scene takes place.

Chaucer's story of Constance, of course, is a relatively late version of the Accused Queen. The earlier folktale had only one malevolent mother; Chaucer has two. In the folktale (I am oversimplifying to a certain extent), the banishment of the heroine is attributed to an incest-minded father; in Chaucer this is supplanted by the proposed marriage with the sultan, although Chaucer—along with Trivet and Gower, his sources—retains Constance's reluctance to talk to anyone about her father.[29] The accusation theme in the folktale centers on the king's evil mother, while Chaucer's treatment (more typical of romance as opposed to folktale) reveals the transitional stage pointed out by Schlauch[30] in which the mother's villainy is supplemented by the introduction of courtly accusers, whose motives (disappointment in love, worldly advancement) and accusations (murder, treason) are more comprehensible to the sophisticated mind than the motives and charges of the malevolent mother (a vague resentment leading to accusations of witchcraft and monstrous birth). The final stage in this development is the addition of miscellaneous trials (such as the evil steward's attempted assault on Constance in the boat), which are in harmony with the hagiographical interests of writers like Trivet.

The most obvious correspondence between the folktale of the Accused Queen and our ballad, "The Lass of Roch Royal," is, of course, the picture we get of the forlorn maid sailing the seas alone. (According to Ebsworth,[31] the "Ocram" broadside has a woodcut of a ship on it.) But the two stories are much closer together than that. The folktale has a mother who cuts the communication lines between her son and his wife by forging letters; the ballad mother accomplishes the same thing by pretending

29. Texts of the story of Constance by Trivet and Gower, together with a discussion of their relation to Chaucer's version, are conveniently printed in Margaret Schlauch, "The Man of Law's Tale," in W. F. Bryan and Germaine Dempster (eds.), *Sources and Analogues of Chaucer's Canterbury Tales* (Chicago, 1941), pp. 155–206.

30. *Chaucer's Constance and Accused Queens*, chap. iv.

31. *Roxburghe Ballads*, VI, 615.

to be her son when she answers the door. In both cases the girl has to depart with her young son aboard ship. When the king returns and discovers the truth, he has his mother executed and searches in vain for his beloved. Lord Gregory curses his mother and mourns for the lass, supposing her to be drowned. One other feature of the folktale is particularly significant when compared with the ballad. The statement in the ballad that the lass is banished from all her kin becomes the more impressive when we realize that it harks back to a version of the Accused Queen story more primitive than Chaucer's—to a version, that is, in which the heroine's banishment is attributed to an incestuous father. But, of course, the ballad as we know it clearly implies (A6–8) that the banishment can be accounted for as owing to the family's indignation at the lass's affair with Gregory. The provision of a ship for the lass by her father (D6, Scott MS 6–10) is probably a modern embellishment.

Not only are the two narratives similar in structure, but there is also a close correspondence in method of treatment. When the lass announces the birth of her babe (whether imminent or already accomplished), the mother denounces her (D11):

Awa, awa, you ill woman,
    You've na come her for gude,
You're but a witch, or wile warlock,
    Or mermaid o the flude.

Here is Chaucer's description of the forged letter sent to King Alla by Donegild, his mother (*Canterbury Tales*, B 750–756):

The lettre spak the queene delivered was
Of so horrible a feendly creature
That in the castel noon so hardy was
That any while dorste ther endure.
The mooder was an elf, by aventure
Ycomen, by charmes or by sorcerie,
And every wight hateth hir compaignye.[32]

As has already been mentioned, pathos reaches its peak in the ballad when, after the mother (speaking as her son) has ordered the girl to

32. Chaucer quotations are from Robinson (ed.), *Chaucer's Complete Works*. Trivet (Bryan and Dempster, *Sources and Analogues of Chaucer's Canterbury Tales*, p. 173) has the mother write in the letter that Constance is an evil spirit in the form of a woman (*maueise espirit en fourme de femme*). In Gower she writes: "Thi wif, which is of faierie" (Bryan and Dempster, p. 190; *Confessio Amantis*, II, 964).

7. The eighteenth century   231

leave, the latter asks who will shoe her foot, etc. In Chaucer's story the high moment of pathos comes for Constance in these justly famous lines (B 645–651):

> Have ye nat seyn somtyme a pale face,
> Among a prees, of hym that hath be lad
> Toward his deeth, wher as hym gat no grace,
> And swich a colour in his face hath had,
> Men myghte knowe his face that was bistad,
> Amonges alle the faces in that route?
> So stant Custance, and looketh hire aboute.

The lines just quoted are an exact counterpart of the "shoe my foot" stanzas of our ballad. A detailed comparison of such passages in cognate ballads and romances would, I think, lead to valuable critical conclusions about the similarities and differences to be observed when the devices of traditional ballad poetry are compared with the conscious art of a poet such as Chaucer.

To the question "who's to be father of my child?" the ballad mother replies ironically ("Ocram" st. 19): " . . . let God be father of your child, / For Lord Gregory is none." Chaucer is, of course, not interested in this kind of exploration of the evil mother's character; the spotlight is always on Constance. But the notion of divine protection is given considerable emphasis (B 631–635):

> Allas! Custance, thou hast no champioun,
> Ne fighte kanstow noght, so weylaway!
> But he that starf for our redempcioun,
> And boond Sathan (and yet lith ther he lay),
> So be thy stronge champion this day!

Constance then gets down on her knees and prays to God. But more specifically applicable to the child is her appeal to the Virgin (B 850–854):

> Now, lady bright, to whom alle woful cryen,
> Thow glorie of womanhede, thow faire may,
> Thow haven of refut, brighte sterre of day,
> Rewe on my child, that of thy gentillesse,
> Rewest on every reweful in distresse.

Very striking use is made of the young child himself in both Chaucer and the ballad. The latter pictures the lass standing at the door calling for her truelove (D8):

The night was dark, an the win blew caul,
    An her love was fast asleep,
An the bairn that was in her twa arms
    Fu sair began to weep.

It is interesting to compare this with Chaucer's description of Constance (B 834–840):

Her litel child lay wepying in hir arm,
And knelynge, pitously to hym she seyde,
'Pees, litel sone, I wol do thee noon harm.'
With that hir coverchief of hir heed she breyde,
And over his litel eyen she it leyde,
And in hir arm she lulleth it ful faste,
And into hevene hire eyen up she caste.

All of these correspondences, both in structure and in treatment of the story, lead me to the conclusion that "The Lass of Roch Royal" properly belongs with the extensive lore and literature of the Accused Queen. Whether this conclusion is of any value for fixing the date of origin of the ballad I hesitate to say. If the theory of one recent critic is correct, the story of the Accused Queen goes back ultimately to the *Clementine Recognitions* of the third century.[33] At the other end of the scale (which is, of course, where ballad scholars now realize they should look), our queen survives, on the inappropriate level of farce, as "Christian Custance," a wealthy widow, in Nicholas Udall's *Roister Doister* (mid-sixteenth century), and, more suitably, as the noble and virtuous Queen Hermione in Shakespeare's *The Winter's Tale*.[34]

Finally I would like to cite one more very significant correspondence between the story of the Accused Queen and our ballad, which represents, I believe, the most reliable type of evidence that can be brought to bear in a study such as the present one. It will be recalled that among the hazards encountered by Constance in Chaucer's "Man of Law's Tale" is the evil steward who attacks her on the ship (B 911–924):

Doun fro the castel comth ther many a wight
To gauren on this ship and on Custance.
But shortly, from the castel, on a nyght,

33. J. Schick, "Die Urquelle der Offa-Konstanze Sage," *Britannica* ("Festschrift Max Förster") (Leipzig, 1929), pp. 31–56. Cited by Schlauch, "The Man of Law's Tale," p. 160, n. 2.

34. Schlauch, *Chaucer's Constance and Accused Queens*, p. 61. I have made no special effort to uncover post-medieval versions of the Accused Queen story. I suspect there are more than a few.

7. The eighteenth century   233

The lordes styward–God yeve hym meschance!—
A theef, that hadde reneyed oure creance,
Cam into ship allone, and seyde he sholde
Hir lemman be, wher-so she wolde or nolde.

Wo was this wrecched womman tho bigon;
Hir child cride, and she cride pitously.
But blisful Marie heelp hire right anon;
For with hir struglyng wel and myghtily
The theef fil over bord al sodeynly,
And in the see he dreynte for vengeance;
And thus hath Crist unwemmed kept Custance.

In the ballad the lass is sailing alone, when (B7):

She hadna saild a league but twa
        O scantly had she three,
Till she met with a rude rover,
        Was sailing on the sea.

This "rude rover," of course, is none other than Chaucer's evil steward. But how does he behave in the ballad? He begins by asking her flattering questions: "O whether is thou the Queen hersel, / Or ane o her maries three?" This might at first suggest that he is about to make overtures to the girl. But he turns out to be merely checking her identity, and his only function is to point the way to Gregory's castle.[35] It is in the performance of this menial function that a final and bitter retribution comes upon the evil steward. In medieval romance the reward for his presumptuous attack on Constance was death by drowning. In the ballad, as punishment for looking upon our heroine with a luxurious eye, he has been turned into an innocuous signpost on the high seas.

35. The fact that he asks her if she is the "Queen hersel" need not be pushed as having any direct connection with the lass's Accused Queen ancestry. Many a ballad heroine, as she passes through the town, is "taken to be some queen." It is interesting to note that Mrs. Brown, with her usual perceptiveness, sensed that the "rude rover" was vestigial and cut him entirely out of the story.

8. Bishop Percy

The story of the making of Bishop Thomas Percy's *Reliques of Ancient English Poetry* (1765) has been eloquently told by Friedman[1] and will not be repeated here. In the present chapter we need only consider those ballads which were collected by Bishop Percy from authentic and previously untapped sources of eighteenth-century ballad tradition. Besides those pieces taken from his own folio manuscript and from earlier broadsides and collections like *The Tea-Table Miscellany*, Percy included in his *Reliques* some eight ballads sent him from Scotland which are among the best and most frequently anthologized of all the Child ballads. Moreover, as a result of the publication of the *Reliques*, Percy received from various contributors between the years 1766 and 1780 a large number of ballads and songs which he kept among his papers with the intention of using them in a subsequent volume. Although Percy's plans for publishing a new collection never materialized, his papers eventually came into the hands of Professor Child, who selected from them more than two dozen texts and fragments for inclusion in his *English and Scottish Popular Ballads*.

Some of the texts preserved in the Percy papers appear to be stall copies, "excellent old songs" like "Dick o the Cow" (185) and "Hobie Noble" (189) which were sent to Percy in 1775 by Roger Halt. A few seem to be imperfect recollections of broadsides preserved in oral tradition. Thus we have two incomplete versions of "Jock o the Side" (187), one collected for Percy by a Mr. William Hadley in 1775 "from the memory of an old person" (187C), and one collected by Percy himself in 1774 from a Mr. Leadbeater (187D). A similar origin may be postulated for the two fine ballads sent in by Miss Fisher of Carlisle in 1780, "Johnie Cock" (114A) and "Archie o Cawfield" (188A). Somewhat less valuable are the texts contributed by Mrs. Barnard, wife of a Bishop of Derry, whose versions of "Fair Margaret and Sweet William" (74B) and "The Death of Queen Jane" (170A) nevertheless testify to the flourishing of these earlier compositions in oral tradition in the eighteenth century.[2]

1. *The Ballad Revival*, pp. 185–232.
2. Mrs. Barnard likewise contributed some stanzas related to "The Famous Flower of Serving-Men" (106), which Child quotes in the introduction to that ballad (*ESPB*, II, 429).

There is also that remarkable oral version of "Hugh Spencer's Feats in France" (158B), discussed in an earlier chapter, communicated to Percy by the Duchess Dowager of Portland.

One of the most important of Percy's contributors was the Reverend P. Parsons of Wye, near Ashford, Kent, whose text of "The Twa Sisters" (10Y) was "taken down from the mouth of the spinning wheel, if I may be allowed the expression," and was first communicated to Percy in 1770. It is a remarkable version in that it is the earliest example of the interlaced refrain which later became so popular in American texts of "The Twa Sisters" (10Y1):

> There was a king lived in the North Country,
> > Hey down down dery down
> There was a king lived in the North Country,
> > And the bough it was bent to me
> There was a king lived in the North Country,
> And he had daughters one, two, three.
> > I'll prove true to my love,
> > If my love will prove true to me.

Except for a fragment of "Fair Margaret and Sweet William" (74C) and the rather slight "Willie o Winsbury" (100D), all the other ballads sent by Parsons are of considerable importance. These are the earliest known versions of "Lord Randall" (12S), "Lord Lovel" (75A), "Lamkin" (93K), and "The Maid Freed from the Gallows" (95A). All seem to be authentic specimens of eighteenth-century oral tradition, untouched by a sophisticated hand.

From the opposite end of the country on the Scottish border came five ballads, sent to Percy by the Reverend Robert Lambe, of Norham, author of "The Laidley Worm of Spindleston Heughs," which Child included as an appendix to "Kemp Owyne" (34App). Because of the pseudo-archaic character of "The Laidley Worm," one might be tempted to doubt the authenticity of Lambe's ballads, yet in fact they seem quite genuine. His "Gude Wallace" (157B) is reminiscent of a chapbook version of about 1745, and "Edom o Gordon" (178C) is fragmentary, but his "Braes o Yarrow" (214D) and "The Broom of Cowdenknows" (217A) are the earliest versions of those ballads. It may be true, as Child remarks, that Lambe's "Jean o Bethelnie" (238F) "is not pure and unvarnished tradition,"[3] as indeed can be seen in the following stanza (238F8):

3. *ESPB*, IV, 338.

'Bonny Earl Ogie, be courteous and kind;
My daughter loves you; must she die in her prime?'
When he read the first lines, a loud laugh gave he;
But or he redd the middle, the tear filld his ee.

But this is the earliest known version of the ballad by several decades, and I suspect it is more likely to be close to the original on which later versions are based, rather than, as Child apparently implies, a traditional ballad that has been polished.[4]

One of Percy's chief correspondents in Edinburgh during the decade following publication of the *Reliques* was George Paton, antiquary, bookseller, and friend of David Herd.[5] In view of Paton's interests, his knowledge, and his contacts in Edinburgh, it is surprising that he contributed only two ballad texts of his own to Percy's growing collection. One of these was a version of "Sir Hugh" (155C) which Paton obtained in 1768 from "a friend," and the other, sent to Percy ten years later, was "Lord Maxwell's Last Goodnight" (195A). This latter ballad is usually remembered because of Lord Byron's indebtedness to it in *Childe Harold*,[6] but it is most remarkable, I think, as an eighteenth-century survival of the "pseudo-ballade." Child prints the text in quatrains, but there is little doubt the original was in octaves (*ababbcdC*), as is suggested by the following two stanzas, which are printed here as one (195A7–8):

'Adue, fair Eskdale, up and doun,
    Wher my poor frends do duell!
The bangisters will beat them doun,
    And will them sore compell.
I'll reveinge the cause mysell,
    Again when I come over the sea;
Adue, my leady and only joy!
    Fore, trust me, I may not stay with the.

The final two lines of the octave are repeated several times in the ballad, reminiscent of the refrain ballads of Richard Sheale's minstrel book (Ashmole 48) considered in an earlier chapter;[7] and the use of the "fare-

4. By placing Lambe's "Jean o Bethel-nie" far down the line (238F), Child editorially discourages recognition of its priority. See Nygard, "Ballads and The Middle Ages," pp. 92 ff.

5. For an account of Paton, together with extracts from the Percy-Paton correspondence, see Hecht, *Songs from Da-*

vid Herd's Manuscripts, pp. 3–29.

6. *ESPB*, IV, 36; Leach, *The Ballad Book*, p. 533; Friedman, *The Ballad Revival*, p. 318.

7. Note that the version of "Lord Maxwell's Last Goodnight" in the Glenriddell MSS (195B) is written in stanzas of eight lines.

well" motif recalls its occurrence in the sixteenth-century minstrel poem "Flodden Field" (168 App), in one of Sheale's songs (LXVIII), and in "Johnie Armstrong" (169C29–31) and "Jock o the Side" (187A20–24). The literary form of "Lord Maxwell's Last Goodnight" and the fact that its story belongs to the early seventeenth century combine to suggest that Paton's text is the first recorded version of a ballad more than 150 years old. If this is correct, then it must be admitted that the preservation of its octave stanzas is a rarity in the history of oral transmission.

The last of the contributors to Percy's unpublished ballad collection is Dr. William Robertson, a Presbyterian minister, best known for his *History of Scotland during the Reigns of Queen Mary and of James VI* (1759), the *History of Charles V* (1769), and *History of America* (1777). In 1762 he was made principal of Edinburgh University. Of all Percy's informants thus far considered Dr. Robertson is the most suspect. His ballad beginning "There came a ghost to Helen's bower," which Child treats as a version of "Lord Lovel" (75I), is actually a composite, as Child recognized,[8] derived from "Sweet William's Ghost" (77), "Death and the Lady," and other pieces involving the deaths of lovers, and its commonplace stanzas involving a messenger boy, the saddling of steeds, love-death, and birk and brier are characteristic of eighteenth-century ballad composition. Much more skilfully put together is Dr. Robertson's version of "The Braes o Yarrow" (214A), although, as Child observes, it too was "somewhat edited" before being sent to Percy. Like several other ballads of this period, it appears to be a narrative re-creation of an earlier lyric, of which a fragment was published by Herd in 1775 (214O). But its sophisticated character is indicated by the introduction of "Douglas," alluding to William Hamilton's poem, and by such antiquarian touches as can be seen in the following stanzas (214A5–6):

'O are ye going to hawke,' she says,
    'As ye ha done before, O?
Or are ye going to weild your brand,
    Upon the braes of Yarrow?'

'O I am not going to hawke,' he says,
    'As I have done before, O,
But for to meet your brother Jhon,
    Upon the braes of Yarrow.'

8. *ESPB*, II, 204. Child calls attention to Dr. Robertson's use of inverted commas to make it look as if certain words have been changed in an otherwise reliable and authentic text (II, 213), a practice which is also evident in his version of "The Braes o Yarrow" (214A).

With all of its polish, however, Robertson's text deserves the place of honor accorded it by Child, for it is typical of a kind of dramatic ballad which was becoming increasingly popular in the later eighteenth century. The sophistication of Dr. Robertson's two versions is of course exceptional and should not be allowed to obscure the remarkable fact that most of the ballads sent to Percy after publication of the *Reliques* were authentic recoveries from oral tradition.

Turning now to the ballads which Percy originally procured for the first edition of the *Reliques*, we find a quite different picture. Very few of these ballads in fact are directly traceable to oral tradition.[9] From Ramsay's *Tea-Table Miscellany* came "The Gaberlunyie Man" (279App), "The Bonny Earl of Murray" (181A), "Sweet William's Ghost" (77A), and "Bonny Barbara Allan" (84A). Some of these seem to have been communicated to Percy in the form of manuscripts sent from Scotland, but in spite of a few orthographic differences, the texts printed in the *Reliques* are clearly Ramsay's. Three other ballads had been published separately in Glasgow in 1755: "Gill Morice" (83F), "Young Waters" (94), and "Edom o Gordon" (178D). This leaves precisely four new texts which Percy obtained in manuscript form from Scotland and which had never been published. They are "Lord Thomas and Fair Annet" (73A), "Edward" (13B), "Sir Patrick Spens" (58A), and "The Jew's Daughter" (155B). Amazingly, all four of these superb anthology pieces seem to have reached Percy in a single precious packet forwarded by John Mac-Gowan from Edinburgh in August, 1763.[10]

As might be expected, critics have not been slow to suggest that the Scottish ballads in the *Reliques*, including those that had been published in Glasgow in 1755, are more literary than traditional, as when Henderson asks rhetorically, "Were *Edom o' Gordon, Edward,* and *Sir Patrick Spens* the work of the same balladist or fakist?"[11] It is indeed very likely that MacGowan's source in Edinburgh was none other than the eminent

9. Friedman remarks in *The Ballad Revival*, p. 226: "Long before, Percy had combed the 'wilds' via letter for survivals of ancient poetry, and from Scotland, mainly thanks to Dalrymple, he gathered into the *Reliques* perhaps a dozen ballads taken up directly from oral sources."

10. Falconer, *Percy-Hailes Correspondence*, p. 48: "Last post was a lucky one indeed, it brought me your very obliging and valued Letter, and at the same time a very interesting packet from Mr. Mac-Gowan. I am fully repaid for waiting for the promised favours of that Gentle-man; he has sent me four ancient poems, three of which are of first-rate merit, and will be great ornaments to my book." (Percy to Dalrymple, Aug. 30, 1763). Could the one Percy excluded from the first rank be "Sir Hugh" (155B)? It is the least artful and most traditional-looking of the four probably included (see *ibid.,* p. 48, n. 1), yet it is first in order of appearance in the *Reliques*.

11. T. F. Henderson, *The Ballad in Literature* (Cambridge, 1912), p. 120; see also Hodgart, *The Ballads*, pp. 108 f.

8. Bishop Percy   239

jurist, David Dalrymple, Lord Hailes (1726–1792), whose interest in balladry is evident not only from the fact that he edited "Edom o Gordon" in 1755, but also from his role as Percy's Scottish expert in the preparation of the *Reliques* for the press. "I am extremely happy," said Percy in a letter to Dalrymple of January 7, 1763, "to find I have the pleasure of corresponding with the Editor of *Edom of Gordon*."[12] Then, after suggesting that the latter ballad might be improved with the addition of a few stanzas from Percy's own folio version of "Captain Car" (178B), he goes on to say:

> Be pleased, sir, to inform me whence you had Edom of Gordon, Gil Morris, (for I presume you also were the Editor of this) and any of the other charming ballads lately printed by Mr. Foulis. You will pardon me, if I suspect that they received some beauties in passing thro' your hands. This was not only an allowable freedom (if they did) but absolutely necessary to render them worthy attention.[13]

In view of Percy's own suspicions, the modern critic may perhaps be forgiven some speculation on the role of Dalrymple in the making or remaking of Percy's Scottish ballads. It is not my purpose to confront directly the question of authorship of these ballads, but, as the following analysis will indicate, I do believe that several of them have a striking similarity of style, striking enough to suggest that they may have been composed or at least retouched by the same expert hand. We may begin by considering the three Glasgow ballads published in 1755, "Gill Morice" (83F), "Young Waters" (94), and "Edom o Gordon" (178D).

In an earlier chapter we had occasion to recognize the Percy folio version of "Child Maurice" (83A) as an assignation ballad in the tradition of "Little Musgrave" (81), differing from the latter mainly in the sudden, dramatic revelation by John Steward's wife that Child Maurice was not her lover but her son. This flash of drama beneath the surface narrative, which John Home was to exploit so successfully on the stage in his tragedy of *Douglas* (1756), is much more fully developed in the Glasgow version of the ballad. The little footpage, for example, who simply delivers Child Maurice's message in the folio text, becomes in the later version an important character in the unfolding of the action.

---

12. Falconer, *Percy-Hailes Correspondence*, p. 18.

13. *Ibid.*, pp. 19–20. Dalrymple's name seems to have been given as editor of only one of the Glasgow ballads, "Edom o Gordon" (178D), but I suspect, like Percy, that his editing did not stop there. In fact I think it very likely that Dalrymple provided the texts of all three.

When Gill Morice tells him to go ask the lady to come to the greenwood, the bonny boy, whose name is Willie, protests on moral grounds, even when his master threatens him (83F4–6):

'O no! Oh no! my master dear,
　　I dare nae for my life;
I'll no gae to the bauld baron's,
　　For to triest furth his wife.'

'My bird Willie, my boy Willie,
　　My dear Willie,' he sayd,
'How can ye strive against the stream?
　　For I sall be obeyd.'

'Bot, O my master dear,' he cry'd,
　　'In grene-wod ye're your lain;
Gi owre sic thochts, I walde ye rede,
　　For fear ye should be tain.'

But when Gill Morice insists and gives him the message, Willie delivers a warning speech of three stanzas in which he agrees to go on the "black errand" but warns his master of the dire outcome, hinting that he may even lend a hand to destiny in his manner of delivering the message (83F12):

'And sen I maun your errand rin,
　　Sae sair against my will,
I'se mak a vow, and keip it trow,
　　It sall be done for ill.'

True to his vow, the boy delivers his message to the lady in the very presence of her husband at the dinner table, in spite of her efforts to warn him (83F19):

The lady stamped wi her foot,
　　And winked wi her ee;
But a' that she coud say or do,
　　Forbidden he wad nae bee.

In desperation the lady suggests that the message is for her maid, who picks up the cue immediately, but the bonny boy will not be diverted and the angry baron sets out in search of Gill Morice.

It should be quite evident that the episode just described has no precedent in the ballad tradition we have been studying. Little footpages may swim streams when the bridge is broken and slack their shoes and run on the green grass, but they do not make pivotal decisions and moral judgments on their masters. The behavior of Willie in this text is a remarkable deviation from traditional practice and implies a dramatic exploration of character better suited to the stage than to the ballad. No doubt it was this same dramatic quality that led Child to suppress the last eight stanzas of "Gill Morice" and put them in the textual notes as an example of eighteenth-century taste.[14] But this is a misleading editorial device, for those eight stanzas are but an extreme example of a technique that is operative in the ballad from beginning to end.

Of the three Glasgow ballads under consideration, "Young Waters" (94) alone exists in a single version. There is of course a long and inferior Buchan text, but Child puts it in an appendix, explaining that he has included it "for much the same reason that thieves are photographed."[15] More recently Bronson, in his edition of the Child ballad tunes, calls attention to certain artificialities in "Young Waters" and concludes that the 1755 text itself "does not seem beyond the powers of an 18th-century Scottish man or woman thoroughly familiar with Scottish popular ballad-style and working upon hints and scraps of tradition, whether native or foreign."[16] I find myself in complete agreement with this judgment and would merely add my conviction that the artificialities which Bronson has noted in "Young Waters" are precisely those we have observed in "Gill Morice" (83F). This can be seen, for example, in the characterization of the "wylie lord" who tempts the queen to speak the fatal words in praise of Young Waters (94, st. 5):

> Out then spake a wylie lord,
> Unto the queen said he,
> 'O tell me wha's the fairest face
> Rides in the company?'

As Bronson remarks, "there is something too clarifying" about this stanza; the motivation of the lord is too explicit. The same could be said of the highly dramatic exchange between the jealous king and the queen. But the technique here is exactly that of the bonny boy Willie in "Gill Morice." It is a technique previously foreign to balladry, and it makes its first appearance in the group of ballads we are now considering.

<hr />

14. Child describes the eight concluding stanzas as being "in the taste of the middle of the last century" (II, 263) and prints them separately (II, 275). Yet the last stanza but one of these eight ("I curse the hand," etc.) finds its way into Motherwell's MS (83E33).

15. *ESPB*, II, 342.

16. Bronson, *The Traditional Tunes of the Child Ballads*, II, 446.

If "Young Waters" is a newly created eighteenth-century ballad, upon what "hints and scraps of tradition" is it based? In my opinion this ballad owes its inspiration to "The Bonny Earl of Murray" (181A), which had appeared in the fourth volume of Ramsay's *Tea-Table Miscellany* (1737). Indeed "Young Waters" is, in a sense, the dramatic realization of a single suggestive stanza in "The Bonny Earl of Murray" (181A5):

> He was a braw gallant,
> > And he playd at the glove;
> And the bonny Earl of Murray,
> > Oh he was the Queen's love!

Even more specifically one can see the influence of its final stanza (181A6),

> Oh lang will his lady
> > Look oer the castle Down,
> Eer she see the Earl of Murray
> > Come sounding thro the town!

in the following lines from "Young Waters" (94, st. 2):

> The queen luikt owre the castle-wa,
> > Beheld baith dale and down,
> And then she saw Young Waters
> > Cum riding to the town.

And it is interesting that the same stanza, used somewhat less effectively,[17] appears also in "Gill Morice" (83F33):

> The lady sat on castil-wa,
> > Beheld baith dale and doun,
> And there she saw Gill Morice head
> > Cum trailing to the toun.

This is a remarkable stylistic development, foreshadowing the "block" composition of what I have referred to as the "mosaic" ballads of the late eighteenth century. In the stanzas quoted above a certain flexibility remains, but the excellence of "The Bonny Earl of Murray" renders precarious the borrowing of its beauties for the creation of new ballads. The introduction of Gill Morice's head in the stanza quoted comes perilously close to bathos. In the latter half of the century, as we shall see, stanzas

---

17. It is interesting to note that a third use of this stanza is deliberately avoided in "Edom o Gordon" (cf. 178A4 with 178D5).

in the treasury of ballad commonplaces tend to petrify and are frequently used as rigid and unvarying units in the composition of ballad mosaics. For the poet of the Glasgow ballads, meanwhile, a limited creative freedom remains; but the successful exploitation of this freedom in the creation of new ballads is contingent on a sensitive awareness of its artistic limits.

As an effort to capture the form and reproduce the impact of traditional balladry, it seems to me that "Young Waters" is superior to "Gill Morice." In part this may be attributable to the fact that "Young Waters," being a much shorter piece, contains fewer of those dramatic episodes such as are found in the other ballad. It has much greater narrative compression. Even more to the point, I think, there is a skilful use of incremental repetition which makes the story less cluttered and allows it a more leisurely development. If, as Bronson suggests, the pathos of the concluding stanzas of "Young Waters" misfires, the incremental ending is nevertheless clearly superior to the conclusion of "Gill Morice," which, as we have noted, Child suppressed in his edition. Here again we may perhaps detect the influence of "The Bonny Earl of Murray," which provides not only the plot but also the technique of incremental repetition that establishes the stylistic superiority of "Young Waters."

The third and final ballad in this group is "Edom o Gordon" (178D), fortunately preserved in several other versions of unmistakable authenticity. The earliest, as we have noted in a former chapter, appears in a sixteenth-century manuscript, a second in the Percy folio, and a third was sent to Percy by Robert Lambe in 1766. Few ballads have such solid evidence of preservation in oral tradition for nearly two hundred years. If Dalrymple's "Edom o Gordon" is the best of the three Glasgow texts, this is at least in part because it is strongly traditional, with relatively few signs of artful re-creation.

The excellence of "Edom o Gordon" is evident in its opening stanza (178D1),

> It fell about the Martinmas,
>> When the wind blew schrile and cauld,
> Said Edom o Gordon to his men,
>> We maun draw to a hald.

which is remarkably close to the sixteenth-century MS version of "Captain Car" (178A1):

> It befell at Martynmas,
>> When wether waxed colde,

Captaine Care said to his men,
    We must go take a holde.

The economy of this beginning is especially striking if we compare it with
what Bronson calls the density and "self-conscious archaism"[18] of the first
stanza of "Young Waters" (94, st. 1):

About Yule, when the wind blew cule,
    And the round tables began,
A there is cum to our king's court
    Mony a well-favourd man.

Indeed I suspect that this is an artful adaptation of the opening stanza
of "Edom o Gordon," for our analysis thus far strongly suggests a close
stylistic relationship among the three Glasgow ballads.

    A comparison of "Edom o Gordon" with "Captain Car" offers interest-
ing evidence of the evolution of ballad style which we have been tracing.
It will be recalled that the earlier text was one of our first examples of a
ballad composed to fit a known melody; except for the repetitive choric
comment in stanzas beginning "Fye upon the . . . ," there was little if any
of the narrative symmetry characteristic of the new minstrelsy, and of
course there was none of the functional repetition associated with the
pre- and post-minstrelsy periods. In accordance with what we have seen
to be the increasing tendency of eighteenth-century ballads, therefore, it
is not surprising to discover that Dalrymple's edition of "Edom o Gordon"
contains typical examples of incremental repetition, as can be observed in
the following comparisons.

    The arrival of Captain Car and his men at the lady's castle is described
in a single stanza which provides a dramatic contrast between the domestic tranquility of the supper table and the hostile gang surrounding
the home (178A7):

They wer no soner at supper sett,
    Then after said the grace,
Or Captaine Care and all his men
    Wer lighte aboute the place.

In the eighteenth-century Glasgow text this stanza is doubled and provided with incremental repetition (178D3-4):

18. Bronson, *The Traditional Tunes of
the Child Ballads*, II, 446. Bronson was
likewise struck by the similarity of the
beginning stanzas of "Young Waters" and
"Edom o Gordon," though he drew no
conclusion from it.

8. Bishop Percy   245

She had nae sooner busket her sell,
  Nor putten on her gown,
Till Edom o Gordon and his men
  Were round about the town.

They had nae sooner sitten down,
  Nor sooner said the grace,
Till Edom o Gordon and his men
  Were closed about the place.

A similar change is evident in the lady's conversation with the villain.
"Gyue ouer thi howsse, thou lady gay," says Captain Car, and she replies,
"I will not geue ouer my hous" in two subsequent but unlinked stanzas. In
the Glasgow version, however, this conversation has developed a rigid
parallelism (178D7–10):

'Cum down to me, ye lady fair,
  Cum down to me; let's see;
This night ye's ly by my ain side,
  The morn my bride sall be.'

'I winnae cum down, ye fals Gordon,
  I winnae cum down to thee;
I winnae forsake my ane dear lord,
  That is sae far frae me.'

'Gi up your house, ye fair lady,
  Gi up your house to me,
Or I will burn yoursel therein,
  Bot and your babies three.'

'I winnae gie up, you fals Gordon,
  To nae sik traitor as thee,
Tho you should burn mysel therein,
  Bot and my babies three.'

Other instances of this kind of development, typical of later balladry,
could be cited. The single stanza in "Captain Car," for example, alluding
to the treachery of John Hamleton (178A21), becomes three parallel
stanzas with incremental repetition in "Edom o Gordon" (178D12–14).
The general effect of these changes is to increase the emotional intensity
of the earlier text. Gordon's men move into the town and then close about
the place; Gordon first entices the lady, then threatens her; and treach-

erous Jock first lets in the smoke, then the fire. These devices are the result, as I have suggested, of the increased importance of melody in the shaping of ballads in the eighteenth century and contribute significantly to their attractiveness as long as they are used with restraint and discrimination.

Although it is unmistakably traditional, "Edom o Gordon" shows some signs of modernization similar to those we have observed in the other two ballads in this group. In editing the text Child did not suppress any of the stanzas, but he recognized the presence of certain "deplorable interpolations," particularly following the description of the death of the lady's daughter on the point of Edom's spear (178D19–23), and to these should perhaps be added two stanzas describing the lady's "fair speeches" and Gordon's "rage of wrath" (178D5–6). Most intriguing of all, however, is the problem of the ending, for here we have a rare opportunity to observe a ballad in the process of revision.

In the original ballad of "Captain Car" the villain and his men escape unharmed and Lord Hamilton, when he arrives, can only exclaim in grief (178A29–30):

'Fye vpon the, Captaine Care,
    And all thy blody bande!
Thou haste slayne my lady gay,
    More worth then all thy lande.

'If thou had ought eny ill will,' he saith,
    'Thou shoulde haue taken my lyffe,
And haue saved my children thre,
    All and my louesome wyffe.'

The Percy folio MS version, unfortunately, is defective, but enough of the ending is preserved to show that the lord very likely avenged his wife's death (178B19–21):

But when he looket this writing on,
    Lord, in his hart he was woe!
Saies, I will find thee, Captaine Carre,
    Wether thou ryde or goe!

Buske yee, bowne yee, my merrymen all,
    With tempered swords of steele,
For till I haue found out Captaine Carre,
    My hart it is nothing weele.

But when he came to Dractons-borrow,
    So long ere it was day,
And ther he found him Captaine Carre;
    That night he ment to stay.

    ❊   ❊   ❊   ❊   ❊   ❊

The Glasgow text differs from both of these earlier versions in that the lord arrives at the burning castle before Gordon and his men have left the scene. A terrible battle ensues, after which the grief-stricken husband throws himself in the fire (178D27–29):

But mony were the mudie men
    Lay gasping on the grien;
For o fifty men that Edom brought out
    There were but five ged heme.

And mony were the mudie men
    Lay gasping on the grien,
And mony were the fair ladys
    Lay lemanless at heme.

And round and round the waes he went,
    Their ashes for to view;
At last into the flames he flew,
    And bad the world adieu.

This ending is almost certainly modern, and seems based in part on the often reprinted broadside version of "Chevy Chase," particularly such stanzas as these (162B29, 54):

They closed full fast on euerye side,
    noe slacknes there was found,
But many a gallant gentleman
    lay gasping on the ground.

    . . . .

Of fifteen hundred Englishmen
    went home but fifty-three;
The rest in Cheuy Chase were slaine,
    vnder the greenwoode tree.

The lord's suicide is of course completely untraditional and is quite similar to those excursions into melodrama which we have noticed in "Young Waters" and particularly in "Gill Morice." In this connection it is interesting that Percy, in a letter to Dalrymple of February 28, 1764, criticized the ending of "Edom o Gordon" as follows:[19]

> I wish there is not something unnatural, at least *outrèe* in the conclusion, of the Lady's Husband's leaping into the flames; (which by the bye can hardly be supposed still burning at his return from persuing Edom o' Gordon): what if that stanza is wholly omitted, and we draw a veil over the husband's situation after having revenged her death; as the judicious painter unable to express the grief of Agamemnon properly, covered it from view. The Ballad will end very well, at
>
> > And Mony were the weiping dames
> > > Lay lemanless at hame.
>
> You dislike my two stanzas; but I think some such line as this
>
> > *Ein wood[x] wi' fel despair*   [x]i.e. mad.
>
> should be inserted, if we retain the husband's catastrophe; nothing but supposing that his grief rendered him distracted, can account for such an incident; which after all, looks like a modern, artificial contrivance: and will always look so, express it how we will.

Although Dalrymple's letters to Percy do not survive, the fortunate preservation of Percy's copy of the *Reliques* has saved for us a revised ending for "Edom of Gordon" contributed by Dalrymple:

And mony wer the mudie men,
> Lay gasping on the grèin:
For o' fifty men, that Edom brocht out,
> But five returnd again.

And mony were the mudie men,
> He left to grin and grane:
And mony were the weiping dames,
> Lay lemanless at hame.

Then back to his lady and babes he hied,
> Their esches dear to find:
Ah! lever I'd find those dear eschès,
> Than a' the gowd of Inde.

And round, and round the wa's he went
> Ein wood wi' fell despair:

---

19. Falconer, *Percy-Hailes Correspon-   dence*, pp. 68–69.

Then lap into the brenning flames,
And word spaik nevir mair.[20]

It is evident that Dalrymple was unwilling to give up the suicide ending and simply inserted a single stanza, perhaps suggested by the folio text (178B12), to account for the lord's return to the burning castle. But Percy finally rejected Dalrymple's conclusion and inserted in the *Reliques* an ending of his own based on the version in the folio MS:

He wrang his hands, he rent his hair,
And wept in teenefu' muid:
'O traitors, for this cruel deid
Ye sall weep teirs o' bluid.'

And after the Gordon he is gane,
Sa fast as he might drie;
And soon i' the Gordon's foul hartis bluid,
He's wroken his dear ladie.[21]

Whichever ending the modern reader may prefer, the friendly argument of Percy and Dalrymple over the conclusion of "Edom o' Gordon" is a fascinating instance of poetic re-creation and should serve to prepare us for the rather striking literary quality of the four new Scottish ballads included in Percy's *Reliques*: "Lord Thomas and Fair Annet" (73A), "Edward" (13B), "Sir Patrick Spens" (58A), and "Sir Hugh, or, The Jew's Daughter" (155B).

Of the four ballads just mentioned that came to Percy in a single package from Edinburgh, only one exists in an earlier version, namely, "Lord Thomas and Fair Annet," which had appeared as "Lord Thomas and Fair Ellinor" in a seventeenth-century broadside and was frequently reprinted. In his edition Child gives the Edinburgh text the place of honor, calling it "the Scottish traditional copy" and declaring it to be "one of the most beautiful of our ballads, and indeed of all ballads."[22] More recently, however, Hodgart cites it as "an example of intervention by a gifted poet" and says that "Child was rash in calling it 'the Scottish traditional copy,' though his description of it as 'one of the most beautiful of all ballads' is certainly just."[23] This seems to me an accurate judgment,

20. *Ibid.*, p. 169: "In Percy's own copy of the *Reliques* (now in the Harvard University Library) occur four additional stanzas of 'Edom o Gordon' contributed by Lord Hailes . . . across the top of the page, Percy has written: 'The following Stanzas by Sir David Dalrymple were rejected.'" For a more elegant ending, see Ian A. Gordon (ed.), *Shenstone's Miscellany, 1759–1763* (Oxford, 1952), pp. 78–87, 154–155, notes.
21. *Reliques* (4th ed., 1794), I, 100.
22. *ESPB*, II, 180.
23. Hodgart, *The Ballads*, p. 105.

confirmed or at least supported by Bronson's observation that there is "no firm anchorage for any musical tradition for 'Lord Thomas and Fair Annie' among Scottish folk-singers."[24] On the other hand, I question Hodgart's conclusion that the author of the Scottish text combined two forms of the ballad assumed to exist in tradition at that time. In his classification of versions into two groups,[25] Hodgart ignores chronology and thus fails to consider the possibility that his group one, of which the earliest representative is "Sweet Willie and Fair Annie" (73E) in Jamieson's *Popular Ballads and Songs* (Edinburgh 1806), is derived from the poetic version in Percy's *Reliques,* and, still more important, that the latter is an impressive re-creation of the seventeenth-century broadside.

The broadside version tells the original story of "Lord Thomas and Fair Ellinor" with great economy and with a trace of the structural symmetry which we have seen to be characteristic of the new minstrelsy. Thomas asks his mother if he should marry the brown girl, and Ellinor asks her mother if she should attend Thomas' wedding. The two scenes are set forth in parallel stanzas (73D2–3, 8–10) so as to sharpen the contrast between Thomas' obedience and Ellinor's disobedience. At the wedding, moreover, it is Ellinor who insults the brown girl and thus precipitates the tragedy. In the Scottish version the case is quite different.

It is not easy to describe precisely the changes that have occurred in the Scottish version of "Lord Thomas" (73A), for the poet has made a fundamental alteration in the main characters which affects the entire narrative structure. One thing that prompted this change in conception was perhaps a dissatisfaction over Thomas' spineless compliance with his mother's instruction to marry the brown girl in the original story. The lovers' quarrel with which the Scottish ballad opens thus prepares the listener for Thomas' final acceptance of his mother's advice. This change of course introduces a strained relationship between Thomas and Annet, so that his journey to tell her the news (in the broadside) is no longer appropriate, and the poet therefore solves the problem by omitting that episode and by having Annet's father simply order her to go with him to attend the wedding. Another basic change is made because of the poet's apparent dissatisfaction with the antagonism displayed by Ellinor in defying her mother's command not to go to the wedding and insulting the bride when she gets there. This unpleasant side of the heroine's personality is avoided by eliminating the episode in which she seeks her

24. Bronson, *The Traditional Tunes of the Child Ballads,* II, 88.

25. Hodgart, *The Ballads,* p. 88.

mother's advice and by having the brown bride insult fair Annet first, so as to justify the latter's devastating reply.

The fundamental changes in characterization just described are skilfully reinforced by some very striking innovations in the style of the Scottish ballad. The broadside, for example, had conveyed a sense of Ellinor's majesty and beauty in a single stanza (73D11):

> She cloathed herself in gallant attyre,
>   And her merry men all in green,
> And as they rid thorough everye towne,
>   They took her to have been a queene.

In the Scottish version this stanza is replaced by a brilliant, visual realization of the heroine and her procession (73A14–20):

> 'My maides, gae to my dressing-roome,
>   And dress to me my hair;
> Whaireir yee laid a plait before,
>   See yee lay ten times mair.

> 'My maids, gae to my dressing-room,
>   And dress to me my smock;
> The one half is o the holland fine,
>   The other o needle-work.'

> The horse Fair Annet rade upon,
>   He amblit like the wind;
> Wi siller he was shod before,
>   Wi burning gowd behind.

> Four and twanty siller bells
>   Wer a' tyed till his mane,
> And yae tift o the norland wind,
>   They tinkled ane by ane.

> Four and twanty gay gude knichts
>   Rade by Fair Annet's side,
> And four and twanty fair ladies,
>   As gin she had bin a bride.

> And whan she cam to Marie's kirk,
>   She sat on Marie's stean:
> The cleading that Fair Annet had on
>   It skinkled in their een.

And whan she cam into the kirk,
    She shimmerd like the sun;
The belt that was about her waist
    Was a' wi pearles bedone.

Accustomed as we are to think that descriptive passages like this one are typical of traditional ballad style, it is somewhat surprising to realize that the particular style of this passage from "Lord Thomas and Fair Annet" is virtually unknown in ballads collected before the publication of Percy's *Reliques.* The nearest resemblance to it, in fact, can be seen in "Young Waters," one of the Glasgow texts considered earlier in this chapter (94, sts. 3–4):

His footmen they did rin before,
    His horsemen rade behind;
Ane mantel of the burning gowd
    Did keip him frae the wind.

Gowden-graithd his horse before,
    And siller-shod behind;
The horse Young Waters rade upon
    Was fleeter than the wind.

But in spite of this I am not trying to say that the style of these ballads is mere poetic invention, for although it does represent a new development in eighteenth-century balladry, it remains in some sense traditional. It is a style that is analogous to the colorful pageantry of "Will Stewart and John" (107, sts. 49–50) and the aureate descriptions of "Child Waters" (63A18 ff.), but it is in no sense an imitation of these. What we are observing, I think, is a fresh realization of the possibilities of expression in traditional style.

Other changes in the Scottish "Lord Thomas," while perhaps less significant and effective than the major passage just considered, are nevertheless typical of eighteenth-century tendencies we have noticed. Thomas consults not only his mother but also his brother and sister in a series of rigidly parallel stanzas (A4–11) expanding the simple question and answer of the broadside; and the visible signs of Thomas' love for Annet are described in two stanzas (A21–22) designed to prepare the way for the brown girl's insulting question. Furthermore, the barbarous decapitation of the bride is replaced by a stabbing, and Lord Thomas' wordless suicide in the earlier text is given a melodramatic touch in revision (73A28):

'Now stay for me, dear Annet,' he sed,
    'Now stay, my dear,' he cry'd;
Then strake the dagger untill his heart,
    And fell deid by her side.

To regard this stanza as providing "a richer background of folklore" seems to me a misapprehension.[26] What we have here is precisely the kind of dramatic emphasis that is characteristic of the three Glasgow ballads, notably "Gill Morice" (83F), except that the "Lord Thomas" stanza is much more restrained and decorous. Finally it is interesting to note, in view of the imperfect conclusions of the three earlier ballads, that the Scottish "Lord Thomas" ends effectively with birk and brier growing from the lovers' graves, a motif adapted from "Fair Margaret and Sweet William" (74A18–19) and destined to be used again and again in ballads of the late eighteenth century.[27] In many ways "Lord Thomas and Fair Annet" is reminiscent of the Glasgow ballads of 1755, but it clearly surpasses them as an example of traditional ballad style. If the same poet is responsible for all four texts, we must acknowledge that his art has matured considerably in the eight-year period that separates "Lord Thomas" from the earlier ballads.

The three remaining Scottish ballads, "Edward" (13B), "Sir Patrick Spens" (58A), and "Sir Hugh, or, The Jew's Daughter" (155B), universally regarded as sterling specimens of the popular ballad, were completely unknown to the world before their publication in the *Reliques* in 1765. The form of "Edward" is unique among the ballads we are considering, and its literary origin has been fully demonstrated by Bronson.[28] But the complete reliance on dialogue to unfold the story, and Edward's sudden implication of his mother in the murder of his father at the end, serve well to illustrate the tendency toward drama in eighteenth-century balladry that we have been considering (13B7):

'And what wul ye leive to your ain mither deir,
        Edward, Edward?
And what wul ye leive to your ain mither deir?
    My deir son, now tell me O.'

---

26. *Ibid.*, p. 107, following Wimberly, *Folklore in the English and Scottish Ballads*, p. 30.

27. The birk and brier in the Scottish "Lord Thomas" (73A29–30) is perhaps anticipated in Elizabeth Cochrane's text of "The Lass of Roch Royal" (76A35),

although I am inclined to believe that 1730 is too early an estimate of the date of that songbook.

28. B. H. Bronson, "Edward, Edward: A Scottish Ballad," *SFQ*, IV (1940), 1–13, 159–61.

'The curse of hell frae me sall ye beir,
    Mither, mither,
The curse of hell frae me sall ye beir,
    Sic counseils ye gave to me O.'

Whereas the art of "Edward" is embodied in a unique, inimitable form, "Sir Patrick Spens" achieves artistic success within the confines of the conventional ballad stanza. What we have here is not imitation or the use of specific commonplaces but rather a skilled and subtle echoing of earlier ballad styles (58A1–2):

The king sits in Dumferling toune,
    Drinking the blude-reid wine:
'O whar will I get guid sailor,
    To sail this schip of mine?'

Up and spak an eldern knicht,
    Sat at the kings richt kne:
'Sir Patrick Spence is the best sailor
    That sails upon the se.'

Few ballads begin with such dramatic suddenness, but the stanzas themselves are almost casually traditional, as may be seen, for example, if we compare them with the following lines taken from "A Gest of Robyn Hode" (117, sts. 359, 367):

The kynge was wonder wroth withall,
    And swore by the Trynyte,
'I wolde I had Robyn Hode,
    With eyen I myght hym se.'

. . . .

Than bespake a proude fostere,
    That stode by our kynges kne:
Yf ye wyll se good Robyn,
    Ye must do after me.

Even closer to the eldern knicht is the wylie lord of "Young Waters" (94, st. 5):

Out then spake a wylie lord,
    Unto the queen said he,
'O tell me wha's the fairest face
    Rides in the company?'

And yet the very comparison underscores the superiority of "Sir Patrick Spens," in which the all too evident malice of the lord is removed and the motive of the knight left ambiguous.

Perhaps the most conventional feature of "Sir Patrick Spens" is the device of the written message in the form of a letter from the king (58A3–4):

> The king has written a braid letter,
>   And signd it wi his hand,
> And sent it to Sir Patrick Spence,
>   Was walking on the sand.
>
> The first line that Sir Patrick red,
>   A loud lauch lauched he;
> The next line that Sir Patrick red,
>   The teir blinded his ee.

We have already had occasion to notice the occurrence of this device in earlier minstrel compositions, particularly "Lady Bessie" in the folio manuscript,[29] whence it finds its way into seventeenth-century ballads like "Johnie Armstrong" (169A4):

> The king he writt an a letter then,
>   A letter which was large and long;
> He signed it with his owne hand,
>   And he promised to doe him no wrong.

The mixed emotions of the recipient are also anticipated in the folio version of "The Lord of Lorn" (271A85):

> The first looke he looked the letter vpon,
>   Lo! he wept full bitterly;
> The second looke he looked it vpon,
>   Said, False steward, woe be to thee!

But the recognition of these stanzas as commonplaces merely calls attention to their increased intensity and effectiveness in the later ballad. As MacEdward Leach remarks, "the ballad of 'Sir Patrick Spens' proves that these commonplaces can be manipulated to produce highly artistic effects."[30] To this I would only add that these artistic effects are the peculiar achievement of ballad "mosaics" in the latter half of the eighteenth century, of which "Sir Patrick Spens" is an outstanding example.

29. Hales and Furnivall, *The Bishop Percy Folio Manuscript*, III, 319 ff. See chap. v, above.

30. *The Ballad Book*, pp. 22–23.

Students of the ballad have often observed that actual narrative finds little space in "Sir Patrick Spens" and that the account of the shipwreck is confined to a single faultless stanza (58A8):

O our Scots nobles wer richt laith
 To weet their cork-heild schoone;
Bot lang owre a' the play wer playd,
 Thair hats they swam aboone.

This kind of ironic vision tends to be rare in traditional balladry, but it is not unlike that vivid couplet in an English sea ballad, "The Golden Vanity," describing the enemy crew at cards, blissfully unaware that their ship is sinking (286A7):

Some ware at cards, and some at dice,
Until the salt water flashd in their eyes.

This has a similar irony, but the Scottish stanza is cast in a different metrical and rhetorical mold, very similar in fact to the following stanza from "Edom o Gordon" (178D26):

And some they raid, and some they ran,
 Fu fast out-owr the plain,
But lang, lang eer he coud get up
 They were a' deid and slain.

It is tempting to see these lines as the work of a young poet in the apprentice stage, who achieves maturity in the superior style of "Sir Patrick Spens."

One other echo from tradition lends support to the notion that a single poetic intelligence lies behind the Scottish ballads we are considering. I have already indicated what seems to me the indebtedness of "Young Waters" to "The Bonny Earl of Murray." If these Scottish ballads be regarded as the work of one poet, therefore, it may be more than coincidence that the same influence suggests itself in the present case. Compare, for example, the last stanza of "The Bonny Earl of Murray" (181A6),

Oh lang will his lady
 Look oer the castle Down,
Eer she see the Earl of Murray
 Come sounding thro the town!

with the following stanza from "Sir Patrick Spens" (58A9):

8. Bishop Percy 257

> O lang, lang may their ladies sit
> Wi thair fans into their hand,
> Or eir they se Sir Patrick Spence
> Cum sailing to the land.

Far from being merely imitative, this is a brilliant re-creation of the earlier stanza, a poetic achievement we have almost come to expect of the Scottish master. Little wonder that Percy should inquire, in his letter to Sir David Dalrymple of August 30, 1763:

> I have received the Ballad of *Sir Patrick Spence*. Pray who was this warrior; in what aera of history did he live? Where may one meet with any account of him?—I have put this question to Mr MacGowan: which I here repeat, because I am fond of the poem, and would pick up information concerning it from every quarter.[31]

The final ballad in the group we are considering from Percy's *Reliques* is "Sir Hugh, or, The Jew's Daughter" (155), based on the thirteenth-century legend of Hugh of Lincoln, but perhaps best known as an analogue of Chaucer's "Prioress' Tale" of the young child allegedly slain by the Jews for his devotion to the Virgin. Several good early texts of the ballad survive. In addition to the original version in the *Reliques* (155B), there is one among the Percy papers sent in by George Paton of Edinburgh in 1768–1769 (155C); another in David Herd's manuscripts which was published in Herd's *Scottish Songs* in 1776 (155D); and, last but not least, a text obtained from Mrs. Brown of Falkland in 1800 by Robert Jamieson and published in 1806 in his *Popular Ballads and Songs* (155A). "Sir Hugh" is an appropriate ballad with which to conclude the present chapter, for in our study of its early versions we shall have a preview of the two main sources of balladry yet to be considered: David Herd and Mrs. Brown of Falkland.

The account of Hugh of Lincoln first appears under the year 1255 in the Annals of Waverley,[32] and it is undoubtedly for this reason that Child places "Sir Hugh" at the head of his series of "historical" ballads, immediately preceding "Queen Eleanor's Confession" (156), which he regarded on the basis of internal evidence to have been composed considerably later than the time of Queen Eleanor herself. But are we to suppose that "Sir Hugh" in some form or other has been in continuous existence from the year 1255? This is apparently what Child thought:

---

31. Falconer, *Percy-Hailes Correspondence*, p. 50.

32. *ESPB*, III, 235.

The English ballads [of "Sir Hugh"], the oldest of which were recovered about the middle of the last century, must, in the course of five hundred years of tradition, have departed considerably from the early form; in all of them the boy comes to his death for breaking a Jew's window, and at the hands of the Jew's daughter.[33]

It seems to me quite unlikely, however, that such a ballad could have lasted in tradition for five hundred years leaving no trace of its existence, only to emerge suddenly from obscurity with the publication of the *Reliques* in 1765. "Sir Hugh" is skilfully constructed in traditional ballad form, but like "Young Waters" and "Sir Patrick Spens," its structure and style mark it as a new creation of the Scottish master.

Of all the ballads thus far examined, "Sir Hugh" has the most plausible antique surface, and it therefore tends to elude efforts to discover the sources of its inspiration. The opening stanza, for example, skilfully suggests a partial breakdown in meaning and in the form of obscure proper names (155B1):

The rain rins doun through Mirry-land toune,
    Sae dois it doune the Pa:
Sae dois the lads of Mirry-land toune,
    Whan they play at the ba.

Percy remarks in his note to this ballad: "As for Mirry-land Town, it is probably a corruption of Milan (called by the Dutch Meylandt) Town: The Pa is evidently the river Po: altho' the Adige, not the Po, runs thro' Milan."[34] For someone as perceptive as Percy, this remark sounds almost like a parody of antiquarian ballad commentaries. Having already referred to the legend of Hugh of Lincoln, I suppose Percy is here graciously leaving it to others to discover, as indeed they do, that "Mirry-land toune" is a corruption of "merry Lincoln." Apart from the meaning of this stanza, whatever it may be, it is certainly an ingenious choice to begin the ballad, oddly but effectively reminiscent of the lyrical stanzas often prefixed to the rhymes of Robin Hood, as can be seen in the opening of "Robin Hood and the Monk" (119, sts. 1–2):

In somer, when þe shawes be sheyne,
    And leves be large and long,
Hit is full mery in feyre foreste
    To here þe foulys song:

33. *ESPB*, III, 239.   34. *Reliques* (4th ed., 1794), I, 29.

To se þe dere draw to þe dale,
   And leve þe hilles hee,
And shadow hem in þe leves grene,
   Vnder the grene-wode tre.

In an analogous way, the lads of Mirry-land toun playing ball in the rain set the stage for the beguiling of Sir Hugh, and yet they have no real part in the story. They seem to be part of a lyric prelude.

Although for reasons given above it is difficult to be sure, I suspect that "Sir Hugh" owes its general shape and form to "The Cruel Mother" (20), a seventeenth-century ballad discussed in an earlier chapter. This is the story of a duke's daughter who gives birth to two pretty babes and then murders them and buries them in the greenwood. But the babes come again as revenants, warning their mother that she will be consigned to hell for her crime. That this ballad was still alive and circulating in the eighteenth century is attested by two fragments, one preserved in David Herd's MSS (20A), and the other in James Johnson's *The Scots Musical Museum* (20B). The narrative patterns of "The Cruel Mother" and "Sir Hugh" are quite similar: both divide roughly in the middle, part one depicting the infanticide, and part two giving the revenant ending. Although traces of the influence of other ballads are occasionally evident, indebtedness to "The Cruel Mother" seems to me fundamental.

The slaying of Sir Hugh is thus described in the *Reliques* version (155B4):

And scho has taine out a little pen-knife,
   And low down by her gair;
Scho has twin'd the yong thing and his life,
   A word he nevir spak mair.

It is interesting to compare this with a stanza of "The Cruel Mother" in Johnson's *Museum* (20B3):

She's taen out her little pen-knife,
   Fine flowers in the valley
And twinnd the sweet babe o its life.
   And the green leaves they grow rarely

By this comparison it is possible to see how the creator of "Sir Hugh" has converted a couplet stanza into a quatrain by replacing the refrain of the older ballad with fillers of the type we have already noted in our earlier discussion of the "weak" line of late medieval minstrelsy. The final line of the quatrain, "a word he nevir spak mair," is recognizable as the last line of David Mallet's "William and Margaret," which occurs in Dalrymple's revision of "Edom o Gordon" (178D30) quoted above, and likewise in "Lord Thomas and Fair Annet" (73A25).

A different kind of adaptation of couplet to quatrain is evident in the description of the burial. I quote first from the broadside version, "The Duke's Daughter's Cruelty" (20O9):

> She dug a grave, it was long and deep,
> *Come bend and bear away the bows of yew*
> And there she laid them in to sleep.
> *Gentle hearts, be to me true*

With this compare the burial of Sir Hugh (155B7):

> Scho rowd him in a cake of lead,
> Bade him lie stil and sleip;
> Scho cast him in a deip draw-well,
> Was fifty fadom deip.

But not all of the descriptions are related to passages in "The Cruel Mother." One is reminded of the bleeding scene in "The Death of Robin Hood" (120A17),

> And first it bled, the thicke, thicke bloode,
> And afterwards the thinne,
> And well then wist good Robin Hoode
> Treason there was within.

in the stabbing of Sir Hugh (155B5):

> And out and cam the thick, thick bluid;
> And out and cam the thin,
> And out and cam the bonny herts bluid;
> Thair was nae life left in.

It is, finally, a curious fact that the second part or revenant episode of "Sir Hugh" seems scarcely indebted at all to "The Cruel Mother." But it is worth noting that the revenant portion of the latter ballad begins with a stanza (20O11),

> As she was a going by her father's hall,
> *Come bend and bear away the bows of yew*
> She see three children a playing at ball.
> *Gentle hearts, be to me true*

8. Bishop Percy   261

which may in part have suggested the rather puzzling first stanza of "Sir Hugh" already discussed wherein the lads of Mirry-land town are playing at the ball.[35]

The absence of influence of "The Cruel Mother" in the latter half of "Sir Hugh" can be explained, I think, by the poet's shift in midstream to another revenant ballad as his primary source of inspiration. "Sweet William's Ghost," as we have seen in an earlier chapter, is found in the 1740 edition of Ramsay's *Tea-Table Miscellany*, thus confirming that it was in existence well before the time of Percy's *Reliques*. But I suspect that the form in which this ballad was known to the Scottish author of "Sir Hugh" was similar to Herd's text which, as we have already noted, shows greater signs of antiquity than Ramsay's. Compare, for example, the beginning of the revenant episode in Herd's version (77B1),

> Whan bells war rung, an mass was sung,
> A wat a' man to bed were gone,
> Clark Sanders came to Margret's window,
> With mony a sad sigh and groan.

with the equivalent stanza in "Sir Hugh" (155B8):

> Whan bells wer rung, and mass was sung,
> And every lady went hame,
> Than ilka lady had her yong sonne,
> But Lady Helen had nane.

It seems unlikely that this is a mere sharing of ballad commonplaces, first, because both stanzas initiate revenant episodes, and second, because this motif does not in fact become commonplace until the time of Mrs. Brown, well after the publication of the *Reliques*.[36] Moreover, Sander's macabre response to Margaret's questions at the end of Herd's ballad (77B15),

> 'Cold meal is my covering owre,
> But an my winding sheet;
> The dew it falls na sooner down
> Then ay it is full weet.'

---

35. Some later versions of "The Cruel Mother" begin with the ball-playing stanza; see 20K, L, N, the version in the Wilkie MS (*ESPB*, IV, 451), and Findlay's MSS (V, 211); also "Lady Mary Ann" in *The Scots Musical Museum*, No. 377 (mentioned by Child, I, 226), which is Burns's adaptation of "My Love is Long A-Growing" in Herd's MSS (see Hecht, *Songs from David Herd's Manuscripts*, pp. 145, 299). For the possible connection with "The Bitter Withy," see below.

36. The only other occurrence of the "when bells were rung" motif before Mrs. Brown (according to Child, *ESPB*, V, 474) is in Herd's version of "Lord Ingram and Chiel Wyet" (66C26).

seems in essence to lie behind Sir Hugh's reply to his mother (155B12–13):

'The lead is wondrous heavy, mither,
    The well is wondrous deip;
A keen pen-knife sticks in my hert,
    A word I dounae speik.

'Gae hame, gae hame, my mither deir,
    Fetch me my windling sheet,
And at the back o Mirry-land toun,
    It's thair we twa sall meet.'

Thus while we must acknowledge that the revenant theme has been radically and skilfully revised to meet the needs of the legend, it appears likely that the most impressive of the revenant ballads has contributed something to the making of "Sir Hugh."

George Paton's text of "Sir Hugh" (155C), sent to Percy in 1768 or 1769, introduces a change in the story which becomes a part of nearly all subsequent versions. The ball game, which in the *Reliques* version had no narrative function, becomes in Paton's text the occasion for the encounter with the Jew's daughter (155C1–2):

Four and twenty bonny boys
    War playing at the ba;
Then up and started sweet Sir Hew,
    The flower amang them a'.

He hit the ba a kick wi's fit,
    And kept it wi his knee,
That up into the Jew's window
    He gart the bonny ba flee.

This prompts the Jew's daughter to use the ball as a means of enticing the boy in, though ultimately she has to resort to the apple, as in the earlier text. Paton's version also expands and improves on the somewhat melodramatic stanza of the original (155B6),

Scho laid him on a dressing-borde,
    And drest him like a swine,
And laughing said, Gae nou and pley
    With your sweit play-feres nine.

by replacing it with the following two stanzas describing the murder (155C7–8):

> She wyl'd him into ae chamber,
>   She wyl'd him into twa,
> She wyl'd him to her ain chamber,
>   The fairest o them a'.

> She laid him on a dressing-board,
>   Where she did sometimes dine;
> She put a penknife in his heart,
>   And dressed him like a swine.

The boy then bleeds the thick, thick blood, and the first part of the ballad ends, like the *Reliques* version, with his body being cast into the draw-well.

A curious change occurs in the revenant portion of Paton's ballad which seems in part a singer's mistake and in part a sophisticated revision. The first thing one notices is that the transitional stanza of the original, beginning "Whan bells wer rung and mass was sung," has dropped out of its place and appears, slightly revised, as the last stanza of the later text. Such a dislocation, with resultant loss of an important transition, probably led to an accidental linking of the last stanza of part one with the first stanza of part two in the mind of the singer, especially since both have similar opening phrases (155B7, 9):

> Scho rowd him in a cake of lead,
>   Bade him lie stil and sleip;
> Scho cast him in a deip draw-well,
>   Was fifty fadom deip.

> . . . .

> Scho rowd hir mantel hir about,
>   And sair, sair gan she weip,
> And she ran into the Jewis castel,
>   Whan they wer all asleip.

What happens in Paton's text, naturally enough, is that the second of these stanzas is taken to refer not to Sir Hugh's mother, but to the Jew's daughter, and therefore it is revised as follows (155C11):

> She's tane her mantle about her head,
>   Her pike-staff in her hand,
> And prayed Heaven to be her guide
>   Unto some uncouth land.

Surely this is a sophisticated revision! So far as I am aware, no other version of "Sir Hugh" sends the Jew's daughter on a pilgrimage to escape prosecution for murder, or to do penance for her crime, whichever may be implied.

Other differences in the Paton text are rather slight, and in some respects it remains closer to the original than any other version. It retains such dubious archaisms as "Mirryland town" and "play-feres," and even adds a gothic touch of its own in having Sir Hugh promise to meet his mother "at the *birks* of Mirryland town." But despite these hints of antiquarian editing, I nevertheless think the text shows unmistakable signs of melodic influence. Not only does the dislocation already discussed seem to be the result of a memory lapse, but the passage describing the mother's search for her son Hugh gives every appearance of having been sung into symmetry (155C12–14):

His mither she cam to the Jew's castle,
    And there ran thryse about:
'O sweet Sir Hew, gif ye be here,
    I pray ye to me speak.'

She cam into the Jew's garden,
    And there ran thryse about:
'O sweet Sir Hew, gif ye be here,
    I pray ye to me speak.'

She cam unto the Jew's draw-well,
    And there ran thryse about:
'O sweet Sir Hew, gif ye be here,
    I pray ye to me speak.'

The only distinctive thing about Herd's text of "Sir Hugh" (155D) is that it totally lacks the revenant episode, and therefore it ends, like Paton's, with the transitional stanza (155D10):

Whan bells was rung, and mass was sung,
    And a' men bound to bed,
Every lady got hame her son,
    But sweet Sir Hugh was dead.

Otherwise Herd's text is very close to Paton's and thus strongly confirms the existence of a version of "Sir Hugh" in Scottish oral tradition in the decade following publication of the *Reliques*. Furthermore, it completely lacks the signs of antiquarian editing which were noted above. As we shall see, the purity of this text is characteristic of the ballads collected by David Herd.

8. Bishop Percy   265

Mrs. Brown of Falkland, who gave her version of "Sir Hugh" to Jamieson in 1800, must be assumed to be acquainted with the two previously published texts, both having been included in Herd's *Scottish Songs* (1776), with which she was certainly familiar.[37] On the other hand, we can be reasonably sure that she had no knowledge of the unpublished version that Percy obtained from George Paton, which thus takes on added importance as a check on the authenticity of Mrs. Brown's variations.

The first half of Mrs. Brown's "Sir Hugh" has one new stanza, describing the boy's approach to the Jew's castle (A3), which seems patterned after the symmetrical stanzas in Paton's text (C12–14), thus suggesting a connection between the two versions in oral tradition. But in general Mrs. Brown is inclined to modify or compress rather than expand. In her text, for example, Sir Hugh no longer pleads that he cannot enter the castle without his playmates; instead he gives a quite different and more ominous excuse (155A5):

'How will I come up? How can I come up?
    How can I come up to thee?
For as ye did to my auld father,
    The same ye'll do to me.'

The superiority of Mrs. Brown's text, moreover, is especially evident in its compression of the two stanzas in Paton and Herd describing the murder (C7–8, D7–8) into a single stanza which skilfully exploits the order of climax (155A7):

She's led him in through ae dark door,
    And sae has she thro nine;
She's laid him on a dressing-table,
    And stickit him like a swine.

Besides the narrative economy, there is a gothic touch here in the "dark doors" through which the Jew's daughter entices Sir Hugh. One is reminded of Dr. Robert Anderson's statement, in his letter to Percy of September 14, 1800, that Mrs. Brown "reads everything in the marvelous way," and it is interesting to speculate that her Jew's castle may owe its dark doors to *The Castle of Otranto*.[38]

---

37. *Scottish Songs* (1776), I, 96–98, 155–157. Among Child's papers relating to Mrs. Brown in Harvard College Library (HCL 25241.37.5) is a transcript of Mrs. Brown's letter to Jamieson in which she refers to Herd's book (appendix to Child's copy of Jamieson-Brown MS, p. xv).

38. Nichols' *Illustrations of the Literary History of the Eighteenth Century*, VII, 89 f. Horace Walpole's *The Castle of Otranto* was published in 1765.

There is no dislocation of stanzas in Mrs. Brown's version of the revenant ending of "Sir Hugh," but in other respects it is very close to Paton's unpublished text. Something similar to Paton's curious pilgrimage stanza (C11) is preserved by Mrs. Brown (A11), but the latter correctly attaches it to Hugh's mother, not the Jew's daughter. Paton's symmetrical stanzas describing the mother's search for her son (C12–14) have their counterpart in the Brown version (A12–14), but the parallelism is less rigid and incremental repetition replaces the mere reiteration of formulas. This passage illustrates well the fact, as we shall see, that Mrs. Brown tends to re-create her ballads rather than merely transmit them. But perhaps the most dramatic of Mrs. Brown's changes is the new ending which she provides. Besides the added lines in which the corpse meets Lady Maisry "at the back o merry Lincoln" as promised (A16), we have the following six-line stanza with which the ballad concludes (155A17):

And a' the bells o merry Lincoln
    Without men's hands were rung,
And a' the books o merry Lincoln
    Were read without man's tongue,
And neer was such a burial
    Sin Adam's days begun.

One cannot fail to be impressed by the aptness, the inevitability, of this conclusion. Speaking of the version in the *Reliques*, Percy had remarked: "The conclusion of this ballad appears to be wanting: what it probably contained may be seen in Chaucer."[39] If Percy intended this as a challenge, we must acknowledge that Mrs. Brown's ending is a worthy response, which captures the spirit of the "Prioress' Tale" without directly imitating it. The fragility of this ending, however, is evident in the fact that it does not survive in later versions of the ballad.

Of the seven ballads in the *Reliques* sent to Percy from Scotland, "Sir Hugh" is unique in that it seems to have been sung from the moment of its first appearance.[40] I will go farther and say that it is the one new ballad in this group that may have been originally composed with a specific tune

---

39. *Reliques* (4th ed., 1794), I, 29.
40. Its popularity can be measured by the lists of traditional survivals in England (Margaret Dean-Smith, *A Guide to English Folk Song Collections* [Liverpool, 1954], p. 85, "Little Sir Hugh/ William") and in America (Coffin, *The British Traditional Ballad in North America*, p. 107). I myself know a single verse

of "Sir Hugh" unrecorded elsewhere, which I heard from my mother, who learned it as a child in Monroe, N.C., *ca.* 1893:

My little son Hugh, if you're in here,
    As I suppose you to be,
Hark unto your dear mother's voice,
    Who stands and waits for thee.

in mind. For this reason it provides us with a rare opportunity to observe the remarkable ways in which melody can influence the evolution of a particular ballad, and hence we may conclude the present chapter by tracing this influence, even though it means going beyond the limits of the present history to include a few nineteenth-century texts.

It will be recalled that the earliest version of "Sir Hugh" has an opening stanza that is curiously archaic and seemingly detached from the rest of the ballad (155B1):

> The rain rins doun through Mirry-land toune,
>> Sae dois it doune the Pa;
> Sae dois the lads of Mirry-land toune,
>> Whan they play at the ba.

And while playing at the ball, as we have seen, is not uncommon in balladry, it is a little unusual when combined with rainfall. The popular carol known as "The Bitter Withy," however, does in fact have a similar opening stanza:[41]

> As it fell out on a Holy day,
>> The drops of rain did fall, did fall,
> Our Saviour asked leave of His mother Mary
>> If he might go play at ball.

This suggests the possibility, at least, that "Sir Hugh" was originally created and shaped to fit the melodic pattern of "The Bitter Withy." Of course one difficulty with this supposition is the fact that our earliest known fragment of the carol was published in 1868, over a century after publication of "Sir Hugh" (155B) in the *Reliques*. But this problem is more apparent than real, for, as we have noted in an earlier chapter on the folksong tradition, the much greater "stability of occasion" for the singing of religious songs has allowed unrecorded survivals of carols over a longer period of time than has been possible in the case of balladry.

Even if it is safe, as I think it is, to assume the existence of "The Bitter Withy" in the mid-eighteenth century, the fact that it and "Sir Hugh" have similar opening stanzas would scarcely suffice to establish a connection between the two, nor do all versions of "Sir Hugh" possess the rainfall stanza. There are several nineteenth-century texts, however, containing evidence which curiously suggests that "The Bitter Withy" was leaving its stamp on the ballad of "Sir Hugh."

The first nineteenth-century version of "Sir Hugh," in only five stan-

41. Reprinted in Leach, *The Ballad Book*, p. 689.

zas, was published in 1814, and it contains a particularly interesting addition to the boy's original reason for refusing to enter the Jew's castle (155I4):

'I durst not come, I durst not go,
    Without my play-fellowes all;
For if my mother should chance to know,
    She'd cause my blood to fall.'

At first glance this excuse seems ominously ambiguous, but another version makes the meaning clear (155J4):

'I dare not come, nor I will not come,
    Without my schoolfellows come all;
For I shall be beaten when I go home
    For losing of my ball.'

The boy's fear that his mother will beat him when he goes home is of course suggestive of what actually happens to the child Jesus in "The Bitter Withy." But taken alone this slight change in motivation could scarcely be attributed to influence of the carol.

Motherwell's version of our ballad, published in 1827, does not refer to the threat of a beating by the mother, but it does have the following curious and seemingly irrelevant final stanza (155E22):

O the broom, the bonny, bonny broom,
    The broom that makes full sore,
A woman's mercy is very little,
    But a man's mercy is more.

In a note to this stanza Motherwell remarks: "This stanza, though meant for a moral, seems to have little business here, and we are at a loss to make sense of the second line."[42] But the late Miss Gilchrist is surely right in explaining it as a quatrain from "The Bitter Withy":[43]

O the withy, the withy, the bitter withy,
    That caused me to smart, to smart
And the withy it shall be and the very first tree,
    Shall perish all at the heart.

42. William Motherwell, *Minstrelsy, Ancient and Modern* (Glasgow, 1827), p. 55, n. 2.
43. *Journal of the Folk Song Society*, XIV (1910), 43. Miss Gilchrist suggests that the "Sir Hugh" stanza may represent the original ending of "The Bitter Withy."

I cannot believe she is correct, however, in thinking that "Sir Hugh" is the model on which "The Bitter Withy" is based. The stanza quoted here is from the version obtained by Vaughan Williams, *Journal of the Folk Song Society*, VIII (1906), 205.

It seems to me that this is decisive evidence of the melodic influence of "The Bitter Withy," which in turn supports what we have inferred from the rainfall stanza and the threatened beating by the boy's mother. Although the actual tune of the versions of "Sir Hugh" quoted above is not preserved, the outlines of its magnetic field can be seen in these remarkable changes in the ballad's form.

A final example of melodic influence on "Sir Hugh" can be seen in a version obtained in Ireland and published in 1849. Here we find a fascinating transformation of the "pilgrimage" stanza discussed earlier, describing the mother as she prepares to go in search of her son (155F8):

> She put her mantle about her head,
>> Tuk a little rod in her han,
> An she says, Sir Hugh, if I fin you here,
>> I will bate you for stayin so long.

There can be little doubt that the anxious mother searching for Hugh has taken on the character of the Virgin Mary bent on punishing her child and that the rod in her hand is a branch of "The Bitter Withy."

9. David Herd

The Scottish ballad collector David Herd (1732–1810) grew up in the village of Marykirk in southwest Kincardineshire, but he spent most of his life as an accountant's clerk in Edinburgh.[1] Both his rural background and his long tenure as a respected member of the "Knights Companions of the Cape," an Edinburgh social club, help to explain his close contact with the ballad tradition. The purpose of the Cape Club was, as Herd describes it:

> to pass the evening socially with a set of select companions in an agreeable but at the same time a rational and frugal manner; for this purpose beer or porter were their liquors, from fourpence to sixpence each the extent of their usual expence, conversation and a song their amusement. . . .[2]

Significantly, Herd's official club name was "Sir Scrape Graysteel," no doubt alluding to *Eger, Grime, and Graysteel,* a romance treated in an earlier chapter of this history.[3] In addition to the usual evenings spent in conviviality, the knights of the club occasionally staged celebrations in memory of great men, such as Shakespeare and the Scottish poet James Thomson, in honor of whom odes were composed and sung "by musical knights." Meetings were likewise held to pay respects to the deceased, one for example in 1773 when

> a solemn dirge composed for the occasion by Sir Precenter [the poet Robert Fergusson] and sett to music by Sir Sobersides was performed by Sir Sobersides, Sir Fender and Sir Precenter, after which the evening concluded with drinking to the memory of all the deceased knights respectively, the Hall being fitted up suitable to the occasion.[4]

1. For a sketch of Herd's life see Hecht, *Songs from David Herd's Manuscripts,* pp. 30–65.
2. *Ibid.,* p. 36.
3. See chapter v above for a discussion of *Eger, Grime and Graysteel,* a romance in the Percy folio manuscript. Scott alludes to David Herd as "Dr. Graysteel" in his novel *The Antiquary* (1816), chap. 30 (Lang edition, p. 393): "He then took out his memorandum-book and wrote down: 'Kelso convoy,—said to be a step and a half ower the threshold. Authority —Caxon. *Quaere*—Whence derived? *Mem.* To write to Dr. Graysteel upon the subject." Caldwell, the editor of *Eger and Grime,* refers to the popularity of Graysteel as a nickname in Scotland (pp. 6 ff.)
4. Hecht, *Songs from David Herd's Manuscripts,* p. 41.

Against this background of Edinburgh club life David Herd's ballads may profitably be considered.

The Herd manuscripts, to which we have already referred in earlier chapters, contain by far the largest collection of Scottish ballads and songs yet assembled. By no means all of these were published in Herd's lifetime, but the manuscripts circulated freely, considering their value, and were known to several important men of letters in the last decades of the century, notably Bishop Percy, Joseph Ritson, Robert Burns, and Sir Walter Scott. Herd's *Scottish Songs*, of course, reached a much larger circle of readers and ballad lovers, including Mrs. Brown of Falkland. The first edition was published in Edinburgh in 1769, and a much larger second edition in two volumes appeared in 1776.[5]

Before turning to the ballads themselves we may briefly notice the songs in Herd's manuscripts, edited and published by Hecht in 1904. The antique flavor of the collection is indicated by the inclusion of three songs from J. Forbes's *Aberdeen Cantus* (1662), the first of which is identified by Herd as one of the songs listed in the famous *Complaint of Scotland* (1549).[6] "I am to court a wife" (ix) is recognizable as a form of "Billy Boy," and "Had I the Wyte" (xx) implies a domestic romance like that in the beginning of "The Kitchie Boy" (252). Lyrics on the order of "Green Grows the Rashes O" (xxi) are well represented. At least one of the songs, "My love is long a-growing," (xxxix), is really the fragment of a ballad, a full text of which is printed by James Maidment in *A North Countrie Garland* under the title "The Young Laird of Craigstoun." Modern versions of "A-Growing" survive, with beautiful melodies, and it is unfortunate that Child did not include this ballad in his edition.[7]

5. A complete bibliographical description of Herd's two editions is given in *ibid.*, pp. 65–69. In the following discussion I use Hecht's edition of the songs and the Glasgow reprint (1869) of Herd's second edition of the *Ancient and Modern Scottish Songs, Heroic Ballads, etc.*

6. Hecht, *Songs from David Herd's Manuscripts*, p. 91.

7. See Hodgart, *The Ballads*, pp. 21–23, which prints a Somerset text entitled "Still Growing" collected by Cecil Sharp. The earliest evidence of this remarkable ballad is a tune called "Long a-growing" preserved, without words, in the Guthrie manuscript dated about 1650–1670, which is preserved in the University Library, Edinburgh (MS Laing III. 111). The solution to the tablature of this MS was not known to James C. Dick, *The Songs of Robert Burns* (London, 1903), p. xl, though it is now said to have been deciphered: see Henry George Farmer's introduction to the modern reprint of Dick's *Songs* (Hatboro, Pa., 1962). The "Young Laird of Craigstoun," in James A. Maidment's *North Countrie Garland* (Edinburgh, 1824), pp. 21–24, was taken from the mid-eighteenth-century MS of Reverend Robert Scott, Glenbucket Parish. I am indebted to my student, Edgar G. Leimbacher Jr., for information contained in his detailed study of this ballad. Leimbacher found nearly two-dozen versions, British and American, and more than a half-dozen current recordings, including a rendition of "The Trees They Do Grow High" by Joan Baez on Vanguard VSD-2097.

The first part of Herd's *Scottish Songs*, entitled "Heroic Ballads and Fragments," owes much to Ramsay's *Tea-Table Miscellany* and Percy's *Reliques*. To the former he was ultimately indebted for "Bonny Barbara Allan" (84A), "Bonny Earl of Murray" (181A), "William's Ghost" (77A), and "Willie's drown'd in Yarrow" (215A). From the *Reliques* Herd prints all seven ballads of the Scottish master,[8] plus a version of "Chevy-Chase" (162B) and "Fair Margaret and Sweet William" (74A). Other pieces, of course, like "Lady Bothwell's Lament" and "Gilderoy," are likewise from the *Reliques*, though they are not ballads by the Child standard. Most of the songs, however, of which my favorite is "Macpherson's Rant," are Scottish and are Herd's own contribution, many obviously from oral sources. The Scottish editor could indeed boast, in the preface to his first edition, that "the only collection upon our plan, consisting entirely of Scots songs, is the Orpheus Caledonius, published by William Thomson in 1733."[9]

When all of the reprints, poems, and songs are set aside, however, the number of original ballad texts collected by Herd, including those preserved only in his manuscripts, is no less than forty-six, much larger than any other collection we have reviewed except for the Percy folio. Of these forty-six, there are twelve ballads that exist in earlier versions, five which are found in other versions contemporary with or slightly earlier than Herd, and twenty-nine which appear first in Herd's published or unpublished collections.[10]

The earliest of Herd's ballads is "The Battle of Otterburn" (161B) which, as we have seen, is preserved in a manuscript of the mid-sixteenth century. Unfortunately, as Child apparently suspected, Herd's version is almost certainly a modern reconstruction of the original and quite inferior to it.[11] Three in this first group, however, "The Baffled Knight" (112D), "The Death of Queen Jane" (170C), and "The Broom of Cowdenknows" (217B), are based on early broadsides, and a fourth, "The Cruel Mother" (20A), though fragmentary, is a lyric survival, as we have observed, of the late seventeenth-century broadside, "The Duke's Daugh-

8. The seven ballads are Child 83F, 94, 178D, 73A, 13B, 58A, and 155B, all discussed above in chapter viii. For Herd's own classification of the contents of his MS, see Hecht, *Songs from David Herd's Manuscripts*, pp. 77–87.
9. Quoted in *ibid.*, pp. 66–67.
10. Twelve ballads existing in earlier versions are 4C, 5G, 20A, 76BF, 77B, 112D, 161B, 170C, 204M, 217B, 227d, 279B. The five found in contemporary versions are 58B, 93P, 100B, 155D, 214O. The twenty-nine first appearing in Herd's collections (including two versions of 11, 68, 69, 221) are 11G, 11H, 14B, 38A, 39C, 42B, 43B, 46A, 50, 51A, 62D, 64C, 66C, 68A, 68G, 69A-77B, 69B, 88A, 91B, 182B, 196 frag, 210A, 213ef, 220A, 221A, 221B, 236 App, 241 frag, 248a, 274A, 275A, 277 frag, 305A.
11. *ESPB*, III, 294.

ter's Cruelty." Early eighteenth-century broadsides are probably represented in Herd by "Lady Isabel and the Elf-Knight" (4C), "Gil Brenton" (5G), "The Lass of Roch Royal" (76B), "Bonny Lizie Baillie" (227d), and "The Jolly Beggar" (279B). With the exception of "Bonny Lizie Baillie" (227d), which seems to be merely an imperfectly recalled broadside text, all of these ballads show signs of having come from oral tradition. There are indeed a few traces of antiquarian influence, as in the fragmentary version of "The Lass of Roch Royal" (76F7–8):

And when she saw the stately tower,
    Shynand sae cleere and bricht,
Whilk proud defies the jawing wave,
    Built on a rock a hicht,

Sche sailed it round, and sailed it sound,
    And loud, loud cried she,
'Now break, now break, ye fairy charms,
    And let the prisoner free.'

And it is tempting to suppose that the "fragment" of "Jamie Douglas" (204M) is an effort to construct a "heroic ballad" out of the folksong "Waly, Waly," which had been published earlier in Ramsay's *Tea-Table Miscellany*. But in general the ballads of this group support the conclusion that Herd's texts are solidly traditional.

Of the five Herd ballads found in other versions of about the same date, "Willie o Winsbury" (100B), "Sir Hugh" (155D), and "The Braes o Yarrow" (214O) are clearly derived from oral tradition. The case is not so clear, however, for "Sir Patrick Spens" (58B), which merely looks like the *Reliques* version marred by the tampering of an amateur, and "Lamkin" (93P), which has been so thoroughly rewritten that Child found it necessary to reject eleven of its nineteen stanzas.[12] In Herd's version of the latter ballad, Lammikin, who never received his wages for building Lord Weire's castill, threatens to burn it with fire and vows a "black revenge." In spite of this Lord Weire decides to go hunting in the good greenwood, even after his wife has an ominous and prophetic dream:

'Yestrene, yestrene, I dreamt my bower
    Of red, red blude was fu;
Gin ye gang to this black hunting,
    I sall hae caus to rue.'

12. *ESPB*, II, 340.

The five concluding stanzas, which Child also suppressed, begin with an extravagant speech by the lady when she discovers the murder of her child:

> And when she saw the red, red blude,
>   A loud scrich scriched she:
> 'O monster, monster, spare the child
>   Wha never skaithed thee.'

Both stanzas quoted above are patterned after "Sir Patrick Spens," and both contain melodramatic features like those we have observed, for example, in "Child Maurice" (83). Little wonder that Mrs. Brown of Falkland remarks, in her letter to Jamieson of September 15, 1800: "As to the fragment of Lamekin, upon reading over the edition of it that is in Herd's collection I find that mine differs from it very materially. . . . "[13]

We now come to the ballads which appear for the first time in Herd's collection. About half of these seem to be based ultimately on broadside or garland texts typical of the later eighteenth century and will not be dealt with here.[14] There are more than a dozen ballads of romance and tragedy, however, which constitute a distinctive group and are well worth considering. It is difficult to define precisely the features which these ballads have in common, but their archaic atmosphere and melodramatic action are often suggestive of the gothic novel. Perhaps they may best be compared with those "restored" gothic ruins which were the delight of landscape artists in the eighteenth and nineteenth centuries. In any case their symmetrical narratives and commonplace stanzas and themes illustrate beautifully the block composition of eighteenth-century ballad mosaics.

Two of Herd's dozen or so "originals," namely "The Cruel Brother" (11G, H) and "Babylon" (14B), are in couplet form with flower refrain and appear to be modeled after "The Twa Sisters" (10) and "The Cruel Mother" (20), both of which, as we have seen, were first recovered in the seventeenth century. It is of course possible that "The Cruel Brother" and "Babylon" are equally old, but I suspect they are not. For one thing they seem to have been influenced by the "Edward" (13) or "Lord Randal" (12) type of ballad, especially in the case of "The Cruel Brother,"

13. Quoted from Child's transcription of the Jamieson-Brown MS, Appendix, p. xv, in Harvard College Library MS 25241.37.5.
14. The best example is "Fair Mary of Wallington" (91B), which exists in a garland version of 1775 (91A) and also one by Mrs. Brown (91C). For an excellent discussion of these, see Bronson, *The Traditional Tunes of the Child Ballads*, II, 417.

with its use of the climax of relations, a motif unknown in English and Scottish balladry before the eighteenth century. The bride's willing of the gallows to her brother John in "The Cruel Brother" is especially reminiscent of the ending of "Lord Randal," while the two superfluous stanzas at the end surely echo Edward's bequest to his bairns and his wife in the *Reliques* version of that ballad (13B6).

Even more indicative of an eighteenth-century origin for "The Cruel Brother" and "Babylon" is the almost mathematical symmetry of their narratives. This can be seen in a comparison with earlier couplet ballads. "The Twa Sisters," for example, tends to develop incremental repetition in the eighteenth century, as can be seen when we compare the single stanza of the broadside devoted to the drowning girl's appeal (10A3),

> 'O sister, O sister, take me by the gowne,
> And drawe me up upon the dry ground.'

with Mrs. Brown's expansion of the same (10B11–13):

> 'O sister, sister, tak my han,
> And Ise mack you heir to a' my lan.
>
> 'O sister, sister, tak my middle,
> An yes get my goud and my gouden girdle.
>
> 'O sister, sister, save my life,
> An I swear Ise never be nae man's wife.'

But it is important to notice that Mrs. Brown's incremental repetition is an overlay which does not affect the basic narrative structure of "The Twa Sisters." The same could be said for "The Cruel Mother." When we look at "The Cruel Brother," however, the case is quite different (11G1–10):

> There was three ladys in a ha,
> *Fine flowers i the valley*
> There came three lords amang them a',
> *Wi the red, green and the yellow*
>
> The first of them was clad in red:
> 'O lady fair, will you be my bride?'
>
> The second of them was clad in green:
> 'O lady fair, will you be my queen?'

The third of them was clad in yellow:
'O lady fair, will you be my marrow?'

'You must ask my father dear,
Likewise the mother that did me bear.'

'You must ask my sister Ann,
And not forget my brother John.'

'I have askt thy father dear,
Likewise thy mother that did thee bear.

'I have askt thy sister Ann,
But I forgot thy brother John.'

Her father led her through the ha,
Her mother dancd before them a'.

Her sister Ann led her through the closs,
Her brother John put her on her horse.

This is a remarkable example of the power which melody seems to have exerted over narrative in eighteenth-century balladry. One notices first of all how the tricolored refrain has produced a rainbow of three suitors when only one is needed. But the most distinctive feature of "The Cruel Brother" is the way in which the plot itself is constructed of unvarying mathematical increments. The action can only be described as choreographic, and the dance is interrupted for but one swift moment in the middle (11G11–12):

'You are high and I am low;
Let me have a kiss before you go.'

She was louting down to kiss him sweet,
Wi his penknife he wounded her deep.

After this the slow, deliberate pace is resumed (11G13–14),

'O lead me over into yon stile,
That I may stop and breath a while.

'O lead me over to yon stair,
For there I'll ly and bleed ne mair.'

and the ballad ends with the bride's leisurely will and testament, a whole stanza being devoted to each member of the family. "The Cruel Brother" is skilfully wrought with an art that is epitomized in the brother's *double-entendre*: "You are high and I am low."

The symmetrical structure of "Babylon" (14B) is even more obvious than that of "The Cruel Brother" just considered, perhaps because "Babylon" has a less substantial plot and is artistically inferior. Three sisters, picking flowers, are threatened by a banished man, who kills two of them. The choreography of the whole ballad can easily be forecast in its description of the first encounter (14B3–6):

> He has taen the eldest by the hand,
> He has turned her about and bade her stand.
>
> 'Now whether will ye be a banisht man's wife,
> Or will ye be sticked wi my pen-knife?'
>
> 'I will na be ca'd a banished man's wife,
> I'll rather be sticked wi your pen-knife.'
>
> And he has taen out his little pen-knife,
> And frae this lady he has taen the life.

The next stanza begins with "He has taen the second by the hand," and the outcome is sufficiently predictable for any self-respecting ballad singer to compose his own ending, as in fact many of them did in the nineteenth century. Herd's version ends with the third girl defying the banished man, but later versions either suggest that the man is her brother (14C), or they have him commit suicide when he learns of the relationship (14A, D), or they have the girl's real brother rescue her from the banished man at the last moment (14E).

Both "The Cruel Brother" and "Babylon" thus seem by their style and structure to be eighteenth-century creations in imitation of earlier couplet ballads. Although not particularly archaic, they exhibit a consciousness of earlier tradition and are skilfully constructed with a symmetry that probably owes much to the melodic pattern on which they were based. The same may be said of Herd's quatrain ballads, except that the latter, as we shall see, are often curiously antiquarian in form and content.

Of the thirteen ballads of fairy lore which Child groups together as numbers 32–44 in his edition, the four earliest are "The Wee Wee Man" (38A), "Tam Lin" (39C), "Clerk Colvill" (42B), and "The Broomfield Hill" (43B), all first appearing in David Herd's collection. Prior to this time very little fairy lore had found its way into balladry, except for what can be seen obliquely in "Riddles Wisely Expounded" (1) and "The Elfin Knight" (2). Why the sudden appearance of so many fairy ballads in the latter half of the eighteenth century? The reason, I suspect, is that these are new ballads, composed in response to a growing interest in the folklore of popular tradition. They are not, of course, created out of whole cloth. "The Wee Wee Man," for example, bears a close resemblance to a metrical piece in eight-line stanzas found in a fourteenth-century manuscript, but it is altogether unlikely that Herd's text is the fruit of four hundred years of oral transmission.[15]

It should be emphasized that the folklore of the fairy ballads seems based on authentic traditional beliefs, as is particularly evident in the shape-shifting motif of "Tam Lin" and the mermaid in "Clerk Colvill." What marks these ballads as late productions is not their subject matter but rather their sophistication and self-conscious style. In "Tam Lin," for example, lest the hearer fail to grasp the supernatural status of the girl's lover, Thomas is made to explain (39C4–5):

'Full pleasant is the fairy land,
    And happy there to dwell;
I am a fairy, lyth and limb,
    Fair maiden, view me well.

'O pleasant is the fairy land,
    How happy there to dwell!
But ay at every seven years end
    We're a' dung down to hell.

This contrasts very sharply with the unexplained battle of wits in "Riddles Wisely Expounded" (1) and "The Elfin Knight" (2), neither of which bothers to discourse on the otherworld characters involved in the dialogues. The most we get are brief identifications, as in the opening stanza of "Inter diabolus et virgo":[16]

Wol 3e here a wonder thynge
Betwyxt a mayd and þe fovle fende?

There was, of course, no need to explain the status of the devil in the

15. The MS poem is given as an appendix to "The Wee Wee Man" (ESPB, I, 333–334), but Child remarks in his introduction that "there is no reason for deriving the ballad from the poem in this instance" (I, 330). The Cotton MS, Julius A. V, contains a translation of Langtoft's Chronicle by Robert of Brunne, and two sets of prophecies of Merlin. The poem in the Cotton MS introduces a series of prophecies which are not included in Child's text. These are followed by "Des suffrances de Guil. Longespée pris par les Saracens."
16. ESPB, V, 283.

fifteenth century, and indeed even less information is given us in the later ballad of the elfin knight, who merely sits on yon hill blowing his horn (2A1).

Another indication of modernity in the fairy ballads is to be seen in their adaptation of features from earlier and more popular pieces. In "Clerk Colvill" (42B), for example, the traditional mermaid has been domesticated so that she is first seen washing at a well, reminiscent of the setting of "The Maid and the Palmer" (21). That the well-washing scene had already become a stock narrative "tableau" can be seen in the mid-eighteenth-century chapbook version of "Gude Wallace" (157A2). Moreover in the final stanza of "Clerk Colvill," the will and testament theme of "Edward" and the rhetorical farewell of "Barbara Allan" seem to be echoed in the words of the dying man (42B10):

'O mother, mother, braid my hair;
    My lusty lady, make my bed;
O brother, take my sword and spear,
    For I have seen the false mermaid.'

Judgment of the antiquity of "Clerk Colvill" has inevitably been affected by its relation to the great Danish ballad of "Elveskud," which spread throughout Western Europe beginning in the sixteenth century.[17] The relationship is undeniable, but can scarcely be used to argue an early date for the English versions. The possibility of a connection between "Clerk Colvill" and "Giles Collin," however, does offer a means of getting at the problem. The latter ballad, under the title "Lady Alice" (85), was first recovered by Child in the nineteenth century, but the recent publication of William Shenstone's "Miscellany" (1759–1763) has brought to light a much earlier version which begins,[18]

Giles Collin came home unto his mother,
    O Mother come bind my head
For before eight o'clock in the morning
    O Mother, I shall be dead.

suggesting that this ballad is actually a conclusion to "Clerk Colvill," as is in fact confirmed in the American versions.[19] Such a connection with "Giles Collin" would therefore presuppose the existence of a version of

17. *ESPB*, I, 374 ff.
18. Gordon, *Shenstone's Miscellany 1759–1763*, p. 18.
19. See Coffin, *The British Traditional Ballad in North America*, "Lady Alice," pp. 86–88; also Bronson, *The Traditional Tunes of the Child Ballads*, II, 392.

"Clerk Colvill" as early as 1759–1763, at least six years before its publication in Herd's *Songs* (1769). A date much earlier than this, however, seems precluded by the pseudo-archaic and imitative style of the ballad as we know it.

One other fairy ballad, "The Broomfield Hill" (43), offers interesting confirmation of our earlier conjecture that antiquarian interests stimulated the composition of texts in this eighteenth-century group. A girl accepts a wager with her would-be lover that she can go to yon bonny greenwood and a maiden return. Going to the wood, she finds the lover asleep, and, strewing him with flowers to make known her presence, she escapes untouched. The lover rebukes his steed for not waking him. Herd's text is very slight—only six stanzas—and may be simply a fragmentary recollection of a contemporary broadside (43F) which gives the story in much greater detail.[20] The significant point to observe, however, is that neither the broadside nor Herd's version contains any hint of the supernatural. Not until Sir Walter Scott introduces the witch-woman in his second version of the ballad (43Aa) do we find the magical elements that led Child to assign it to this group. All of this suggests that Herd's text is a pastourelle in the tradition of "The Baffled Knight" (112) which Scott (or his informant) transformed into a story of witchcraft.[21] We shall find the same kind of interest in the supernatural and the occult in the ballads of Mrs. Brown of Falkland.

Passing over "Captain Wedderburn's Courtship" (46A), discussed in chapter ii above, we come to two little-known ballads, "The Bonny Hind" (50) and "Lizie Wan" (51A). Neither could be called an artistic success, but both are interesting as imitations of earlier developments in eighteenth-century balladry, especially the dramatic features of "Gil Morrice" (83F) and "Edward" (13B). In "The Bonny Hind" a maid meets a squire who takes her by the hand and deprives her of her maidenhead. When the maid, following the traditional practice, asks the squire his name, he answers truthfully and we thus discover that the lovers are brother and sister. The girl stabs herself to death, and her brother buries her among the hollins green. Grief-stricken, he returns home where, unable to tell the truth, he pretends to have lost a bonny hind beneath yon hollin tree. His father takes this literally and offers him the choice of the whole herd in his park, but the boy says (51, sts. 16, 17),

20. The broadside was printed by John White who died in 1769 (see *ESPB*, V, 145).

21. I am indebted to a study of "Broomfield Hill" by a former student, Frances W. Starr, for some valuable insights. Analogues containing the charm-induced sleep motif are cited by Child, *ESPB*, I, 391 ff.

'I care na for your hyns, my lord,
    I care na for your fee;
But O and O for my bonny hyn,
    Beneath the hollin tree!'

to which the father replies in the final stanza:

'O were ye at your sister's bower,
    Your sister fair to see,
Ye'll think na mair of your bonny hyn
    Beneath the hollin tree.'

The symbolic function of the hollin tree is similar to the braken-bush of Herd's "Battle of Otterburn" (161B11–12), but I think the symbolism is more successful in this case. Above all one is struck by the obviously contrived dramatic irony of the father's reply in the last stanza. This kind of drama, first found in "Child Maurice" (83), is quite common in ballads of the latter half of the eighteenth century.

In Herd's text of "Lizie Wan" (51A), the incest theme is given a further development. Lizie Wan's brother Geordy kills his sister when she informs him that she carries his child between her two sides. When Geordy comes to his mother's bower she questions him in the manner of "Edward" (13) and he eventually confesses what he has done. He says he will set his foot in a bottomless boat and never return till the sun and the moon shall dance on the green. Dramatic as are the events described, however, "Lizie Wan" is less effective than "The Bonny Hind" and far inferior to "Edward," which is the source of its inspiration. Just as any attempt to spell out the story implied by Hemingway's "The Killers" is doomed to failure, so this spelling out of the "Edward" ballad in "Lizie Wan" could not hope to succeed. Since the murder is explicitly related in the opening stanzas, the following dialogue between mother and son is robbed of its dramatic force.

The two ballads just considered are similar in that both strive for dramatic effect, but they differ in their method of construction. "The Bonny Hind" converts a pastourelle in the tradition of "The Knight and the Shepherd's Daughter" (110) into a drama of incest, while "Lizie Wan" makes explicit the dramatic implications of the mother-son dialogue in "Edward." In both ballads the effects are contrived, and it is unlikely that either has been long in oral tradition. Curiously, "The Bonny Hind" is one of the rare texts in Herd's collection for which a source is mentioned in the MS: "Copied from the mouth of a milkmaid, by W. L., in 1771."[22] One is reminded of the practice of Sir Thomas Malory, who frequently introduces his own additions to the French Arthurian texts with the phrase, "as the French book saith . . . ."

The ballads to which Child assigned numbers in the sixties are for the most part connected with medieval romance, as we have already noticed in the Percy folio versions of "Sir Aldingar" (59), "King Estmere" (60), "Sir Cawline" (61), "Child Waters" (63), and "Glasgerion" (67), all of which appeared in the *Reliques* in 1765. Percy himself wrote a continuation to "Sir Cawline," published as the second part of that ballad, so that a "revival" of romance ballads stimulated by publication of the *Reliques* might well be expected, and in this regard Herd does not disappoint us. Five of his texts belong in this romance group, namely, "Fair Annie" (62D), "Fair Janet" (64C), "Lord Ingram and Chiel Wyet" (66C), "Young Hunting" (68A), and "Clerk Saunders" (69A–77B), the first two being published in his *Songs* (1769), and the latter three preserved in manuscript.[23] In addition to the influence of the *Reliques*, these five texts exhibit an indebtedness to other romantic ballads still alive in tradition. "Fair Janet," for example, begins with this stanza (64C1),

Livd ance twa luvers in yon dale,
    And they luvd ither weel;
Frae evning late to morning aire
    Of luving luvd their fill.

which echoes the beginning of "Lord Thomas and Fair Annet" (73A):

Lord Thomas and Fair Annet
    Sate a' day on a hill;
Whan night was cum, and sun was sett,
    They had not talkt their fill.

On the other hand, like "The Lass of Roch Royal" (76), which we have seen to be a type of Accused Queen story, two of these new Herd ballads also show interesting connections with medieval narrative, "Fair Annie" resembling Chaucer's "Clerk's Tale" of patient Griselda, and "Lord Ingram and Chiel Wyet" reminding us of the January–May motif of the "Merchant's Tale." In the latter, Chaucer describes the old man's exuberance in bed with his young bride,

22. *ESPB*, I, 446.
23. A fragmentary version of "Young Hunting" (68G) was published in Herd's *Songs* (1776), I, 148.

9. David Herd   283

The slakke skyn aboute his nekke shaketh,
Whil that he sang, so chaunteth he and craketh.
But God woot what that May thoughte in hir herte,
Whan she hym saugh up sittynge in his sherte,
In his nyght-cappe, and with his nekke lene;
She preyseth nat his playyng worth a bene.[24]

which parallels the following stanzas in "Lord Ingram and Chiel Wyet"
(66C27-28):

Was na it a fell thing for to see,
    Twa heads lye on a coad,
Lady Maisdrey like the moten goud,
    Auld Ingram like a toad?

He turnd his face unto the stock,
    And sound he fell asleep;
She turnd her fair face unto the wa,
    And sa't tears she did weep.

Apart from its January-May motif, however, which resembles the
"Merchant's Tale" only in a general way, "Lord Ingram and Chiel Wyet"
is particularly interesting as a typical example of eighteenth-century
"block" composition. Formulas that were used flexibly by the Scottish
master now seem in "Lord Ingram" to have hardened into fixed stanzas,
no longer subject to change, and along with these comes an increasing
structural parallelism that we have found to be characteristic of this
period. Beneath the simple mosaic surface, however, is a rather complex
narrative. Lady Maisdry rejects Ingram's marriage proposals by telling
him frankly that she has slept with his nephew Wayets. Nevertheless, old
Ingram presses his suit by showering the girl and her whole family with
expensive presents. Concluding that she will be compelled to marry the
old man, Maisdry invites her lover Wayets to the wedding. In a sense
what we have here is "Lord Thomas and Fair Annet" with the sexes
reversed. Both ballads describe an impressive bridal procession, and in
both a quarrel breaks out at the church; but no violence occurs in the
Herd ballad, for although Wayets jokingly casts doubt on the bride's
virginity, he answers evasively when Lord Ingram questions him. During
the wedding night, when Maisdry confesses that she is with child, old

24. *The Canterbury Tales*, in Robinson   (E), 1849-1854.
(ed.), *Chaucer's Complete Works*, IV

284

Ingram accepts the news calmly, inviting the distracted girl to "father that bairn on me."

The leisurely pace of the narrative of "Lord Ingram," similar to the *Reliques* version of "Lord Thomas and Fair Annet" (73A), is evident in the five stanzas needed to describe the old man's gifts to the family (66C4–8) and in the twelve stanzas taken up with Maisdry's message to Wayets and his response to it (C9–20). Here the verbal-message theme, as Jones terms it,[25] assumes the fixed and inflexible form that we find in Principal Robertson's composite text of "Lord Lovel" (75I) and the garland version of "Fair Mary of Wallington" (91A), both of which begin in the manner of "Lord Ingram" (66C9–10):

'Whare will I get a bonny boy,
    Wad fain wun hos and shoon,
That wud rin on to my Wayets,
    And quickly cume again?'

'Here am I, a bonny boy,
    Wad fain wun hoes and shoon,
Wha wull rin on to your Wayets,
    And quickly cume again.'

This is followed by the "look-out" stanza of "Captain Car" (178) and "The Bonny Earl of Murray" (181), used so effectively by the Scottish master, but now employed for the pedestrian purpose of allowing Wayets to glimpse the approaching messenger (66C12):

Lord Wayets lay our his castle wa,
    Beheld baith dale and down,
And he beheld a bonny boy
    Cume rinnen to the town.

How are the mighty fallen—when a mere messenger boy replaces the awesome Captain Car and the noble Earl of Murray! Thus we see that in eighteenth-century ballad tradition, the artistic successes of yesterday are used without fear or favor in the block composition of today's ballads. It will be observed, moreover, that the individual stanzas which comprise the verbal-message theme come from a variety of sources. The "look-out" stanza just quoted, for example, is followed by a traditional inquiry, "what news, what news," in the manner of "Lord Thomas"

25. Jones, "Commonplace and Memorization." For details of the verbal-message theme see p. 112, n. 31.

(73D6), and this in turn by a curiously inappropriate stanza, similar to one in the "Lord Lovel" composite (75I),[26] in which the anxious lover asks (66C14):

'O is my ladie's fauldis brunt?
　Or is her towrs wun?
Or is my Maisdrey lighter yet
　A dear dochter or sun?'

And finally Lord Wayets, like the bold baron of "Child Maurice" (83F23), responds to news of the wedding with appropriate violence (66C17):

He dung the boord up wi his fit,
　Sae did he wi his tae;
The silver cup that sat upon 't
　I the fire he gard it flee:
'O what na a lord in a' Scotland
　Dare marry my Maisdrey?'

From the above analysis it is evident that commonplace themes like the verbal-message are strung together in a series of stanzas from miscellaneous sources. The ultimate development in this evolutionary process, of course, is that the stanza sequence itself becomes rigid and the entire verbal-message theme is regarded as a fixed unit in ballad composition. This stage is reached in the late eighteenth and early nineteenth century, especially in the ballads of Peter Buchan, which, however, fall mercifully outside the chronological limits of the present history.

The two remaining ballads in this romance group, "Young Hunting" (68) and "Clerk Saunders" (69), do not strike the same note of modernity that we have detected in the other three. Indeed, as we observed in the earlier discussion of revenant balladry, "Clerk Saunders" radiates a genuine and impressive antiquity. On the other hand, the age of "Young Hunting" is more of a problem. Though in some ways archaic, it nevertheless looks very much like a composite, pieced together skilfully from narrative themes and stanzas of earlier ballads. It is possible, however, that "Young Hunting," like "Young Andrew" (48) considered in an earlier chapter, is based on a real incident of some antiquity and that what seems to be pieced together is in fact a composite prelude designed to supply what

26. Child thought stanzas 4–11 of Principal Robertson's composite came from Mrs. Brown's ballad "Lady Maisry" (65A18–24; see *ESPB*, II, 204). But the particular stanza containing the anxious questions (75I8) seems designed as the speech of a husband separated from his wife and is therefore better suited to Principal Robertson's text than to "Lady Maisry" or "Lord Ingram."

was not known, that is, the motive and method of the actual murder. The known facts of the story—if this hypothesis is correct—would be the search for and recovery of the body from Clyde Water, which is indeed the most distinctive part of the ballad. The ordeal by fire which saves the girl falsely accused and burns the murderess is less likely to be part of the original story. Its antiquarian quality reminds one of the pilgrimage vow in "Old Robin of Portingale" (80, st. 32). But the use of candles to locate the corpse in the water has a ring of authenticity.

The imaginative re-creation of the prelude to the murder in "Young Hunting" owes much, as Nygard has shown,[27] to the famous international ballad which in Child is called "Lady Isabel and the Elf-Knight" (4). A connection between the two is not surprising, since in both a knight is slain by his lady-love. In "Lady Isabel" he is actually drowned by her, of course, whereas in "Young Hunting" he is first stabbed to death and then put in the water as a means of concealment. But the most striking development is the use of the talking bird in "Young Hunting" as the agent for exposing the murderess to the authorities, which is a much more functional role than that of the superfluous parrot appearing at the end of "Lady Isabel." This might be taken as evidence that the conception of the bird preceded that of the parrot, and hence that "Lady Isabel" borrowed from "Young Hunting"—a possibility which Nygard entertains— but I am inclined to think otherwise, mainly because the talking bird in "Young Hunting" is but one of several otherwise unrelated elements which make up the composite prelude. Let us now notice what these elements are, and if possible where they come from.

The first question apparently faced by our hypothetical composer of "Young Hunting" is a universal one: why did she do it? The motive is therefore provided in the opening stanzas (68A1–2):

'O lady, rock never your young son young
    One hour longer for me,
For I have a sweetheart in Garlick's Wells
    I love thrice better than thee.

'The very sols of my love's feet
    Is whiter then thy face:'
'But nevertheless na, Young Hunting,
    Ye'l stay wi me all night.'

27. Nygard, *The Ballad of Heer Hale-wijn*, pp. 284–286 and p. 336, n. 16. Nygard carefully qualifies his observations on the possible relationship of Child 4 and 68.

The child is an addition, referred to nowhere else, but the basic attitude expressed by Young Hunting is that of Lord Thomas (73D14):

> 'Despise her not, Fair Ellin,' he sayd,
> 'Despise her not now unto mee;
> For better I love thy little finger
> Than all her whole body.'

But as frequently happens in ballad composites, the borrowed motif fits imperfectly into its new setting. Lord Thomas was forced into a choice by the presence of both fair Ellen and the brown girl at the wedding, and though he states his preference for Ellen decidedly, he also urgently suggests that she not taunt the bride. It is a very human crisis. Young Hunting's abrupt rejection of his lady, however, is sudden and unmotivated. This kind of thing need not be a defect, but it is often the result of borrowing, and its artistic success is usually fortuitous rather than calculated, as I think is the case here in "Young Hunting."

The composer next had to ask the question: how did she do it? To answer this he appears to have taken a hint or two from another ballad murderess, the Jew's daughter in "Sir Hugh" (155B). Enticing him into her abode, the lady gets Young Hunting drunk as a swine[28] and takes him to her bed (68A6),

> And she has minded her on a little penknife,
> That hangs low down by her gare,
> And she has gin him Young Hunting
> A deep wound and a sare.

which resembles the murder of Sir Hugh (155B4):

> And scho has taine out a little pen-knife,
> And low down by her gair;
> Scho has twin'd the yong thing and his life,
> A word he nevir spak mair.

Even the talking bird episode, derived mainly it would seem from "Lady Isabel," receives a touch from "Sir Hugh." This is evident in the stanza in which the bird refuses to be enticed to light down on the lady's hand. The bird says (68A11):

---

28. With the swine reference in "Young Hunting" compare "Sir Hugh" (155B6): "Scho laid him on a dressing-borde,/And drest him like a swine."

'I winna light down, I shanna light down,
   I winna light on thy hand;
For soon, soon wad ye do to me
   As ye done to Young Hunting.'

One is reminded of Sir Hugh's response to the Jew's daughter in the *Reliques* version (155B2),

'I winnae cum in, I cannae cum in,
   Without my play-feres nine.'

or perhaps still more of this stanza from Mrs. Brown (155A5):

'How will I come up? How can I come up?
   How can I come up to thee?
For as ye did to my auld father,
   The same ye'll do to me.'

Unable to catch the bird, the lady then ingeniously dresses the corpse so as to escape detection (68A12),

She has booted an spird him Young Hunting
   As he had been gan to ride,
A hunting-horn about his neck,
   An the sharp sourd by his side.

which seems very much like an imaginative expansion of a stanza from "Bonnie James Campbell" (210A2):

Sadled and bridled,
   and bonie rode he;
Hame came horse, hame came sadle,
   but neer hame cam he.

This last would perhaps be an extravagant hypothesis, were it not for the subsequent oath of innocence sworn by the lady, particularly the form it takes in Herd's second version (68G7),

And she sware by the grass sae greene,
   Sae did she by the corn,
That she had not seen Earl Richard
   Sen yesterday at morn.

9. David Herd   289

which may possibly have been suggested by the lament of Bonnie James Campbell's wife (210A4):[29]

'My house is unbigged,
   my barn's unbeen,
My corn's unshorn,
   my meadow grows green.'

There is nothing in earlier balladry, however, to account for the dramatic climax of the story, which relates the discovery of Young Hunting's body by the divers with the aid of divining candles floated on the water at night (68A23):

Thay left off their ducking o the day,
   And ducked upon the night,
And where that sakeless knight lay slain,
   The candles shone full bright.

This lurid scene is the peculiar property of "Young Hunting," as distinctive in its way as is the devouring wolf in "Young Andrew." It is the historical event for which all else in the ballad is an imaginative preparation. MacEdward Leach speaks of "the tendency in the ballad to pass quickly over the first half of the plot—the unstable situation—to come to the second—the solution," and quite rightly gives "Lord Randal" and "The Cruel Brother" as examples. "The folk are not concerned with why," he says, "for they are not introspective or analytical. Rather they are concerned with the drama of the moment and the character's reaction to it."[30] But a composite ballad like "Young Hunting" reflects a strong interest in character and motive, suggesting that it is indeed an artistic creation that has not yet felt the shaping influence of oral tradition.

We may conclude the present chapter with one final example of an eighteenth-century ballad composite, namely "Young Johnstone" (88A), first published in Herd's *Songs* in 1769. In this ballad a knight, nameless in Herd's text, has killed his lady's only brother, but she nevertheless helps him escape his pursuers by hiding him in her secret bower while she serves bread and wine to the four and twenty armed knights who are pursuing him. She also tells these knights that the man they are seeking has already passed by. They thank her for the refreshments, and one of them wishes aloud that he had her fair body, implying I suppose that

---

29. The oath motif itself had appeared earlier in "Glasgerion" (67A18).

30. Leach, *The Ballad Book*, pp. 3 f.

these men are not members of her family. When they have (presumably) departed, the lady goes to the secret bower to meet her husband, and here the ballad concludes dramatically with four swift stanzas (88A10–3):

> Then she's gane to her secret bower,
> Her husband dear to meet;
> But he drew out his bloody sword,
> And wounded her sae deep.
>
> 'What aileth thee now, good my lord?
> What aileth thee at me?
> Have you not got my father's gold,
> But and my mother's fee?'
>
> 'Now live, now live, my fair lady,
> O live but half an hour,
> There's neer a leech in fair Scotland
> But shall be at thy bower.'
>
> 'How can I live? how shall I live?
> How can I live for thee?
> See you not where my red heart's blood
> Runs trickling down my knee?'

Why does he stab her? Is she accusing him of killing her for her money? Is his remorse genuine? The ballad ends with such questions still reverberating. Child remarks, "Awake or waking, Young Johnstone's first instinct is as duly to stab as a bull-dog's is to bite."[31] On the other hand, Bronson protests, "It seems probable that the makers of this song were more concerned with telling a tale of tragic error than they were with depicting the psychology of a rash and headstrong ruffian."[32] While not necessarily disagreeing with either of these statements, I identify "Young Johnstone" specifically as a gothic drama, a tour de force inspired by the *Reliques* version of "Edward" (13B) and pieced together with the help of "Lord Thomas and Fair Ellinor" (73D) and "Edom o Gordon" (178D).[33] Unlike "Young Hunting," it gives no indication whatever of any connection with real events; its setting is the Middle Ages as envisioned by an eighteenth-century antiquarian imagination. The secret bower that figures in the story is probably conceived as one of those hidden rooms frequently

---

31. *ESPB*, II, 288.
32. Bronson, *The Traditional Tunes of the Child Ballads*, II, 411.
33. The influence of Edward in "Young Johnstone" is fundamental, but particular echoes may be detected in 88A2–3. For traces of "Edom o Gordon," compare 88A4 with 178D5, and 88A5 with 178D3–4.

found in English manor houses, popularly said to have been used for the concealment of the family priest after the Reformation, and hence known as "the priest's hole."

As a tour de force "Young Johnstone" is an unqualified success. Its dramatic ending, as we have seen, invites speculation, and it is interesting to note that Motherwell's version responds to this challenge by adding two final stanzas which are worthy of being treated as a part of the original ballad (88B26–27):

'But take thy harp into thy hand,
    And harp out owre yon plain,
And neer think mair on thy true-love
    Than if she had never been.'

He hadna weel been out o the stable,
    And on his saddle set,
Till four and twenty broad arrows
    Were thrilling in his heart.

Are the lady's last words sincerely self-abnegating? Or is she in her dying moment trying to make sure he leaves? If the latter, why does she want him to leave? for his safety? Or did she secretly arrange an ambush with the four and twenty knights? Did he, after all, know this, and is this why he stabbed her? But if that is the case, then why does he ride to his death? The questions reverberate endlessly. Motherwell's version testifies eloquently to the recognition of "Young Johnstone" as a gothic drama in later ballad tradition.

Who could have composed the original ballad of "Young Johnstone"? It is a highly skilled piece of work, almost certainly by a poet in close touch with the ballad tradition. A possible stylistic clue is his tendency to use repeated questions, as in the last stanza of the Herd text of 1769 already quoted, and in the following stanza near the beginning (88A2):

'How can I byde? how dare I byde?
    How can I byde with thee?
Have I not killd thy ae brother?
    Thou hadst nae mair but he.'

This structural pattern first appears in a text considered in a previous chapter in George Paton's version of "Sir Hugh," obtained from a friend and sent to Percy in 1768 or 1769 (155C15):

'How can I speak, how dare I speak,
    How can I speak to thee?
The Jew's penknife sticks in my heart,
    I canna speak to thee.'

If we knew the identity of Paton's "friend," we might well know who was the composer of "Young Johnstone." Whatever his name, I am reasonably confident that he was a member of that remarkable social club in Edinburgh to which David Herd belonged, the "Knights Companions of the Cape."

10. Mrs. Brown of Falkland

The most important single contributor to the canon of English and Scottish ballads was Anna Gordon Brown (1747–1810), a native of Aberdeen, whose husband was the Reverend Andrew Brown, minister at Falkland.[1] Her father was Professor Thomas Gordon of King's College, Aberdeen, and her mother came from a singing family of the Scottish highlands, in the Braemar district. In addition to her mother, Mrs. Brown seems to have been particularly influenced in her childhood by her aunt, Mrs. Farquharson, whom Professor Gordon describes as follows in a letter to Alexander Fraser Tytler of January 19, 1793: "Being maternally fond of my children when young, she had them much about her, and was much with us. Her songs and tales of chivalry and love were a high entertainment to their young imaginations."[2] It was in this fertile environment, no doubt, that young Anna Gordon's talent for ballad singing first began to develop. We should observe, by the way, that the social setting for ballad singing here described is far different from that of the era of the new minstrelsy of the fifteenth or sixteenth centuries, and that even Allan Ramsay's gentleman of the Armstrong family seems to have retired, leaving the field to the ladies of the household. These changes affecting the "stability of occasion" of ballad recitation have of course been a constant factor in the evolutionary development being sketched in the present history, and the new social context of the "singing family" of the late eighteenth century is inevitably reflected, as we shall see, in the ballads of Mrs. Brown. Yet it is interesting to note, even at this late date, that an important feature of minstrelsy was preserved in the Gordon family as described by the professor, namely Mrs. Farquharson's "songs and tales of chivalry and love."[3]

---

1. See Bertrand H. Bronson, "Mrs. Brown and the Ballad," *California Folklore Quarterly*, IV (1945), 129–140. Manuscripts and correspondence relating to Mrs. Brown are conveniently assembled in Harvard College Library MS 25241.37.5. I am also indebted to a former student, Dr. Conny E. Nelson, whose unpublished study of "Thomas Rymer" first interested me in Mrs. Brown as a ballad informant.

2. Harvard College Library MS 25241.-37.6, pp. 13–15.

3. Without trying to make too much of Professor Gordon's words, it nevertheless may be significant that he mentions songs and tales together as parts of a single repertoire. This accords well with the almost exclusively narrative character of the texts in Mrs. Brown's MSS as compared, say, with those of David Herd's MSS.

Three principal manuscripts of Mrs. Brown's ballads are preserved. The first of these, known today as the Jamieson-Brown MS, contained twenty ballad texts without music and was originally compiled in 1783 at the request of the musicologist William Tytler. Later that same year Tytler asked Mrs. Brown for the music to these ballads, and this request resulted in the transcribing of a second manuscript, somewhat different from the first and containing only fifteen ballads, this time with musical notations, which is known as the William Tytler-Brown MS. Concerning this latter MS, Mrs. Brown remarks,

> My Father ordered Bob Scott [her nephew, later professor of Greek at Aberdeen], then a very young boy & a mere novice in musick to try to do it & he & I set to work, but found the business so crabbed that in order to abridge our labours a little we selected what we thought the best of the Ballads whose tunes being added in the best manner we could were sent [to Mr. Tytler].[4]

Seventeen years later, in 1800, when Walter Scott was collecting materials for his *Minstrelsy of the Scottish Border* (1802), he obtained the William Tytler-Brown MS and fortunately at the same time induced Alexander Fraser Tytler (whose father, William Tytler, had died in 1792) to persuade Mrs. Brown to transcribe a third set of ballads, now known as the Alexander Fraser Tytler-Brown MS. This MS contained only nine texts and no music. Later in the same year (1800), Mrs. Brown met Robert Jamieson, whose edition of *Popular Ballads and Songs* was destined to appear in Edinburgh in 1806. As a result of this meeting and through subsequent correspondence Mrs. Brown contributed six more texts (again without music) which Jamieson included in his edition.

The Jamieson-Brown MS (J-B), so called because it was given to Robert Jamieson and used by him in his *Popular Ballads and Songs*, is now among the David Laing papers in the University of Edinburgh Library. William Tytler's Brown MS (WT-B) was lost and therefore is not represented in Francis J. Child's edition except for two texts preserved in family copies and single stanzas from each of the remaining ballads quoted by Robert Anderson in his letter to Bishop Percy.[5] Fortunately, however, a transcript of the manuscript, including music, was made by Joseph Ritson, and this copy of WT-B was obtained by Dr. A. S. W. Rosen-

---

4. Quoted by Bronson, "Mrs. Brown and the Ballad," p. 130.
5. Nichols' *Illustrations of the Literary History of the Eighteenth Century*, VII, 89 f. The two ballads preserved in other copies by the Tytler family are "Willie's Lady" (6), and "Clerk Colvill" (42A).

bach and presented to the Harvard College Library in December, 1920.[6] The Alexander Fraser Tytler-Brown MS (AFT-B) has been preserved among the papers of the Fraser-Tytler family and is still kept at Aldourie Castle, Inverness.[7]

In view of the complexity of the relationship of the three collections of Mrs. Brown's ballads, I provide below a table showing the contents of each manuscript.[8] This table reveals at a glance that fourteen of the twenty texts originally copied down in J-B reappear in WT-B as preserved by Ritson. On the other hand, only two of the nine ballads in AFT-B are represented in the earlier Brown repertoire: "Child Waters" (63) and "The Lass of Roch Royal" (76). This means that the following table lists twenty-seven ballads in forty-four versions. In most cases of duplication, Child incorporated variants in his textual notes at the end of each ballad section. In two instances, however—"Young Beichan" (53AC) and "The Lass of Roch Royal" (76DE)—Child printed both texts as being sufficiently different to constitute two distinct versions.

In addition to the twenty-seven ballads preserved in J-B, WT-B, and AFT-B, Mrs. Brown furnished Jamieson with six more ballads for publication, as we have seen, in his *Popular Ballads and Songs* (1806):

"Lamkin"	93A
"Willie and Earl Richard's Daughter"	102A
"Sir Hugh, or, The Jew's Daughter"	155A
"The Baron of Brackley"	203C
"The Mother's Malison"	216B
"Bonny Baby Livingston"	222A

6. I am indebted to the Harvard College Library for use of a microfilm of the Brown MSS, and to my student, Mr. Shohachi Fukuda, whose collations of the Ritson MS have been very helpful to me in the preparation of this chapter.

7. I have learned from Dr. E. F. D. Roberts, assistant keeper, National Library of Scotland, Edinburgh, that the William Tytler MS has recently turned up and is at Aldourie Castle along with the AFT-B MS. Both MSS are available in Xerox copies in the National Library (Accession 3640). I have not had an opportunity to check Ritson's copy, used in this chapter, with the original WT-B MS.

8. The table is an adaptation of one made by Kittredge in HCL MS 25241.-

37.6, pp. 68–69. Mr. Fukuda (see n. 6, above), in his unpublished study of Ritson-Tytler, points out that the numbering of ballads in William Tytler's MS as given in Dr. Anderson's letter does not agree with that of the Ritson copy. Fukuda concludes: "But the difference is only that Ritson's Nos. 2 and 3 are Anderson's 13 and 14. Ritson's order is probably the original one. The assumption may be supported by the fact that Alexander Fraser Tytler made a transcript of 'Willie's Lady' and 'Clerk Colven' which are Ritson's Nos. 1 and 2. It is more likely that Fraser Tytler picked up the first two and did not care for more, than that he chose Nos. 1 and 13." For this reason I have used the Ritson numbering for WT-B in the table.

Ballad	Child no.	J-B MS (1783)	WT-B MS (1783)	AFT-B MS (1800)
"Rose the Red and White Lily"	103A	1	8	
"Johnie Scot"	99A	2	4	
"Willie o Douglas Dale"	101A	3	10	
"Young Beichan"	53C	4	7	
"Young Beichan"	53A	5		
"The Gay Goshawk"	96A	6	6	
"Brown Adam"	98A	7	3	
"Lady Elspat"	247	8	12	
"Fair Annie"	62E	9		
"Child Waters"	63B	10		9
"Lady Maisry"	65A	11	14	
"The Lass of Roch Royal"	76DE	12		2
"Kemp Owyne"	34B	13	11	
"King Henry"	32	14	13	
"Willie's Lady"	6	15	1	
"Gil Brenton"	5A	16	5	
"Brown Robin"	97A	17	9	
"The Twa Sisters"	10B	18	15	
"Allison Gross"	35	19		
"The Bonny Birdy"	82	20		
"Thomas Rymer"	37A			1
"Fause Foodrage"	89A			3
"Jellon Grame"	90A			4
"Fair Mary of Wallington"	91C			5
"Bonny Bee Hom"	92A			6
"The Kitchie-Boy"	252C			7
"The Cruel Brother"	11A			8
"Clerk Colvill"	42A		2	

This brings Mrs. Brown's total to thirty-three ballads in fifty-one versions.[9] The actual number is of course less significant than the quality of the texts. As the above tables reveal, Child gave Mrs. Brown's version the place of honor in twenty-four out of thirty-three cases.[10] Moreover, when

9. "Bonny Baby Livingston" (222A) exists in two versions by Mrs. Brown, as will be explained below in the discussion of that ballad.

10. By "place of honor" I mean ballads in first position (designated by the letter "A") or those existing only in Mrs. Brown's repertoire. Ballads *not* given this honor are 10B, 62E, 63B, 76DE, 91C, 203C, 216B, 252C.

we remember the broad spectrum of folksong in earlier collections—even David Herd's—it is striking to note that Mrs. Brown's texts are all ballads without exception. For the first time in our survey of the tradition we have encountered a MS collection the contents of which define the ballad exactly as does Child's edition. There can be little doubt that Mrs. Brown of Falkland is one of the most important contributors to the canon of English and Scottish balladry.

Ten of Mrs. Brown's thirty-three ballads are found in earlier versions, and hence most of these have been discussed in previous chapters. It is interesting to observe, however, that only two of them are of any great antiquity: "The Twa Sisters" (10) and "Child Waters" (63). Moreover, the former had been frequently reprinted in late seventeenth- and eighteenth-century collections, and the latter, "Child Waters," though it is known only through the Percy folio MS, had been printed by Percy in his *Reliques* (1765). It is highly unlikely that Anna Gordon's singing family carried on an oral tradition totally independent of these printed sources.[11] The remainder of Mrs. Brown's ballads, about two dozen, are originals, first found in her repertoire. In most cases later versions are also known, but five of them are uniquely preserved in the Brown MSS and are not found elsewhere.[12] The following discussion of Mrs. Brown's ballads will deal with themes (magic and witchcraft), structure (commonplaces), and genre (romance), while at the same time the chronological development of Mrs. Brown herself as a ballad composer will not be ignored.

One of the most striking interests of Mrs. Brown, judging by her repertoire, was in stories of folklore, magic, and witchcraft. She was anticipated, as we have seen in the preceding chapter, by David Herd's ballads of fairy lore, such as "Tam Lin" (39C), and in fact her version of "Clerk Colvill" (42A) seems closely related to its predecessor in Herd's *Scottish Songs*. But her interest in such folklore goes far beyond Herd's. Nearly a third of Mrs. Brown's ballads contain some form of magic or witchcraft as an important feature of the plot. Such a concentration of similar themes is unprecedented in earlier balladry and can scarcely be accidental.

Mrs. Brown's interest in the supernatural is verified by the fact that several ballads with no trace of magic or witchcraft acquire these themes in her versions. "The Lass of Roch Royal" (76), for example, has a heroine

11. Other ballads with versions predating Mrs. Brown are 5, 11, 42, 62, 76, 91, 93, 155. Some of these will appear in subsequent discussion.

12. Ballads uniquely preserved by Mrs. Brown are 6, 32, 35, 82, 247. All of these belong to her early period (1783).

who is denounced by Lord Gregory's mother as a "base creature," but it is only in Mrs. Brown's texts that the girl is reviled as an otherworld being (76D11):

> 'Awa, awa, you ill woman,
>> You've na come here for gude,
> You're but a witch, or wile warlock,
>> Or mermaid o the flude.'

Similarly, as noted in an earlier chapter, Mrs. Brown's version of "Gil Brenton" (5A) introduces an elaborate chastity test (5A15–26) and a miraculous talking bed to expose the bride's deception (5A27–32), neither of which can be found in any previous version. The obliging household familiar, "Billy-Blin," first appears in the ballads of Mrs. Brown,[13] notably in her longer version of "Young Beichan" (53C), where he is obviously intrusive, since he does not appear in any other version of that ballad.[14]

It is perhaps suggestive that two of Mrs. Brown's "witchcraft" ballads, "Willie's Lady" (6) and "King Henry" (32), first appeared in Matthew Gregory Lewis' *Tales of Wonder* (1801). Lewis was the notorious author of *The Monk* (1796), that masterpiece of gothic horror so widely imitated in the nineteenth century, and it is easy to see how these two ballads of the supernatural would appeal to him. The spell against childbirth used by the witch-mother on the bride in "Willie's Lady" is a widespread motif in folk tradition, as Child has shown, but the particular realization of it by Mrs. Brown in "Willie's Lady" seems indebted to "Gil Brenton" (5A). It is interesting that both of these are couplet ballads and have very similar opening stanzas. The symmetrical structure and rigid repetitions of "Willie's Lady," however, mark it as a late couplet ballad of a type very similar to "The Cruel Brother" (11), discussed in the last chapter. Although much less interesting from a structural point of view, "King Henry" (32), the other ballad that caught Lewis' eye, is nevertheless a skilful eighteenth-century treatment of the loathly lady theme in "The Marriage of Sir Gawain" (31) and Chaucer's "Wife of Bath's Tale."

Nearly all of the ballads of magic and witchcraft belong to Mrs. Brown's early period (1783), and for the most part they are artistically

---

13. In *ESPB*, I, 67, Child identifies Billy-Blin with Burlow-Beanie in "King Arthur and King Cornwall" (30, sts. 60 ff.), and he may be right (see *ESPB*, I, 297 f.), but the "foule feende" (30, st. 59) of the earlier ballad seems only remotely connected with Mrs. Brown's household familiar.

14. Billy-Blin also appears in "Willie's Lady" (6), discussed briefly below, and may have been intended in "Gil Brenton" (5A29–32), since he is specifically mentioned in Cromek's version of this passage (5C44–47). But he is not found in the earliest versions of "Gil Brenton" (5EG).

inferior. Very little can be said, for example, on behalf of "Kemp Owyne" (34B) or "Allison Gross" (35). It is only when these are compared with "The Laidley Worm of Spindleston Heughs" (34 App) that Mrs. Brown's superiority to the Reverend Robert Lambe of Norham as an antiquarian becomes evident.

There is one late ballad of witchcraft, "The Mother's Malison, or, Clyde's Water" (216B), communicated by Mrs. Brown to Jamieson in September, 1800. Willie tells his mother that he is determined to visit May Margaret in spite of the stormy night. The mother threatens to drown him, by her curse, in Clyde's water, if he goes. Of course Willie leaves anyway, in defiance of his mother's curse. As he rides o'er yon high, high hill, he hears the roar of Clyde's water. Crossing safely, he comes to Margaret's door and tirls at the pin. He pleads in vain with her to let him in (216B10–11):

'O open the door to me, Margaret!
    O open and lat me in!
For my boots are full o Clyde's water
    And frozen to the brim.'

'I darena open the door to you,
    Nor darena lat you in,
For my mither she is fast asleep,
    And I darena mak nae din.'

Margaret continues to make excuses, saying there is not space for him inside, the rooms are occupied, etc. Seeing there is no hope, Willie bids her a melodramatic farewell (216B15):

'O fare ye weel, then, May Margaret,
    Sin better manna be;
I've win my mither's malison,
    Coming this nicht to thee.'

He then rides away and plunges into Clyde's water. The mother's curse is thus effective. Clearly this gothic tale is conceived as a counterpart to "The Lass of Roch Royal," in which the lass similarly pleads for admittance (76E9):

'O open the door, Love Gregor,' she says,
    'O open, and let me in;
For the wind blaws thro my yellow hair,
    And the rain draps oer my chin.'

300

Echoes of other ballads and songs are evident also, notably the "Yarrow" ballads (214, 215), "Sweet William's Ghost" (77), and perhaps a trace of the folksong, "Go 'way from my Window." Indeed "The Mother's Malison," while not by any means great art, is a remarkable example of the late eighteenth-century ballad composite. It is also a good illustration of Mrs. Brown's abiding interest in magic and witchcraft.

There is a second group of ballads by Mrs. Brown having very slight narratives, usually telling how true lovers struggle successfully against great odds. Their view of love and marriage is obviously feminine and reflects the changed social conditions, already referred to, affecting the composition and re-creation of ballads. Their general outlook, their morality, is that of the middle-class "singing family" of the period. They are of particular relevance to the present discussion, however, because their thinness of narrative helps to reveal certain structural features characteristic of late eighteenth-century ballad composition.

Concerning the conventional morality of Mrs. Brown's ballads it should be said, first of all, that she is by no means a Victorian before her time. Certain changes in her text of "Clerk Colvill" (42A) play down the sex encounter with the mermaid, but these changes can be attributed, as Ritson's transcript of WT-B shows, to the delicacy of Mr. Tytler rather than Mrs. Brown![15] On the other hand, it is quite clear that there were limits to the kind of ballad she would admit to her repertoire. That she knew "Little Musgrave and Lady Barnard" (81) is obviously implied by her lyrical ballad, "The Bonny Birdy" (82), as Child recognized,[16] but the former ballad, with its flamboyant tale of adultery, is nowhere to be found in her MSS.

Most of the rather slight love ballads belong to Mrs. Brown's early period and usually involve some form of elopement or abduction, as can be found, for example, in "Willie o Douglas Dale" (101A). If any single traditional ballad of an earlier age could be said to have provided the

---

15. Kittredge remarks (HCL MS 25241.37.6, p. 95): "Comparison with MS. R. shows that Mr. William Fraser Tytler's transcript of Willie's Lady varies from MS WT in almost every stanza, but only in minute particulars; whereas he has changed Clark Colven (*pudoris causa*) strikingly." In the transcript printed by Child, Clark Colven's affair with the mermaid is described as follows (42A6):

He's taen her by the milk-white hand,
    He's taen her by the sleeve sae green,

And he's forgotten his gay ladie,
    And away with the fair maiden.

Ritson's copy of the same stanza, however, reads:

He's taen her by the milk-white hand,
    And likewise by the grass-green sleeve
An' laid her down upon the green,
    Nor of his lady speer'd he leave.

16. *ESPB*, II, 260.

basic inspiration for Mrs. Brown's love ballads, it must have been "Child Waters," which, as we have seen, Mrs. Brown knew in a form similar to that published in Percy's *Reliques*. Indeed, "Willie o Douglas Dale" (101A) is in some respects an anti-"Child Waters," a remaking of the old ballad from the feminine point of view. Willie gets the king's daughter with child, but he promises to take her to Scotland and make her a lady. On their way through the forest the girl goes into labor, and Willie makes her a bed of leaves. While in her pains she asks him to blow the horn to summon her father, but he refuses, offering her the horn and thus forcing her to choose between her family and him. The girl at last bears a bonny young son, and Willie finds a shepherdess to accompany them and nurse the child. The ship then takes them to Scotland, where the couple live happily ever after as the lord and lady of Douglas Dale.

The conversion from "Child Waters" to "Willie o Douglas Dale" completely eliminates the disciplined biblical tone which made the earlier ballad so reminiscent of Chaucer's "Clerk's Tale." The inscrutable objectivity of Child Waters is replaced by the solicitousness of Willie, whose only harshness (refusal to blow the horn) is designed to preserve the lady's loyalty to him. Is the girl with child? Willie will make her a lady in Scotland. Is she crying? He will make her a soft bed. Does she crave berries and a drink of water? He will fetch them. Obviously this is the way Child Waters should have behaved. In this connection it is interesting that in Mrs. Brown's version of "Child Waters" (63B) the character of Lord John is clearly modified in the direction of Willie, and Burd Ellen tends to show more spirit than fair Ellen, her medieval predecessor in the Percy folio version (63A). Here the effect of social change is once more evident. The shift from the masculine tradition of minstrelsy to the feminine emphasis of the singing family had a subtle but profound effect on both the creation and re-creation of ballads. Before the time of Mrs. Brown it would be difficult to imagine a ballad devoting six stanzas to the procuring of a suitable nurse for the newborn child, as is the case in "Willie o Douglas Dale" (101A26–31).

The relationship of "Willie o Douglas Dale" to "Child Waters" is confirmed by an occasional echo of the older ballad in its offspring. An example is Ellen's announcement to her lover that she is pregnant (63A2–3):

> Saies, Christ you saue, good Chyld Waters!
> > Sayes, Christ you saue and see!
> My girdle of gold, which was too longe,
> > Is now too short ffor mee.

'And all is with one chyld of yours,
    I ffeele sturre att my side;
My gowne of greene, it is to strayght;
    Before it was to wide.'

In "Willie o Douglas Dale" the king's daughter informs Willie of her condition in similar language (101A9):

'O narrow, narrow's my gown, Willy,
    That wont to be sae wide;
An short, short is my coats, Willy,
    That wont to be sae side;
An gane is a' my fair colour,
    An low laid is my pride.'

Another instance of similarity is evident in the description of the child's birth, except that in this case Mrs. Brown borrows from her own version of "Child Waters" rather than the original. It will be recalled that in the Percy folio text Child Waters is completely impassive while Ellen gives birth to the child, whereas Lord John in Mrs. Brown's version rushes to the stable, breaks down the door, and takes immediate charge of the situation (63B35):

Up he has taen his bonny young son,
    An gard wash him wi the milk;
And up has he taen his fair lady,
    Gard row her in the silk.

In like manner Willie assists his beloved in the later ballad (101A25):

O up has he tane his bonny young son,
    An washn him wi the milk,
An up has he tane his gay lady,
    An rowd her i the silk.

The inappropriateness of this stanza to the austere greenwood setting of "Willie o Douglas Dale" merely reinforces what is already evident, namely, that the stanza is here a borrowing and fits more naturally into the aristocratic scenery of "Child Waters."

It is worth noting, with reference to the social changes affecting balladry in the eighteenth century, that the same feminine touch we have seen above is evident in Mrs. Brown's two Robin Hood ballads, "Rose the Red and White Lily" (103A) and "Willie and Earl Richard's Daughter" (102A). In fact, I suspect it was this unmistakably feminine point of view that led Child to refuse these two pieces a place in the Robin Hood canon. Yet "Rose the Red and White Lily," though it draws motifs from folktale as well as balladry, is clearly inspired by "Robin Hood and Maid Marian" (150). The other ballad, "Willie and Earl Richard's Daughter" (120A), had it not been for Child's bias, might more properly be called "The Birth of Robin Hood," which is in fact its title in Jamieson's *Popular Ballads and Songs from Tradition*. This is one of Mrs. Brown's later ballads, which Jamieson obtained from her in the summer of 1800, and it draws extensively on the greenwood episode of "Willie o Douglas Dale" (101A1–24; cf. 102A1–9) in order to depict the birth of Robin Hood. It is perhaps not irrelevant to recall that five years earlier Joseph Ritson had published his *Robin Hood*, a two-volume collection of poems, songs, and ballads about the celebrated outlaw. It is highly appropriate, therefore, that the missing ballad of his birth be supplied by Mrs. Brown (102A17–18):

> An mony ane sings o grass, o grass,
>> And mony ane sings o corn,
> And mony ane sings o Robin Hood
>> Kens little whare he was born.

> It wasna in the ha, the ha,
>> Nor in the painted bower,
> But it was in the gude green wood,
>> Amang the lily-flower.

The most characteristic ballads of true love from Mrs. Brown's early repertoire, are those numbered 96–99 in Child's edition: "The Gay Goshawk" (96A), "Brown Robin" (97A), "Brown Adam" (98A), and "Johnie Scot" (99A), to which should be added "Lady Maisry" (65A), and "Lady Elspat" (247). These ballads provide the most interesting examples of Mrs. Brown's use of commonplace stanzas in establishing patterns of narrative structure.

Although "Lady Maisry" (65A) differs from the rest of the ballads in this group by virtue of its tragic ending, it shares with them the frequent use of commonplace stanzas in the "block" composition of its narrative. Maisry refuses all Scottish suitors because, as she tells them, she has given her love to an English lord. A kitchy-boy overhears this and tells her brother, who threatens Maisry with death unless she gives up the Englishman, Lord William. When she refuses, her brother orders a fire built to burn his sister. Maisry manages to send a bonny boy to Lord William, who arrives, however, too late to rescue her from the fire.

304

The structure of "Lady Maisry" is such as to require two messengers, one the kitchy-boy who goes to the brother, and the other the bonny boy who is sent to Lord William. The verbal-message theme is quite common, as Jones has shown,[17] but it is interesting to note in this case how Mrs. Brown has worked variations on the theme. The bonny boy sent by Maisry is for the most part a conventional messenger. He swims the stream when the bridge is broken, slacks his shoes and runs in the green grass, and leaps the castle wall in his anxiety to complete the errand. As we have observed, this is the behavior of the traditional messenger boy, whose origin is perhaps traceable to the little page of "Little Musgrave and Lady Barnard" (81A8–12). Furthermore, in subsequent ballads the theme lengthens and picks up added features. The person to whom the message is directed, for example, will often ask certain conventional questions, as in Principal Robertson's "Lord Lovel" (75I8):

'Is there onny of my castles broken down,
    Or onny of my towers won?
Or is Fair Helen brought to bed
    Of a doughter or a son?'

To this the bonny boy replies in the negative and then delivers his message.[18] Similar questions are asked by Lord Wayets in Herd's version of "Lord Ingram and Chiel Wyet" (66C14), and in Mrs. Brown's "Lady Maisry" the questions are put to the boy by Lord William (65A23–24):

'O is my biggins broken, boy?
    Or is my towers won?
Or is my lady lighter yet,
    Of a dear daughter or son?'

'Your biggin is na broken sir,
    Nor is your towers won;
But the fairest lady in a' the lan
    For you this day maun burn.'

It is to the credit of Mrs. Brown that the boy's reply, instead of being a mere negative repetition of the preceding stanza, as in other ballads, includes the climactic announcement of the burning of Maisry. We have already seen an example of this skilled sense of climax operating in her version of "Sir Hugh" (155A7).

17. "Commonplace and Memorization."
18. Dr. Robertson's "Lord Lovel" (75I) is so thoroughly dominated by commonplaces that it ends the message theme without giving the message—which does not, however, prevent the lord from crying, "Gar saddle me the black," etc., and riding to meet the comely corpse of Fair Helen.

To conclude the messenger sequence, one generally finds either the action-packed stanza in which the lord overturns the dining table, as in "Gil Morrice" (83F23) and "Lord Ingram" (66C17), the "saddle me the black" stanza in Robertson's version of "Lord Lovel" (75I10), or both stanzas combined, as in "Fair Mary of Wallington" (91A22, 24; B20, 22).[19] In "Lady Maisry" Mrs. Brown chooses the second of these alternatives and then adds to the conventional stanza two highly original ones which skilfully depict the agonizing tardiness of the would-be rescuer and the hysterical optimism of the doomed girl (65A25–27):

'O saddle me the black, the black,
    Or saddle me the brown;
O saddle me the swiftest steed
    That ever rade frae a town.'

Or he was near a mile awa,
    She heard his wild horse sneeze:
Mend up the fire, my false brother,
    It's na come to my knees.'

O whan he lighted at the gate,
    She heard his bridle ring:
'Mend up the fire, my false brother,
    It's far yet frae my chin.'

The occasional tendency to break free of the grip of commonplace stanzas which we have just noted in "Lady Maisry" should remind us that Mrs. Brown's ballads often have a superiority of style which distinguishes them from the *rifacimenti* of the late eighteenth and early nineteenth century. Her style is of course traditional, but it frequently preserves the best features of ballad diction from the past, something which I think is attributable to the example of superior early ballads like "Child Waters," the general influence of which on Mrs. Brown we have already observed. More than anything else, Mrs. Brown seems to have been impressed by the leisurely, lingering style of "Child Waters," as can be seen in the following stanzas from the Percy folio version (63A22–23):

There were four and twenty ladyes,
    Were playing att the ball,

19. For chronological development of the "saddle me the black" commonplace, see 200A9, G6; 237, st. 4; 76A3, 26, 28; 76B23; 75I10; 91A24; 91B22; 65A25; 222A28.

And Ellen, was the ffairest ladye,
    Must bring his steed to the stall.

There were four and twenty faire ladyes
    Was playing att the chesse;
And Ellen, shee was the ffairest ladye,
    Must bring his horsse to grasse.

In her own version of "Child Waters" Mrs. Brown lovingly reworked lines
like the ones just quoted (63B19–20) and added similar new passages of
her own. These are not always successful—it is dangerous to tamper with
a ballad as excellent as "Child Waters"—but they illustrate well her interest in important matters of ballad style. In the folio version, for example, Ellen's crossing of the water is described as follows (63A15–16):

But when shee came to the waters side,
    Shee sayled to the chinne:
'Except the lord of heauen be my speed,
    Now must I learne to swime.'

The salt waters bare vp Ellens clothes,
    Our ladye bare vpp her chinne,
And Child Waters was a woe man, good Lord,
    To ssee Faire Ellen swime.

Mrs. Brown replaces these two stanzas with three of her own (63B7–9):

But the firstin stap the lady stappit,
    The water came til her knee;
'Ohon, alas!' said the lady,
    'This water's oer deep for me.'

The nextin stap the lady stappit,
    The water came till her middle;
An sighin says that gay lady,
    I've wat my gouden girdle.

The nextin stap that lady stappit,
    The water came till her pap;
An the bairn that was in her twa sides
    For caul begane to quake.

The lingering style with which Mrs. Brown experiments in "Child
Waters" undergoes further development in the group of ballads we are
now considering. We find the same repetitive technique, for example, in
the following description of the courting of Lady Maisry (65A2–4):

O they hae courted Lady Maisry
    Wi a' kin kind of things;
An they hae sought her Lady Maisry
    Wi brotches an wi' rings.

An they ha sought her Lady Maisry
    Frae father and frae mother;
An they ha sought her Lady Maisry
    Frae sister an frae brother.

An they ha followed her Lady Maisry
    Thro chamber an thro ha;
But a' that they coud say to her,
    Her answer still was Na.

The effect of this technique is given an added dimension, however, at the close of the ballad. Lord William has arrived too late to save the lady from burning, and so he vents his helpless rage with vows of revenge and suicide in the last two stanzas (65A30–31):

O I'll gar burn for you, Maisry,
    Your father an your mother;
An I'll gar burn for you, Maisry,
    Your sister and your brother.

'An I'll gar burn for you, Maisry,
    The chief of a' your kin;
An the last bonfire that I come to,
    Mysel I will cast in.'

The occurrence of these parallel passages at the beginning and end has a sharply unifying effect and dramatizes the contrast between the civilized opening and the violent conclusion of the ballad.

Mrs. Brown's ballad "The Gay Goshawk" (96A) has a bird as a messenger instead of a bonny boy, but in style and structure it is in many ways similar to "Lady Maisry." Acting on instructions from his love-sick Scottish master, the goshawk delivers a letter to his truelove south of the border, pleading that he will die without her love. The girl tells her father of a wish to be buried in Scotland, and then she promptly takes a sleeping potion that makes her appear to be dead. As the funeral procession moves north the Scottish lover comes to meet it, whereupon the "corpse" miraculously comes alive and the lovers escape into Scotland.

Something of the lingering technique of "Child Waters" is reflected in

"The Gay Goshawk," as in the following passage in which the lover gives the goshawk a description of his lady (96A5–6):

'An four and twenty ladies fair
    Will wash and go to kirk,
But well shall ye my true-love ken,
    For she wears goud on her skirt.

'An four and twenty gay ladies
    Will to the mass repair,
But well sall ye my true-love ken,
    For she wears goud on her hair.'

The same technique takes on a more complicated function later, however, in the girl's request, spoken to her father, for funeral arrangements in case of her death (96A17–18):

'An the firstin kirk that ye come till,
    Ye gar the bells be rung,
An the nextin kirk that ye come till,
    Ye gar the mess be sung.

'An the thirdin kirk that ye come till,
    You deal gold for my sake,
An the fourthin kirk that ye come till,
    You tarry there till night.'

When it appears that the girl has died, the family makes the necessary arrangements and her instructions for the funeral are carried out to the letter (96A24–26):

The firstin kirk that they came till,
    They gard the bells be rung,
And the nextin kirk that they came till,
    They gard the mess be sung.

The thirdin kirk that they came till,
    They dealt gold for her sake,
And the fourthin kirk that they came till,
    Lo, there they met her make!

'Lay down, lay down the bigly bier,
    Lat me the dead look on;'
Wi cherry cheeks and ruby lips
    She lay an smil'd on him.

The ingenuity of this use of incremental repetition is indeed remarkable. Not only do we learn dramatically that the funeral procession has served as an assignation, but, in an inspired departure from the repetitive pattern, the ballad achieves a superb climax when the "corpse" smiles on her lover. This last is a sophisticated parody of the traditional love-death motif ("Set down, set down that comely corpse"), and as such it summarizes the gay spirit appropriate to this story of a funeral which is turned into a wedding.

Certainly "The Gay Goshawk" is Mrs. Brown at her best, but its style and structure is no different from many other less successful ballads in her repertoire, such as "Brown Robin" (97A), "Brown Adam" (98A), and "Johnie Scot" (99A). The first of these, "Brown Robin," is clearly an inferior piece of work, perhaps composed whimsically without serious attention to artistic detail. Hints of the repetitive style are evident, but they are not developed. Nevertheless, the story itself, in which Brown Robin escapes from his lady's bower dressed as a woman, is perhaps symbolic of the feminine influence of the singing family which we have noted.

Scarcely more impressive is "Brown Adam" (98A), a blacksmith whose humble calling is given a kind of dignity in the following stanza (98A2):

His hammer's o the beaten gold,
    His study's o the steel,
His fingers white are my delite,
    He blows his bellows well.

But the composer is not really devoting his (or her) concentrated attention to this ballad. Thus in describing the banishment of Robin to the greenwood it is simpler just to lift ready-made stanzas from "Lady Maisry" (65A2–4, 30–31) and change them slightly (98A3–4):

But they ha banishd him Brown Adam
    Frae father and frae mither,
An they ha banishd him Brown Adam
    Frae sister and frae brither.

And they ha banishd Brown Adam
    Frae the flowr o a' his kin;
An he's biggit a bowr i the good green wood
    Betwen his lady an him.

In his study of "Commonplace and Memorization in the Oral Tradition of the English and Scottish Popular Ballads," Jones finds that "Johnie Scot" (99) "is composed almost entirely of seven-stress and fourteen-stress commonplaces, especially in its central section which contains the verbal-message theme comprising nearly a third of the ballad."[20] This is certainly true, and hence it is not surprising that "Johnie Scot" is artistically inferior to such ballads as "Lady Maisry" and "The Gay Goshawk." From the very first stanza (modeled on the opening stanza of "Willie o Douglas Dale") "Johnie Scot" is filled with echoes of other ballads. The most interesting of these for our present purpose is a passage, similar to the funeral procession of "The Gay Goshawk," but in this ballad describing the march of Johnie's men to rescue his true love (99A22–23):

> The firstin town that they came till,
>   They gard the bells be rung;
> And the nextin town that they came till,
>   They gard the mess be sung.
>
> The thirdin town that they came till,
>   They gard the drums beat roun;
> The king but an his nobles a'
>   Was startld at the soun.

The use of the repetitive style here is effective in suggesting the inexorable march of Johnie and his men, but of course it lacks the complexity of function we have observed in the funeral procession of "The Gay Goshawk." Nevertheless, this is a fascinating example of the evolution of ballad style. What begins in "Child Waters" as a stylistic trait develops an important structural function in "The Gay Goshawk" and finally "freezes" into a ballad commonplace in "Johnie Scot."[21]

All of the love ballads in the group just considered belong to Mrs. Brown's early period,[22] so that the question naturally arises whether there are any changes in style or the use of commonplaces observable in her later ballads. The final answer to this question can only be given in the light of her romance ballads, the last group to be considered in this chapter, but before turning to these it will be well to give some attention to the one love ballad excluded from the previous discussion, since it was

20. "Commonplace and Memorization," p. 108. Jones goes on to relate his observations on the structure of "Johnie Scot" to a theory of oral composition, and he draws on all versions of the ballad, not just Mrs. Brown's.

21. The technique under discussion is not the peculiar property of Mrs. Brown. Compare, for example, a similar development in Herd's text of "Fair Mary of Wallington" (91B23–25).

22. The exception is "The Birth of Robin Hood" (102A).

first obtained from Mrs. Brown by Jamieson in the summer of 1800. The ballad is "Bonny Baby Livingston" (222A), and it is particularly valuable because, although a late ballad, it survives in two forms, one text having been taken down by Jamieson directly from Mrs. Brown's recitation, and the other preserved in a letter from Mrs. Brown to Jamieson dated September 15, 1800, in which she remarks:

> On the other page you will find the whole ballad of Bonny Baby Livingston. I found upon recollection that I had the whole story in my memory, and thought it better to write it out entire, as what I repeated to you was, I think, more imperfect.[23]

In spite of this proffered revision, Jamieson printed his original transcription in *Popular Ballads and Songs from Tradition*, but Professor Child, in his edition, prints the revision, adding the variant readings from Jamieson in the textual notes, so that both versions are readily available to the modern reader.

Bonny Baby Livingston of Dundee is stolen away by a highlander, Glenlion, who wishes to make her his bride, but the girl cares nothing for the pastoral delights of the highlands and wishes she were back home. Glenlion's brother John advises him to scorn the lass, but his three sisters comfort her and help her send a message to her true love, Johny Hay, at Dundee. Johny and his merry men ride to Glenlion's castle, and, while his men keep the gate, Johny escapes with Baby Livingston to the consternation of the highlanders. The last stanza is a carefree taunt (222A41):

'Awa, Glenlion! fy for shame!
   Gae hide ye in some den!
You've lettn your bride be stown frae you,
   For a' your armed men.'

The ballad is an excellent one, composed in a gay and frolicsome spirit. It is Mrs. Brown's answer to "Jock o the Side" (187).

The most remarkable thing about the structure of "Bonny Baby Livingston" is that although it is replete with commonplaces, including the message theme, the stanzas are in some cases carefully altered so as to conceal their commonplace character. It is as if Mrs. Brown had become self-conscious in the intervening years about the use of such stanzas in her ballads. One can see this kind of alteration in the changes Mrs. Brown made in her letter to Jamieson, as when, for example, she revises "He's carried her oer yon hich hich hill," an echo of the Yarrow ballads,[24] to

23. *ESPB*, IV, 238.
24. See 214D6; also 216B6 (Mrs. Brown).

312

read "He's carried her oer hills and muirs" (222A4), a more generalized description. An even clearer case is her revision of the message theme, which she originally recited to Jamieson as follows (222Ab21–23):

And gin I had a bonny boy
    To help me in my need,
That he might rin to bonny Dundee,
    And come again wi speed.

And they hae gotten a bonny boy
    Their errand for to gang,
And bade him run to bonny Dundee
    And nae to tarry lang.

The boy he ran oer muir and dale,
    As fast as he coud flee,
And eer the sun was twa hours height
    The boy was at Dundee.

In itself this original form of the message theme is a departure from what we have seen to be the usual formula beginning "O whare will I get a bonny boy." Gone are the broken bridges, the green grass, the leaping oer castle wall. But these departures from tradition pale into insignificance when compared with the revision and expansion of this passage in the revised text which Mrs. Brown sent in her letter to Jamieson (222Aa20–26):

O she's got paper, pen, and ink,
    And candle that she might see,
And she has written a broad letter
    To Johny at Dundee.

And she has gotten a bonny boy,
    That was baith swift and strang,
Wi philabeg and bonnet blue,
    Her errand for to gang.

'O boy, gin ye'd my blessing win
    And help me in my need,
Run wi this letter to my love,
    And bid him come wi speed.

'And here's a chain of good red gowd,
    And gowdn guineas three,
And when you've well your errand done,
    You'll get them for your fee.'

The boy he ran oer hill and dale,
    Fast as a bird coud flee,
And eer the sun was twa hours height
    The boy was at Dundee.

And when he came to Johny's door
    He knocked loud and sair;
Then Johny to the window came,
    And loudly cry'd, 'Wha's there?'

'O here's a letter I have brought,
    Which ye maun quickly read,
And, gin ye woud your lady save,
    Gang back wi me wi speed.'

Here is undoubtedly the most colorful of all the bonny boys in ballad tradition. The care that has gone into this portrait strongly suggests that Mrs. Brown, in her later period, has developed a new style which, for lack of a better term, might be designated "baroque." She still seems to compose instinctively by block stanzas in the customary eighteenth-century manner, but in her latest ballads, plagued perhaps by an increased literary consciousness as composer, she quickly disguises her commonplaces beneath elaborate cross-patterns of baroque detail. The fortunate preservation of two versions of her "Bonny Baby Livingston" has enabled us to observe in slow motion this fascinating process of stylistic revision.

The last group of Mrs. Brown's ballads to be considered are the romances, which are found in the Alexander Fraser Tytler-Brown MS drawn up in 1800 for Mr. Tytler at the suggestion of Sir Walter Scott. It is a curious fact that, with the exception of "Young Beichan" (53A,C), two versions of which were known to Mrs. Brown in 1783, all of the romance ballads belong to her later period. Indeed the doubts that have been expressed from time to time about the authenticity of Mrs. Brown's repertoire very likely were suggested by the more "literary" ballads of the AFT-B MS. Dr. Robert Anderson, in a letter to Bishop Percy of September 14, 1800, tells the bishop something about Mrs. Brown and encloses a copy of "Child Waters" (63Bb), transcribed from AFT-B "by a little girl at my elbow." Anderson then goes on to say:

I accompanied Mr Jamieson to my friend [Walter] Scott's house in the country [Abbotsford, near Ercildoun], for the sake of bringing the collectors to a good understanding. I then took on me to hint my suspicion of modern manufacture, in which Scott had

314

secretly anticipated me. Mrs Brown is fond of ballad poetry, writes verses, and reads everything in the marvelous way. Yet her character places her above the suspicion of literary imposture; but it is wonderful how she should happen to be the depository of so many curious and valuable ballads.[25]

That there are grounds for such suspicions in Mrs. Brown's romance ballads cannot be denied. But it is important, I think, that we keep in mind a distinction between her native flair for block composition and her more rational desire for literary elegance, the two sides of her creative effort which we have seen operating in "Bonny Baby Livingston" (222A).

The ballad of "Young Beichan" (53) is one that I have known for many years in a version with the title "Lord Bateman," as sung by Pleaz Mobley of Manchester, Kentucky.[26] As a result it looms large in my imagination as a kind of archetype of the romance ballad. I suspect that Mrs. Brown had something of this feeling about it. She provides two versions in the Jamieson-Brown MS of 1783. One of these, which Child gives the place of honor (53A), seems to be the original, perhaps based ultimately on a lost broadside, and the other appears to be Mrs. Brown's re-creation (53C). No version earlier than Mrs. Brown's is known to exist, but the ballad has since become tremendously popular, both in Britain and America.

Young Beichan sails from London and is imprisoned by a Moor, whose daughter frees him on condition he will marry her within seven years. She gives him bread and wine, and he returns to London. After seven long years the girl sails to London and reaches Young Beichan's gates just as he is about to marry another. Beichan returns the young bride to her mother and declares he will marry the Moorish lady.

The story just summarized is from what I take to be the original or broadside version of "Young Beichan" (53A), an assumption which is confirmed by its resemblance to a text dated 1791 and preserved in the Glenriddell MSS (53B). Yet a comparison of these two suggests that even Mrs. Brown's "original" has been retouched to some extent, especially in the description of the reunion of the lovers and the pathetic appeal of the Moorish lady (53A19–21):

25. Nichols' *Illustrations of the Literary History of the Eighteenth Century*, VII, 89 f. James A. H. Murray, in the introduction to his edition of *Thomas of Erceldoune* (EETS, O.S. 61 [London, 1875]), pp. lii f., doubts that "Thomas Rymer" was handed down in oral tradition, "even without the additional particulars that the source of the verses was that Mt. Athos

of antique ballads, Mrs. Brown's MS." Concerning Scott's suspicions, see Child, *ESPB*, II, 296.

26. Library of Congress, *Archive of American Folk Song*, Album 12, "Anglo-American Songs and Ballads," 56A & B. Recorded at Harrogate, Tenn., 1943, by Artus M. Moser. This album is now available on LP.

O quickly ran he down the stair,
　　O fifteen steps he has made but three;
He's tane his bonny love in his arms,
　　An a wot he kissd her tenderly.

'O hae you tane a bonny bride?
　　An hae you quite forsaken me?
An hae ye quite forgotten her
　　That gae you life an liberty?'

She's lookit oer her left shoulder
　　To hide the tears stood in her ee;
'Now fare thee well, Young Bicham,' she says,
　　'I'll strive to think nae mair on thee.'

For the most part, however, Mrs. Brown preserves the compact, fast-moving narrative of the hypothetical broadside.

The twenty-three stanzas of the original are expanded to thirty-six in Mrs. Brown's re-creation of "Young Beichan" (53C).[27] The shorter version plunges swiftly into the story, taking but a single stanza for the hero to be carried abroad, imprisoned, and tortured (53A1):

In London city was Bicham born,
　　He longd strange countries for to see,
But he was taen by a savage Moor,
　　Who handld him right cruely.

By comparison Mrs. Brown's beginning is almost leisurely, and indeed it is more characteristic of what we normally consider to be ballad style (53C1–2):

Young Bekie was as brave a knight
　　As ever saild the sea;
An he's doen him to the court of France,
　　To serve for meat and fee.

---

27. MS Ritson clears up the mystery of "Young Betrice," which Child thought (*ESPB*, II, 377) might be a version of "Hugh Spencer" (158). It is actually "Young Bekie" (53C), "differing only in details from the copy of that piece in MS J-B . . . , but affording two additional stanzas, one after stanza 17, the other after stanza 29" (Kittredge, HCL MS 25241.37.6, pp. 92 f.). The two additional stanzas are:

17a. Ye put nae money in your pocket,
　　But barely guineas three,
And that to gie to the proud porter,
　　To bid him speak you wi'.
　　. . . . .

29a. It's nae to anger the king, he says,
　　Nor yet to vex your grace,
But the blackest bit o' the sole o'
　　her fit
Is whiter nor your face.

He had nae been i the court of France
    A twelvemonth nor sae long,
Til he fell in love with the king's daughter,
    An was thrown in prison strong.

Here we see Mrs. Brown using her instinctive or "natural" method of block composition, such as she employs, for example, in "Johnie Scot" (99A1–2),

O Johney was as brave a knight
    As ever saild the sea,
An he's done him to the English court,
    To serve for meat and fee.

He had nae been in fair England
    But yet a little while,
Untill the kingis ae daughter
    To Johney proves wi chil.

and in "Willie o Douglas Dale" (101A1–2):

O Willy was as brave a lord
    As ever saild the sea,
And he has gane to the English court,
    To serve for meat and fee.

He had nae been at the kingis court
    A twelvemonth and a day,
Till he longd for a sight o the king's daughter,
    But ane he coud never see.

In our earlier consideration of the revised "Child Walters" (63B) we noted a tendency on the part of Mrs. Brown to develop and expand the lingering style and incremental repetition of that ballad. Something of the same tendency is observable in her revision of "Young Beichan," particularly in the conversation between the hero and the girl just before she sets him free. The usual broadside form of the exchange, preserved to this day in American versions like Pleaz Mobley's,[28] is a simple question and answer (53A5–6):

28. Here is Pleaz Mobley's version of the question and answer:
  "Have you got house, have you got land, sir,
    Do you hold yourself of high degree,
  What would you give the Turkish lady
    If out of prison I'll set you free?"

"Well, I've got house and I've got land, love,
Half of Northumberland belongs to me,
I'll give it all to the Turkish lady
    If out of prison you'll set me free."

'O hae ye ony lands or rents,
    Or citys in your ain country,
Coud free you out of prison strong,
    An coud maintain a lady free?'

'O London city is my own,
    An other citys twa or three,
Coud loose me out o prison strong,
    An coud maintain a lady free.'

In Mrs. Brown's revision, however, there is no conversation. Instead the girl overhears Beichan bewailing his fate (53C4–5):

'O gin a lady woud borrow me,
    At her stirrup-foot I woud rin;
Or gin a widow wad borrow me,
    I woud swear to be her son.

Or gin a virgin woud borrow me,
    I woud wed her wi a ring;
I'd gi her ha's, I'd gie her bowers,
    The bonny towrs o Linne.'

This is of course precisely what we have observed in tracing the development of Mrs. Brown's early ballad style.

After releasing Beichan from prison, the Moor's daughter (in the original version) thoughtfully provides him with a loaf of bread and a flask of Spanish wine (53A8), a favor which she nostalgically reminds him of, at least in the Glenriddel version, when she comes to his gate in London after seven long years (53B13, 17). Mrs. Brown replaces this motif with a somewhat gothic passage which points prophetically toward the baroque style of her later ballads (53C8–10):

O whan she saw him, Young Bekie,
    Her heart was wondrous sair!
For the mice but an the bold rottons
    Had eaten his yallow hair.

She's gien him a shaver for his beard,
    A comber till his hair,
Five hunder pound in his pocket,
    To spen, an nae to spair.

318

She's gien him a steed was good in need,
    An a saddle o royal bone,
A leash o hounds o ae litter,
    An Hector called one.

This kind of detail is more suited to *The Monk* or *The Castle of Otronto* than to a ballad. It is similar to the mention of a forced marriage, a unique feature of this revision, which prevents Beichan from keeping his vow (53C12–13), and which Child calls a "far-fetched allegation."[29]

Another unique contribution of Mrs. Brown to "Young Beichan," already alluded to in this chapter, is her introduction of the household familiar, Billy Blin, as the agent who induces the girl to sail to London (53C14–15):

O it fell once upon a day
    Burd Isbel fell asleep,
An up it starts the Belly Blin,
    An stood at her bed-feet.

'O waken, waken, Burd Isbel,
    How can you sleep so soun,
Whan this is Bekie's wedding day,
    An the marriage gain on?'

This, I think, is easily Mrs. Brown's most effective use of the Billy Blin, especially in view of the dream setting, borrowed perhaps from "Fair Margaret and Sweet William" (74A5). Moreover, at this point Mrs. Brown deliberately slows down the fast pace of the narrative by having the Billy Blin give Burd Isbel detailed instructions concerning the sea voyage (53C16–19):

'Ye do ye to your mither's bowr,
    Think neither sin nor shame;
And ye tak twa o your mither's marys,
    To keep ye frae thinking lang.

'Ye dress yoursel in the red scarlet,
    An your marys in dainty green,
An ye pit girdles about your middles
    Woud buy an earldome.

29. *ESPB*, I, 461. By introducing the forced marriage, however, I think Mrs. Brown was merely defending the character of young Beichan, just as Child himself does (*ibid.*): "I have little doubt that, if we could go back far enough, we should find that he [Beichan] had all along been faithful at heart."

10. Mrs. Brown of Falkland   319

'O ye gang down by yon sea-side,
    An down by yon sea-stran;
Sae bonny will the Hollans boats
    Come rowin till your han.

'Ye set your milk-white foot abord,
    Cry, Hail ye, Domine!
An I shal be the steerer o't,
    To row you oer the sea.'

As with the funeral procession in "The Gay Goshawk," Billy Blin's instructions are repeated in narrative form in the four following stanzas,
beginning "She's tane her till her mither's bowr . . . ." The overall effect
of this addition is to provide a resplendent, pageant-like procession reminiscent of fair Annet's journey to Lord Thomas' wedding (73A13–20),
and the lingering style of the whole passage contrasts vividly with the
otherwise swift movement of the story.

A final revision that should be mentioned involves the recognition
scene near the end of the ballad. Having eliminated the bread and wine
motif, Mrs. Brown substitutes a stanza from the procession scene which
is somewhat daringly repeated a third time in the words of the porter
telling of Burd Isbel's arrival (53C28):

'There's ane o them dressd in red scarlet,
    And twa in dainty green,
An they hae girdles about their middles
    Woud buy an earldome.'

This general description of the three ladies is apparently enough to suggest to Beichan that the visitor is Burd Isbel, but when he races down
the stairs to greet her, Isbel is ready with further proof, echoing the account of his escape from prison quoted above (53C33–34):

'I gae you a steed was good in need,
    An a saddle o royal bone,
A leash o hounds o ae litter,
    An Hector called one.'

It was well kent what the lady said,
    That it wasnae a lee,
For at ilka word the lady spake,
    The hound fell at her knee.

This recognition device is of course traditional.[30] But note particularly the preparation that is made for it in the ballad. The porter's description of the three ladies and Isbel's own recital of her gifts to Beichan provide a kind of functional narrative symmetry reminiscent of the technique of late medieval minstrelsy. It is remarkable to find this example of the older style in a ballad of the late eighteenth century. Without doubt Mrs. Brown's re-creation of "Young Beichan" contains a fascinating variety of techniques, with some passages that illustrate her early style at its best, and others that foreshadow the baroque style destined to become increasingly important in the romance ballads of her later period.

The AFT-B MS made by Mrs. Brown in 1800 contains romance ballads almost exclusively. In thus using the term "romance" I mean to suggest those ballads that seem connected in some fairly definite way with the medieval romance tradition. Thus we have seen, for example, that "Child Waters" (63B) is related to Chaucer's "Clerk's Tale" of patient Griselda, and "The Lass of Roch Royal" (76E) fits the pattern of the Accused Queen found in the "Man of Law's Tale" of Constance. The only two ballads in AFT-B that cannot be made to fit into the romance category are "The Cruel Brother" (11A) and "Fair Mary of Wallington" (91C), the latter based on a garland text of about 1775.[31] This leaves five ballads in the romance category to be considered briefly by way of concluding the third and last main group of Mrs. Brown's ballads.

Undoubtedly the most excellent as well as the best known of the romance ballads is "Thomas Rymer" (37A), based on the medieval romance of *Thomas of Erceldoun*. For this reason it may seem surprising, in the light of the previous discussion, to observe that Mrs. Brown's ballad of "Thomas Rymer" is almost completely devoid of the distinctive features of style so manifest in the earlier ballads already considered. The explanation for this, I believe, is that "Thomas Rymer" is composed directly from the romance rather than from a generalized conception of the story. I do not mean this in a derogatory way, however, for the re-creation of the romance as a ballad is skilfully done. The description of the queen of elfland in *Thomas of Erceldoun*, for example, occupies the equivalent of six ballad stanzas (37App5–10):

30. *ESPB*, I, 457, n. It is also a popular feature of the Tristan legend.

31. Bronson, in *The Traditional Tunes of the Child Ballads*, II, 417, calls attention to the close relationship between Herd's and Mrs. Brown's versions of "Fair Mary of Wallington" (91B, C): "Herd's copy could be artificially blown out from a variant like Mrs. Brown's, as has been suggested above; on the other hand, Mrs. Brown's could be deliberately extracted, with the exercise of taste and judgment, from a longer text. It does not seem likely, in this case, that mere forgetfulness would account for so neat a result."

Hir palfraye was a dappill graye,
　　Swylke one ne saghe I neuer none;
Als dose Þe sonne on someres daye,
　　Þat faire lady hir selfe scho schone.

Hir selle it was of roelle bone,
　　Ffull semely was Þat syghte to see;
Stefly sett with precyous stones,
　　And compaste all with crapotee;

Stones of oryente, grete plente.
　　Hir hare abowte hir hede it hange;
Scho rade ouer Þat lange lee;
　　A whylle scho blewe, a-noÞer scho sange.

Hir garthes of nobyll sylke Þay were,
　　The bukylls were of berelle stone,
Hir steraps were of crystalle clere,
　　And all with perelle ouer-by-gone.

Hir payetrelle was of irale fyne,
　　Hir cropoure was of orphare,
And als clere golde hir brydill it schone;
　　One aythir syde hange bellys three.

Scho led three grehoundis in a leesshe,
　　And seuene raches by hir Þay rone;
Scho bare an horne abowte hir halse,
　　And vndir hir belte full many a flone.

This is reduced to a single stanza in the ballad that perfectly epitomizes the otherworld character of the lady (37A2):

Her skirt was of the grass-green silk,
　　Her mantel of the velvet fine,
At ilka tett of her horse's mane
　　Hung fifty silver bells and nine.

It is this ability to catch the spirit of the romance while compressing it into ballad form that is responsible for the success of "Thomas Rymer," for in matters of style and narrative structure the ballad is wholly untraditional.

In sharp contrast to "Thomas Rymer" are two ballads that seem perhaps the least successful of Mrs. Brown's romances, namely "Fause

Foodrage" (89A) and "Jellon Grame" (90A). Her failure here, I think, is attributable to her effort to imitate the pseudo-archaic style of "Hardy-knute," Lady Wardlaw's forgery, which originally appeared in 1719 but was frequently reprinted during the century.[32] "Fause Foodrage" seems designed to supply a ballad the existence of which might be inferred from a tale mentioned in *The Complaint of Scotland*, and "Jellon Grame" is a "dramatic" ballad in the tradition of "Child Maurice" (83). Child's comment on the former of these can well serve as a criticism of them both: "while not calling in question the substantial genuineness of the ballad, we must admit that the form in which we have received it is an enfeebled one, without much flavor or color . . . ."[33]

Passing over "Bonny Bee Hom" (92A), which is a very slight ballad inspired by "The Lowlands of Holland" in Herd's *Scottish Songs*[34] with the addition of a ring motif from "Hind Horn" (17), we come to the final romance ballad, "The Kitchie-Boy" (252C). A noble lady falls in love with her father's footboy, sweet Willie, and, since her father of course would never knowingly allow them to marry, she provides the boy with money for a ship in which he is to sail abroad, returning after a brief absence disguised as a nobleman's son. In this capacity he can then presumably ask for the lady's hand. Before he leaves, she gives him a ring and asks him to wear it until the day he dies. Willie then obediently sails abroad and lands on the coast of Spain, where a lady of high degree falls in love with him as she sees him walking up and down. In order to make an impression, she dresses in a red gold mantle and, accompanied by her maries, goes down to the shore where Willie is and with a smile invites him to dine with her. When Willie protests that he is ready to return to his own country, the lady makes several efforts to tempt him to stay, promising him towns and castles, and offering him a ring. He refuses all temptations, insisting that he intends to remain true to his lady-love at home. When Willie returns to his native strand, his lady's father takes him to be some Lord, and, inviting him in to dine, agrees readily when Willie asks to marry his daughter. But Willie has blacked his face, so that when the lady meets them at the gate, she does not recognize the dark-skinned stranger as her beloved footboy. Later, when they are alone, Willie removes the disguise for his bride's benefit, but the groom's identi-

---

32. Reprinted in Herd, *Scottish Songs* (1776), I, 119–131. Child discusses Mrs. Brown's possible indebtedness to the poem (*ESPB*, II, 296): "It is quite possible that Mrs. Brown may unconsciously have adopted this verse from the tiresome and affected Hardyknute, so much esteemed in her day." It seems to me even probable that she did, though not "unconsciously."

33. *ESPB*, II, 296.

34. Edition of 1776, II, 2.

ty is kept from her father for seven years. Finally, at a christening feast, they tell the bride's father, who takes the deception in good spirit (252C37):

> And her father laughd aboon the rest,
>> And said, My daughter, you're nae to blame;
> For you've married for love, and no for land,
>> So a' my gowd is yours to claim.

Child regarded this ballad as a modern adaptation of "Hind Horn" (17), basing his conclusion at least to some extent on later versions like that in the Skene MS (252A) which expands the ring motif and even adds two stanzas from "Hind Horn" (252A33–34). At the same time Child recognized that certain features of the story did not fit the "Hind Horn" narrative: "In particular of the hero's having his choice of two women it is more like the *gest* of 'King Horn,' or 'Horn Childe and Maiden Rimnild;' but an independent invention of the Spanish lady is not beyond the humble ability of the composer of 'The Kitchie-Boy.' "[35] On the other hand, while it is undeniable that this ballad acquires stanzas and echoes from "Hind Horn" in the later versions, I venture to suggest that Mrs. Brown's version—the earliest—is a romance ballad inspired by "Young Beichan" (53A, C) and that the Moor's daughter is the model for the kitchie-boy's Spanish lady.

Apart from a general similarity of narrative structure, the relationship between "Young Beichan" and "The Kitchie Boy" is suggested by the sharing of an occasional motif or turn of phrase. Both the Moor's daughter and the Spanish lady, for example, offer the hero a drink of Spanish wine (53A8; 252C16), and just as the Moorish girl "set her foot on good ship-board" (53A10) to sail to London, so Willie "set his foot on good ship-board" (252C26) to return to his true love. But the most significant example of the connection appears in the Spanish lady's temptation of Willie (252C11–15), a scene inspired by Mrs. Brown's own description of Burd Isbel's procession to the seastrand in her re-created version of "Young Beichan" (53C16–23). Both ladies are dressed in red and are accompanied by their maries. As an added touch, perhaps from "Thomas Rymer" (37A3–4) or "The Lass of Roch Royal" (76B8), Willie takes the Spanish lady to be some queen (252C14). In the subsequent temptation Willie's fidelity is shown to be flawless in a scene comparable to the testing of the lady in "Brown Adam" (98A9–15).

35. *ESPB*, IV, 401.

A final example of similarity comes to mind when we recall that Mrs. Brown's re-creation of "Young Beichan" is distinguished by a remarkable revival of the symmetrical narrative of minstrelsy, employing functional repetitions to dramatize the recognition scene at the end. A similar functional repetition leading to a recognition occurs in "The Kitchie-Boy," except that in this instance the parallel is between the temptation and recognition scenes. The Spanish lady's testing of sweet Willie begins with the following exchange (252C16–18):

> Says, Ye maun leave your bonny ship
>   And go this day wi me and dine,
> And you shall eat the baken meat,
>   And you shall drink the Spanish wine.
>
> 'I canna leave my bonny ship,
>   Nor go this day to dine wi thee,
> For a' my sails are ready bent
>   To bear me back to my ain countrie.'
>
> 'O gin you'd forsake your bonny ship
>   And wed a ladie of this countrie,
> I would make you lord of a' this town,
>   And towns and castles twa or three.'

Willie successfully resists these and other temptations, and returns to his native shore, where his true love's father initiates a similar conversation (252C28–30):

> Says, Will ye leave your bonny ship
>   And come wi me this day to dine?
> And you shall eat the baken meat,
>   And you shall drink the claret wine.
>
> 'O I will leave my bonny ship,
>   And gladly go wi you to dine,
> And I woud gie thrice three thousand pounds
>   That your fair daughter were but mine.'
>
> 'O gin ye will part wi your bonny ship
>   And wed a ladie of this countrie,
> I will gie you my ae daughter,
>   Gin she'll consent your bride to be.'

To be sure, the parallels here are somewhat forced, and the repetition serves merely to accentuate the somewhat ambiguous fidelity of the kitchie-boy, but the technique is quite similar to that used in "Young Beichan" (53C), a ballad which indeed seems to have had an important and lasting influence on Mrs. Brown as ballad composer.

Having completed our review of the main groups of ballads in Mrs. Brown's repertoire, it is tempting to speculate on possible explanations for the wide variation in quality which we have observed. Among the earlier pieces we find not only distinguished ballads like "The Gay Goshawk" but also the pathetic "Lady Elspat," just as in her later period we find not only "Thomas Rymer" but also, regrettably, "Fause Foodrage." Of course it might be argued that even major poets—like Wordsworth for example—exhibit great variation in the quality of their work, even though, unlike Mrs. Brown, they compose under the discipline of public awareness of their authorship.[36] There may be something to this argument. But I think there is another possible explanation, which will emerge in the following brief analysis of "Lamkin" (93A), a late ballad of Mrs. Brown's not previously considered.

It is certainly true that "Lamkin" must have existed in tradition many years before Mrs. Brown sent her version to Jamieson in 1800.[37] The earliest recovered text (93K), somewhat fragmentary, was sent to Percy by the Rev. Mr. Parsons in 1775, and Herd's contaminated version (93P) appeared in the second edition of *Scottish Songs* in 1776. Moreover, echoes of "Lamkin" in Mrs. Brown's "Lady Elspat" (247, sts. 4, 6) suggest that she may have known the ballad as early as 1783, even though it is not preserved in her MS and survives only in Jamieson's *Popular Ballads and Songs* (1806).

According to Mrs. Brown's text, Lamkin is a mason who built Lord Wearie's castle. When the lord refuses to pay him, he exacts a terrible revenge. While Lord Wearie is away, and with the help of the family nurse, the mason enters the castle and murders the lord's wife and baby boy. When the lord returns and discovers the deed, Lamkin and the nurse are executed. As this brief summary indicates, "Lamkin" is an atrocity ballad and belongs in the tradition of "Young Hunting" (68). Its dis-

36. Mrs. Brown, in her letter to Jamieson of December 2, 1802, expresses resentment toward Sir Walter Scott for referring to her by name in his *Minstrelsy* (1802).

37. Mrs. Brown offers in her letter to Jamieson of September 15, 1800, to send "Lamkin," and hence she probably sent it to him soon after that date, though we do not have the actual text or letter of transmittal. It is printed in Jamieson, *Popular Ballads and Songs* (1806), I, 176, and there attributed to Mrs. Brown.

tinctive feature—like the concealment and discovery of Young Hunting's body—is the double murder, and in particular the device of stabbing the young baby so that its cries will bring the mother downstairs to her death. If the ballad is based on real or reported events, this grisly scene must have constituted the beginning and end of the story as known in the community. All else seems to be imported to provide a setting and motivation for the violence. The earliest version, for example, says nothing of the lord's refusal of payment, and in fact no motive whatever is given. We are told merely (93K1):

> My lord said to my lady,
>> when he went from home,
> Take care of Long Longkin,
>> he lies in the lone.

Nor is there any hint in this text of the execution of Lamkin or burning of the nurse at the stake. Instead it ends in a family massacre, with an endlessly rotating series of daughters descending the stairs (93K8–12):

> 'Come down, Lady Betty,
>> the flower of all your kin,
> And see your mother's heart's blood,
>> so freely running.
>
> Down came Lady Betty,
>> her heart full of woe:
> 'Oh take my life, Longkin,
>> and let my mother go.'
>
> 'Come down, Lady Nelly,
>> the flower of all your kin,
> And see your sister's heart's blood,
>> so freely running.'
>
> Down came Lady Nelly,
>> her heart full of woe:
> 'Oh take my life, Longkin,
>> and let my sister go.'
>
> 'Come down, Lady Jenny, etc.

One suspects either that the hypnotic rhythm of the spinning wheel has taken over here or that this version of the ballad has been turned into a "scare" song like "There Was an Old Woman All Skin and Bones."

10. Mrs. Brown of Falkland   327

In spite of the corruptions in Herd's "Lammikin"[38] discussed in the preceding chapter, the Herd version is much closer to that of Mrs. Brown. It has the same motive for murder (failure to pay wages) and even a similarity of detail, such as the little wicket (a shot-window in Mrs. Brown) through which Lamkin gains entry into the castle, although it lacks any reference to the lord's return or the execution of Lamkin and the nurse. As we have seen, Mrs. Brown was familiar with Herd's text and commented on it in a letter to Jamieson, so that she may well have used it to some extent in shaping her own version of "Lamkin." But if this be true, we can only conclude—Ritson to the contrary—that Mrs. Brown has managed to turn lead into gold.

The nature of Mrs. Brown's achievement in "Lamkin" can be seen both in her improvement of elements already present in the ballad and in her additions to it. Her device for removing Lord Wearie from the scene via a sea journey, for instance, is far superior to the rather arbitrary hunt in the greenwood of Herd's text. The differing methods of building suspense in the two versions is likewise instructive. Herd uses the conventional ominous dream motif, cast in the artificial style which Child rightly deplored:

'Yestrene, yestrene, I dreamt my bower
    Of red, red blude was fu;
Gin ye gang to this black hunting,
    I sall hae caus to rue.'

'Wha looks to dreams, my winsome dame?
    Ye hae nae caus to feare:'
And syne he's kist her comely cheik,
    And syne the starting teare.[39]

Mrs. Brown uses none of this (except one line, "I sall hae caus to rue," which she assigns to Lamkin, 93A4) and instead picks up a hint from a later stanza which in Herd's text reads as follows:

'Now where's the lady of this castle?
    nurse, tell to Lammikin:'
'She's sewing up intill her bowir,'
    the fals nourrice she sung.[40]

38. As already mentioned, Herd's "Lammikin" is dissected by Child, the stanzas he regarded as authentic being printed in regular position (93P), and the others in the textual notes (ESPB, II, 340). The complete ballad, lacking one stanza, (93P4), is in Herd's Scottish Songs (1776), I, 145–148.

39. Herd, Scottish Songs (1776), I, 146, sts. 5 and 6.

40. Ibid., I, 147, st. 9 (93P3).

In Mrs. Brown's version this brief exchange between Lamkin and the nurse is dramatically expanded (93A8–11):

'O whare's a' the men o this house,
    that ca me Lamkin?'
'They're at the barn-well thrashing;
    't will be lang ere they come in.'

'And whare's the women o this house,
    that ca me Lamkin?'
'They're at the far well washing;
    't will be lang ere they come in.'

'And whare's the bairns o this house,
    that ca me Lamkin?'
'They're at the school reading;
    't will be night or they come hame.'

'O whare's the lady o this house,
    that ca's me Lamkin?'
'She's up in her bower sewing,
    but we soon can bring her down.'

This is of course precisely the kind of incremental repetition that we have seen to be a hallmark of Mrs. Brown's style. But whereas in "Child Waters" its effect is leisurely and majestic, in "Lamkin" it serves admirably both to set the stage for the murder and to create an atmosphere of suspense.

At this point in the narrative Herd's text starts the action with another exchange between Lamkin and the nurse:

What sall we do, what sall we say,
    to gar her cum there down?'
'We'll nip the baby in the cradle,
    the fals nourrice she sung.

Lammikin nipped the bonie babe,
    while loud fals nourice sings;
Lammikin nipped the bony babe,
    while hich the red blude springs.[41]

Here is Mrs. Brown's version of the same passage (93A12–13):

41. These two stanzas are in Child (93P4–5); the first is in Herd's MSS, but not in his *Scottish Songs*.

Then Lamkin's tane a sharp knife,
    that hang down by his gaire,
And he has gien the bonny babe
    a deep wound and a sair.

Then Lamkin he rocked,
    and the fause nourice sang,
Till frae ilkae bore o the cradle
    the red blood out sprang.

The first of these is a commonplace taken perhaps from "Young Hunting" (68A6), but the second is a superb example of Mrs. Brown's mastery of the order of climax in stanza construction, similar to what we have already observed, for instance, in her version of "Sir Hugh" (155A7).

There is much more that is distinctive about Mrs. Brown's "Lamkin," such as the reference at the end to burning at the stake—probably suggested by the trial by fire in "Young Hunting" (68A25–27)—but perhaps her most characteristic and effective touch is the stanza describing how the lady descends the stairs to see why the baby is crying (93A18):

O the firsten step she steppit,
    she steppit on a stane;
But the neisten step she steppit,
    she met him Lamkin.

This style is by now familiar to us; but the skilfully calculated effect of horror achieved here is completely unlike that of incremental passages that we have observed in her other ballads and hence underscores the variety of effects Mrs. Brown is capable of producing with this single basic technique.

Returning to the question of unevenness in quality of Mrs. Brown's texts, it seems to me that the best of them, like "Lamkin," are usually known to exist in earlier tradition. This is true of "Gil Brenton" (5A), "The Twa Sisters" (10B), "The Cruel Brother" (11A), "The Lass of Roch Royal" (76D, E), "Fair Mary of Wallington" (91C), and "Sir Hugh" (155A), all excellent ballads. The superiority of "Thomas Rymer" (37A), as I have suggested, is attributable in part at least to its close dependence on the romance of *Thomas of Erceldoun*. The one exception appears to be "The Gay Goshawk" (96A). At the risk of seeming to rig the evidence to fit my theory, I will suggest that in this one instance Mrs. Brown's version may be based on an earlier traditional form of the ballad which happens not to have been recorded.

330

From what I have just said it might be thought that I am depriving Mrs. Brown of any significant artistic role in the composition of her ballads. Nothing could be further from the truth. One of the most striking things we have observed in the present chapter is that her style, although unmistakably traditional, is also distinctively her own. This stylistic harmony cannot be explained by coincidence. All I am suggesting is that she seems to have had difficulty when composing new ballads, and that she is at her best with those already existing in tradition. In short, she is better at re-creation than she is at creation. Yet except for that poet who composed the Scottish masterpieces for Percy's *Reliques*, no one has contributed more to English and Scottish balladry than Mrs. Brown of Falkland.

10. Mrs. Brown of Falkland   331

Conclusion

Of making many books there is no end, and much study is a weariness of the flesh. Ballads were meant to be sung. Yet they are also an inseparable part of literary history and have experienced a development analogous to that of other literary genres. More attention ought to be devoted to this development. The present ballad history, therefore, imperfect as it is, has implications for the future of ballad studies which I would like to mention briefly by way of conclusion.

One obvious need is for a study of balladry in the modern period. The monumental work done by collectors since the time of Francis J. Child has prepared the way for a new assessment of folksong and ballad in the nineteenth and twentieth centuries. An earlier generation looked upon modern times as an era of decline and fall for the ballad tradition. But those of us who have been privileged to live through the singing sixties know better. Thanks to the artistry and dedication of modern minstrels like Pete Seeger, a new vitality has been restored to ballad and folksong. Even the element of radical social protest, largely dormant since the rhymes of Robin Hood in the fifteenth century, has made a strong comeback. The current revival, aided enormously by the electronic revolution, has been sketched by Josh Dunson in *Freedom in the Air* (New York, 1965). I continue to hope, however, that a scholar of sufficiently catholic taste will be found who can chronicle the evolution of balladry from Sir Walter Scott to Bob Dylan.

Finally I would like to refer to the acute need that exists for an anthology that will make possible the study of the evolution of ballad style in the classroom. At the present time all ballad books stand in the shadow of Child's collection, and not one of them could be conveniently used for study of the literary history of balladry. What we need is a ballad book in which the texts are ordered chronologically and grouped according to sources within each time period. Perhaps the plans now being made for a modern edition of Child's great work can include a new chronological ordering of the materials in the manner I have suggested. If this is done, I believe that students of the ballad and folksong will shake off the hypnotic effect of the old, arbitrary arrangement of Child's texts and will experience a new freedom in the continually fascinating study of the popular ballad.

Bibliography

Manuscripts

Cambridge. Trinity College MS B.14.39 (*ca.* 1250). Judas (23).

Cambridge. University Library MS Ee. iv. 35 (*ca.* 1500). Robin Hood and the Potter (121), and The King and the Barker (273 App I).

Cambridge. University Library MS Ff. 5.48 (*ca.* 1450). Robin Hood and the Monk (119), and Thomas of Erceldoun (37 App).

London. British Museum MSS Additional 22311–22312 (David Herd's Manuscripts).

London. British Museum Additional MS 27879 (*ca.* 1650), (Percy Folio Manuscript).

London. British Museum MS Additional 31042 (Childhood of Jesus).

London. British Museum MS Cotton Vespasian A. xxv (*ca.* 1600). Captain Car (178).

London. British Museum MS Sloane 2593 (*ca.* 1450). St. Stephen and Herod (22), Robyn and Gandeleyn (115), I Have a Yong Suster, etc.

Oxford. Balliol College MS 354 (Richard Hill's commonplace book).

Oxford. Bodleian Library MS Ashmole 48 (*ca.* 1557–1565). The Hunting of the Cheviot (162).

Oxford. Corpus Christi College MS 255 (*ca.* 1550–1570). King John and the Bishop (45).

Scotland. Mrs. Anna Gordon Brown of Falkland. Manuscripts.

Jamieson-Brown MS (J-B), in David Laing Papers, University of Edinburgh Library (1783).

William Tytler's Brown MS (WT-B), Aldourie Castle (1783); Joseph Ritson's copy of WT-B in Harvard College Library.

Alexander Fraser Tytler-Brown MS (AFT-B), Aldourie Castle (1800).

Cambridge, Mass. Harvard College Library MS 25241.37.5/6. Manuscripts of Mrs. Brown of Falkland, with notes by G. L. Kittredge.

Books and articles

Adolf, Helen. *Visio Pacis: Holy City and Grail.* Pennsylvania State University Press, 1960.

The Apocryphal New Testament. Trans. M. R. James. Oxford, 1924.

Arden of Feversham (anon.), reprinted in C. F. Tucker Brooke, *The Shakespeare Apocrypha*. Oxford, 1908.

Auerbach, Erich. *Scenes from the Drama of European Literature*. New York, 1959.

Awntyrs of Arthure at the Terne Wathelyne, ed. F. J. Amours in *Scottish Alliterative Poems*. Edinburgh, 1897 (Scottish Text Society, v. 21).

Barry, Phillips. "The Bridge of Sunbeams," *Journal of American Folklore*, XXVII (1914), 77–89.

Batho, Edith C. "The Life of Christ in the Ballads," *Essays and Studies by Members of the English Association*, IX, 70–97.

Beaumont, Francis, and John Fletcher. *Knight of the Burning Pestle*. London, 1611.

Bennett, H. S. "The Author and his Public in the Fourteenth and Fifteenth Centuries," *Essays and Studies*, XXIII (1937), 7–24.

Billings, A. H. *A Guide to the Middle English Metrical Romances*. New York, 1901.

Bland, D. S. "The Evolution of 'Chevy Chase' and 'The Battle of Otterburn,'" *Notes and Queries*, CXCVI (1951), 160 f.

Bland, D. S. "'Macbeth' and 'The Battle of Otterburn,'" *Notes and Queries*, CXCIV (1949), 335 f.

Boddeker, R. "Englische Lieder und Balladen aus dem 16. Jahrhundert," *Jahrbuch für romanische und englische Sprache und Literatur*, N.F. II (1875), 81–105, 210–239, 347–367; concluded in III (1876), 92–129.

Bronson, Bertrand H. "Edward, Edward: A Scottish Ballad," *Southern Folklore Quarterly*, IV (1940), 1–13, 159–161.

Bronson, Bertrand H. "The Interdependence of Ballad Tunes and Texts," *California Folklore Quarterly* (now *Western Folklore*), III (1944), 185–207.

Bronson, Bertrand H. "Mrs. Brown and the Ballad," *California Folklore Quarterly* (now *Western Folklore*), IV (1945), 129–140.

Bronson, Bertrand H. *The Traditional Tunes of the Child Ballads*. Princeton, 1959–.

Brown, Carleton. *English Lyrics of the Thirteenth Century*. Oxford, 1932.

Brown, Carleton. *Religious Lyrics of the Fifteenth Century*. Oxford, 1939.

Brown, E. K. *Rhythm in the Novel*. Toronto, 1950.

Bruce, J. D. *The Evolution of Arthurian Romance from the Beginnings down to the Year 1300*. 2 vols. Göttingen, 1923.

Burns, Robert. *The Poetry of Robert Burns*, ed. W. E. Henley and T. F. Henderson. London, n.d.

Burns, Robert. *The Songs of Robert Burns*, ed. James C. Dick. London, 1903; repr. Hatboro, Pa., 1962.

Chambers, E. K. *English Literature at the Close of the Middle Ages.* Oxford, 1945.

Chaucer, Geoffrey. *The Works of Geoffrey Chaucer*, ed. F. N. Robinson. 2nd edition. Boston, 1957.

Child, Francis J. *The English and Scottish Popular Ballads.* 5 vols. Boston and New York, 1882–1898; repr. New York, 1956.

Childhood of Jesus, ed. C. Horstmann, in *Archiv*, LXXIV (1885), 327–339.

Chrétien de Troyes. *Arthurian Romances.* Trans. W. W. Comfort. London, 1914 (Everyman, 698).

Chrétien de Troyes. *Der Percevalroman*, ed. Alfons Hilka. Halle: M. Niemeyer, 1932.

Chrétien de Troyes. *Le Roman de Perceval ou Le Conte du Graal*, ed. William Roach. Geneva: Librairie Droz, 1956 (Textes Litteraires Français).

Chrétien de Troyes. *The Story of the Grail.* Trans. Robert W. Linker. Chapel Hill, 1960.

Christophersen, Paul. *The Ballad of Sir Aldingar.* Oxford, 1952.

Coffin, Tristram P. *The British Traditional Ballad in North America* (rev. ed.). Philadelphia, 1963.

Coffin, Tristram P. "Mary Hamilton and the Anglo-American Ballad as an Art Form," *Journal of American Folklore*, LXX (1957), 208–14.

A Collection of Old Ballads (anon.). 3 vols. London, 1723–25.

The Complaynt of Scotlande, A.D. 1549, ed. James A. H. Murray. (*Early English Text Society, Extra Series, 17–18.*) London, 1872.

Cornelius, Roberta D. "A New Text of an Old Ballad," *Publications of the Modern Language Association*, XLVI (1931), 1025–33.

Cornish Drama. *The Ancient Cornish Drama*, ed. Edwin Norris. 2 vols. Oxford, 1859.

Cursor Mundi, ed. Richard Morris. (*Early English Text Society, Original Series*, 57, 59, 62, 66, 68.) London, 1874–78.

Dean-Smith, Margaret. *A Guide to English Folk Song Collections, 1822–1952.* Liverpool, 1954.

Death and Liffe, ed. J. H. Hanford and J. M. Steadman, in *Studies in Philology*, XV (1918), 223–294.

336

Defoe, Daniel. *The Apparition of Mrs. Veal*. London, 1706.

Delony, Thomas. *The Works of Thomas Delony*, ed. Francis O. Mann. Oxford, 1912.

A Dictionary of Middle English Musical Terms, ed. H. H. Carter and George B. Gerhard. Bloomington, 1961.

Donaldson, E. Talbot. *Piers Plowman: The C-Text and Its Poet*. New Haven, 1949.

Dunson, Josh. *Freedom in the Air*. New York, 1965.

The Early South English Legendary, ed. C. Horstmann. (*Early English Text Society, Original Series*, 87.) London, 1887.

Eger and Grime, ed. James R. Caldwell. Cambridge, 1933 (*Harvard Studies in Comparative Literature*, vol. IX).

English Nativity Plays, ed. S. B. Hemingway. New Haven, 1909 (*Yale Studies in English*, XXXVIII).

Erasmus, Desiderius. *Erasmi Apothegmata*. Trans. Nicholas Udall. London, 1542.

Fehr, B. "Die Lieder der Hs. Sloane 2593," *Archiv*, CIX (1902), 33–70.

Flugel, Ewald. "Zur Chronologie der englischen Balladen," *Anglia*, XXI (1899), 312–358.

Foster, Idris Ll. "Culhwch and Olwen and Rhonabwy's Dream," *Arthurian Literature in the Middle Ages*, ed. R. S. Loomis. Oxford, 1959.

Fowler, David C. "An Accused Queen in 'The Lass of Roch Royal' (Child 76)," *Journal of American Folklore*, 71 (1958), 553–63.

Fowler, David C. "The Date of the Cornish *Ordinalia*," *Mediaeval Studies*, XXIII (1961), 91–125.

Fowler, David C. " 'The Hunting of the Cheviot' and 'The Battle of Otterburn,' " *Western Folklore*, XXV (1966), 165–71.

Fowler, David C. "Toward a Literary History of the Popular Ballad," *New York Folklore Quarterly*, XXI (1965), 123–141.

Fowler, David C. *Piers the Plowman: Literary Relations of the A and B Texts*. Seattle, 1961.

Fowler, David C. *Prowess and Charity in the Perceval of Chrétien de Troyes*. Seattle, 1959.

Friedman, Albert B. *The Ballad Revival. Studies in the Influence of Popular on Sophisticated Poetry*. Chicago, 1961.

Friedman, Albert B. "A New Version of 'Musselburgh Field,' " *Journal of American Folklore*, LXVI (1953), 74–77.

Friedman, Albert B. *The Viking Book of Folk Ballads of the English-Speaking World.* New York, 1956; reprinted, 1963.

Gammer Gurton's Garland, or, The Nursery Parnassus. London, 1810.

Gerould, G. H. "The Ballad of the Bitter Withy," *Publications of the Modern Language Association,* XXIII (1908), 141–167.

Gesta Romanorum. *The Early English Versions of the Gesta Romanorum,* ed. Sidney J. H. Herrtage. (*Early English Text Society, Extra Series,* 33.) London, 1879.

Gilchrist, Anne G. " 'Death and the Lady' in English Balladry," *Journal of the English Folk Dance and Song Society,* IV (1941), 37–48.

Gilchrist, Anne G. and Lucy E. Broadwood, "The Bitter Withy," *Journal of the Folk-Song Society,* XIV (June, 1910), 38–45.

Graves, Janet M. " 'The Holy Well': A Medieval Religious Ballad," *Western Folklore,* XXVI (1967), 13–26.

Greene, Richard L. *The Early English Carols.* Oxford, 1935.

Greene, Richard L. "The Meaning of the Corpus Christi Carol," *Medium Aevum,* XXIX (1960), 10–21.

Greene, Richard L. "The Traditional Survival of Two Medieval Carols," *English Literary History,* VII (1940), 223–238.

Greig, Gavin. *Last Leaves of Traditional Ballads . . . Collected . . . by the Late Gavin Greig,* ed. A. Keith. Aberdeen, 1925.

Gummere, Francis B. *Old English Ballads.* Boston, 1894.

Hartshorne, Charles Henry. *Ancient Metrical Tales.* London, 1829.

Hazlitt, W. Carew. *Remains of the Early Popular Poetry of England.* 4 vols. London, 1864–66.

Henderson, T. F. *The Ballad in Literature.* Cambridge, 1912.

Herd, David. *Ancient and Modern Scottish Songs.* 2 vols. Edinburgh, 1776.

Herd, David. Songs from David Herd's Manuscripts, ed. Hans Hecht. Edinburgh, 1904.

Hodgart, M. J. C. *The Ballads.* London, 1950.

Hollander, John. *The Untuning of the Sky.* Princeton, 1961.

Holmes, Urban T., Jr., and Sister M. Amelia Klenke. *Chrétien, Troyes, and the Grail.* Chapel Hill, 1959.

Holzknecht, K. J. *Literary Patronage in the Middle Ages.* Philadelphia, 1923.

Home, John. *Douglas.* London, 1756.

Hulbert, James R. "A Hypothesis concerning the Alliterative Revival," *Modern Philology,* XXVIII (1931), 405–22.

Hulbert, James R. "The Sources of St. Erkenwald and the Trental of Gregory," *Modern Philology*, XVI (1919), 485–93.

Jamieson, Robert. *Popular Ballads and Songs*. 2 vols. Edinburgh, 1806.

Johnson, James. *The Scots Musical Museum*. 6 vols. Edinburgh, 1787–1803.

Jones, James H. "Commonplace and Memorization in the Oral Tradition of the English and Scottish Popular Ballads," *Journal of American Folklore*, 74 (1961), 97–112.

Keen, Maurice. *The Outlaws of Medieval Legend*. Toronto, 1961.

Knoblock, J. A. " 'The Gypsy Laddie' (Child 200): An Unrecognized Child of Medieval Romance," *Western Folklore*, XIX (1960), 35–45.

Laneham, Robert. *Robert Laneham's Letter*, ed. F. J. Furnivall. London, 1907.

Leach, MacEdward. *The Ballad Book*. New York, 1955.

Leach, MacEdward and Tristram P. Coffin (eds.). *The Critics and the Ballad*. Carbondale, Ill., 1961.

Le May, Sister Marie d. L. *The Allegory of the Christ Knight in English Literature*. Washington, D. C., 1932.

Lengert, Oscar. "Die Schottische Romanze 'Roswall and Lillian,' " *Englische Studien*, XVI (1892), 321–356.

Lewis, Matthew Gregory. *The Monk*. London, 1796.

Lewis, Matthew Gregory. *Tales of Wonder*. London, 1801.

Loomis, R. S. (ed.). *Arthurian Literature in the Middle Ages*. Oxford, 1959.

The Mabinogion. Trans. Lady Charlotte Guest (Everyman, 97). London, 1906.

Maidment, James. *A North Countrie Garland*. Edinburgh, 1824.

Malory, Sir Thomas. *Morte Darthur*, edited as *The Works of Sir Thomas Malory*, by Eugène Vinaver. Oxford, 1954.

Manning, Stephen. "I Syng of a Myden," *Publications of the Modern Language Association*, LXXV (1960), 8–12.

Medieval Romances, ed. R. S. Loomis and L. H. Loomis. New York, 1957 (Modern Library, 133).

Motherwell, William. *Minstrelsy, Ancient and Modern*. 2 vols. Glascow, 1827.

Muscatine, Charles. "Form, Texture, and Meaning in Chaucer's *Knight's Tale*," *Publications of the Modern Language Association*, LXV (1950), 911–929.

Myrk, John. *Myrc's Duties of a Parish Priest*, ed. E. Peacock. (*Early English Text Society, Original Series*, 31.) London, 1868.

Nessler, Karl. *Geschichte der Ballade "Chevy Chase."* Berlin, 1911.

Nichols, John. *Illustrations of the Literary History of the Eighteenth Century.* 8 vols. (vols. VII and VIII by John Bowyer Nichols). London, 1817–58.

The Northern Passion, ed. F. A. Foster. (*Early English Text Society, Original Series*, 145, 147.) London, 1912–13.

Nygard, Holger. *The Ballad of Heer Halewijn. Its Forms and Variations in Western Europe. A Study of the History and Nature of a Ballad Tradition.* Helsinki (Folklore Fellows Communications no. 169) and Knoxville, 1958.

Nygard, Holger. "Ballads and the Middle Ages," *Tennessee Studies in Literature*, V (1960), 85–96.

Nygard, Holger. "Popular Ballad and Medieval Romance," in *Folklore International: essays in traditional literature, belief and custom in honor of Wayland Debs Hand*, ed. D. K. Wilgus. Folklore Associates, Inc. Hatboro, Pennsylvania, 1967. Pp. 161–173.

Patch, Howard R. *The Other World According to Descriptions in Medieval Literature.* Cambridge, Mass., 1950.

Pearl, ed. E. V. Gordon. Oxford, 1953.

Percy, Thomas. *Bishop Percy's Folio Manuscript*, ed. J. W. Hales and F. J. Furnivall. 3 vols. and Supplement of "Loose and Humorous Songs." London, 1867–68.

Percy, Thomas. *The Correspondence of Thomas Percy and David Dalrymple, Lord Hailes*, ed. A. F. Falconer. Baton Rouge, La., 1954.

Percy, Thomas. *The Percy Letters*, ed. David Nichol Smith and Cleanth Brooks. Baton Rouge, La., 1944.

Percy, Thomas. *Reliques of Ancient English Poetry.* 3 vols. London, 1765; numerous later editions.

Piers the Plowman. A Critical Edition of the A-Version, ed. T. A. Knott and D. C. Fowler. Baltimore, 1952.

Piers the Plowman, in Three Parallel Texts, ed. W. W. Skeat. 2 vols. Oxford, 1886.

Puttenham, George. *The Arte of English Poesie*, ed. G. D. Willcock and A. Walker. Cambridge, 1936.

Quinn, Esther. *The Quest of Seth.* Chicago, 1962.

Ramsay, Allan. *The Ever Green: A Collection of Scots Poems Wrote by the Ingenious before 1600.* 2 vols. Edinburgh, 1724; reprinted 1874.

Ramsay, Allan. *The Tea-Table Miscellany.* 4 vols. Edinburgh, 1723–1737; many subsequent editions.

Rastell, John. *The Interlude of the Four Elements,* ed. J. O. Halliwell. London, 1848 (Percy Society, 22).

Rastell, John. *The Nature of the Four Elements,* ed. John S. Farmer. London, 1908 (Tudor Facsimile Texts).

Ravenscroft, Thomas. *Pammelia, Deutromelia, Melismata.* London, 1609–11; repr. American Folklore Society, Inc., Philadelphia, 1961.

Ritson, Joseph. *Ancient Englëish Metrical Romanceës.* London, 1802.

Ritson, Joseph. *Ancient Songs from the Time of King Henry the Third to the Revolution.* London, 1790.

Robbins, R. H. *Secular Lyrics of the XIVth and XVth Centuries.* Oxford, 1952.

Robertson, D. W. Jr. "The Doctrine of Charity in Mediaeval Literary Gardens," *Speculum,* XXVI (1951), 24–49.

Robertson, D. W. Jr. *Preface to Chaucer.* Princeton, 1962.

Rollins, Hyder E. "Concerning Bodleian MS. Ashmole 48," *Modern Language Notes,* XXXIV (1919), 340–51.

Rollins, Hyder E. "William Elderton, Elizabethan Actor and Ballad-Writer," *Studies in Philology,* XVII (1920), 199–245.

Roman de la Rose, ed. E. Langlois. 5 vols. Paris, 1914–24 (Publications de la Société des Anciens Textes Français).

Roswall and Lillian. Edinburgh, 1663.

Routley, Erik. *The English Carol.* London, 1958.

The Roxburghe Ballads, ed. William Chappell (vols. I–III) and J. W. Edsworth (vols. IV–VIII). Hertford, 1883–96 (Ballad Society).

Sandys, William. *Christmas Carols, Ancient and Modern.* London, 1833.

Schick, J. "Die Urquelle der Offa-Konstanze Sage," *Britannica* ("Festschrift Max Förster"). Leipzig, 1929, pp. 31–56.

Schlauch, Margaret. *Chaucer's Constance and Accused Queens.* New York, 1927.

Scott, Sir Walter. *The Antiquary.* Edinburgh, 1816.

Scott, Sir Walter. *Minstrelsy of the Scottish Border.* Edinburgh, 1802–3; and later editions.

Scouten, Arthur H. "An Early Printed Report on the Apparition of Mrs. Veal," *Review of English Studies,* VI (1955), 259–63.

Shenstone, William. *Shenstone's Miscellany 1759–1763*, ed. Ian A. Gordon. Oxford, 1952.

Sidgwick, Frank. "The Bitter Withy," *Notes & Queries*, 10th ser., IV (July 29, 1905), 84.

Simeone, W. E. "The May Games and the Robin Hood Legend," *Journal of American Folklore*, 64 (1951), 265–274.

Solomon and Marcolf. *Salomon et Marcolfus*, ed. Walter Benary. Heidelberg, 1914.

Sources and Analogues of Chaucer's Canterbury Tales, ed. W. F. Bryan and Germaine Dempster. Chicago, 1941.

Sylvester, Joshua. *A Garland of Christmas Carols*. London, 1861.

Taylor, Archer. *"Edward" and "Sven I Rosengård."* Chicago, 1931.

Taylor, Donald S. "The Lineage and Birth of Sir Aldingar," *Journal of American Folklore*, 65 (1952), 139–147.

Thomas of Erceldoun, ed. James A. H. Murray. (*Early English Text Society, Original Series*, 61.) London, 1875.

Tolkien, J. R. R. *The Hobbit*. London, 1937.

Tottel's Miscellany. London, 1557.

Tristan and Iseult. *The Romance of Tristan and Iseult*, as retold by Joseph Bedier. New York, 1945 (Anchor, A2).

Udall, Nicholas. *Roister Doister*. London, ca. 1567.

Van Duzee, Mabel. *A Medieval Romance of Friendship: Eger and Grime*. New York, 1963.

Walpole, Horace. *The Castle of Otranto*. London, 1765.

Watkin-Jones, A. "Bishop Percy and the Scottish Ballads," *Essays and Studies by Members of the English Association*, vol. XVIII (1933), 110–121.

Wells, Evelyn K. "Corpus Christi Carol," *Journal of the English Folk Dance and Song Society*, IV, 3 (1942), 122 f.

White, T. H. *The Sword in the Stone*. New York, 1939.

Wilgus, D. K. *Anglo-American Folksong Scholarship since 1898*. New Brunswick, N. J., 1959.

Wimberly, Lowry C. *Folklore in the English and Scottish Ballads*. New York, 1928.

Wright, Thomas. *Songs and Carols, Now First Printed from a Manuscript of the Fifteenth Century*. London, 1847.

Wright, Thomas. *Songs and Carols from a Manuscript in the British Museum of the Fifteenth Century*. London, 1856.

Wright, Thomas. *Songs and Ballads, with Other Short Poems, Chiefly of the Reign of Philip and Mary.* London, 1860.

Zimmer, Heinrich. *The King and the Corpse.* New York, 1948 (Bollingen Series, XI).

Recordings

Baez, Joan. "Joan Baez Vol. 2," Vanguard VSD–2097. Twelve inch LP recording.

Flanders, Helen Hartness. "Eight Traditional British-American Ballads," Helen Hartness Flanders Collection, Middlebury College, Middlebury, Vermont. (New England Folksong Series No. 1.) Twelve inch LP recording.

Library of Congress. Archive of American Folk Song. Collection of field recordings.

MacColl, Ewan and A. L. Lloyd. *English and Scottish Popular Ballads,* ed. Kenneth S. Goldstein, Riverside RLP 12–621 ff. Twelve inch LP recordings.

Index

ABC of Aristotle, The, 80
Aberdeen Cantus, 272
"Abu Kasem's Slippers," 154
"Adam Bell, Clim of the Clough, and William of Cloudesly" (116), 71
"Adam lay I-bowndyn," 36
Addison, Joseph, 4
Adolf, Helen, 72n.
"Agincourte Battell," 147
Aldourie Castle, 296
"Allison Gross" (35), 297, 300
"Amongst the Mirtles," 152
Amours, F. J., 201n.
Ancient and Modern Scots Songs, 210
Anderson, Dr. Robert, 266, 296n., 314–315
Annals of Waverly, 94
Antiquary, The, 271n.
Apology for Poetry, 12–13
"Apparition of Mrs. Veal, The," 191
"Archie o Cawfield" (188), 235
Archive of American Folk Song, 126n., 315n.
Arden of Feversham, 171
"Are Women Faire," 152
Armstrong family, 16
Art of English Poesie, The, 102
Arthurian ballads, 160–161
Arthurian cycle, 8–10, 72–73
"As I went throw a gardyn grene," 36
"As It befell One Saturday," 159n.
Ashmole MS, *see* Oxford, Bodleian Library MS Ashmole 48.
Auchinleck MS, 8
Auerbach, Erich, 62n.
"Ave maris stella," 36
Awntyrs of Arthure at the Terne Wathelyne, 201–202, 206n.

"Babylon" (14), 275–276, 278
Baez, Joan, 272n.
"Baffled Knight, The" (112), 20, 29, 30, 273, 281
Ballads: American versions, 4n.; in Percy folio MS, 158–182; pseudo-ballads, 237, revenant, 183–206, Scandinavian, 14, 211, 280
—, composition of: "block" composition, 167, 284, 285, 304, 317; "commonplace stanzas," 208, 304, 311, 312, 330; "stability of occasion," 21, 42, 44n., 268, 294
—, structure of: mosaics, 16, 243–244,

256; narrative symmetry, 9, 10, 12, 16, 65, 73, 88, 122, 146, 211–213, 245, 267, 275–277, 299, 321, 325; parallelism, 16, 124, 141, 284; repetition, 17, 32, 38, 73, 86, 177, 208–209, 211–212, 220, 244–245, 267, 276–277, 292, 299, 301–311, 317, 325; stanza form, 9, 46, 133, 137–139, 151, 202, 237, 299; refrain, 6n., 12, 13, 14, 211
—, themes in: accused queen, 218, 228–230, 233, 283, 321; contest of wits, 22, 279; love-death, 187, 224, 226–227, 238, 310; loathly lady, 299; memento mori, 191; message, 177, 238, 241–242, 256, 313; ominous dream, 177, 228, 274, 328; riddles, 20, 21–23; supernatural contest, 30–31; vow of austerities, 136, 187, 194; wedding tasks, 23–24
"Banks of the Ohio, The," 172
"Barbara Allan," *see* "Bonny Barbara Allan" (84)
Barnard, Mrs. (wife of Bishop of Derry), 296
Barry, Phillips, 51n.
Batho, Edith C., 12n., 51, 60n., 62–62n.
"Battle of Otterburn, The" (161), 13n., 95, 97, 273, 282
Beaumont, John, 187
Bedier, Joseph, 198n.
"Beggar-Laddie, The" (280), 208
"Bell My Wife," 152
Benary, Walter, 155
Bennett, H. S., 81n.
"Bewick and Graham" (211), 215–217
Bible, 7, 45, 50, 62, 186
—, Old Testament: Genesis, 23, 185; Genesis 3:22, 51; Job, 181; Song of Solomon, 62, 63; Isaiah 11:6, 48; Isaiah 14:13, 193; Daniel 3:24–25, 44
—, New Testament, 7, 184; Luke 16:19–31, 45; John 4:6–26, 43; John 19:34, 61; John 20:17, 196; I Corinthians 15: 22, 46
—, Apocrypha, 11n., 45, 46, 47, 50n., 184n., 185–186
Billings, A. H., 8n.
"Billy-Blin," 299
"Billy Boy," 272
"Bitter Withy, The," 20, 42–43, 44n., 51–54, 262n., 268–270
Bland, D. S., 108n.
"Blind Beggar of Bednall Green," 155

344

Index   345

Index   347

Vaux, Thomas Lord, 96
Vision literature, medieval, 193
Vinaver, Eugene, 192n., 198n.
Vlach, Kathleen, 51n.

Waller, Edmund, 152
Wallys, John, 96, 99, 100
Walpole, Horace, 266n.
"Waly, Waly, Gin Love Be Bony" (204), 207, 274
War of the Roses, 8
Wardlaw, Lady, 323
Watertoune, Thomas, 96
Watkin-Jones, A., 18n.
"Wee Wee Man, The" (38), 278–279
Wells, Evelyn K., 59
White, John, 281n.
White, T. H., 22
"White Rose and Red," 147, 164
Whitman, Walt, 152
"Wife of Usher's Well, The" (79), 190
Wilgus, D. K., 4, 65
"Will Stewart and John" (107), 15, 143, 167–170, 253
"William and Margaret," 261
Williams, Vaughan, 269n.
"Willie and Earl Richard's Daughter" (102), 296, 304

"Willie o Douglas Dale" (101), 297, 301, 302–304, 311, 317
"Willie o Winsbury" (100), 236, 274
"Willie's drown'd in Yarrow" (215), 273
"Willie's Lady" (6), 295, 296n., 297, 299
Wilkie MS, 262n.
Wimberly, Lowry C., 183, 184, 188, 193, 196, 202, 205n., 254n.
Wither, George, 152
Wordsworth, William, 152
Wright, Thomas, 11, 33–34, 100, 102n., 106n., 152, 158n.

"Yarrow" ballads (214, 215), 236, 238, 274, 301
"Young Andrew" (48), 171–172, 175, 286, 290
"Young Beichan" (53) ("Lord Bateman"), 296, 297, 299, 314–316, 324
"Young Hunting" (68), 195n., 283–291, 330
"Young Johnstone" (88), 290–292
"Young Laird of Craigstone," 272n.
"Young Waters" (94), 239, 242–253, 257, 259

Zimmer, Heinrich, 154